BRUNNER/MAZEL PSYCHOSOCIAL STRESS SERIES No. 12

MENTAL HEALTH RESPONSE to MASS EMERGENCIES

Theory and Practice

Edited by

Mary Lystad, Ph.D.

BRUNNER/MAZEL, *Publishers* • New York

Library of Congress Cataloging-in-Publication Data

Mental health response to mass emergencies : theory and practice /
    edited by Mary Lystad.
        p. cm.—(Brunner/Mazel psychosocial stress series ; no. 12)
        Includes bibliographies and indexes.
        ISBN 0-87630-514-1
        1. Disaster victims—Mental health.   2. Disaster victims—Mental
    health services.   3. Disaster relief.   4. Disasters—Psychological
    aspects.   I. Lystad, Mary H.   II. Series.
        [DNLM: 1. Crisis Intervention.   2. Disasters.   3. Emergency
    Medical Services—organization & administration.   4. Mental Health
    Services—organization & administration.   W1 BR917TB no. 12 / WM 30
    M55314]
    RC451.4.D57M46 1988   362.2'8—dc19   88-5025
    DNLM/DLC   CIP
    for Library of Congress

Copyright © 1988 by Mary Lystad

Published by
BRUNNER/MAZEL, INC.
19 Union Square
New York, New York 10003

MANUFACTURED IN THE UNITED STATES OF AMERICA

10 9 8 7 6 5 4 3 2 1

MENTAL HEALTH RESPONSE to MASS EMERGENCIES

Theory and Practice

Brunner/Mazel Psychosocial Stress Series
Charles R. Figley, Ph.D., Series Editor

1. *Stress Disorders Among Vietnam Veterans*, Edited by Charles R. Figley, Ph.D.
2. *Stress and the Family Vol. 1: Coping with Normative Transitions*, Edited by Hamilton I. McCubbin, Ph.D., and Charles R. Figley, Ph.D.
3. *Stress and the Family Vol. 2: Coping with Catastrophe*, Edited by Charles R. Figley, Ph.D., and Hamilton I. McCubbin, Ph.D.
4. *Trauma and Its Wake: The Study and Treatment of Post-Traumatic Stress Disorder*, Edited by Charles R. Figley, Ph.D.
5. *Post-Traumatic Stress Disorder and the War Veteran Patient*, Edited by William E. Kelly, M.D.
6. *The Crime Victim's Book, Second Edition*, By Morton Bard, Ph.D., and Dawn Sangrey
7. *Stress and Coping in Time of War: Generalizations from the Israeli Experience*, Edited by Norman A. Milgram, Ph.D.
8. *Trauma and Its Wake Vol. 2: Traumatic Stress Theory, Research, and Intervention*, Edited by Charles R. Figley, Ph.D.
9. *Stress and Addiction*, Edited by Edward Gottheil, M.D., Ph.D., Keith A. Druley, Ph.D., Steven Pashko, Ph.D., and Stephen P. Weinstein, Ph.D.
10. *Vietnam: A Casebook*, By Jacob D. Lindy, M.D., in collaboration with Bonnie L. Green, Ph.D., Mary C. Grace, M.Ed., M.S., John A. MacLeod, M.D., and Louis Spitz, M.D.
11. *Post-Traumatic Therapy and Victims of Violence*, Edited by Frank M. Ochberg, M.D.

Editorial Note

The Psychosocial Stress Book Series Editorial Board proudly welcomes this volume to the Series. We are satisfied that this book will make an important contribution to the Series and to the social sciences in general.

The Series strives to develop and publish books that in some way make a significant contribution to the understanding and management of the psychosocial stress-reaction paradigm. In particular, books in the Series are designed to advance the work of clinicians, researchers, and other professionals involved in the varied aspects of human services. These professionals are challenged to help clients confront, cope with and, in some cases, become enriched by various psychosocial stressors, such as mass emergencies.

Books in the Series focus on the stress associated with a wide variety of psychosocial events. Collectively, the books in the Series have focused on the immediate and long-term psychosocial consequences of extraordinary stressors such as war, divorce, parenting, separation, racism, social isolation, acute illness, drug addiction, death, sudden unemployment, rape, natural disasters, incest, and crime victimization.

This book, as with every other book proposed for the Series, is subjected to an intensive review by the Editorial Board. As a "refereed" book series, this ensures that only the most important contributions are published. Indeed, the quality and significance of the Series are a product of the nationally and internationally respected group of scholars who compose the Editorial Board. Like the readership, the Board represents the fields of general medicine, pediatrics, psychiatry, nursing, psychology, sociology, social work, family therapy, political science, and anthropology.

This present volume, number 12 in the Series, focuses on a wide variety of psychosocial stressors: natural and manmade disasters, including war. Different from previous volumes, this book directs attention to public education and planning programs for preventing and ameliorating the deleterious consequences of mass emergencies.

Dr. Mary Lystad, the editor of this volume, is an internationally known mental health administrator and scientist, currently Chief of the Emergency Services Branch of the United States National Institute of Mental Health. This is the primary U.S. agency that awards grants for mental health services to victims of mass emergencies and for research that will contribute knowledge to improve such services. Dr. Lystad is author of numerous scholarly publications. With these credentials it is therefore not surprising that she was able to attract so many well-known scholars and clinician-scholars to contribute to this unique volume. Indeed, 26 highly regarded scholars have contributed 15 chapters divided among three interrelated parts.

The volume begins with Dr. Lystad's introduction. Here she provides a useful perspective on the field, along with a preview of the chapters to follow. Her final section is especially valuable, discussing the implications from this collection with regard to research needs, service needs, and social policy. Among other things, it points to the directions she hopes to lead her Emergency Services Branch as well as the emergency services area in general.

We are especially pleased to welcome Dr. Lystad's book as the latest addition to the Psychosocial Stress Book Series. It provides not only a solid, scientific contribution to the field, but also needed direction for researchers, clinicians, and policymakers. This book continues the tradition of the Series, providing a new orientation for thinking about human behavior under extraordinary conditions. These books provide an integrated set of resources for scholars and practitioners interested in how and why some individuals and social systems exposed to stressful situations improve and grow stronger and more vibrant, while others do not.

The Editorial Board welcomes your reactions to this and to all of the books in the Series. We also welcome any proposals you may have for other books appropriate for the Series.

Charles R. Figley, Ph.D.
Series Editor
Purdue University
West Lafayette, Indiana

To Gilbert Fowler White
who brought us together and encouraged our research
and our interventions on behalf of disaster victims.

Contents

Contributors

Robert Bolin, Ph.D.
Associate Professor, Department of Sociology/Anthropology, New Mexico State University, Las Cruces, New Mexico

Raquel E. Cohen, M.D., M.P.H.
Professor of Psychiatry, University of Miami School of Medicine, Miami, Florida

Evelyn Payne Davis
Vice President, Community Education Services, Children's Television Workshop, New York, New York

Christine Dunning, Ph.D.
Associate Professor, Department of Governmental Affairs, University of Wisconsin, Milwaukee, Wisconsin

Joe Gelsomino, Ph.D.
Clinical Field Manager—East, Readjustment Counseling Service, Veterans Administration Medical Center, Bay Pines, Florida

H. Allen Handford, M.D.
Associate Professor of Psychiatry, The Pennsylvania State University College of Medicine, Hershey, Pennsylvania

Joyce D. Kales, M.D.
Professor of Psychiatry, The Pennsylvania State University College of Medicine, Hershey, Pennsylvania

Robert S. Laufer, Ph. D.
Associate Professor of Sociology, Brooklyn College/Graduate Center, City University of New York, New York City, New York

Bruno R. Lima, M.D., M.P.H.
Assistant Professor, Departments of Psychiatry and Mental Hygiene, Johns Hopkins Schools of Medicine and Public Health, Baltimore, Maryland

Julio Lozano, M.D.
Assistant Professor, Department of Psychiatry, University Javeriana School of Medicine, Bogota, Colombia

Jairo Luna, M.D.
Former Director, Health Department, State of Tolima, Colombia

Mary Lystad, Ph.D.
Chief, Emergency Services Branch, National Institute of Mental Health, Rockville, Maryland

David W. Mackey, M.A.
Team Leader, Tampa Vet Center, Tampa, Florida

Enos D. Martin, M.D.
Associate Professor of Psychiatry, The Pennsylvania State University College of Medicine, Hershey, Pennsylvania

Armond T. Mascelli, M.S.W.
Manager, Operations and Technical Support, Disaster Services, American Red Cross National Headquarters, Washington, D.C.

Dennis S. Mileti, Ph.D.
Professor of Sociology and Director, Hazards Assessment Laboratory, Colorado State University, Fort Collins, Colorado

Joanne M. Nigg, Ph.D.
Director, Office of Hazards Studies, and Associate Professor, School of Public Affairs, Arizona State University, Tempe, Arizona

Carol S. North, M.D.
Post-doctoral Fellow and Clinical Instructor, Department of Psychiatry, Washington University School of Medicine, St. Louis, Missouri

Ronald W. Perry, Ph.D.
Professor, School of Public Affairs, Arizona State University, Tempe, Arizona

Jack N. Peuler, M.S.W.
Program Manager, San Mateo County Mental Health Services, San Mateo, California

Paul C. Price, A.B.
Research Assistant, Department of Psychiatry, Washington University School of Medicine, St. Louis, Missouri

Hernan Santacruz, M.D.
Assistant Professor, Department of Psychiatry, University Javeriana School of Medicine, Bogota, Colombia

Elizabeth M. Smith, Ph.D.
Research Associate Professor of Psychiatry, Washington University School of Medicine, St. Louis, Missouri

John H. Sorensen, Ph.D.
Energy Division, Oak Ridge National Laboratory, Oak Ridge, Tennessee

James L. Titchener, M.D.
Professor of Psychiatry, University of Cincinnati, Cincinnati, Ohio

George J. Warheit, Ph.D.
Professor of Sociology, University of Miami, Coral Gables, Florida

Preface

In the last two decades, three groups of experts have focused increased attention on psychological responses of individuals, communities, and governments to a range of mass emergencies. One group includes those clinical and social researchers who study human response to stressful life events, the usual problems of everyday living, and the unusual problems resulting from catastrophes in the physical and social environment. These academics are developing a body of knowledge on how people react and how they cope with environmental crises, including human-induced crises. In so doing, they are able to address basic questions about human behavior and social organization.

A second group consists of mental health professionals who see their roles as service providers not only to the mentally ill in institutions or community-based clinics, but also to essentially normal persons in abnormal situations, and they offer such help in non-health care settings. Some, but not all, of these persons carry out research on victim responses and service delivery as well.

A third group of individuals focusing on human response to mass emergencies is made up of legislators and policymakers. They have established several national relief efforts, including Public Law 93-288, the Disaster Relief Act of 1974, which provides Federal funds for victims of Presidentially-declared disasters, affording crisis counseling services, along with food, housing, unemployment compensation, and other basic assistance to individuals and families.

The purpose of this book is threefold. Part I brings together what is known of individual and community responses to mass emergencies. It addresses theoretical and methodological issues, research findings, and research needs. Part II describes and analyzes innovative social and clinical intervention programs, focusing on their assumptions, organization, and service delivery techniques. Part III addresses issues in public education and planning to assist individuals, community organizations, and Federal, State and local governments in emergency preparedness and response.

xv

The book is designed primarily for planners and administrators charged with responding to an array of emergency needs in the emergency health and mental health fields. It also is of utility to researchers curious about the state of the art in theory and practice. It is a collaborative effort of researchers, service providers, and emergency planners and administrators who have come together to share their findings, their experiences, and their concerns for the future. These authors address a range of emergencies, including natural disasters, technological accidents, and war-related incidents. Similarities and differences between human response to, service delivery for, and preparedness planning on different types of emergencies are addressed.

My appreciation is extended to the authors of these chapters who share their expertise, their commitment, and their questions about emergency mental health. Appreciation is also given to Ann Alhadeff, Executive Editor of Brunner/Mazel, and to Charles Figley, Editor of the Psychosocial Stress Series, for their steadfast, understanding support.

Mary Lystad, Ph.D.

Perspectives on Human Response to Mass Emergencies

MARY LYSTAD

INTRODUCTION TO THE PROBLEM

Humans have been victimized by disasters throughout recorded history. An earthquake in Syria in 526 A.D. claimed 250,000 lives. Floods and tidal waves in the Hwang-ho River in China in 1931 claimed approximately 3.7 million lives. A more recent natural disaster was the earthquake in Tangshan, China, in 1976, which took over 655,000 lives. Still more recently, a serious industrial accident in Bhopal, India, in 1984 resulted in over 2000 dead and tens of thousands injured following release of a deadly toxic gas. The atomic bomb explosion in Hiroshima, Japan, in 1945 killed over 200,000 persons.

Large-scale efforts in disaster relief are relatively new in human history. The International Red Cross, established in Geneva in 1863 by Henry Dunant, encouraged the establishment of the American Red Cross (ARC) by Clara Barton in 1881. In its 1986 reporting year, the American Red Cross responded to 43,658 disaster incidents and expended $122,669,696 for domestic and foreign disaster preparedness and relief activities (ARC, 1986). In its 1986 reporting year, the Federal Emergency Management Agency (FEMA) (1987) responded to 30 presidentially declared disasters and obligated $648,011,810 in funds for disaster relief. In that same reporting year, the National Institute of Mental Health (NIMH) (1986a) responded to nine presidentially declared disasters, for which FEMA obligated $1,885,654 for mental health services to victims.

Knowledge about human response to mass emergencies has increased significantly in the last 30 years, although, as several authors in this volume point out, there remain critical theoretical and methodological problems in research on the subject. Typological categorization of disasters has been repeatedly attempted and yet the field lacks a single agreed-upon definition of disaster as well as a comprehensive typology of disaster characteristics and consequences. The early distinctions between natural disasters ("Acts of God") and technological disasters ("Acts of Man") have given way to realization that the two events are not clearly separable and that responses to such events are not clearly different. A natural event, such as flooding, can cause the spread of poisonous chemicals (such as dioxin in Times Beach, Missouri, 1982), and a technological accident, such as a dam break, can cause massive flooding (Buffalo Creek, West Virginia, 1972). Technological breakthroughs have allowed purposeful disasters, such as nuclear warfare (Hiroshima and Nagasaki, Japan, 1945).

There have been several theoretical approaches to disaster research, grounded in the academic disciplines of the researchers. Clinicians most often take a psychological trauma perspective emanating from in-depth interviews with primarily self-selected victims. Sociologists, on the other hand, most often take a social organization perspective, focusing on social organization and community support in a disaster based on random samples of victims.

A third approach is used by some social psychologists and sociologists (Bolin, 1985; Dohrenwend & Dohrenwend, 1981; Warheit, 1985; and others), who look at stressful life events and their impacts on human emotions and behaviors. Stress is usually conceptualized as a process in which an event (stressor) subjects an individual or group to demands which require the individual to respond in some fashion. When demands exceed the capacity of the individual or group to respond, stress occurs.

The Dohrenwends (1981) link stressful life events, as they are affected by social situations and personal dispositions, to health and mental health consequences for individuals. They offer several hypotheses about these linkages. One is a hypothesis of straightforward cause and effect: Stressful life events result in adverse health changes. Two more hypotheses concern the exacerbation of stressful life events by social and personal dispositions: The combination of factors results in adverse health changes. A fourth hypothesis proposes that symptoms of adverse health changes lead to stressful life events, which, in turn, increase the degree of adverse health changes.

Warheit (1985) offers a more dynamic model encompassing the systematic relationships among life events, coping resources, stress, and stress outcomes. The Warheit model postulates that stressful events arise from five sources: 1) the individual's biological constitution; 2) the individual's psychological characteristics; 3) the social structure; 4) the culture; and 5) the geophysical environment.

In terms of biological factors, age and physical and mental abilities have been hypothesized as significantly related to the stress of emergencies. It is hypothesized that young children are more vulnerable because of their attachment to the mother/caretaker (Farberow & Gordon, 1986). Attachment behavior is intense until after the third birthday; it is especially apt to be aroused when the child is ill, fatigued, or afraid. At such times the child searches for the care and comfort of person and place that are most familiar. Separation, or threat of separation, from an attachment figure is seen as a particular vulnerability of children.

The frail elderly and the physically ill have been hypothesized to be more vulnerable because they are less able to care for themselves and are more economically dependent, although research findings have not borne out significantly greater stress levels (Kilijanek & Drabek, 1979; Warheit, 1985). The mentally ill, because of their weak coping skills, have been hypothesized to be more vulnerable, although again research data do not support significant stress consequences (Ahearn, 1981; Warheit, 1985). The conditions under which those with physical and psychological vulnerabilities are adversely affected by disaster need further investigation.

Theoretical formulations that relate psychological response to mass disaster events focus on perception, personality characteristics, and social behaviors. Slovic et al. (1979) focus on the perception of risk in disaster situations, hypothesizing that persons who perceive the risk as great are more likely to heed warnings and take some individual action to avoid or ameliorate consequences than those who do not. In the case of technological risks, those who perceive the risk as great are also more likely to blame the government for policies which allow the risk to occur.

Glenn (1979) looks at the personality characteristics of disaster victims. In reviewing published research, he reports that individual and group reactions to natural disasters differ by disaster phases (warnings, threats, and impacts) and that responses are dependent upon predisaster coping skills. Schulberg (1974) refers to the adaptive capacities of victims as an important factor in the probability of personal crisis in disaster conditions.

Social behaviors are examined by Taylor (1978), who constructs hypotheses regarding the importance of political, economic, and family interactions and supports. Her variable, "political supports," refers to functions served by public figures at disaster sites. "Economic supports" are defined as financial institutions that provide funds in aid of recovery of the community. "Family supports" refers to the functioning of family members in warning system evacuation and extended family assistance.

Theoretical formulations regarding social responses to disaster—community supports, planning, and preparedness—have been reviewed by Kreps (1981), who looks at the findings of two long-term disaster research programs. The first, sponsored by the National Academy of Sciences and the National Research Council in the 1950s, is exemplified by the work of Barton (1969), who uses a general sociological framework for analyzing individual and organizational behavior in disaster situations. This led Barton to postulate the existence of a two-part emergency social system. The first part of the system involves individual patterns of adaptive and nonadaptive reactions to stress, particularly the motivational basis of various types of helping behavior (e.g., altruism and close relationship to the victim); these discrete patterns of individual behavior are conceptually aggregated to reflect the community's informal "mass assault" on disaster-generated needs. The second part of the system is the community's formal organizational structure. Here Barton broadens his initial discussion of the individual basis of helping behavior by examining a community-based model of collective assistance.

The second long-term program of social research discussed by Kreps (1981) is that of the Disaster Research Center (DRC), which began in the 1960s at Ohio State University and continues now at the University of Delaware. Studies conducted by the DRC have used an organizational level of analysis, looking at local disaster-relevant organizations and emergency groups with particular attention to emergency responses and planning for such responses. Quarantelli and Dynes (1977), the two dominant figures in that program, felt that previous theoretical efforts to link ideas of individual and social system response were unsuccessful without the full development of a framework for analyzing organizational response. They have emphasized a planning perspective to determine what can and should be done in advance of disasters to deal with their consequences. The DRC has consistently argued for a flexible approach to disaster planning and preparedness at the local level.

Cultural theories related to disaster have looked at the importance of cross-cultural differences in response to and recovery from the event. Roth (1970) suggests use of a number of factors in cross-cultural research: the degree of societal differentiation, level of technology, historical tradition, and the dominant value orientation in the affected society. Quarantelli (1954) and Wenger et al. (1975) have identified disaster myths as important cultural variables. Such myths include the belief that panic and looting are major problems after disaster. These authors argue that the myths inhibit proper disaster response and they have sought to dispel such myths and to encourage the mass media to also dispel them.

Bolin and Bolton (1986), studying four disasters, found significant differences in disaster response and recovery among cultural groups, stemming from a complex interplay of class and ethnicity. Poor families and large families had the most trouble acquiring adequate aid and recovering from disaster; members of ethnic minorities, particularly blacks and Hispanics, were more likely to belong to such families. They used multiple aid sources in their efforts to recoup losses; yet they still more often than whites evaluated the aid received as inadequate, and their economic recovery was slower. These researchers observed that certain ethnic/cultural traditions tended to keep some victims out of the formal aid network: for example, the tradition of self-help among members of the Mormon Church, the tradition of family and self-reliance of Japanese-Americans. Bolin and Bolton stress the importance of recovery policies which are responsive to social inequalities and value orientations among populations groups.

Further theoretical formulations about stress involve a geophysical dimension. They focus on the disaster event itself. Frederick (1980) and others have theorized that technological disasters create more mental stress than do natural disasters because they are defined not as originating from God but as originating from human actions. Still other theoreticians differentiate among phases of a disaster. Baker (1964) distinguishes between more frequent immediate psychological effects of the disaster experience and less frequent long-term consequences of disaster for the individual. Others have looked at the magnitude of the disaster's impact. Kastenbaum (1974), for example, hypothesizes a significant difference between those disasters that affect the individual's whole environment and those that affect only a part of it.

Emergency situations are particularly useful for the study of the emotional and physical effects of stress. Emergencies provide a natural setting in which to research the phenomenon. The earlier stress studies, conducted in laboratory settings using aversive stimuli such as electric shocks or noise bursts as stressors, are less informative than more recent disaster studies about long-term responses to real life crises of varying magnitudes. Natural and technological emergencies also, because they are uncommon events primarily outside of the individual's control, are less likely than common and controllable stressful events, such as divorce or job loss, to offer confusing relationships between the event and symptoms of an illness. The disaster event could not be a consequence of illness.

But there are considerable methodological problems related to the study of emergencies. Drabek (1970) points out that, because disasters are unpredictable, researchers face difficulties in research preparation, random sampling, beginning data collection too late, and gaining local cooperation. From the start, researchers must decide on what to observe and where to collect data and must define their unit of analysis. Drabek offers the concept of "environmental disruption" to include manmade and natural calamities and to place disaster investigation within a broader perspective for viewing individual and collective responses. His recommendations for future research include: using ongoing research teams, bridging of field and laboratory investigations, strengthening of sampling procedures, and emphasizing the comparisons of different situations.

Perry and Lindell (1978) relate the inconsistencies in research findings on psychological consequences of emergencies to methodological difficulties. The authors conclude: 1) the frequently used "after only" survey design reflects an inappropriate conception of what the research questions should be; and 2) some short-term psychological consequences of natural disasters probably do occur, but research designs have been inadequate in determining whether the consequences are wholly positive or negative, or whether they persist over the long term. The authors advocate the development of study designs which account for base rates of psychological disorders and theoretical frameworks which provide explicit logics for developing comparable operational definitions.

Green (1982) further emphasizes the need for future research to seek greater comparability between methods employed and proposes that this be accomplished by the use of standardized test instruments and by requiring researchers to be explicit about their methods and their populations.

Methodological problems are particularly troublesome in evaluation studies of prevention and treatment programs following disasters. Solomon (in press) discusses the advantages and disadvantages of three basic approaches available for evaluating formal interventions for disaster-induced mental health disorders: controlled clinical trials, field studies, and quasi-experimental designs which combine elements of both. She concludes that in some cases the latter approach may be the most feasible research strategy. An investigator could use field study methods to first identify victims at highest risk for psychopathology. Then a variety of outreach strategies could be targeted to these victims. Individuals reached by the different methods could be referred to a particular mental health provider who would then randomly assign victims to either of two intervention models. This design permits comparison of short- and long-term outcomes of differing interventions for high-risk individuals. Such a strategy deserves further exploration.

In this volume, theoretical and methodological issues in the study of natural and technological disasters and war-related events are explored further. Refined theoretical models of the relationship of life events to stress, of public response to warnings, and of the integration of mental health care into emergency aid are presented. Methodological refinements in the study of human responses to a disaster event and to organizational management of that event are offered. An epidemiological study designed to minimize some of the methodological problems already discussed is described. Further, exemplary social and clinical intervention programs, and public education and planning programs are discussed.

INDIVIDUAL AND COMMUNITY RESPONSES TO DISASTER

Part I of this book includes chapters by researchers who have studied human responses to a range of emergencies. They look at theoretical assumptions, methodological approaches, measures used, populations interviewed, and research outcomes in terms of consistency of findings and utility of findings in the planning of services to victims.

Warheit, in Chapter 1, notes considerable variation in schools of thought about psychological consequences of disaster on victims. He feels the sources of such contradictory findings are: 1) differences in the definition of disaster used; 2) differences in the definition of mental health used (i.e., as emotional stress versus emotional illness); 3) research orientations (i.e., sociologists focus on macro-level social structural variables, psychiatrists focus on micro-level individual psychopathology); 4) confusion between agent generated (disaster) and response generated (organizational response efforts) consequences; and 5) the absence of an integrated theoretical model.

Warheit offers a theoretical model which represents systematic relationships among life events, coping resources, stress, and stress outcomes as they occur in a temporal context. A research design based on this model would necessitate obtaining information on all of its various components; it would also require analytic procedures that could test relationships within and between the variables. There is no single piece of research in the scientific literature that approaches the rigor imposed by the comprehensive, integrated model which he offers. Nonetheless, the model is useful as a framework for looking at variables to be considered in addressing the relationship of disasters and mental health and for analyzing research findings on disaster and mental health.

Warheit believes that future efforts to move the field of inquiry forward require researchers to place less emphasis on the general questions that have dominated a great deal of interest over the last 20 years—i.e., whether or not disasters produce negative mental health consequences. They must now ask specific questions about types of effects produced by types of disaster agents on types of population subgroups. He also feels that standardized instruments capable of identifying a broad spectrum of disorders ranging from subclinical conditions, such as demoralization, to the kinds of specific disorders delineated by the Diagnostic and Statistical Manual of Mental Disorders, Third Edition (DSM-III), American Psychiatric Association, 1980, are needed.

Bolin, in Chapter 2, reviews the research literature on human response to natural disasters and asks specific questions. He argues that potential mental health impacts involve three major categories of phenomenon: the event itself, victim characteristics, and social responses to the event. Bolin focuses on research dealing with event characteristics and social responses.

In terms of event characteristics, Bolin reports that the literature indicates heightened stress levels to be associated with:

1. disasters with sudden, unanticipated onsets;
2. disasters in which victims are unfamiliar with, and unprepared for, impact;
3. disasters where victims are exposed to life-threatening situations and/or witness the death of others;
4. disasters that impact a large segment of a local population when accompanied with widespread property damage;
5. disasters that are followed by a continued threat of recurrence.

Bolin believes that these findings appear also to be true of nonnatural disasters.

In terms of response characteristics, Bolin writes that the literature suggests that heightened stress levels are associated with:

1. evacuations in which families are separated, or in which there is a lack of consensus on the decision to evacuate;
2. emergency shelter stays that are protracted or the center for interpersonal conflict;
3. evacuations that are poorly managed or expose victims to continuing environmental threats;
4. temporary housing that is perceived as dangerous or inadequate;
5. failure to establish stable temporary housing;
6. temporary housing or relocation programs that socially isolate victims from their old communities and neighborhoods;
7. exclusion of victims from or their failure to qualify for formal aid programs.

Bolin believes that some of these findings apply to nonnatural disasters as well.

In Chapter 3, Smith, North, and Price discuss human responses to technological disasters. These authors, like Handford, Martin, and Kales in Part II, realize that, in an expanding technological world, technological accidents become more frequent. From their review of the literature of such accidents, Smith and associates report findings of a wide range of psychiatric disturbance and a wide range of methods of studying victim response. The differences in victim response, the authors suggest, may be attributable to how, when, and on whom the data were collected rather than on type of event. The authors stress the importance of looking at individual symptoms as well as at clinically diagnosable psychiatric syndromes. Inattention to individual symptoms could result in overlooking very distressed individuals within an otherwise essentially normal population.

The authors perceive the existing literature as revealing of three categories of risk factors: individual factors, situational factors, and agent-related factors. In terms of individual risk factors, the only one that has consistently been found to affect response to disaster is that of preexisting psychiatric diagnosis, although the dynamics of this relationship are unclear.

In terms of situational risk factors, the one found most relevant is the degree of the victim's involvement with the disaster agent. As for agent-related risk factors, the severity and totality of the stress (disaster) supercede the intrapsychic predisposition as a determinant of neurotic stress response. These authors cite the conclusions of Hocking (1970), from study of war-related stress, that at the far end of the continuum of stressful situations, predisposing psychological factors become irrelevant, since all individuals break down under extreme stress.

Smith et al. report on Smith's epidemiological study of an area, affected by two types of disaster, which fortuitously had been the site of a careful evaluation of psychiatric status just before disaster occurred. This study offered a rare opportunity to return to previously known respondents affected by disaster and to determine whether exposure to floods or tornadoes, or notification of long-standing exposure to either dioxin or radioactive well water, had affected their psychiatric status. This effect could be judged by comparing changes in their mental health status with changes in the mental health status of a control group. (Disasters occurred near St. Louis, Missouri, in 1982.) The study found little evidence that either type of disaster agent caused the onset of mental disorders, caused remitted disorders to relapse, preserved symptoms of disorders, or caused new symptoms to appear (with the exception of post-traumatic stress disorder: PTSD).

Laufer, in Chapter 4, looks at psychosocial responses to war and war-related events in contemporary society. The author points out that research in this area focuses on early adult exposure to a catastrophic stress and that as such it generates a major clash with established clinical theory committed to the impact of childhood trauma and developmental patterns in the shaping of adult lives. The perspective of this chapter, based on evidence accumulated over the last two decades on the holocaust, World War II, Korea, and Vietnam, indicates that war stress plays a decisive role in postwar adult development, but that predisposing factors play a significant role in particular patterns of psychosocial response in individuals exposed to warfare.

Laufer distinguishes war from other catastrophic trauma because it involves the purposeful destruction of human beings to achieve the objective of collective dominance of one social system over another or among groups within social systems. War is also distinguished from other catastrophes by the fact that efforts to impose dominance through resort to warfare or through rebellion against authority takes place over time, i.e., it is a process.

Those who survive war, the author writes, must cope with that trauma in its variegated forms through their life course. Laufer looks at the trauma during the readjustment period, and in early, middle, and late adulthood of survivors. His systematic exploration of lifetime effects is a critical addition to the study of environmental stress.

The author writes that research indicates depression, anxiety, phobic symptomatology and disorder, and substance abuse, as well as divorce, intergenerational conflict, antisocial behavior and career deficits, are all related to exposure to war stress among veteran, prisoner of war, and targeted civilian populations. Further, there is some evidence that in these populations the largest proportion of the incidence of psychopathology occurs in early adult development, though there is also evidence of some incidence of psychopathology even during late adulthood. Thus, it appears that disruptive symptomatology and psychopathology are persistent parts of the life course of war's victims.

SOCIAL AND CLINICAL INTERVENTION PROGRAMS

Part II of this volume describes different intervention programs for different kinds of victims of different kinds of disasters. Though the programs differ by intervention, victim, and disaster variables, they share common assumptions. They assume that most victims are from normal populations under abnormal environmental stress, and that community outreach by mental health professionals is helpful in relieving stress and preventing some serious mental health consequences.

These programs share common strategies. They avoid the label of "mentally ill" in dealing with victims. They use a crisis intervention model to address the immediate problem rather than a traditional psychotherapy model of addressing lifetime adjustment. They deliver strategic outreach and services where the people actually are — in disaster assistance centers, in relocation areas of mobile home parks, in community agencies; they do not just wait for people to come to ask for help.

Funding for these programs comes from private and public sources at local, State, and Federal levels. Of the private sources, American Red Cross local chapters address a large proportion of the smaller disasters. They are often assisted by other volunteer groups, sometimes church-based, which routinely supply food, clothing, and shelter. The American Red Cross has 2,800 community-based chapters, and it is usual for other neighboring Red Cross chapters or other private organizations within a locality or State to assist when needed (see Mascelli in this volume).

On the national level, the American Red Cross has promoted the National Committee of Voluntary Organizations. Its membership includes, in addition to ARC: the American Radio Relay League; Ananda Marga Universal Relief Team; B'nai B'rith; Boy Scouts of America; Christian Reformed World Relief Committee; Church of the Brethren; Church World Service; The Episcopal Church Presiding Bishop's Fund for World Relief; Lutheran Council in the U.S.A.; Mennonite Disaster Service; National Association for the Advancement of Colored People; National Catholic Disaster Relief Committee; National Conference of Catholic Charities; Presbyterian Church in the United States Crisis Fund; REACT International; The Salvation Army; Seventh-Day Adventist Community Services; Society of St. Vincent de Paul; Southern Baptist Commission Convention Home Mission Board; United Methodist Committee on Relief and the National Division: Board of Global Ministries; United Methodist Church; The United Presbyterian Church; U.S.A. World Relief, Emergency, and Resettlement Services; and Volunteers of America (ARC, 1982).

While most member organizations use volunteers, they usually are trained by the individual agency or the American Red Cross. Many of the agencies have a religious affiliation, and they coordinate with ARC and sometimes FEMA as well. These agencies often have distinct advantages of prior knowledge of the communities in which they are working, of not carrying a "mental illness" label, and of being able to operate without cumbersome forms and files.

Of the public sources, local community agencies handle small disasters. For disasters beyond their capabilities, assistance from adjacent communities or from the State may be secured. The Federal government comes into play when there is a presidentially declared disaster. If such a disaster is primarily from natural causes, FEMA can provide funds for public assistance, temporary housing, disaster unemployment assistance, and individual and family grants.

Because the focus of this book is on mental health services, FEMA's role in this regard will be detailed. The Disaster Relief Act Amendments of 1974, Public Law 93-288, Section 413, authorizes the President, through the National Institute of Mental Health, to provide training and services to alleviate mental health problems caused or exacerbated by major disasters. The actual program has been developed in cooperation between FEMA and NIMH and is funded by FEMA. Assistance under this program is limited to presidentially declared major disasters. The program is designed to supplement the available resources and services of State and local governments, but support for crisis counseling services to disaster victims may be granted for up to 11 months following a disaster if these services cannot be provided by existing agency programs (NIMH, 1986b).

The Federal government also has a role in technological and war-related emergencies. The Environmental Protection Agency (EPA) is the lead agency for hazardous waste disasters and provides for public involvement in its Superfund Program, which is charged with cleanup of hazardous waste. Public involvement includes communication of information and outreach and dialogue about public concerns, questions, and preferences. EPA maintains that public comment and involvement have significantly influenced EPA's plans for cleanups in a number of instances and that citizens have provided EPA with valuable input about conditions at particular sites (EPA, 1986).

In terms of war-related events, the Veterans Administration has a broad-based mental health program for war veterans. Originally labeled "Operation Outreach" at its inception in 1979, it involves intervention and prevention services to Vietnam veterans (Blank, 1982; Gelsomino & Mackey, this volume).

Still other Federal agencies become involved in the protection of citizens following emergencies. Among them are the agencies of the United States Public Health Service: Alcohol, Drug Abuse, and Mental Health Administration; Centers for Disease Control; Food and Drug Administration; Health Resources and Services Administration; and the National Institutes of Health. The National Oceanic and Atmospheric Administration (NOAA) produces valuable pamphlets for adults and children on protective stances for natural disasters. All Departments of the Executive Branch of Government can become involved and their roles focus on various aspects of public safety and concern. How they perform their jobs directly affects the mental health of the public they are dealing with.

Mascelli, in Chapter 5, describes the long history of American Red Cross involvement with a wide variety of emergencies and disasters, beginning with the 1881 forest fires in Michigan. In 1905 the disaster response and relief efforts of ARC were recognized by a Congressional charter which mandates cooperation with the U.S. government in matters pertaining to the Geneva Conventions for the protection of war victims. This charter requires that Red Cross serve as a communication between members of the armed forces and their families at home, that it provide aid to sick and wounded in time of war, and that it carry on a program of voluntary relief for victims of disasters. The Disaster Relief Acts of 1950, 1969, and 1974 further recognized the roles and responsibilities of ARC in time of disaster and established lines of communication between the Red Cross and the Federal government in the areas of disaster planning, preparedness, response, and relief.

Of particular interest is Mascelli's discussion of future ARC directions. The first involves further focus in the area of technological disasters. The Red Cross has over the last decade noted a sharp increase in hazardous material incidents that require sheltering of local residents and has isolated some factors in technological disasters to be addressed in planning of services.

A second future intention of ARC is to direct more attention to needs of disaster victims and stress management assistance to disaster relief workers. Federal funds, as has been noted, are available for such assistance in presidentially declared disasters. Because of shrinking community mental health center budgets, local funds are seldom adequate in the vast majority of disasters that are not presidentially declared. It is of major importance that the Red Cross is considering the provision of psychological assistance as well as material assistance to victims. It is also significant that, given its far-reaching activities in the area of disaster relief, it is focusing on the mental health needs of its own workers as well as of victims.

Titchener, in Chapter 6, views natural and technological disasters as the cause of immense suffering and perhaps lifelong scars for some victims. He emphasizes the importance of having a mental health professional involved in the highest level of disaster planning and policy making before disaster strikes, and in the highest level of community response direction and reintegration following disaster. The mental health professional, he feels, should have a role entirely different from any previously held; more than a mere consultant or advisor, the professional should have decision-making and supervisory responsibility.

One example of psychiatric expertise in disaster response comes from the Mexico City earthquake of 1985. Titchener reports that psychoanalysts there found that television and radio stations filled their hours with images of agony and death, overwhelming and disorganizing persons in rural and urban areas. These psychoanalysts recognized the power of the media for ego-weakening; they sought to use it for ego-strengthening. They employed TV and radio for other messages—advising victims to communicate with each other, describing stress response syndromes, and announcing training courses for disaster workers.

Titchener sees crisis intervention as beginning with community outreach. After the Beverly Hills Supper Club fire (in Ohio, 1976) a group of 10 professionals in the area, most with some disaster experience, gathered after midnight to consider what was happening and what needs were greatest. When they had ascertained that there were few physical injuries and many deaths, they decided that the need for psychiatric services was at the place where over 150 corpses had been assembled for identification. Titchener and his colleagues went to a temporary morgue in a large armory that had sufficient floor space to lay out this many corpses. They worked for four days, with teams of six to eight mental health professionals. On the armory floor these teams had a presence, walking up and down the rows of corpses, standing at the official desk, talking to persons in private rooms in neighboring buildings. Titchener characterizes their activity as "aggressively hanging around." He points out that such crisis counseling is extremely difficult because victims, emergency workers, and the governmental system tend to avoid the emotional issues and believe that avoidance is the best course.

In Chapter 7, Handford, Martin, and Kales look at a range of technologically generated disasters made possible by the discovery of nuclear energy: the atomic bombing of Japan (1945); the nuclear plant accidents at Three Mile Island (1979) and Chernobyl (1986); and work site accidents such as those at Love Canal, New York (discovered 1978), Times Beach, Missouri (1982), and Bhopal, India (1984), which occurred with the release of toxic chemicals into the environment of industrial plants and sometimes to surrounding communities beyond.

The authors' discussion of transportation accidents points out that the greatest disaster in the United States during the 20th century, apart from war, has been the production of some 50,000 victims a year from automobile highway accidents.

Like Titchener, Handford et al. emphasize the importance of mental health professionals being involved in the planning processes conducted by emergency management at Federal, State, and local levels. Also like Titchener, these authors urge creative use of mass media, guarding against sensationalism and presenting calm, factual information about normal human reactions to stress and about available mental health services, including crisis lines and walk-in clinics.

Handford et al. promote outreach intervention. They write that, initially, contact is best made through the provision of direct, nonprofessional assistance in meeting basic human needs. Mental health workers in disasters are in a position to be most effective if they are directly involved in rescue or relocation operations. A mental health worker might make early contact by riding in an evacuation vehicle with children and their parents. There questions could be answered, stories could be told, songs could be sung about what everyone is experiencing—all devices for reducing anxiety by allowing for acceptable expression of feelings. Similarly in shelters, crayons and paper could be provided to allow for expression of fantasies about the technological accident, since these are often events not visible or easily explained by the victims.

Handford et al. perceive the basic mental health goal as short-term crisis intervention to restore the victim to his/her preaccident state and to enable preexistent support systems such as families and friends again to meet fundamental emotional needs. They identify several populations with special needs: on-site personnel responsible for bringing the disaster under control (they compare rescue teams to war veterans, who also directly observe and experience death or severe injury); children exposed to dramatic scenes of destruction and death; the frail elderly whose daily life routines are severely disrupted; the chronically mentally ill, alcoholic, and drug dependent.

Gelsomino and Mackey, in Chapter 8, describe the Veterans Administration's Vet Center Program which was established in 1979 by an Act of Congress to offer community-based psychosocial services for Vietnam Era veterans in order to deal with the emotional sequelae of the Vietnam War. This intervention program began several years after the last soldier left South Vietnam. The authors believe that both the controversial nature of the war and the lack of contingency planning contributed to the delayed response in planning, and they argue as strongly as do the authors of previous chapters for preparedness prior to any catastrophe.

Upon review of the clinical interventions necessitated by veteran's suffering from the traumas and stressors of combat exposure years earlier, it became abundantly clear that aggressive outreach was necessary to preclude the high incidence and severity levels of PTSD from recurring in any future conflicts that might arise. The Vet Center Program provides a necessary alternative to clinical interventions that rigidly adhere to the more conventional medical model approach to the delivery of mental health services. It is a community-based outreach approach based on a theoretical framework in which the agency's clinicians view themselves not so much as treaters of pathology but rather as facilitators and catalysts of a normal stress recovery process.

Along with this assumption of normalcy is the use of community outreach services. Outreach counselors routinely contact and network with a broad range of community health care and social service agencies as well as with churches and synagogues, themselves good sources of reciprocal referrals on behalf of veterans in need of services. Yet another client referral source that has been quite successful is the criminal justice system.

Peuler, in Chapter 9, focuses on disaster assistance from a community mental health center perspective. Since the local community mental health center is likely to be indigenous to the area impacted, has networks with other public service agencies, and is part of the local government bureaucracy, it is in an excellent position to coordinate services from a community perspective.

The author points out that disaster services are relatively new for public community mental health centers. Given their heavy case loads and low funding levels, there centers prioritize resources to the chronically mentally ill. Thus, it is imperative that agencies write a disaster plan and train staff in the types of services to be delivered to disaster victims when situations make this a new priority.

Community mental health centers, Peuler maintains, must be made aware of disaster training resources at the State and Federal levels. Concomitantly, State Departments of Mental Health should provide leadership and support to local agencies to establish the provision of services after disasters. Further, the author writes, State Offices of Emergency Services and the Federal Emergency Management Agency must continue to require mental health involvement and input as they develop area disaster plans. Peuler sees three disaster service activities for the community mental health center: information, social support, and assessment and treatment interventions.

Peuler emphasizes the need for good self-care on the part of disaster workers. They, too, need to vent feelings and to use debriefing sessions to allow them to adequately continue to serve victims. A debriefing, the author explains, is not a critique. A critique is a meeting in which the incident is discussed, evaluated, and analyzed with regard to procedures, performance, and what could have been improved upon. A debriefing has a different focus: that of dealing with the emotional aspects of the experience.

Cohen, in Chapter 10, discusses services to children following a disaster. She emphasizes that the response to the event must be designed to fit the developmental states of different systems—somatic, psychological, social, and behavioral. Cohen has found that there is a direct relationship between the level achieved in these developmental systems and the ability of the child to deal with stressful events following the disaster.

Cohen also emphasizes the need to plan programs that take into account a number of factors:

- serious disruption of the developmental processes of the child will produce disorganization in all psychological expressions;
- the quality of family relationships will affect the expression of mourning of what was lost;
- intensity of the physical and psychological trauma will influence the mourning process and lengthen the duration of the postdisaster reactions;
- special circumstances surrounding the predisaster life of the child; for example, divorce, new school, or illness will affect the child's reactions, and reactions to these events by other important adults in the child's life will affect the child;
- the multiple changes in the child's environment due to the loss of family following the disaster are of special importance.

But Cohen, like Garmezy (1986) and other researchers studying children under environmental stressors, emphasizes the resilience of children and their considerable ability to cope and recover from difficult circumstances.

For Cohen, early phases of mental health interventions with children involve working directly with families in relocation centers. Any active interactions between the professional and the family that supplements, reinforces, and promotes family systems mechanisms in the new setting are useful. By restoring family adaptive strategies, one assists the child to function more effectively.

In Chapter 11, Dunning focuses on services to disaster workers—police, fire, and emergency medical personnel. There is considerable evidence that emergency situations place extraordinary demands on such personnel and on employing agencies which need to make optimum use of limited resources under difficult conditions. Dunning is concerned that organizational plans be made which take into account the welfare of workers. These plans should focus on: 1) the development of mechanisms to enhance workers' ability to perform optimally at the disaster site; 2) the reduction of the negative impact of disaster management on future organizational functioning, and 3) organizational responsibility for ameliorating negative consequences of disaster work.

Dunning believes strongly in preplanning. While techniques of debriefing workers who have encountered extraordinary conditions have been utilized for some time, Dunning makes the cogent argument that care of workers must start long before the disaster event. A stress diagnostic system and a stress audit should be developed by organizations, especially in situations where stress can never be eliminated. Diagnosis can thus occur prior to the disaster, as the organization monitors situations and incidents that result in obvious indicators of possible psychological injury — chronic illness, turnover, absenteeism, poor performance. The diagnosis and identification of potential job stressors and their manifestations increase the administrator's awareness of and sensitivity to worker concerns.

Dunning stresses the need for agencies to maintain a continuity of concern and care for disaster workers which is not event-limited. This presupposes a commitment on the part of the employing agency to provide adequate training, social support, debriefing, and any needed subsequent mental health care. It incorporates both the concepts of organizational responsibility and the importance of care.

PUBLIC EDUCATION/PLANNING PROGRAMS

Part III of this book looks at prevention measures that can ameliorate or eliminate the negative emotional effects of mass emergencies. The need for educating the public on what to do to protect themselves in emergencies and for educating public organizations on how to respond to emergencies is axiomatic. Some of the difficulties, as well as some of the innovative ways in which the difficulties have been addressed, are described in these chapters. Most of the measures discussed are government-sponsored. Primary responsibility for planning emergency-related programs, for training persons to operate such programs, and for practicing roles and responsibilities in these programs is located within public agencies at the Federal, State, and local levels.

At the Federal level, the Federal Emergency Management Agency, an independent Agency reporting directly to the White House, takes the lead in planning for emergency response. It coordinates with the Environmental Protection Agency, the Department of Defense, the Department of Health and Human Services, and other appropriate Federal agencies.

FEMA has its own National Emergency Training Center in Emmitsburg, Maryland, for the training of emergency administrators and planners at Federal, State, and local levels.

At the State level, each State has an Office of Emergency Services which from the Governor's office coordinates all emergency-related planning of all State Departments. Localities have varying arrangements, often cooperative with nearby localities, for handling small disasters. They have, or should have, specific agreements with State and Federal agencies for situations when additional funds, supplies, and personnel are needed.

In Chapter 12, Davis describes public education programs designed to alert children and their families of the dangers of fire and of other natural hazards, including hurricanes and earthquakes. The programs were developed by the Community Education Services of the Children's Television Workshop, the producer of *Sesame Street* and related programming. Under one contract with FEMA, Children's Television Workshop (CTW) produced a program to teach fire safety to preschoolers. Children are particularly good targets for education because, as Cohen and Peuler point out in accompanying chapters, they bring information back to parents and tend to involve the whole family.

Because television is a medium widely used by preschoolers and because *Sesame Street* has been successful in teaching protective measures to this age group, CTW agreed to explore ways of including important burn prevention/fire safety messages on television. In this activity it paid particular attention to the nature and capabilities of three- to five-year-olds and to the limitations of the television medium itself. In order to carry out the project, CTW went beyond those messages that could be demonstrated safely on television and developed additional materials to help firefighters, parents, and caregivers teach fire safety skills. Songs and skits teaching specific behaviors, along with recommended teaching techniques for their effective use were prepared.

The fire program, which involved research in every phase of production, was so successful that FEMA asked CTW to experiment with messages for children on a range of natural hazards. The general goals for this contractual project are to develop awareness about the nature of natural hazards among children and their families, to motivate children and families to prepare for such emergencies, and to stimulate interest in learning more about natural phenomena.

The public education programs discussed in Chapter 12 are designed to alert persons to the nature of a disaster and the need to plan for protective measures against its future occurrence. A basic purpose of public warning systems, as discussed in Chapter 13 by Mileti and Sorensen, is to elicit protective actions by people who are presently in danger. The authors' focus is on warning systems used by public safety officials to alert the public to a broad range of geological, climatological, technological, and civil disturbance risks. Public health officials also use warning systems against health hazards, such as smoking, drug and alcohol abuse, epidemics of influenza, polio, and AIDS. Warnings—everyday occurrences in the United States—are issued to encourage the public to alter behavior in a variety of protective ways.

Protective actions, Mileti and Sorensen write, do not flow automatically from hearing a warning. An influential intervening factor between hearing and responding to a warning is the situational perception of risk that people hold. Personal perceptions of risk, as well as perceptions about appropriate response actions, influence what people do and do not do in response to warnings. A key purpose of a warning system, therefore, is to provide the public with accurate perceptions of risk from the impending disaster commensurate with the actual or objective nature of the risk, and to provide sound situational perceptions of what to do to prevent personal harm and loss.

Warning systems have had records of success and failure. According to the authors, two factors or determinants affect warning effectiveness: sender, or warning, determinants, and receiver determinants. Sender determinants of importance are the attributes of the message itself, the channels through which the message is conveyed, the frequency of conveyance, and the persons or organizations from which the message comes. Receiver determinants of importance are the receiver's own environment and his/her social, psychological, and physiological attributes.

Mileti and Sorensen conclude that underlying the warning-response process and the effect of sender and receiver determinants on the outcome of that process is the concept of confirmation, which is itself a social process. The available evidence strongly indicates that the first warning response of most people is to seek confirmation of the message; people tend not to believe the news at first blush. Only after confirmation do most people respond positively to the warning. The authors present a model of the causes and effects of public response to warnings of impending disaster, using the concepts discussed.

Chapter 14 by Perry and Nigg focuses on the governmental planning process. These authors echo the message of all those discussing intervention programs: i.e., that effective planning is vital to any successful emergency response operation, whether the disaster agent is natural or technological in origin. Perry and Nigg define the goal of emergency planning as protection of the public from the effects of a hazardous agent.

With reference to organizations and governmental units, they see planning as the pathway to achieving a state of emergency preparedness—the capacity to successfully cope with aberrations in the environment.

These authors emphasize that planning and response processes for any given community are intergovernmental in nature. To develop a comprehensive emergency plan, a community must take into account matters of risk identification, risk assessment, and risk reduction. In some cases, geographical boundaries act to make an emergency an inescapably local problem; planning involves making inventories of local resources—personnel, skills, equipment, and material. In other cases, however, the need for resources effectively to manage a disaster exceeds those available in any given community, and communities are increasingly formalizing agreements for extracommunity assistance primarily to enhance the effectiveness of the emergency response process.

Collaborative arrangements between differing levels of government—municipal, county, State, and Federal—as well as arrangements between governments of the same level are examined by Perry and Nigg. In any community, emergency local government is responsible for managing the event, for determining where shortfalls in management resources exist, and for acquiring supplements. An important means of acquiring supplemental resources is through agreements with other governmental units. These agreements may be horizontal (with units governing similar political jurisdictions) or hierarchical (with units governing larger, inclusive political jurisdictions).

Perry and Nigg view the written plan as a by-product of the planning process which inevitably changes as planning adapts to new threats, new assessments of old threats, and new mechanisms for risk reduction. The written plan should be "a slice of life," reflecting the state of planning at some given point in time. Thus the best plans are concise, clear, well-structured, easily up-dated, and short.

Perry and Nigg state correctly that mental health disaster services have not been well-integrated into the emergency response planning process. In the final Chapter 15, Lima, Santacruz, Lozano, and Luna address ways of accomplishing integration of mental health with health planning in emergencies. The authors focus on planning which utilizes skills of primary care workers, who, they point out, have been effective in providing mental health care in routine clinical situations both in developed and in developing countries. Their capacities for mental health interventions in disasters, particularly in the medium- and long-term care of victims, remained largely unexplored until recently.

Lima's own experience in Colombia followed a major disaster. He had undertaken to design, implement, and evaluate a primary mental health care plan in Colombia in August 1985. Three months later a volcanic eruption in the town of Armero produced a mudslide that resulted in 22,000 dead, 5000 injured, and other thousands of homeless people. The psychiatric hospital of Armero, which represented 87% of the country's psychiatric beds, was totally destroyed, and many of its professional staff were killed. Primary health care workers became paramount in dealing with the tragic results of this disaster.

The authors of this chapter note the difficulties of providing content related to a future disaster that may never occur, in the limited mental health training of the primary care worker. After a disaster strikes, however, the indigenous primary care workers of necessity become involved with its health consequences and are more motivated to develop additional skills to meet the varied health needs of patients. Observed in Armero was the situation where heightened tension and anxiety in the postimpact period facilitated the learning process and created a climate conducive to the optimal development of new skills, knowledge, and attitudes.

Lima et al. advocate design, implementation, and evaluation of a program for developing the primary care worker's capability for active participation in the delivery of mental health care to disaster victims. This involves a series of strategies that include the formulation of a clear national policy on mental health in disasters, the establishment of a specialized unit within the Department of Mental Health, and minimal financial provisions for operating the program.

IMPLICATIONS

The contributors to this volume provide important insights into human response to mass emergencies. They give evidence that environmental stressors of a variety of sources and intensities can and do produce significant emotional stress on human victims and on human service workers responding to these victims. They argue for clinical interventions of a nontraditional nature, focused on normal persons in abnormal stress situations. They place heavy emphasis on mental health planning for interventions and on public education at all governmental levels. These contributors identify specific research, service delivery, and public policy needs for addressing human response to mass emergencies. Some of their far-reaching conclusions are summarized here; these and others are discussed in detail in the ensuing chapters.

Research Needs

Analysis of research findings indicates a need for further refinement of theoretical models so they can be used to construct paradigms to 1) estimate the impact mass emergencies may have on mental health and 2) order findings in the literature. There is a further need to address specific rather than general research questions: What kinds of mental health consequences occur, following what kinds of disaster events, and following what kinds of social responses to disaster? Who in the population are more at risk and why? What mental health and public education programs are effective in mediating the stress of disaster? There is a need for more rigorous methodologies in disaster studies, including wherever possible use of control groups, pre- and postassessments, standarized testing, comparisons among different cultural groups, and longitudinal studies of events.

The study of individual responses to emergencies in relation to life course is essential. Well documented by previous research, for example, is the fact that children's perception of stress and children's coping skills differ by developmental level. Additional research also shows that adults may respond differently to the same stressor in early, middle, and late adulthood. There is a need to study individual responses to disaster in the context of other daily stressors, and to learn more about the effect of accumulated stress on individual coping mechanisms over time. Attention must be paid both to human reactions to environmental stress and to human ability to effect personal and social changes to meet environmental conditions. Finally, there is a need to disseminate research findings to graduate schools and medical schools, so that those planning and conducting interventions are aware of the state of the art, of research findings, and of strengths and limitations of research data.

Service Needs

Mental health services following mass emergencies are provided primarily to a normal population unfamiliar with mental health services. In addressing the needs of this population, it is important to avoid the label of "mental illness," to provide outreach, and to offer nontraditional crisis counseling rather than traditional psychotherapy.

Disaster workers themselves—emergency managers, fire, police, paramedical and medical personnel—who experience the intensity of the disaster directly and for overly prolonged time periods need support services. Four types of service needs are apparent: training in the recognition and interpretation of human responses; organizational support of the work; respite and interventions during or immediately after the disaster; and debriefing after the disaster work is completed.

Among the groups at risk during emergencies are the socially disadvantaged: minorities, the poor, and the frail and poor elderly. These persons are particularly vulnerable because disasters tend to intensify their social disadvantage. They often have cultures different from the mainstream and feel isolated from community supports. Another group at risk is children, because their developmental systems are incomplete and leave them less able to deal with stressful events following disaster and because the death or psychological unavailability of a nurturant person will of itself constitute a developmental interference of a very serious nature.

Local community mental health centers are key sources of mental health services to disaster victims. These agencies have staffs whose skills can be adapted to the needs of disaster victims. They are frequently indigenous to the area impacted and have established networks with other public service agencies and the local government bureaucracy. They are also most aware of all the potential public and private mental health resources in the community and are thus in excellent positions to coordinate services from a community-wide perspective. Their work, though, must be coordinated with overall emergency management response in the community.

The media can be a major resource for the mental health professional. Effective use of the media to provide information about normal human responses to stressful events and about where to go for help is critical. Multimedia services should be used—radio, TV, newspapers, magazines—as well as face-to-face meetings of mental health and health workers, public officials, and the public.

Social Policy

The implications of these chapters for public policy on mental health needs in emergencies cover three areas: planning, public education, and public funding for emergency operations. Planning must take place at Federal, State, and local levels and the planning and response processes for any community must be intergovernmental in nature. Planning should be a continuing process, involving adaptive actions, flexibility, education, and testing of proposed response.

Written plans should be short and concise and amenable to continuous changes. Mental health planning should be included at the highest level of emergency planning and policy making.

Public education is also of importance in prevention of and intervention in the deleterious effects of disaster. A public attitude that demands individual acceptance of major responsibility for one's own safety must be advocated, and the public must be informed clearly and concisely, through multimedia and multicultural networks, of risks and of ways to avoid risks. People respond to warnings through a social process; planning for public warning response should address that process, with the goal of adaptive behaviors.

Finally, there is a need for adequate funding for emergency mental health operations. This funding should include, first of all, funding for longitudinal research on human response to emergencies. It should also include funds for planning and public education, for training of human service workers, and for service delivery programs that provide appropriate and comprehensive responses. In all intervention and prevention programs, funds should be set aside for evaluation. Sustained support on Federal, State, and local levels is critical, if the mental health gains achieved are to be maintained and if progress in the area is to continue.

In the following chapters, the commitment and creativity of mental health professionals who address human needs in mass emergencies are evident. These professionals consistently reach out to other disciplines, as well as to a wide range of public and private agencies, to further research development and service delivery in emergency situations. The chapters also reveal gaps in knowledge and in intervention and prevention programming for human needs. It is hoped that this volume will stimulate the field to continue to address such gaps with energy and expertise.

REFERENCES

American Psychiatric Association (1980). *Diagnostic and Statistical Manual of Mental Disorders, Third Edition,* (DSM-III). Washington, D.C.: American Psychiatric Association.

Ahearn, F. (1981). Disaster mental health: A pre- and post-earthquake comparison of psychiatric admission rates. *The Urban and Social Change Review,* 14(2): 22–28.

American Red Cross (1982). *National Voluntary Organizations Active in Disaster: National Directory.* Washington, D.C.: American Red Cross.

American Red Cross (1986). *Annual Report.* Washington, D.C.: American Red Cross.

American Red Cross (1987). *Recognizing the Needs of the Homeless and the Hungry.* Washington, D.C.: American Red Cross.

Baker, G. (1964). Comments on the present status and the future direction of disaster research. In G. Grosser, H. Wechsler, & M. Greenblatt (Eds.), *The Threat of Impending Disaster.* Cambridge, MA: MIT Press.

Barton, A. (1969). *Communities in Disaster.* New York: Doubleday.

Blank, A. S. (1982). Apocalypse terminable and interminable: Operation outreach for Vietnam Veterans. *Hospital and Community Psychiatry,* 33(11): 913–918.

Bolin, R. (1985). Disaster characteristics and psychosocial impacts. In B. J. Sowder (Ed.), *Disasters and Mental Health: Selected Contemporary Perspectives* (pp. 3–28). Washington, D.C.: DHHS Publication No. (ADM) 85–1421.

Bolin, R., & Bolton, P. (1986). *Race, Religion and Ethnicity in Disaster Recovery.* Boulder, University of Colorado Institute of Behavioral Science.

Dohrenwend, B., & Dohrenwend, B. (Eds.) (1981). *Stressful Life Events and Their Contents.* New York: Prodist.

Drabek, T. (1970). Methodology of studying disasters. *American Behavioral Scientist,* 13(1): 331–343.

Environmental Protection Agency (1986). Public involvement in the Superfund Program, WH/FS–86–004, Washington, D.C. Mimeo.

Farberow, N. & Gordon, N. (1986). *Manual for Child Health Workers in Major Disasters.* Washington, D.C.: DHHS Publication No. (ADM) 86–1070.

Federal Emergency Management Agency (1987). Disaster Assistance Data, SL/DA, Washington, D.C. Mimeo.

Frederick, C. (1980). Effects of natural vs. human-induced violence on victims. *Evaluation and Social Change* (Special Issue), 71–75.

Garmezy, N. (1986). Children under severe stress: Critique and Commentary. *Journal of Child Psychiatry,* 25(3): 384–392.

Glenn, G. (1979). Natural disasters and human behavior: Explanations, research, and models. *Psychology, A Quarterly Journal of Human Behavior,* 16(2): 23–36.

Green, B. (1982). Assessing levels of psychological impairment following disaster. *Journal of Nervous and Mental Diseases,* 170(9): 544–552.

Hocking, F. (1970). Psychiatric aspects of extreme environmental stress. *Diseases of the Nervous System,* 31: 542–545.

Kastenbaum, R. (1974). Disaster, death, and human ecology. *Omega,* 5(1): 65–72.

Kilijanek, T., & Drabek, T. (1979). Assessing long-term impacts of a natural disaster: A focus on the elderly. *Gerontologist,* 19(6): 555–566.

Kreps, G. (1981). The worth of the NAS–NRC and DRC studies of individual and social response to disasters. In J. Wright & P. Rossi (Eds.), *Social science and natural hazards.* Cambridge, MA: ABT Books.

National Institute of Mental Health (1986a). Emergency Services Branch: Annual Report. Rockville, Maryland, National Institute of Mental Health. Mimeo.

National Institute of Mental Health (1986b). Emergency Services Branch: Crisis Counseling Program Description. Rockville, Maryland, National Institute of Mental Health. Mimeo.

Perry, R., & Lindell, M. (1978). The psychological consequences of natural disaster: A review of research on American communities. *Mass Emergencies,* 3(2/3): 105–115.

Quarantelli, E. (1954). The nature and conditions of panic. *American Journal of Sociology,* 60(3): 267–275.

Quarantelli, E., & Dynes, R. (1977). Response to social crisis and disaster. *Annual Review of Sociology,* 3: 23–49.

Roth, R. (1970). Cross-cultural perspectives on disaster response. *American Behavioral Scientist,* 13(3), 440–451.

Schulberg, H. (1974). Disaster, crisis theory, and intervention strategies. *Omega,* 5(1): 77–87.

Slovic, P., Lichtenstein, S., & Fischoff, B. (1979). Images of disaster: Perception and acceptance of risks from nuclear power. In G. Goodman & W. Rowe (Eds.), *Energy Risk Management* (pp. 223–245). London: Academic Press.

Solomon, S. D. (in press). Evaluation and research issues in assessing disaster's effects. In R. Gist & B. Lubin (Eds.), *Psychosocial Aspects of Disaster.* New York: Wiley & Sons.

Taylor, V. (1978). Future directions for study. In E. Quarantelli (Ed.), *Disasters: Theory and Research* (pp. 251–280). Beverly Hills, CA: Sage.

Warheit, B. J. (1985). A propositional paradigm for estimating the impact of disasters on mental health. In B. J. Sowder (Ed.), *Disasters and Mental Health: Selected Contemporary Perspectives* (pp. 196–214). Washington, D.C.: DHHS Publication No. (ADM) 85–1421.

Wenger, D., Dykes, J., Sebok, T. G., & Neff, J. (1975). It's a matter of myths: An empirical examination of individual insight into disaster response. *Mass Emergencies*, 1(1): 33–46.

MENTAL HEALTH RESPONSE to MASS EMERGENCIES

Theory and Practice

PART I

Individual and
Community Responses

1

Disasters and Their Mental Health Consequences: Issues, Findings, and Future Trends

GEORGE J. WARHEIT

A comprehensive analysis of the literature indicates that there are marked disagreements among researchers, scholars and mental health professionals regarding the psychological consequences of disaster events. This lack of consensus is not surprising when one considers these facts. First, there was almost no empirical research done on the topic until after World War II. Second, as will be outlined in detail later, research in the field has been seriously impeded by an absence of theoretical foundations. Third, research has suffered as a consequence of the plethora of definitions used to operationalize the two key concepts: disaster and psychological consequences. And, fourth, the fragmented state of research in the field can be attributed to the fact that not one single group of multidisciplinary researchers has systematically explored the key issues over an extended period of time.

BACKGROUND

Historically, research on disasters and their mental health sequelae has been strongly influenced by the popular press which has suggested that disaster events produce pervasive psychological distress and social disorganization among impacted populations. Moreover, this perception has been perpetuated by researchers/scholars who have relied on anecdotal accounts to characterize the responses that individuals make to disaster situations. For example, Trimble (1985) in describing the relationships between disaster events and post-traumatic stress disorders cites an account of how Samuel Pepys was psychologically terrorized by the great fire of London which occurred in 1666. Notations from Pepys' diary are used to describe his continuing nightmares concerning the fire six months after it had occurred. And, references to his observations regarding the suicidal behaviors of others are used to suggest that they had experienced marked, long-term emotional distress as a consequence of the fire (Trimble, 1985).

Similarly, Trimble (1985) uses anecodatal accounts from the diary of Charles Dickens to illustrate the psychological impact of an event he experienced. Dickens, who was involved in a railway accident in June of 1865, is quoted as saying that at the time of the event "the scenes amongst the dead and dying rendered his hand unsteady." And, sometime after the accident, Dickens wrote: "I am not quite right within, but believe it to be an effect of the railway shaking. . . . I am weak—weak as if I were recovering from a long illness" (Trimble, 1985, p. 7).

In citing these illustrations, I am not suggesting that life-threatening crisis situations cannot produce both short- and long-term emotional trauma. Obviously, they sometimes do. These references are offered only to illustrate the fact that anecdotal accounts have often been used uncritically in the past as a basis for making generalizations about the postdisaster behaviors of the population at large.

A second notion promulgated largely by the mass media suggests that individuals generally do not respond well to crisis events or emergency situations. The research of Wenger et al. (1975) documents the general existence of this belief set. These investigators found that a very large percentage of a community sample agreed with this statement: "Immediately following the impact of a disaster, victims are in a state of shock and unable to cope with the situation themselves."

Quarantelli (1985) has refuted this stereotypic notion and refers to several news accounts to illustrate how unsubstantiated observations have created and perpetuated a number of myths regarding the responses persons make to disaster events. For example, he cites a *Harper's Magazine* article of 1889 which described the survivors of the Johnston, Pennsylvania, flood as being "crazed by their sufferings." And, he quotes from an article published in the *The Saturday Evening Post* which described the aftermath of the hurricane which occurred in Galveston, Texas, in 1900. That article reported that 500 people went "insane almost in unison." More recent accounts of disasters are also used to illustrate how the news media continue to shape the images that many have of human responses to large-scale emergencies. He notes that following a series of floods in 1973 *Newsweek* reported that once the immediate post-impact period was over, "a new reaction starts to appear among victims." A kind of shared psychosis hits just about everyone affected directly or indirectly by the events . . . symptoms of emotional problems become disturbingly obvious; the number of successful suicides rises by about a third; hospital admissions for psychiatric reasons run at double the normal rate; and the frequency of accidents skyrockets (*Newsweek*, January 29, 1973, pp. 62–63, cited in Quarantelli, 1985, p. 184). This author's review of the *Newsweek* article cited by Quarantelli indicated that none of the behaviors described were supported by factual information.

Quarantelli (1985) has also suggested that the notions held by many in the general population concerning postdisaster behaviors are shared by community leaders. And, he cites the work of Wenger et al. (1980) to support his position. These investigators found that the attitudes held by a sample of public officials concerning postdisaster behaviors did not differ markedly from those of the public at large.

Research on disasters and their mental health consequences has been unduly influenced in the past by two very pervasive, persistent and largely unfounded sets of beliefs, i.e., disaster events inevitably produce both short- and long-term psychological traumas in the general population, and individuals do not respond instrumentally or effectively to the demands placed on them by community-wide emergencies. There are, of course, many other factors which have contributed to the present confusion concerning the relationships between disasters and mental health. However, the two notions just identified have produced and maintained a largely unfounded set of beliefs which have served as the context within which much prior research has been conceptualized, conducted, analyzed, and interpreted. The need to move beyond these two conceptions becomes evident as one reviews the literature on disasters and their psychological aftermath.

THE LITERATURE ON DISASTERS AND THEIR CONSEQUENCES

A comprehensive review of the literature on disasters and their psychological consequences has been reported previously by this author (Warheit, 1985). On the basis of this earlier review, Warheit suggested there are four major schools of thought/sets of findings reported in the literature. These are as follows.

One group of scholars/researchers has suggested that disasters tend to produce widespread psychological distress, physical health problems, and social disruptions among the general population and/or chronic psychic traumas and other psychological disorders among some individuals (cf. Tyhurst 1951, 1957; Menninger, 1952; Rosenman, 1956; Wallace, 1956; Wolfenstein, 1957; Glass, 1959; Crawshaw, 1963; Farber, 1967; Lifton, 1967; Krystal, 1968; Kliman, 1973; Schulberg, 1974; Erikson, 1976; Lifton & Olson 1976; Stretton, 1976; Raphael, 1977; Houts et al., 1980(a), 1980(b); Baum et al., 1981; Boyd, 1981; Gleser et al., 1981; Kasl et al., 1981; Figley, 1985).

A second group of researchers/scholars has concluded that disaster events may produce negative mental health and undesirable social consequences among some members of the general population but that these deleterious effects are relatively mild, of short duration, and most often self-remitting (cf. Janis, 1951; Fritz & Marks, 1954; Moore, 1963; Drabek & Stephenson, 1971; Drabek et al., 1973; Hall & Landreth, 1975; Piepert, 1975; Dohrenwend et al., 1979, 1981; Bromet, 1980; Bromet & Dunn, 1981; Bromet et al., 1982).

A third perspective regarding the mental health consequences of disasters maintains that these events can produce either acute or long-term psychiatric disorders/distress, but mostly among those who are particularly vulnerable and/or among those who have had a prior history of mental illness (cf. Fenichel, 1945; Kardiner, 1959; Brown et al., 1973).

A fourth group of researchers/scholars has postulated that disasters may function to produce a strong sense of personal and social stability among members of the impact population (cf. Janis, 1951; Fritz & Marks, 1954; Coleman, 1961; Fritz, 1961; Wilson, 1962; Quarantelli & Dynes, 1973; Quarantelli, 1979; Drabek & Key, 1983).

Possible Sources for These Differences

Given the great diversity of the findings embodied in the research just cited, how can one possibly account for the differences? Without pretense of being exhaustive or definitive, it appears to this writer that the pervasive disagreement in the literature regarding disasters and their mental health consequences can be attributed largely to the following factors.

1. Differences in the definition of the concept disaster. The term disaster has been used in the literature to describe an extensive array of dissimilar events, e.g., earthquakes, fires, floods, air raids, atomic attacks, tornadoes, train and plane crashes, the sinking of ships, explosions, accidents at nuclear power plants, exposure to toxic wastes, and internment in concentration camps. Obviously, these phenomena differ from one another in many important ways, e.g., source, onset, warning time, duration, magnitude, frequency of occurrence, and social context. This definitional confusion has undoubtedly contributed immensely to the disagreement reported in the literature on disasters and their mental health effects.

2. Differences in definition of mental health utilized by various researchers. The literature review also shows a marked disparity in the definitions of mental health consequences employed by different investigators. A great many scholars/researchers have relied on unobtrusive or indirect measures of mental health problems such as impaired interpersonal relationships, suicide rates, increased use of tobacco or alcohol, physical health complaints, e.g., headaches, nausea, gastrointestinal disturbances, and sleep problems (Houts et al., 1981a, 1981b; Gleser et al., 1981; Kasl et al., 1981). Others like Lifton and Olson (1976) have focused on intrapsychic processes such as death anxiety, inner terror, and guilt as indicators of psychiatric distress. At least one group (Baum et al., 1983) used increased adrenal output as an indicator of psychological stress.

Another group of researchers has defined the mental health sequelae of disasters in terms of a condition characterized by Frank (1973) as demoralization. The demoralized person is seen as having a variety of subclinical psychiatric symptoms which include anxiety, depression, and psychoneuroticism, along with feelings of helplessness, hopelessness, despair, sleep problems, and a sense of foreboding. The task force on the behavioral/psychological consequences of the accident at Three Mile Island relied heavily on measures of demoralization to determine the mental health impact of that event (Dohrenwend et al., 1979; Dohrenwend et al., 1981). The measures of demoralization utilized by this group were closely related to the screening instruments developed and utilized by epidemiologists in field surveys of the general population conducted between 1950–1975 (cf. Srole et al., 1962; Langner & Michael, 1963; Leighton et al., 1963; Schwab et al., 1979).

At least two major research efforts have utilized multimethod approaches to determine the psychological impact that disasters have on affected populations. Investigators studying the mental health effects of the Buffalo Creek dam disaster relied on several different sources of information to establish their psychiatric judgments. These included self report symptom measures, semistructured interviews administered by mental health professionals, case history materials, and clinical assessments made by two psychiatrists (Gleser et al., 1981). Similarly, Bromet and her colleagues who studied the psychological status of the population around Three Mile Island following the accident there used modified versions of the Symptom Check List developed by Derogatis et al. (1973) and the Schedule for the Affective Disorders and Schizophrenias developed by Endicott and Spitzer (1978) as measures of mental impairment (Bromet, 1980; Bromet & Dunn 1981; Bromet et al., 1982).

Researchers with a psychiatric/clinical orientation have often tended to focus on the post-traumatic impact that disasters have on some individuals. Figley (1985), for example, has edited a volume in which he and others discussed the diagnosis of Post-Traumatic Stress Disorder (PTSD), outlined in the Diagnostic and Statistical Manual, Third Edition (DSM-III) of the American Psychiatric Association (1980), as an appropriate method for assessing the mental health outcomes occasioned by a wide variety of traumatic events, including disasters. These events are defined within a general framework which emphasizes the role of victimization as leading to PTSD.

The above list could be expanded, but by now the case has been made. The disparate definitions of what constitutes a negative mental health effect and the methods/measures utilized by different researchers to identify these effects has inevitably led to the collection of different kinds of data and to dissimilar analytic foci, interpretations, and conclusions.

3. Research orientations. Some of the variations in the findings reported in the literature can be attributed to the different ideologies and/or orientation of the investigators doing the research. Sociologists have tended to focus on macro-level, social-structural variables within community contexts; psychiatric epidemiologists have relied largely on establishing the prevalence rates of psychopathology among populations by means of psychometric scale scores; and, psychologists/psychiatrists and others with a clinical orientation have focused on the psychic traumas occasioned by "victimization" and/or on the need for mental health services.

These different orientations have been especially problematic inasmuch as they have influenced disaster/mental health research at every level, i.e., theoretical assumptions used to guide the inquiries, sampling methods, data gathering procedures, analytic techniques, and the interpretation of findings. Given these variations, it is not surprising that there is so little consensus in the literature concerning disaster events and their mental health effects.

4. Confusion between agent-generated and response-generated consequences. Researchers at the Disaster Research Center have made a very useful distinction between the problems occasioned by disaster agents versus those produced by organizational efforts to respond to them (Dynes et al., 1981; Quarantelli, 1985). They point out that the activities of public officials and/or the community agencies involved in postdisaster recovery efforts often compound the impact of the event and magnify its consequences.

This author's own research at Three Mile Island and his analysis of the work of others suggest that the near meltdown of the reactor core (the event) did not in itself produce any significant deleterious social or psychological problems for those living in the area. The problems produced, and there were many, occurred largely as a consequence of the responses made by local, state and/or national officials and organizations. Ambiguous, conflicting and erroneous information regarding the event and its potential threat to life and property was given by officials of the power company and by some of the representatives of governmental agencies (Dohrenwend et al., 1981).

In addition, a massive evacuation was initiated which separated family members at a time of perceived crisis. The logistics of relocating thousands of persons resulted in a vast array of events capable of producing psychosocial stress, e.g., highways were clogged, in some places gasoline was in short supply, there was confusion concerning the availability of adequate shelters, and there was no way to tell evacuees how long they would be kept away from their homes and other family members. In short, the research literature on the accident at Three Mile Island indicates that much of the psychological stress associated with the accident were response-generated and chief among these was a pervasive and long lasting distrust of government agencies and public officials (Dohrenwend et al., 1979; 1981).

5. The absence of an integrated theoretical model. As pointed out by this author (Warheit, 1985) and by many others (cf. White & Hass, 1975; Perry & Lindell, 1978; Hartsough, 1985; Green, 1985; Quarantelli, 1985), much of the research on disasters/mental health has been descriptive, atheoretical, and/or narrowly focused on the special interests of individual investigators. Many of the differences among the findings reported reflect the lack of integrated theoretical frameworks both within and between different research groups.

STRESSFUL LIFE EVENTS: A THEORETICAL MODEL

In order to facilitate research development in the field, Warheit (1979, 1985) has suggested a comprehensive paradigm as a framework for future research. The foundations for this model are derived from systems theory and from the literature on stressful life events. Over the past 50 years, researchers from a number of disciplines have sought to identify the processes by which stressors act as precursors to physical and/or mental disorders. And although there have been almost as many definitions of stress as there have been researchers, a common theme has emerged. Most simply stated, stress is commonly conceptualized as an altered state of an organism produced by agents in the psychological, social, cultural, and/or physical environments. It is assumed that this altered state, when unmitigated, produces deleterious physical and/or mental health effects for certain individuals.

The first systematic research on the relationships between psychological stress and illness is generally attributed to Cannon (1928) whose pioneering efforts sought to detail the relationships between such emotional states as fear, anger, pain, and anxiety and subsequent changes in body function. Adolf Mever extended Cannon's work and opened up further research by emphasizing the role of life events in the development of physical and mental disorders (Lief, 1948). Selye's research (1950, 1956) made important theoretical contributions to our understanding of the psychological adaptations to stress. And others influenced the field by focusing on the links between stressors and illness (Wolff et al., 1950; Hinkle & Wolff, 1957).

Over the past two decades, researchers have given increased attention to the qualitative and quantitative relationships between particular classes of life events and their health consequences. The empirical research of Holmes (1967) together with Rahe (1968), Paykel and his colleagues (1971, 1972), the Dohrenwends (1970, 1973), Myers and associates (1972), and Brown and coworkers (1973) are among the most widely cited. However, there have been scores of others whose contributions have added to our knowledge of stressful life events and their relationships to mental and physical health.

Early research on stress and illness tended to regard the relationships as direct and, in many instances, unicausal. As the field has evolved, this simple stimulus-response type model was modified to include coping skills and resource networks as intervening variables. These factors were seen as resources which buffered the individuals from the damaging demands placed on them by stressful events. However, both models have a serious theoretical deficiency: They represent closed systems and, as such, do not depict the dynamic interactions of an organism as it influences and is influenced by its multiple environments. The scientific problems posed by these closed theoretical models are not confined to their conceptual inadequacies; they contain analytic weaknesses as well. The statistical procedures widely used by investigators in the past, while often appropriate for the kinds of data gathered, are inadequate when viewed from contemporary perspectives, e.g., they did not or could not test for interaction effects among stressors, coping resources, and/or other adaptive responses to stress. And, because of design limitations, they could not establish causal patterns among and between the different variables.

The Warheit model is presented in Figure 1. It postulates that stressful events arise from the following sources: (1) the individual's biological constitution; (2) the individual's psychological characteristics; (3) the social structure, including interpersonal relationships; (4) the culture; and (5) the geophysical environment.

The events section encompasses the specific events commonly associated with the stress and crisis event literature, e.g., the death of a child, loss of employment, or a serious physical illness. It also includes events arising from the sociocultural environment, such as the nuclear accident at Three Mile Island, a prolonged economic recession, or the demise of a basic industry because of technological change. Further, it takes into account events whose origins are in the social realm, such as civil disorders, or in the geophysical environment, such as earthquakes, floods, and tornadoes.

The model emphasizes the importance of recognizing that stress responses

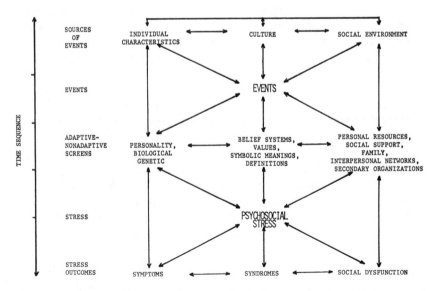

Figure 1. Life events: Sources, adaptations, and outcomes.

involve a dynamic, synergistic interaction of elements that includes the characteristics of the event or events, the idiosyncratic qualities of the individual and his or her personal social structural, and cultural resources. This dynamic, interactive quality of the stress process frequently confounds researchers who seek causal links between events and undesirable personal outcomes. Consider, for example, marital separation or divorce. These events often have been identified, at least implicitly, as the cause of mental health problems. In actuality, an individual's psychological characteristics, such as chronic anxiety or depression, may be underlying factors leading to marital separation or dissolution. And, of course, the marital disruptions may produce new symptoms as well as exacerbate the preexisting ones. Moreover, separation or divorce may represent a loss in the individual's resources which, in turn, can decrease his or her capacity to cope with the problems associated with daily living. Stressful events do not occur within a vacuum, but rather within a complex of interrelated personal, social structural, and cultural environments. Conceptual and analytic models which do not recognize the highly interrelated nature of the responses individuals make to life-crisis events are incomplete and the research results produced by them must be regarded as tentative rather than definitive.

The adaptive screens in the model represent the coping resources available to individuals as they attempt to meet the demands placed on them by life events. These screens include an individual's unique biological and psychological constitutions. They also include social and economic resources, familial and other interpersonal relationships, and the secondary organizations provided by society and community. The culture is also perceived as a valuable coping resource. As Parsons (1951) has pointed out, one of the functions of religion (which he defines as a supraempirical referent) is to transmit systems of belief that give individuals a source of *explanation* and *meaning* for events that cannot be accounted for by society's logic or science.

The model represented by Figure 1 conceptualizes life events, coping behaviors, stress, and illness as highly interactive processes. When a life crisis event occurs, an individual's first line of defense is his or her idiosyncratic characteristics, that is, psychological, physical, and genetic makeup. When an individual's resources are inadequate to deal with the demands occasioned by an event, it is hypothesized that he/she will customarily attempt to extend his/her sources of support, usually by calling for assistance from spouse, children, parents, and/or other family members. When these resources are unavailable or inadequate, individuals turn to other interpersonal networks, such as friends in whom they can confide and/or from whom they can obtain help.

The model suggests, further, that when a person's individual and personal resources are insufficient to meet life-event demands, he/she will attempt to extend those resources by seeking assistance from the social service agencies in the community. If all of these resources prove to be inadequate—as in the case of an incurable, terminal illness—individuals may turn to culturally provided religious beliefs, values, and symbols for comfort, support, and resolution. In practice, of course, when individuals are confronted with crisis-related demands, they normally seek to extend their resources immediately in as wide a circle as possible. Simultaneously, they try to reduce the demands being made on them in ways commensurate with their alternatives and the characteristics of the stressors.

As represented in Figure 1, stress is an altered state of an organism; it occurs when demands exceed an individual's capability to respond. The degree of stress experienced is hypothesized to be a function of the number, frequency, intensity, duration, and priority of the demands placed on an individual in relation to his/her various coping resources. This demand-capability ratio is seen as dynamic, fluctuating, multisystemic, and taking place in a changing temporal context. Moveover, stress is conceptualized as being different from the events that may precipitate it. Events are seen as agents; stress is perceived as an altered state of the organism. And, importantly, stress is different than its outcomes. The latter are viewed as symptoms, syndromes, social dysfunctions, and/or successful adaptation.

The theoretical model represented by Figure 1 reflects the systemic nature of life events, coping mechanisms, stress, and stress outcomes as they occur in a temporal context. A research design based on this model would necessitate obtaining information on all of its various components at several points in time. It also would require analytic procedures that could test for causal relationships within and between the variables. There is, of course, no single piece of research in the scientific literature that approaches the rigor imposed by the comprehensive, integrated, systemic model represented by Figure 1. Moreover, such research is not likely to be seen for a long time, given the current state of development in a number of fields. Nevertheless, the model can be employed as a framework for evaluating prior research findings on disasters and mental health, and elements of it can be used as a paradigm for use in the future.

CURRENT STATE OF KNOWLEDGE

Given the confusion, ambiguity and disagreement found in the literature on disasters and their mental health consequences, what conclusions, if any, can be reached at present? The answer is that there are some areas of general consensus and some areas of unresolved disagreement. These include the following:

1. There is no empirical evidence to justify the stereotypic notion that large-scale, community-wide disasters produce extensive, non-instrumental, panic-like behaviors. This conclusion is based on findings from a variety of studies conducted over the past 35 years. Researchers working in a variety of settings have found that most postdisaster behaviors are purposive and oriented to a restoration of the community to its predisaster state. The fast pace of the search, rescue, and other immediate post-impact phases of recovery reported by some observers in the past may have been misinterpreted/reported as non-purpose, random, panic-like behaviors. In any case, the overwhelming weight of the evidence is that community-wide disaster events do not produce mass hysteria or panic among the general population.

2. An analysis of the literature indicates that community-wide disaster events do not produce an increase in psychotic-type conditions among the general population (Stein, 1974; Bromet, 1980; Dohrenwend et al., 1981; Bromet et al., 1982).

3. The findings on community-wide disasters suggest that these events may increase the prevalence of subclinical symptoms of anxiety, depression, psychoneuroticism, and/or other psychophysiologic complaints among some persons in the general population. However, the little longitudinal information available indicates that most of these symptoms persist for a relatively short period of time and are self-remitting (Marks et al., 1954; Hall & Landreth, 1975; Disaster Research Center, 1976; Melik, 1978; Dohrenwend et al., 1979, 1981; Bromet & Dunn, 1981).

4. The applicable research suggests that community-wide disasters do not significantly increase the psychiatric symptoms and related dysfunctions among those with a previous history of mental health problems (Stein, 1974; Bromet et al., 1982). In addition, the psychological well-being of the elderly does not appear to be especially affected by community disasters (Cohen & Poulshock, 1977; Bell et al., 1978; Huerta & Horton, 1978). These conclusions must be interpreted with extreme caution, however, since the number of studies focusing on the issues have been extremely limited. Presently, we do not know enough about vulnerability to make definitive statements.

5. There is a substantial body of research which indicates that disasters often lead to a sense of personal and social cohesiveness among those in impacted communities. Feelings of solidarity, mutual support, and an

accentuated commitment to common values have been found by many investigators in their community studies of postdisaster situations (cf. Janis, 1951; Marks et al., 1954; Disaster Research Center, 1976; Drabek & Key, 1983).

DISCUSSION

The areas of agreement just listed coincide in many ways with three of the major perspectives regarding the psychological consequences of disasters outlined earlier in this paper. The one exception was found in the cases of vulnerability. Although the research dealing with this issue suggests that the elderly, former mental patients, and/or those in treatment for mental health problems are not at undue risk following large-scale, community-wide disasters, these findings must be regarded as very tentative because of the small number of studies reporting data on these populations.

The finding of considerable empirical support for the three other divergent positions regarding disasters and their consequences suggests that researchers, scholars, and mental health professionals should recognize that there are no definitive, mutually exclusive empirical findings in the literature to support one position against any other. Elements of each may be supported or refuted depending on the theoretical predispositions of the investigators, their methodologies, their modes of analysis, and the emphases of their interpretations. It is apparent that many researchers have emphasized the findings they were looking for and failed to see or report other outcomes which were also present. This process most obviously exists in articles which extrapolate to populations from anecdotal reports. However, it is also evident but less apparent in research which focuses on individuals seeking/receiving mental health services.

Stated most simply, if future efforts are to advance the field of inquiry, researchers must move beyond reliance on undeveloped and untested theoretical assumptions, and beyond the question of whether or not disasters produce negative mental health consequences. At a general level, it is more appropriate now for researchers to ask: What types of effects are produced by various disaster agents? Which subgroups in the population are at greatest risk and why? And, how can the mental health consequences of disasters be prevented or ameliorated most effectively?

In order to address these and similar questions in a scientifically rigorous way, it is important for researchers to recognize that disaster agents are complex phenomena. All floods are not the same. But all floods differ in important ways from tornadoes. And, although each of these agents shares some common characteristics with hurricanes, i.e., high winds and flooding, there are many differences between all of them. These similarities and differences must be taken into account and specified by researchers in the future if their results are to comparable.

The same observations can be made about mental health consequences as phenomena. Attempts to define what constitutes mental health and/or illness have been far from successful in spite of long-term, strenuous efforts on the part of a great many researchers/scholars. Moreover, as with the concept of disaster, future researchers must specify with far greater operational rigor what they are measuring when they refer to mental health/illness. And, in my opinion, they should rely on instruments which have already been developed, tested, and used with large samples of the general population. Further, these instruments should be capable of identifying a broad spectrum of disorders ranging from subclinical conditions (demoralization) at one end of the continuum to the kinds of specific disorders delineated by the DSM-III on the other.

The instrument which probably meets these criteria better than any other at present is the Diagnostic Interview Schedule/Disaster Supplement (DIS/DS) developed by Robins and her colleagues (1981, 1982) for use in the Epidemiologic Catchment Area Programs (ECA) sponsored by the National Institute of Mental Health. For a discussion of ECA projects see Eaton and Kessler (1985) and Smith in this volume. Although not without flaws, the DIS has many of the qualities just noted and, in addition, it provides for the reconstruction of a respondent's psychiatric history and for the making of diagnoses across different time frames. This feature is of value for a number of reasons, not the least of which is that it allows for the systematic examination of many of the issues associated with vulnerability and causality.

Progress in disaster/mental health research depends on much more definitional precision than has been evident in the past. And it depends on the use of standardized methodologies and instrumentation. In addition, the ability of researchers to begin their work as quickly as possible after an event has occurred is of extreme importance.

As observed earlier, one of the major deficiencies in the field has been the absence of any ongoing, multidisciplinary research groups with the skills and resources required to conduct rigorous, systematic inquiries into the issues and to do so over a long period of time. What is needed is a research team or teams similar to the Disaster Research Group appointed by the National Academy of Sciences-National Research Council in 1957 and/or the Disaster Research Center (DRC) originally established at the Ohio State University in 1962 and now located at the University of

Delaware. The initiation of a small number of adequately funded, multi-disciplinary research groups should, in time, dramatically increase our knowledge about a wide range of disaster/crisis events and their relationships to mental health. Advances in theory and methods could also be made by these groups and the field could be moved from its present descriptive mode to quasi-experimental and verificational type studies.

As emphasized throughout this chapter, the relationships between disasters and their mental health consequences are varied and complex. Because of this, conclusions about these relationships defy simplistic, unicausal explanations. Nonetheless, the findings generated to date are powerful enough to warrant the conclusion that these two classes of phenomena are interrelated. This general consensus now makes it possible for us to expand our existing levels of knowledge. However, the field can move forward only if investigators will utilize more rigorous theoretical and methodological models to guide them than were used in the past. And, finally, the securing of new knowledge about disasters and the psychological effects would be greatly facilitated by the presence of a small number of adequately funded, multidisciplinary research groups which could respond to disaster events before and/or immediately following their impact and could do so on a longitudinal basis.

REFERENCES

American Psychiatric Association (1980). *Diagnostic and Statistical Manual of Mental Disorders, Third Edition.* Washington, D.C.: American Psychiatric Association.

Baum, A., Gatchel, R. J., Fleming, R., & Lake, C. (1981). Chronic and Acute Stress Associated with the Three Mile Island Accident and Decontamination: Preliminary Findings of a Longitudinal Study. Unpublished draft report submitted to the Nuclear Regulatory Commission.

Baum, A., Gatchel, R. J., & Schaeffer, M. A. (1983). Emotional, behavioral and physiological effects of chronic stress at Three Mile Island. *Journal of Consulting and Clinical Psychology*, 51(4): 565–572.

Bell, B. D., Kara, B., & Batterson, C. (1978). Service utilization and adjustment patterns of elderly tornado victims in an American disaster. *Mass Emergencies*, 3, 71–81.

Boyd, S. T. (1981). Psychological reactions of disaster victims. *South Africa Medical Journal*, 60: 744–748.

Bromet, E., in collaboration with Parkinson, D., Schulberg, H. C., Dunn, L., & Gondek, P. C. (1980). *Three Mile Island: Mental Health Findings.* NIMH Contract No. 278-79-0048 (SM). Final Report. Rockville, MD: National Institute of Health. Mimeo.

Bromet, E., & Dunn, L. (1981). Mental health of mothers nine months after the Three Mile Island Accident. *The Urban and Social Change Review*, 14(2): 12–15.

Bromet, E., Schulberg, H. C., & Dunn, L. (1982). Reactions of psychiatric patients to the Three Mile Island nuclear accident. *Archives of General Psychiatry*, 39(6): 725–730.

Brown, G. W., Harris, T. O., & Peto, J. (1973). Life events and psychiatric disorders. Part 2: Nature of causal link. *Psychological Medicine*, 3: 159–176.

Cannon, W. B. (1928). The mechanism of emotional disturbance of bodily function. *New England Journal of Medicine*, 198: 877–844.

Cohen, S. C.; and Poulshock, S. W. (1977). Societal response to mass relocation of the elderly: Implications for area agencies on aging. *The Gerontologist*, 17: 262–268.

Coleman, J. (1961). Community disorganization. In R. K. Merton & R. A. Nisbot (Eds.), *Contemporary Social Problems*. New York: Harcourt, Brace and World, pp. 670–722.

Crawshaw, R. (1963). Reactions to disaster. *Archives of General Psychiatry*, 9(2): 157–162.

Derogatis, L. R., Lipman, R. S., & Cooi, L. (1973). SCL-90: An outpatient rating scale— preliminary report. *Psychopharmacology Bulletin*, 9: 13–25.

Disaster Research Center. (1976). Internal Memo on the Xenia Survey Data. Columbus, Ohio: Disaster Research Center, The Ohio State University.

Dohrenwend, B. P., Dohrenwend, B.S., Kasl, V., & Warheit, G. J. (1979). *Report of the Task Force on Behavioral Effects of the President's Commission on the Accident at Three Mile Island*. Washington, D.C.

Dohrenwend, B. P., Dohrenwend, B. S., Warheit, G., et al. (1981). Stress in the community: A report to the President's Commission on the accident at Three Mile Island. *Annals of the New York Academy of Sciences*, 365(4): 159–174.

Dohrenwend, B. S. (1973). Social status and stressful life events. *Journal of Personality and Social Psychology*, 28: 225–235.

Dohrenwend, B. S., & Dohrenwend, B. P. (1970). Class and race as status-related sources of stress. In S. Levine & N. A. Scotho (Eds.), *Social Stress*. Chicago: Aldine, pp. 111–140.

Drabek, T. E., Erickson, P., & Crowe, J. (1973). An evaluation of matched sample in quasi-experimental designs. Paper presented at the Rocky Mountain Social Science Association Annual Meeting, Laramie, WY.

Drabek, T. E., & Key, W. H. (1983). *Conquering Disaster: Family Recovery and Long-Term Consequences*. New York: Academic Press.

Drabek, T., & Stephenson, J. (1971). When disaster strikes. *Journal of Applied Social Psychology*, 1: 187–203.

Dynes, R. R., Quarantelli, E. L., & Kreps, G. A. (1981). A perspective on disaster planning. Report Series No. 11. Columbus, Ohio: Disaster Research Center. The Ohio State University.

Eaton, W. W., & Kessler, L. G. (Eds.). (1985). *Epidemiologic Field Methods in Psychiatry: The NIMH Epidemiological Catchment Area Program*. New York: Academic Press.

Endicott, J., & Spitzer, R. L. (1978). A diagnostic interview: The schedule for affective disorders and schizophrenia. *Archives of General Psychiatry*. 35: 837–844.

Erikson, K. T. (1976). Loss of communality at Buffalo Creek. *American Journal of Psychiatry*, 133(3): 302–305.

Farber, I. (1967). Psychological aspects of mass disasters. *Journal of the National Medical Association*, 59(5): 340–345.

Fenichel, O. (1945). *The Psychoanalytic Theory of Neurosis*. New York: Norton.

Figley, C. R. (Ed.) (1985). *Trauma and Its Wake: The Study and Treatment of Post-Traumatic Stress Disorder*. New York: Brunner/Mazel.

Frank, J. (1973). *Persuasion and Healing*. Baltimore: Johns Hopkins University Press.

Fritz, C. E. (1961). Disaster. In R. Merton & R. Nisbet (Eds.), *Social Problems*. New York: Harcourt, Brace and World, pp. 63–79.

Fritz, C. E., & Marks, E. (1954). The NORC studies of human behavior in disaster. *Journal of Social Issues*, 10: 26–41.

Glass, A. (1959). Psychological considerations in atomic warfare. *U.S. Armed Forces Medical Journal*, 7: 625–638.

Gleser, G. C., Green, B. L., & Winzet, C. (1981). *Prolonged Psychosocial Effects of Disaster: A Study of Buffalo Creek*. New York: Academic Press.

Green, B. L. (1985). Conceptual and methodological issues in assessing the psychological impact of disaster. In B. J. Sowder (Ed.), *Disasters and Mental Health: Selected Contemporary Perspectives*. DHHS Publication No. (ADM) 85-1421, Washington, D.C.: U.S. Government Printing Office.

Hall, P. S., & Landreth, P. S. (1975). Assessing some long term consequences of a natural disaster. *Mass Emergencies*, 1: 55–61.

Hartsough, D. M. (1985). Measurement of the psychological effects of disaster. In J. Laube & S. Murphy (Eds.), *Perspectives on Disaster Recovery* (pp. 22–60). Norwalk, CT: Appleton-Century-Crofts.

Hinkle, L. E., Jr., & Wolffe, H. G. (1957). Health and social environment. In A. H. Leighton, J. A. Clausen, & R. N. Wilson (Eds.), *Experimental Investigations: Explorations in Social Psychiatry.* New York: Basic Books, pp. 105–137.

Holmes, T. H., & Rahe, R. H. (1967). The social readjustment rating scale. *Journal of Psychosomatic Research*, 11: 213–218.

Houts, P. S., Miller, R. W., Tokuhata, G., & Ham, K. S. (1981a). *Health-Related Behavioral Impact of the Three Mile Island Nuclear Incident. Part I.* Report submitted to the TMI Advisory Panel on Health Research Studies of the Pennsylvania State University, College of Medicine.

Houts, P. S., Miller, R. W., Tokuhata, G., & Ham, K. S. (1981b). *Health-Related Behavioral Impact of the Three Mile Island Nuclear Incidents. Part II.* Report submitted to the TMI Advisory Panel on Health Research Studies of the Pennsylvania State University, College of Medicine.

Huerta, F. C., & Horton, R. L. (1978). Coping behavior of elderly flood victims. *The Gerontologist*, 18: 541–546.

Janis, I. (1951). *Air War and Emotional Stress: Psychological Studies of Bombing and Civil Defense.* New York: McGraw-Hill.

Kardiner, A. (1959). Traumatic neuroses of war. In S. Arieti (Ed.), *American Handbook of Psychiatry, Vol. 1.* New York: Basic Books, pp. 245–257.

Kasl, S. V., Chisholm, R. J., & Eskenazi, B. (1981). The impact of the accident at Three Mile Island on the behavior and well-being of nuclear workers: Part I: Perceptions and evaluations, behavioral response and work-related attitudes and feelings. *American Journal of Public Health*, 71(5): 472–495.

Kliman, A. S. (1973). *The Corning Flood Project: Psychological First Aid Following a Natural Disaster.* White Plains, N.Y.: Center for Preventive Psychiatry.

Krystal, H. (Ed.) (1968). *Massive Psychic Trauma.* New York: International Universities Press.

Langner, T. S., & Michael, S. T. (1963). *Life Stress and Mental Illness.* New York: Free Press of Glencoe.

Leighton, D. C., Harding, J. S., Macklin, D. B., Macmillan, A. M., & Leighton, A. H. (1963). *The Character of Danger.* New York: Free Press of Glencoe.

Lief, A. (Ed.) (1948). *The Commonsense Psychiatry of Dr. Adolph Meyer.* New York: McGraw-Hill, pp. 418–422.

Lifton, R. J. (1967). *Death in Life: Survivors of Hiroshima.* New York: Random House.

Lifton, R. J., & Olson, E. (1976). The human meaning of total disaster—The Buffalo Creek experience. *Psychiatry*, 39(1): 1–18.

Marks, E. S., Fritz, C., Bucker, R., et al. (1954). *Human Reactions in Disaster Situations.* Three Volumes. Chicago: National Opinion Research Center, The University of Chicago.

Melick, M. E. (1978). Life changes and illness: Illness behavior of males in the recovery period of a natural disaster. *Journal of Health and Social Behavior*, 19: 335–342.

Menninger, W. C. (1952). Psychological reactions in an emergency (flood). *American Journal of Psychiatry*, 109(2): 128–130.

Moore, H. E. (1963). *Before the Wind: A Study of the Response to Hurricane Carla.* Disaster Study 19. Washington, D.C.: National Academy of Sciences—National Research Council.

Myers, J. K., Lindenthal, J. J., Pepper, M. P., et al. (1972). Life events and mental status: A longitudinal study. *Journal of Health and Social Behavior*, 13: 398–406.

Parsons, T. (1951). *The Social System.* New York: Free Press.

Paykel, E. S., & Uhlenhuth, E. H. (1972). Rating and magnitude of life stress. *Canadian Psychiatric Association Journal*, Special supplement II: 93–100.

Paykel, E. S., Prucoff, B. A., & Uhlenhuth, E. H. (1971). Scaling of life events. *Archives of General Psychiatry*, 25: 340–347.

Perry, R. W., & Lindell, M. K. (1978). The psychological consequences of natural disaster: A review of research on American communities. *Mass Emergencies*, 3: 105–115.

Piepert, J. R. (1975). Mental health studied during Irish violence. *Columbus Dispatch* (Ohio), June 5, p. B–12.

Quarantelli, E. L. (1979). The consequence of disasters for mental health: Conflicting views. Preliminary Paper Series No. 62. Newark: Disaster Research Center, University of Delaware.

Quarantelli, E. L. (1985). An assessment of conflicting views on mental health: The consequences of traumatic events. In C. R. Figley (Ed.), *Trauma and Its Wake: The Study and Treatment of Post-Traumatic Stress Disorder*. New York: Brunner/Mazel, pp. 173–215.

Quarantelli, E. L., & Dynes, R. R. (1973). Response to social crisis and disaster. *Annual Review of Sociology*, 3: 23–49.

Rahe, R. H. (1968). Life change measurement as a predictor of illness. *Proceedings of the Royal Society of Medicine*, 61: 1124–1126.

Raptael, B. (1977). The Granville train disaster—psychological needs and their management. *The Medical Journal of Australia*, 1(9): 303–305.

Robins, L. N., Helzer, J. E., Croughan, J., & Ratcliff, K. S. (1981). National Institute of Mental Health Diagnostic Interview Schedule: Its history, characteristics, and validity. *Archives of General Psychiatry*, 38: 381–389.

Robins, L. N., Helzer, J. E., Ratcliff, K. S., & Seyfried, W. (1982). Validity of the Diagnostic Interview Schedule version III: DSM-III diagnoses. *Psychological Medicine*, 12: 855–870.

Rosenman, S. (1956). The paradox of guilt in disaster victim populations. *The Psychiatric Quarterly Supplement*, 30: 181–221.

Schulberg, H. C. (1974). Disasters, crisis theory and intervention strategies. *Omega*, 5(1): 77–87.

Schwab, J. J., Bell, R. A., Warheit, G. J., & Schwab, R. M. (1979). *Social Order and Mental Health*. New York: Brunner/Mazel Publishers.

Selye, H. (1950). *Stress*. Montreal: Acta.

Selye, H. (1956). *The Stress of Life*. New York: McGraw-Hill.

Srole, L., Langner, T. S., Michael, S. T., Opler, M. K., & Rennie, T. A. (1962). *Mental health in the Metropolis: The Midtown Study. Volume 1*. New York: McGraw Hill.

Stein, S. (1974). An earthquake shakes up a mental health system. In A. Tulipas, C. Attneave, & E. Kingstone (Eds.), *Beyond Clinic Walls*. University, AL: University of Alabama Press.

Stretton, A. (1976). *The Furious Days—The Relief of Darwin*. Sydney and London: William Collins.

Trimble, M. R. (1985). Post-traumatic stress disorder: History of a concept. In C. R. Figley (Ed.), *Trauma and Its Wake: The Study and Treatment of Post-Traumatic Stress Disorder*. New York: Brunner/Mazel, pp. 5–14.

Tyhurst, J. S. (1951). Individual reactions to a community disaster: The natural history of psychiatric phenomenon. *American Journal of Psychiatry*, 107(10): 764–769.

Tyhurst, J. S. (1957). Psychological and sociological aspects of civilian disaster. *Canadian Medical Association Journal*, 76: 385–393.

Wallace, A. F. C. (1956). Tornado in Worcester: *An Exploratory Study of Individual Community Behavior in an Extreme Situation*. Disaster Study No. 3. Washington, D.C.: National Academy of Sciences.

Warheit, G. (1979). Life events, coping, stress and depressive symptomatology. *American Journal of Psychiatry*, 136(4B): 502–507.

Warheit, G. (1985). A propositional paradigm for estimating the impact of disasters on mental health. In B. Sowder (Ed.), *Disasters and Mental Health: Selected Contemporary Perspectives*. Washington, D.C.: DHHS Publication No. (ADM) 85-1421.

Wenger, D. E., Dykes, J., Sebok, T., & Neff, J. (1975). It's a matter of myths: An empirical examination of individual insight into disaster response. *Mass Emergencies*, 1: 33–46.

Wenger, D. E., James, T. F., & Faupel, C. E. (1980). *Disaster Beliefs and Emergency Planning.* Newark, Delaware: Department of Sociology, University of Delaware.

White, G. F., & Haas, J. E. (1975). *Assessment of Research on Natural Hazards.* Boston: MIT Press.

Wilson, R. (1962). Disaster and mental health. In G. W. Baker & D. W. Chapman (Eds.), *Man and Society in Disaster.* New York: Basic Books, pp. 124–150.

Wolfenstein, M. (1957). *Disaster: A Psychological Essay.* Glencoe, IL: The Free Press.

Wolff, H. G., Wolf, S., & Hare, C. (Eds.) (1950). *Life Stress and Bodily Disease.* New York: Research Publications-Association for Research in Nervous and Mental Disease 29.

2

Response to Natural Disasters

ROBERT BOLIN

That natural disasters are associated, in some fashion, with varying degrees and types of psychosocial distress among victims is taken as axiomatic by many researchers in the field. However, beneath that generally shared assumption, there are a number of significant divergences in the literature that deserve careful examination and consideration both by researchers and by those using the existing data base as a guide for planning and delivering mental health services to victims.

In order to address psychosocial impacts of natural disaster, a complex and interdependent set of issues must be considered. At the base is the fundamental question: What are natural disasters and can they be expected to produce different (or any) psychological sequelae compared to other disruptive life events? Beyond this, then, one must consider what type of disaster agents (earthquake, flood, hurricane) and characteristics are the most likely to generate mental health "problems," when, and under what circumstances. This, in turn, raises the issue of what "types" (age, gender, race, etc.) are most vulnerable to disaster-related stressors and under what social conditions. Disasters initiate community-wide collective responses to the event, as well as intensify preexisting social trends and processes (Quarantelli, 1985a). How, then, can these social responses to the disaster, in their own right, affect victims' psychosocial status?

The potential mental health impacts of natural disasters involve the examination of three major categories of phenomena (Bolin, 1985a): event characteristics, victim characteristics, and the types and patterns of social responses to the event and its aftermath. This chapter will review the current state of knowledge on event characteristics and social response stressors as these two categories pertain most directly to the topic of natural disasters. While victim characteristics is an important dimension, it is addressed in detail in Part II of this volume, *Social and Clinical Intervention Programs*, and will receive only cursory treatment here. Most of the literature reviewed specifically refers to the psychosocial impacts of natural disasters and the effects of social responses to those occasions. The reader is referred to the other chapters in this section for reviews of the literature on technological disasters and war. However, in order to illustrate similarities and differences between technological disasters vis-à-vis natural disasters, references will be made as to how individual and collective responses to the two types of disasters may be compared.

Natural disasters, as agents of psychological and social stress, are often, and euphemistically, referred to as "Acts of God," a label which automatically eliminates human agency and culpability from consideration. Further, natural disasters are assumed to be uncontrollable (although many are predictable and avoidable). Conversely, technological and similar disasters caused by humans implicate human negligence, fallibility, or intentionality, giving victims a target of resentment and blame (e.g., Sorensen et al., 1987).

Some have argued, in contrasting the psychosocial impacts of natural vs. technological disasters, that natural disasters typically have an identifiable low point (Baum et al., 1983, p. 337). The notion of a low point suggests a point at which, from the victim's perspective, the "worst is over" and restoration, normalization, and recovery (psychological, social, and physical) can proceed. In contrast, many technological disasters (nuclear plant accidents, toxic contamination, exposure to environmental pollutants) have no necessarily obvious physical impacts, no identifiable "low point," or frequently no discernible short-term negative physical effects on victims (Levine, 1982; Sorensen et al., 1987). Technological disasters are also accompanied by feelings of "dread" and uncertainty which may heighten negative psychosocial effects (e.g., Tierney, 1986). Indeed, Baum et al. (1983) have argued that technological disasters have different types of psychosocial sequelae and are, as a category, inherently more stressful than natural disasters. However, as this chapter illustrates, our current state of knowledge on the specific factors in disaster events that produce negative psychological impacts is sufficiently undeveloped to make many generalizations difficult and premature (cf. Drabek, 1986).

While typological categorization of disaster types and characteristics has been repeatedly attempted (e.g., Barton, 1970; Berren et al., 1980), the field, as yet, lacks a single agreed-upon comprehensive typology of disaster characteristics and consequences (Drabek, 1986). It is necessary, as a result, to address both the generic and situationally specific features of

disaster events when making conclusions about their social and psychological impacts.

Of course, perhaps the most obvious characteristic of natural disasters
is that they have an unambiguous physical impact, resulting in the destruction of property and, sometimes, the traumatic injury and death of
victims. In the psychosocial literature on natural disasters, one most
frequently encounters natural agents such as tornadoes, hurricanes,
earthquakes, floods, mud flows, and volcanic eruptions (see Barton,
1970; Mileti et al., 1975; Drabek, 1986, and White & Haas, 1975, for
representative reviews).

At the risk of blurring clean analytic distinctions, it bears noting that
human actions and intentions can nevertheless play a significant part in
making geophysical and meteorological events into disasters. For example,
if people didn't have a proclivity for building homes on flood plains and in
steep-sided mountain canyons, floods would be floods but not natural
disasters or "Acts of God." The "Dust Bowl" of the 1930s, arguably one of
the most significant "natural disasters" in U.S. history, wouldn't have been
a disaster if farmers hadn't destroyed ground cover while trying to farm
semi-arid lands, thus providing the basis for massive top soil erosion
(Reisner, 1986).

Naturally-occurring geophysical events can provoke additional environmental and structural impacts that are not so clearly "Acts of God."
Earthquakes can ignite massive urban fires while destroying the infra-
structures necessary to fight those fires, as was the case in the 1906 San
Francisco earthquake (Haas et al., 1977). Likewise, riverine floods may
wash toxic waste materials from dump sites into people's homes, effectively
rendering whole neighborhoods uninhabitable in spite of very little physical damage to the homes (e.g., Smith, 1984).

The upshot is that often there is no clear dividing line between natural
disasters and those in which human practices, either intentionally or from
ignorance and neglect, play a role (e.g., Quarantelli, 1985a). How severe a
disaster's impact is may be a property not of the agent per se, but of the
nature, location, construction, social organization, and resources available in human settlements so stricken and how they respond to the event.

These preliminary remarks are intended to remind the reader that
isolating and identifying the sources of psychosocial distress in disaster
occasions is invariably difficult. Broadly, it involves examining the disaster
agent characteristics, victim traits and qualities, and the patterns of social
responses to the event (Bolin, 1985a; Quarantelli, 1985a). An understanding of the existing literature on disaster-related psychosocial stress is best
served by first reviewing the major theoretical approaches used in its

study, along with the range of methodologies that characterize the research. This will be accompanied by a brief overview of disaster typologies to illustrate the range of salient dimensions in disaster agent characteristics.

The remainder of this chapter will focus on three main areas: (1) A review of representative findings from the literature on the psychosocial impacts of natural disasters, and the impacts of social responses to them; (2) An examination of gaps in the literature and weaknesses in the existing data base; (3) A discussion of the implications of the preceding for the provision of mental health services after natural disasters.

THEORETICAL AND METHODOLOGICAL ISSUES

The existing research on psychosocial consequences of disaster presents us with an array of findings and conclusions, a number of them seemingly contradictory. Such conclusions variously support or deny the contention that disasters generate significant mental health impacts among victims (Frederick, 1977). The diversity of findings and resultant controversies over them reflect differences among researchers in theoretical approaches, methodological techniques, and measurement instruments (Perry & Lindell, 1978; Quarantelli, 1985b; Tierney, 1986). Competing theoretical approaches are grounded in different academic disciplines and reflect fundamental underlying paradigmatic differences between those disciplines (cf. Kuhn, 1970). Basic paradigmatic divergences result in different assumptions being made, different questions being asked, and a range of research designs and methodologies being used (Perry & Lindell, 1978; Golec, 1983).

Characteristic, then, of the study of the psychosocial effects of disaster, natural or otherwise, has been a lack of agreement among researchers on how to best study the phenomena (Drabek, 1986). Tierney (1986) argues that there are three basic research traditions in the field.

The first Tierney refers to as the psychological trauma perspective (see also Quarantelli, 1985b). This approach views disasters as producing intense levels of stress as a result of fear, anxieties, death, and exposure to grotesque sites after impact. As a result, psychological trauma may be produced, accompanied by a range of sequelae including post-traumatic stress disorder (Figley, 1985). The focus is on the possibly intense affective and cognitive disruptions that can occur among victims of traumatic events (Green et al., 1985). Disasters, in this context, are seen as one type of traumatic event, sharing features with other stressors such as war, bereavement, violence, terrorism, and the like (Figley, 1985; Baum & Davidson, 1985).

Psychiatrists, psychologists and those in related clinically oriented fields are most likely to operate within this perspective. In-depth interviewing in a case study format is the usual methodological approach for conducting research. A number of studies using this paradigm have been generated regarding the Buffalo Creek (West Virginia) disaster. In that event, a mine company dam collapsed, creating a catastrophic flash flood that destroyed a number of Appalachian mountain communities and created a significant incidence of psychological trauma (Lifton & Olson, 1976; Titchener & Kapp, 1976; Erikson, 1976; Gleser et al., 1981).

In contrast, sociologists have tended to take what Tierney (1986) describes as a "neo-Durkheimian" approach, in reference to the French sociologist who stressed social solidarity and cohesion as the basis of psychological well-being. As recent reviews of the disaster literature indicate, the bulk of available disaster research has, thus far, been produced by sociologists working within this tradition (e.g., Mileti et al., 1975; Drabek, 1986).

At the core of this sociologically oriented perspective is the idea that disasters create a condition of heightened cohesiveness and social solidarity, resulting in a "therapeutic community" with a strong altruistic orientation, sense of collective purpose, and interpersonal cooperation and assistance (Fritz, 1961; Barton, 1970). Consequently, the morale of victims is frequently found to have been sustained, or even improved, by the disaster (Drabek & Key, 1984). Research by "neo-Durkheimians" has tended to minimize the negative psychosocial impacts of disaster, assuming, rather, that disasters don't produce psychological problems outside of short-term, transitory, upsets (Perry & Lindell, 1978). More serious psychological effects are seen as being generated, if at all, by the failure of the therapeutic community to emerge or by the isolation of victims from the salutary effects of that community (Western & Milne, 1979).

The newest paradigm that has developed in the field of disaster research looks at disasters as "stressful life events," and examines the full range of social and psychological effects that victims experience as a consequence (Tierney, 1986). This perspective draws on social-psychological work on life changes, developmental tasks, and accompanying stress-related phenomena (e.g., Holmes & Rahe, 1967; Selye, 1976; Pearlin & Schooler, 1978).

The perspective also directs attention to the use of social resources in mediating the impacts of stressful life events. Most recently this has taken the form of research on the use of social support as a "stress buffer," augmenting victims' coping capacities and resources (Kahn & Antonucci, 1980). While of increasing importance in disaster research, as yet few major studies have relied solely on this perspective. Elements of this approach are beginning to find their way into the research of some sociologists working in the area of psychosocial impacts (Bolin, 1983; Bolin, 1986a; Melick, 1978). The utility of this perspective is that it facilitates consideration of the role of social networks and extrafamilial ties in responding to disaster induced demands (e.g., Drabek & Key, 1984).

It should be noted that Tierney's (1986) typology, while useful in interpreting existing literature on disaster effects, is simply a heuristic device (cf. Quarantelli, 1985b). In fact, boundaries between these perspectives are by no means always clear and researchers utilize elements of more than one perspective. Clinicians, for example, may draw on the stressful life events literature in discussing the psychological trauma of disaster (e.g., Lindy & Grace, 1985).

These competing theoretical perspectives are accompanied by divergences in the methods of research utilized. As noted, those in the psychological trauma tradition tend to rely on clinical, in-depth interviews with victims. In such studies, victims are often self-selected or contacted through various outreach programs. They are victims, in other words, who are seeking out help for emotional strains and problems; hence, they are not necessarily representative of all victims. Data from the Buffalo Creek disaster were gathered from participants in a lawsuit against the coal company held to be responsible for the collapse of a dam (Lifton & Olson, 1976). Based on such samples of victims, studies in this tradition suggest that severe psychological impairment from disaster trauma is not unusual (e.g., Gleser et al., 1981; cf. Quarantelli, 1985b). Of course, many of the studies in this tradition are not based on natural disasters, but rather on dam collapses, fires, transportation accidents, and the like (e.g., Lindy et al., 1984; Lindy & Titchener, 1983).

Sociologically oriented researchers (the neo-Durkheimians) have focused on community-wide disasters and tended to use random samples of victims, thereby including subjects with a wide range of losses and impacts rather than only the severely impacted (Bolin & Bolton, 1986; Quarantelli, 1985b). Few studies have used either control groups of non-victims or have any pre-impact data beyond that derived from victim recall (cf. Bolin, 1982, and Drabek & Key, 1984, for exceptions). Given sampling differences, comparisons of findings between the several traditions is not always possible and may account for differing conclusions (Perry & Lindell, 1978).

A final area of methodological differences among the approaches is in the area of instruments used to measure psychological trauma and psychosocial impacts. A brief review of studies indicates the use of a wide range of standardized psychometric instruments, including the following:

the Demoralization scale (Dohrenwend et al., 1979); the General Health Questionnaire (Parker, 1977); Langner Index of Psychological Stress (Houts et al., 1980); the Psychiatric Evaluation Form (Gleser et al., 1981); the Symptom Checklist (Logue et al., 1981); Social Readjustment Rating Scale (Holmes & Rahe, 1967); Diagnostic Interview Schedule-Disaster Supplement (Smith, 1984).

The lack of a unified approach to measurement often confounds attempts at comparisons between studies vis à vis the incidence, frequency, and severity of psychosocial stress in disaster victims. Sociologists, in turn, often use no specific index, but rather create their own, based on preexisting scales, to measure psychosocial distress and more general problems in living (Bolin, 1982).

While a lack of consensus on theory and methods in studying psychosocial stress is problematic, there is an apparent unifying theme in much of the research—the notion of *stress* (e.g., Selye, 1976). Stress is conceptualized as a process in which an event (the stressor) subjects an individual or collectivity to demands which require the individual to respond in some fashion (Baum & Davidson, 1985). When demands exceed the person's or group's capacity to respond, stress is said to be the consequence (Haas & Drabek, 1973; Drabek & Key, 1984).

Disaster thus may be seen as one type of stress event, one that can create emotional sequelae for some victims unable to cope adequately with the event's demands. In Lazarus and Cohen's (1977) typology of environmentally induced stressors, natural disasters are categorized as "cataclysmic events" (cf. Figley, 1985)—sudden, destructive physical phenomena that affect comparatively large numbers of persons and necessitate significant effort on the part of those involved to cope with demands.

Much of the available literature on natural disasters, whether focusing on individual psychological reactions (Gleser et al., 1981), family disruption and response (Drabek & Key, 1984), or community-wide organizational responses (Haas & Drabek, 1973), utilizes notions of stress and imbalances in demand/response capability ratios (Quarantelli, 1985a).

NATURAL DISASTERS AND PSYCHOSOCIAL STRESS

Two questions will be addressed in this section before reviewing findings from the literature. First, what are the relevant physical characteristics of natural disasters that are salient to the study of psychosocial stress? Second, what is the range of psychosocial sequelae that have been associated with natural disasters?

Characteristics of Natural Disasters

Natural disasters are characterized according to a number of character-istics of dimensions each agent type possesses. Barton (1970) suggests that important features of agents include: speed of onset (from slow, as in droughts, to sudden, as in earthquakes); scope of impact (limited, as in some tornadoes, to widespread, as in hurricanes); duration of impact (short, as in tornadoes and earthquakes, to long-term, as in crescive floods and droughts); predictability (low, as in earthquakes, to high, as in hurri-canes and floods); intensity of impact (minimal, as in droughts, to intense, as in tornadoes, major earthquakes, and volcanic eruptions; threat of recurrence (low, as in some types of floods, to high, as in earthquakes) (cf. Berren et al., 1980). Of course, cataclysmic geophysical events or meteo-rological events become disasters only at the point that they involve human settlements and subject them to death, injury, and property destruction.

Disasters may also be analyzed temporally, according to the phase of the event. Natural disasters (unlike many types of technological ones) are typically preceded by a warning period, the time between the detection of threat and actual impact in which persons are advised of the threat condition. Evacuation, if it occurs, will take place most often during this period. The emergency period entails the impact of the agent and the immediate post-impact responses. The rehabilitation phase involves the restoration of basic services (water, electricity, phone) and the utilization of temporary sheltering of displaced victims (Quarantelli, 1985a). The final, or recovery, phase encompasses all the activities undertaken by survivors and support networks (both personal and institutional) to reestablish a "normal" or stable setting, whether or not it recovers to its predisaster state (Haas et al., 1977).

Psychosocial Sequelae

Related to the type and phases of disaster impact is the range of psychosocial impacts reported in the literature. An array of symptoms from persistent psychopathologies to less severe and more transitory mental health problems (depression, anxiety, substance abuse, phobias) to general "problems in living" (Taylor et al., 1976) have been noted in various studies (Tierney, 1986). "Problems in living" refers to the innu-merable practical demands and stresses that many victims confront in the course of responding to the disaster, such as physical cleanup, coping with injuries, financial problems, difficulties with aid bureaucracies, lack of leisure time, disrupted social networks—in a word, the unavoidable has-sles of day-to-day living in a disrupted physical and social environment.

Bolin (1985a) suggests that the psychosocial impacts of disaster can be categorized into cognitive, emotional, psychosomatic, and social dimensions. Perhaps the classic statement on cognitive dysfunction is Wallace's (1956) description of the "disaster syndrome." Wallace used the term to describe the dazed and shocked behavior exhibited by victims of violent and unexpected disasters. Sociologists are likely to view such cognitive distortions as transitory and not requiring interventions. More clinically oriented researchers consider this psychic numbing as potential precursor to deeper cognitive dysfunction. (Figley, 1985; Zusman, 1976).

General emotional or affective responses to impact encompass a wide range of symptoms. Phobias, anxieties, fears, depression, and loss of affect are variously mentioned in the literature for a number of disasters, including: hurricanes (Bates et al., 1963), earthquakes (Greenson & Mintz, 1972), tornadoes (Bolin, 1982), hailstorms (Leivesley, 1977), and floods (Ollendick & Hoffman, 1982). Severe or more intense disasters have been associated with deeper states of depression among some victims (Hocking, 1965; Knaus, 1975).

In situations where property destruction is extensive or there is a high death rate, grief reactions and bereavement may be encountered. While grief is most common as an emotional response to the deaths of family or friends (e.g., Lifton & Olson, 1976), the loss of home, pets, or personal possessions may also produce grief-like responses and depression (Bolin 1986a; Fried, 1963; Erikson, 1976).

Physical and psychosomatic illnesses are relatively commonplace after disaster (Logue et al., 1981). Most frequently reported are insomnia and related sleep disturbances, nightmares, hypertension, and sexual dysfunction (Church, 1974; Logue et al., 1979; Gleser et al., 1981).

At the level of interpersonal behavior, disasters have been associated with a number of reported problems. Victims who are depressed may withdraw from contacts with others and retreat from dealing with instrumental activities to help in recovery (Bolin, 1986a). Irritability, anger, frustration, and phobias may disrupt interaction patterns within families and create obstacles to recovery (Erikson, 1976; Bolin, 1982).

The preceding illustrates the range of potential impacts and responses to natural disaster. Under what conditions such impacts occur and during what phase of the disaster can now be examined.

PSYCHOSOCIAL IMPACTS: A REVIEW OF FINDINGS

Disasters initiate a complex set of social processes, as well as intensifying preexisting social and economic trends in impacted communities. In considering the literature on psychosocial effects, there are two basic dimensions that must be distinguished. One is the psychological impacts engendered by the threat of, or actual impact of, a natural disaster. This would include all the stresses associated with being in a high risk situation as well as the traumatic effects of physical impact (property destruction, injury, death, horror, and terror).

The second dimension encompasses the stresses and demands associated with the social responses to the disaster event. There is ample evidence in the literature that how individuals and collectivities respond to disasters can become a significant source of psychosocial stress, *independent of agent impact effects*. Social responses such as evacuation, living in temporary housing, relocation, aid seeking, and the like can create stresses that are in addition to the stresses created by the physical impacts of the event. Quarantelli (1985a) refers to the social stresses as response-generated demands. The distinction between response-generated and disaster-generated demands is analytically useful. For disaster victims, of course, all the stresses and demands of an impact and its aftermath are cumulative and experienced as part of a continuing series of problems and tasks that require dealing with (Golec, 1983). Failure to adequately cope with these demands can result in varying levels of psychosocial stress (e.g., Quarantelli, 1985a).

Disaster Impact Characteristics

The features of natural disaster that may be associated with mental health impacts include: pre-impact threat; unexpectedness of impact and rapidity of involvement; scope of destruction; duration of impact; threat of sudden recurrence; exposure to death (e.g., Baum & Davidson, 1985; Berren et al., 1980; Warheit, 1985).

Because many natural disasters are detectable prior to impact, they allow warnings to be issued (Drabek, 1986). With a warning period, victims may experience a period of threat and a sense of vulnerability while anticipating impact. In contrast, many technological disasters (chemical spills, transportation accidents, nuclear plant failures) allow no warning period and don't necessarily have immediate detectable impacts [in the case of nuclear accidents] (e.g., Sorensen et al., 1987).

In general, disasters which allow little or no warning (earthquakes and volcanic eruptions) may be inherently more stressful than those that can be detected and for which warnings can be issued (e.g., hurricanes and some types of floods and tornadoes). Many natural disasters are such that watches and warnings can be issued from minutes to days ahead of predicted impact (Drabek, 1986). Warnings allow individuals to undertake actions to reduce the likelihood of personal injury and property loss (e.g., Bates et al., 1963). A warning period also allows anticipatory socialization to occur, which reduces the stressfulness of the impact should it occur (Pearlin & Schooler, 1978; Kessler, 1979). Thus, disasters preceded by adequate warnings, other things being equal, are less likely to produce psychological distress.

Of course, as much of the risk perception literature illustrates, the accurate warning of an impending disaster may bear little relationship to individuals' perceptions of personal risk and vulnerability (Mileti, 1980; Turner et al., 1986; Slovic et al., 1979; Withey, 1976). As Covello (1983) has indicated in reference to technological hazards, individuals tend to underestimate the hazardousness of their environments. Transient psychosocial stress is more likely to be exacerbated in conditions of ambiguous threat, when expected impacts are delayed, or when the predicted disaster simply fails to occur (e.g., Withey, 1976; Mileti et al., 1975; Lazarus, 1966). Wolfenstein (1957) has suggested that the tendency to interpret hazardous situations as nonthreatening is a strategy used by some to reduce the dissonance associated with being at personal risk (cf. Withey, 1976).

Because natural disaster threats are less ambiguous and the nature of the agents is often familiar they are considered by some to be intrinsically less stressful than technological disasters (Sorensen et al., 1987; Baum & Davidson, 1985). While the true threat of a disaster inheres in the physical nature of the event, perceived threat is a subjective assessment of risk by potential victims, and may or may not be a "realistic" evaluation of the situation (Mileti, 1980).

The unexpectedness of a disaster is inversely related to the available warning period. Unexpected, sudden events allow no time for either mental or physical preparation for impact, increasing the stressful nature of the event (assuming that impact itself is relatively intense or violent) (e.g., Warheit, 1985). However few natural disasters are completely unexpected. Tornadoes are preceded by stormy weather, floods by heavy rains or snowmelt. Technological disasters, by comparison, are usually unexpected, and thus more likely to be stressful (Baum & Davidson, 1985).

Quarantelli (1985a) draws a distinction between the unexpectedness of a disaster and the rapidity of involvement of a population. Slow-onset disasters such as droughts or crescive floods only gradually involve populations in their impacts. For example, a slowly flooding river, forecast weeks in advance, may gradually rise out of its banks and progressively inundate homes and neighborhoods as it crests. Victims of such floods are able to observe the slow rise of the river, remove possessions to safe areas, and even sandbag around their homes to hold off the flood. For these victims, the disaster only very gradually "involves" them in its effects.

In areas of the country where such floods are a recurrent event (i.e., the Southeast and parts of the Midwest), they become almost routine events in local cultures. Disaster subcultures, as these routinized adaptations are referred to (Weller & Wenger, 1973; Hannigan & Kueneman, 1978), provide normative guidelines for appropriate responses, thus eliminating much of the potential stressfulness of the disaster (cf. Britton, 1981).

Conversely, disasters that rapidly involve populations are likely to be perceived as crisis events and, consequently, also likely to produce negative psychological effects (Quarantelli, 1985a.) The rapidity of involvement, while often associated with sudden disasters, can vary independently. As Quarantelli (1985a) writes:

> Mental health effects stem not from how long in some chronological sense people have available to act [in response to disaster], but rather from whether they perceive themselves as having to hurry to save threatened values, as being in a "crisis." (p. 61)

Flash floods (Miller et al., 1981; Erikson, 1976), volcanic eruptions (Leik et al., 1982), tornadoes (Bolin, 1982, Drabek & Key, 1984), and earthquakes (Bolton, 1979) are typical agents that can rapidly involve populations in the crisis. For example, Bolin (1982) describes a tornado that moved through a community at some 40 m.p.h., with winds in excess of 250 m.p.h. and an impact zone a mile wide and several miles long, that destroyed thousands of homes, killed dozens, and rendered several thousand families homeless almost instantly. In such a crisis event, hundreds or thousands are suddenly involved, and it may produce widespread, if transitory, psychological effects (Bolin, 1982).

Another key variable in estimating psychosocial impacts is the scope of destruction. What appears to be central in this dimension is what *proportion* of a local population is involved in the disaster (Warheit, 1985). The scope also determines the proportion of the community that is left undamaged. A tornado, for example, that destroys a few hundred homes in a rural community of two thousand may have different psychosocial impacts than the same amount of tornado damage in a city of half a million. Although there are a number of qualifiers that make firm conclusions impossible (cf. Bolin, 1985a), it would appear that the greater the ratio of damaged to undamaged areas in a community, the greater the likelihood of negative psychological effects (e.g., Quarantelli, 1985a). Disasters that have a large scope of impact may produce long-term social or physical changes in the community, changes which can become a source of chronic stress (Parker, 1977).

The Buffalo Creek disaster, although not an "Act of God," is representative of disasters that involve a large proportion of a local population. In that dam collapse and resultant flood, whole communities were destroyed, resulting in widespread psychological trauma (Erikson, 1976). Part of the trauma of that event was derived from the fact that victims had no intact part of their community in which to seek refuge and solace (e.g., Lifton & Olson, 1976; Lindy & Grace, 1985).

The duration of impact is yet another disaster characteristic that is implicated as a possible source of stress (Berren et al., 1980). Many natural disasters have an acute, relatively short-term impact phase (e.g., earthquakes, tornadoes). Floods and hurricanes generally have a somewhat longer impact phase, sometimes lasting hours or days (White & Haas, 1975). It has been suggested that for equally intense impacts a longer impact period will be experienced as more stressful (Baum et al., 1983). The reference is the length of impact of the physical agent, *not* the length of the crisis that the event occasions. The latter is an independent secondary dimension to be considered below. Technological disasters such as chemical accidents or radiation releases are more likely than natural disasters to be perceived as having a protracted impact period (Baum & Davidson, 1985; Levine, 1982; Sorensen et al., 1987).

The threat of recurrence of a disaster has been found to be a source of stress in some natural disasters (Barton, 1970). The threat of recurrence, in terms of psychosocial stress, is determined by victim perceptions of continued or renewed vulnerability rather than by objective probabilities of event recurrence. The threat of recurrence, if perceived as likely, creates a situation of chronic stress on victims, increasing the likelihood of identifiable mental health effects (Warheit, 1985). Earthquakes and volcanic eruptions frequently present victims with relatively unambiguous "reminders" of the possibility of event recurrence through the typical periods of heightened seismic activity in the aftermath. Major earthquakes are followed by major and minor aftershocks that can continue for a year or more, creating a sense of vulnerability amongst victims (e.g., Bolin & Bolton, 1986; Greenson & Mintz, 1972).

Cyclical or seasonal fear of recurrence has also been noted in the literature. Bolin (1982) found increased levels of stress among tornado victims at the onset of tornado season the year following a major tornado in one Texas town. The stress was related to anxieties victims had over continuing personal vulnerability.

Of all disaster impact characteristics, the one most frequently associated with significant levels of psychosocial stress is the exposure to death or acute life-threatening situations (Green, 1982; Gleser et al., 1981). Extreme events involving physical forces that place victims in life-threatening situations have been associated with relatively serious psychological disturbances, including psychopathologies (Green, 1985).

Sudden, violent disasters are those most likely to produce such life-threatening situations (e.g., tornadoes, flashfloods, earthquakes). Victims of disaster who just manage to "escape with their lives" are more likely to be traumatized by the event than those who may witness the event, but are themselves not at personal risk (Bolin, 1985a).

However, in studies of three powerful and deadly flashfloods (Big Thompson, Colorado, Rapid City, South Dakota, Buffalo Creek, West Virginia), it was only in the last that significant levels of psychological disturbances were identified. This is notable because of the many *event* similarities they had, including: a significant death toll, impact occurring while many were asleep, highly destructive impacts, and the fact that the disasters were sudden and unexpected (Miller et al., 1981; Bolin, 1976; Erikson, 1976).

A number of factors seemed to conspire to make the Buffalo Creek disaster the source of high levels of psychological trauma. One of the factors prevalent at that site but less so at the two other sites was the exposure of survivors to the deaths of others. It should be pointed out that the death toll was actually greater in Rapid City than in Buffalo Creek (Bolin, 1976; Erikson, 1976), but a much smaller portion of the total population was involved. The scope of the destruction in Buffalo Creek was such that many victims witnessed the deaths of others or were exposed to mutilated corpses (Lifton & Olson, 1976; Titchener & Kapp, 1976). The horror of the deaths of others appears as an important determinant of psychopathologies diagnosed after that disaster (Gleser et al., 1981). The deaths of others was a persistent theme in the nightmares of survivors, as well as a source of "survivor guilt" and severe grief reactions (Gleser et al., 1981). Of course, as Quarantelli (1985b) has argued, the Buffalo Creek disaster is highly atypical, and thus may not be representative of more common disaster impacts.

Of all the disaster characteristics reviewed, exposure to life-threatening events and to deaths is perhaps the most traumatic for survivors. None of these dimensions of disaster operates in isolation, but rather they constitute a complex set of existential features that victims experience in highly variable ways. For example, a victim of an earthquake who is trapped in a collapsed building for several days may experience a completely different disaster than someone who escaped from the same building and watched it collapse from the safety of the street. One cannot objectively identify impact characteristics and presume certain types of psychosocial impacts without a thorough qualitative understanding of how victims perceived the impact.

To summarize the preceding, keeping in mind the many contingencies involved, it has been suggested that heightened stress levels are associated with:

1. Disasters with sudden, unanticipated onsets, particularly those that rapidly involve victims in the crisis situation (e.g., Quarantelli, 1985a).
2. Disasters in which victims are unfamiliar with, and unprepared for impact (e.g., Warheit, 1985).
3. Disasters where victims are exposed to life-threatening situations and/or witness the death of others (e.g., Drabek, 1986).
4. Disasters which impact a large segment of a local population when accompanied by widespread property damage (Erikson, 1976).
5. Disasters that are followed by a continuing threat of recurrence, resulting in a prolonged period of threat (Bolin, 1985a).

It is not being suggested that such characteristics pertain only to natural disasters. Disaster events from whatever source share generic characteristics (Quarantelli, 1985a). Natural disasters are distinctive primarily in the types of social responses that they initiate. Also, the stressfulness of any disaster event depends on the coping resources of victims, their ability to access social support, and the nature of the responses of the community and society to the disaster (Bolin, 1985b).

Response-Generated Demands

The social responses to disaster have been studied extensively by sociologists and that literature constitutes a significant portion of all disaster research (Drabek, 1986; Quarantelli, 1985b). How families, communities, and societies respond to the threat of disaster or to disaster impact can become stressors in themselves. Disasters create situations in which many demands may be made on victims (evacuation, search and rescue, seeking shelter), and those demands may continue for some time after the impact effects have subsided. Four common social response processes have been identified as potential sources of psychosocial stress: evacuation/emergency shelter, temporary housing, victim relocation, and recovery and reconstruction (e.g., Bolin, 1985b).

Evacuation/emergency shelter. While it is beyond the scope of this chapter to review all of the evacuation literature (cf. Quarantelli, 1982; Perry et al., 1980; Drabek, 1986), some findings vis à vis psychosocial effects can be identified. Evacuation from a hazardous area, finding emergency shelter, and ultimately returning to one's home is a common social process. It is most usually observed in response to hurricanes, floods, volcanic activity, and forest/brush fires. Many recent large scale evacuations have been documented in response to technological disasters such as Three Mile Island (TMI) (Sorensen et al., 1987) and Chernobyl (Dudley, 1986).

Evacuation is comparatively non-stressful if victims are able to evacuate as family units, to receive emergency shelter in the homes of kin or friends, *and* to return to their own homes in due time (Quarantelli, 1982; Drabek, 1986). Evacuating as a family to the homes of friends or family provides evacuees with a socially supportive milieu. Mass evacuations per se should not be viewed as inherently stressful.

Evacuations in which families are accidentally or intentionally split up, or in which families are not able to stay together in emergency shelters, can become a source of psychosocial stress (Instituut voor Sociaal Onderzoek, 1955; Drabek & Boggs, 1968). Recent research on potential stresses associated with family separation during evacuation come from studies of the TMI accident. Given the ambiguous nature of TMI's threat/impact and contradictory evacuation advice, some families had difficulties in reaching agreement on the need or desirability to evacuate. Such lack of consensus and the resulting family separations were responsible for at least short-term stresses and anxiety (Bromet & Dunn, 1981; Sorensen et al., 1987).

When evacuation procedures are poorly managed by emergency service organizations, or when emergency shelters themselves are in the impact zone, victims have been noted to experience transient fears and anxieties, as well as anger over the process (Bolin, 1986b). As Quarantelli (1985a) writes, " . . . some possible psychological effects on evacuees stem not from the direct impact of the disaster agent, but from having to adjust to the actions (or inactions) of organized helpers" (p. 128). Anxieties may also be intensified if victims cannot or are not allowed to return to their homes in a reasonable period (Parker, 1977; Bates et al., 1963).

Where victims go when they evacuate may have an effect on their psychosocial status, but there is little in the literature to permit any firm conclusions (e.g., Quarantelli, 1982). Mass public shelters, such as those established by the Red Cross, are frequently avoided by evacuees who have options to go elsewhere (e.g., friends' homes, motels, etc.). Hence, public shelters tend to be used disproportionately by evacuees of lower socioeconomic status. In natural disasters such as floods or hurricanes, the stay in emergency shelter may be only a matter of hours or days, and is not likely to be experienced as exceptionally stressful.

In natural disasters, the majority of evacuees go to the homes of friends or kin, avoiding group shelters entirely (Drabek, 1986). There are a few instances in the literature in which evacuees are given shelter in the homes of strangers (e.g., Instituut voor Sociaal Onderzoek, 1955). Such arrangements, while rare, appear more stressful and conflict-ridden than typical emergency shelter arrangements.

The length of time that a family hosts evacuating kin or friends is linked in some studies to heightened stress levels. In American society, with its emphasis on privacy as a dominant family value, relationships between host and evacuee families can begin to deteriorate notably if they persist beyond a few weeks (Bolin, 1982). Typically, levels of interpersonal conflict begin to rise over issues of crowding, money, and privacy (Bolin, 1982; Bolin & Bolton, 1986). However, such lengthy stays are unusual as victims are usually able to secure some form of temporary housing or are able to return to their old homes (e.g., Golec, 1983).

Temporary housing. Following destructive natural disasters, many victims seek temporary housing while they either search for new permanent housing or rebuild their former homes. Quarantelli (1982) sees temporary housing as part of a process, not a "thing," one that involves the actions of disaster victims with those of various local, state, and federal agencies and programs. Temporary housing often provides the victim family with an environment in which to begin to confront the disruptions and turmoil in daily living which the disaster created (Bolin, 1982). Temporary shelter also gives victims a private place to reestablish family routines after staying in crowded mass shelters or with a host family (e.g., Golec, 1983). However, temporary housing can become a source of additional stress, often more protracted and difficult to adjust to than the initial disaster impact that created the need for the housing to begin with.

In the United States, temporary housing is provided in federally declared disasters to all qualified victims under the auspices of the Federal Emergency Management Agency (FEMA). While the provision of rent-free or low-cost temporary housing gives victims transitional shelter, it is sometimes the source of protracted psychosocial stress (e.g., Gleser, 1981). If temporary housing is situated in areas away from familiar neighborhoods, transportation routes, shopping areas, and schools, or if the housing is inadequate for victims' minimum needs, it presents victims with a continuing source of disruption of their daily lives and routines (Trainer & Bolin, 1976; Davis, 1975). Taken by themselves, such disruptions may be relatively minor, but they can also contribute to the many other demands victims face on a day-to-day basis in recovery.

In some circumstances, temporary housing becomes an obstacle to the utilization of informal support networks, particularly if temporary housing is located outside of the disaster-stricken community (Parker, 1977; Bolin, 1986b). Disruptions of social support networks can deny victims an important source of affective and instrumental assistance in coping with disaster-related demands (Solomon, 1985; Kahn & Antonucci, 1980).

Evidence for the potentially stressful effects of temporary housing in U.S. disasters primarily relates to the use of mobile homes as housing (Quarantelli, 1982). At least three factors appear to be related to the stressful nature of trailers under FEMA's auspices: the size and construction of the trailers; the social composition of the trailer courts where they are situated; the bureaucratic monitoring and interventions by agency representatives and contractors.

Several studies have reported the trailers to be: too small for some families' needs; fire hazards; unheated; without adequate plumbing or sewage hook ups; situated in areas that victims feel are unsafe (e.g., Bolin, 1982; Erikson, 1976; Golec, 1983). Any of these factors can range from a minor annoyance to a significant disruptive force.

More important than possible structural inadequacies of the trailers, victim complaints often focus on the social makeup of the trailer camps themselves. (Not all trailers are located in victim only courts; some are placed in existing mobile home parks and some are placed on private lots.) Because the trailers are distributed to qualified applicants on a "first come-first served" basis, the courts are often socially heterogeneous. Consequently, victims report feeling isolated and alienated, as well as fearful of neighbors (Bolin, 1982; Erikson, 1976). The camps typically lack the sense of collective purpose and high morale that is observed in the wake of natural disasters (Quarantelli, 1985c).

Occupants of federally sponsored trailers have their cases continually reviewed by agency personnel to assess their eligibility to remain in the rent-free housing. As Golec (1983) writes, victim families after the Teton dam disaster were ". . . regularly interrupted, with and without writs of entry, by a long list of official and unofficial workers on some disaster mission" (p. 263) (see also Bolin, 1982). Much of the bureaucratic intrusion angers and frustrates victims. It is seen as a type of official harassment, one that contributes to their sense of victimization.

Little is known of the impact of other forms of temporary housing in terms of psychosocial stress (Quarantelli, 1985c). Trailers are used in federally declared disasters only when apartments and rental homes aren't available in adequate numbers to house victims of mass disasters. What can be derived from the available research is that housing that isolates a victim from familiar neighborhoods and informal social support networks may become a source of chronic stress for some (Parker, 1977; Bolin, 1985b; Gleser et al., 1981). The persistent nature of the stressors is intensified when victims are not able to establish stable temporary housing, but rather are required to change residences frequently (Bolin & Bolton, 1986).

Relocation. When victims are relocated away from an impacted community, evidence suggests that psychological distress may be a consequence (Garrison, 1985). Disaster-caused relocation creates a number of existential demands on victims including: having to deal with disaster relevant bureaucracies; employment difficulties; problems in locating permanent housing; adjusting to new neighborhoods; establishing new social relationships; and being deprived of access to former social support networks (Milne, 1977; Sowder, 1985; Garrison, 1985). Parker (1977) terms such demands "relocation stressors" and indicates that they can become a significant source of psychological distress among relocatees (p. 385).

Best evidence for the psychosocial impacts of relocation is found in a series of studies done after cyclone Tracy destroyed much of Darwin, Australia. The Darwin disaster provides interesting insights into relocation because some victims remained in the destroyed community while others were resettled in distant communities. The studies suggest that those who could not return to Darwin suffered the highest stress levels and had notably higher incidence of mental health problems (Milne, 1977; Western & Milne, 1979; Parker, 1977). Milne's (1979) study of the Darwin relocation concludes:

> . . . the total traumatic effect on the Non-Returned Evacuees was the resultant of two sets of factors: the primary [cyclone] impact, and the alienation from the social and physical environment to which they had become adapted. . . . What the Stayers *gained* and what the Non-Returneds *missed*, was the *therapeutic effect* of being inside the post-disaster community. *(Emphasis in original)* (p. 121)

This statement identifies two factors that have been shown to mitigate the stress effects associated with natural disasters: social support and the "therapeutic community" as referred to by Milne.

As noted earlier, it is well established in the sociological literature that following natural disasters a temporary increase in morale, social solidarity, altruism, and helping behaviors emerges (Barton, 1970; Golec, 1983; Drabek, 1986). This postdisaster ethos of collective purpose in confronting a community-wide challenge appears to assist victims in coping with the numerous problems in recovery that they are inevitably confronted with. During the therapeutic phase, social and material support is made available from official sources, and mutual aid is widespread and normatively sanctioned (Golec, 1983; Drabek & Key, 1984; Drabek, 1986).

Natural disasters are more likely to be followed by a therapeutic community phase than are technological disasters. Natural disasters are events that tend to give rise to a community consensus, albeit often short-lived, whereas studies of human-caused disasters indicate that they are more prone to creating conflict and dissension (Levine, 1982; Sorensen et al., 1987; Walsh, 1984). The early phases of natural disasters, during which the therapeutic community arises, do not seem to involve class, economic, and political interests as brazenly as do failures in technological systems such as TMI (Kasperson & Pijawka, 1985). Of course, in the later stages of natural disaster, political and economic conflicts begin to reassert themselves as the therapeutic community subsides (e.g., Bolin, 1982; Quarantelli & Dynes, 1985).

Informal social support after disasters derives from two main sources: that given by individual family members to each other and that given by networks of kin and friends. Each "buffers" the stress of disaster-generated and response-generated demands on the victims (Kahn & Antonucci, 1980; Lindy & Grace, 1985). Conversely, social responses to disasters that disrupt victim access to that support (e.g., relocation) increase the likelihood of psychological distress (Solomon, 1985; Ahearn & Castellon, 1979; Milne, 1977).

Because a primary source of social support is from one family member to another, the death or injury of family members can constitute a significant disruption of such intrafamilial support. Erikson (1976), in his study of the Buffalo Creek disaster, has suggested that the high death rate within primary groups interfered with the traditional functioning of support, adding to the severity of grief and bereavement.

Children, in particular, have been found to be vulnerable to distress caused by deaths in the family or kin group (Perry & Perry, 1959; Blaufarb & Levine, 1982). Children have also been reported to suffer separation anxieties when separated from family members after disaster (Bolin, 1982; Singer, 1982).

Phenomena such as relocation, living in certain types of temporary housing, disrupted support networks, and increased financial burdens are potentially cumulative in their effect on victims. Garrison (1985) indicates that these psychosocial stresses can be intensified in situations where victims feel they cannot control the relocation process (cf. Parker, 1977). The feeling of a loss of control is associated with higher rates of depression and anxiety in victim populations (Folkman, 1984; Bolin, 1986a).

Recovery and reconstruction. Of all phases of disaster, long-term recovery is perhaps the least studied, particularly in reference to enduring psychosocial impacts and delayed stress reactions. The problems in living that accompany recovery are essentially continuations of many earlier response-generated demands. These would include difficulties in reestablishing satisfactory housing, increased indebtedness associated with reconstruction, interruption of employment patterns of family members, time constraints on leisure and visitation, adjustments to new neighborhoods, altered family routines, and the like (e.g., Trainer & Bolin, 1976; Bolin & Bolton, 1986; Drabek & Key, 1984; Golec, 1983).

The recovery phase, during which families and communities rebuild and attempt to return to some form of "normal," will be least stressful when the financial and material support available is adequate to the needs of victims (Haas et al., 1977; Bolin, 1982). Research on long-term recovery (one to two years postimpact) has demonstrated that the receipt of *adequate* state and federal aid is positively correlated with psychosocial recovery (Bolin, 1982, 1986b). The failure to receive adequate aid in the recovery period has been associated with persistent emotional strains lasting more than one year after impact (Bolin, 1982).

What is significant in this is that some groups of victims appear more likely than others to *not* receive adequate aid and to experience greater psychosocial adjustment difficulties as a result. Recent research has identified the poor and minorities (blacks and Hispanics), as well as those with large families, as having the fewest coping resources (Bolin & Bolton, 1986). That research concludes, regarding minorities, that they:

> . . . have greater numbers of dependents, . . . less money in savings
> . . . and fewer personal resources. . . . Such families are under stress
> even prior to the disaster and have fewer capacities (material, social
> or psychological) to cope with additional demands. (p. 222)

Those in socially disadvantaged positions prior to disaster may have those disadvantages deepened in the aftermath, thus being more likely to experience prolonged psychosocial distress (Bolin & Bolton, 1986).

The recovery and reconstruction process can alter the cultural and spatial qualities of a locale, particularly in the case of highly destructive disasters with a wide scope of impact (Dudasik, 1980). The disruption of familiar community and neighborhood patterns can create the need for victims to make additional adjustments to their environments. Because the reconstruction process may last considerably longer than the initial therapeutic phase, what were seen as minor annoyances (construction activities, torn-up streets, trailer camps, etc.) may become less well tolerated as reconstruction continues (Bolin, 1982; Golec, 1983). Because the physical reconstruction of a community is often more rapid than the social and psychological recovery of victims, some may feel alienated from the ongoing community recovery process (Bolin, 1982). As Golec (1983) terms it, a "secondary disaster" may occur for those victims excluded from the aid and recovery processes who may continue to ". . . experience loss and disruption as an enduring and possibly permanent condition of existence" (p. 265). However, enduring psychosocial impacts on victims who are marginal to the overall recovery process in communities have not been studied extensively (e.g., Golec, 1983; Green, 1985).

While the discussion has thus far stressed negative impacts of disaster-caused and response-generated stresses on victims, some sociological literature has emphasized their positive effects on individual and family functioning (Drabek, 1986). The myriad problems and demands confronted by disaster-stricken families may become the basis for greater family solidarity and higher levels of marital satisfaction (Drabek & Key, 1984; Leik et al., 1982).

To briefly reiterate major points on psychological impacts of response-generated demands, the following are noted:

1. Evacuations in which families are separated or in which there is a lack of consensus on the decision to evacuate are more likely to be stressful (Drabek, 1986).
2. Emergency shelter is unlikely to be perceived as stressful unless the stays are protracted or the shelters become a center for interpersonal conflict (Bolin, 1986a).
3. Evacuations that are poorly managed or that expose victims to continuing environmental threats will increase stress levels (Quarantelli, 1985a).
4. Temporary housing will heighten psychosocial distress if it is perceived as dangerous, inadequate, or located in socially heterogeneous camps (Erickson, 1976).

5. The failure to establish stable temporary housing may constitute a chronic stressor after community-wide disasters (Gleser et al., 1981).
6. Any temporary housing or relocation programs that socially isolate victims from their old communities and neighborhoods may have negative psychosocial impacts (Parker, 1977).
7. Victims who are excluded from or fail to qualify for formal aid programs are likely to experience long-term difficulties in their economic and psychosocial recovery (Bolin, 1982).

NEEDED RESEARCH

In spite of the tremendous growth in disaster studies in the past decade (cf. Drabek, 1986; Mileti et al., 1975), there are still a number of gaps in the data base that make drawing unqualified conclusions problematic. Although there is a general consensus as to the dimensions and characteristics of disaster relevant to the study of psychosocial stress (e.g., Sowder, 1985), as yet there is no typological model to categorize and order the multitude of findings in the literature (cf. Warheit, 1985).

Because researchers often come from different disciplinary backgrounds, there is a lack of methodological standardization that makes comparing findings difficult (Quarantelli, 1985b; Green et al., 1985). More research is needed that utilizes random sampling techniques in impacted communities. It would seem important to obtain measurements on victims with a range of impacts and losses, not just of those seeking mental health services or who are contacted through outreach programs. Multisite comparisons, utilizing standardized instruments, are also needed to help determine, within the framework of a single study, how different disaster characteristics interact with different patterns of community response in producing or mitigating psychosocial stress.

There are almost no studies available that use pre- and post-impact assessments of mental health status of disaster victims, except in a post-hoc fashion (Drabek & Key, 1984). This is a significant methodological challenge and until it is suitably met it will be difficult to unequivocally assess disaster-generated psychological impacts. Similarly, few studies have utilized control groups in their assessments of disaster-generated effects (e.g., Drabek & Key, 1984; Bolin, 1982).

To better understand the influence of culture on coping strategies of disaster victims, studies utilizing crosscultural research are also desirable (e.g., Haas et al., 1977; Pelanda, 1982). Crosscultural analyses could provide more insights into how cultural values, kinship systems, and community structures affect the psychological impact of natural disaster (Bates, 1982; Trainer & Bolin, 1976; Loizos, 1977).

Lastly, more research is needed on the psychosocial impacts of so-called response-generated demands. Evidence reviewed here suggests that social actions (or their lack) in response to natural disaster may constitute a significant and persistent source of stress on some victims. Research designs need to be developed to better conceptualize and measure the relative effects of disaster-related demands and social response demands on the psychosocial status of victims. In cases where disaster relief and recovery efforts are ineffective, discriminatory, or badly managed, persistent emotional distress has been documented (Bolin, 1982; Golec, 1983).

IMPLICATIONS

This review has identified areas in which there is some agreement in the literature on the psychological impacts of natural disaster. However, the fact that there are also conflicting conclusions and disagreements in the research base suggests that disciplinary approaches and biases play a role in those conclusions (Quarantelli, 1985b; Tierney, 1986).

For those concerned with the provision of mental health services after natural disaster, several points are relevant. The trauma potential of disaster is less based on the characteristics of the impact (speed of onset, intensity, scope) than on the individual's or family's particular experiences with the disaster *and* with the social processes that the event engenders.

Because natural disasters often create a therapeutic response phase (unlike technological disasters), mental health services for victims often go unused (Tierney, 1986). Demands on victims change over time, both quantitatively and qualitatively, as do potential psychosocial stresses (Green, 1985). Any changes in the structure of the impacted community, due to relocation, temporary housing, housing shortages, high death rates, increased unemployment, and the like, may become chronic stressors (e.g., Garrison, 1985). Likewise, postdisaster social responses that disrupt informal social support networks are potentially significant sources of psychological stress. Conversely, because natural disasters may create a therapeutic community response, the stress effects of the event may be buffered, under conditions of adequate aid and support.

It is within this ambiguous and paradoxical situation of heightened social support *and* intensified demand levels that mental health programs for victims must function. Because the delivery of mental health services is discussed extensively in accompanying chapters, only a few points will be made here.

Studies indicate that mental health programs offered to the victims of natural disaster will go unused unless considerable effort is made to contact victims through outreach programs. Also, if the term "mental health" appears in the title of the program, victims will be reluctant to utilize services (Tierney & Baisden, 1979) because of the stigma attached to it in some areas (Ahearn & Cohen, 1984).

Mental health programs may have their greatest utility in nontraditional roles such as assisting with referrals in Disaster Assistance Centers, helping victims fill out aid application forms, providing transportation, helping to mobilize support networks, offering stress reduction workshops, and providing victims with an opportunity to ventilate feelings (Kliman, 1976; Hartsough, 1982; Tierney, 1986).

Socially disadvantaged groups, including minorities, the poor, the homeless, and the unemployed, are most vulnerable to disaster and response-generated demands. Disasters tend to perpetuate or intensify such social inequities. The long-term effects of natural disasters depend on the social, political, and economic patterns of inequality in the larger society, as well as on the particular circumstances of the disaster (Quarantelli, 1985b). It is difficult for conventional mental health services to redress problems generated by larger societal inequities. For disadvantaged groups, then, the negative effects of natural disaster may be mitigated more by advocacy services, community organizers, and social change than by counseling alone.

Overall, the effective delivery of mental health services depends on an awareness of predisaster social conditions in the community and an understanding of how the disaster event *and* the social responses to it can create conditions that will produce transient or chronic stresses on victims.

BIBLIOGRAPHY

Ahearn, F. (1981). Disaster mental health: A pre-post and post-earthquake comparison of psychiatric admission rates. *The Urban and Social Change Review,* 14(2): 22–28.

Ahearn, F., & Castellon, S. (1979). Mental health problems following a disaster situation. *Acta Psiquiatrica y Psicologica de America Latina,* 25: 58–68.

Ahearn, F., & Cohen, R. (1984). Disasters and mental health: An annotated bibliography. DHHS Publication No. (ADM) 84–1311. Washington, D.C.

Barton, A. (1970). *Communities in Disaster.* Garden City, N.Y.: Doubleday.

Bates, F. (Ed) (1982). Recovery Change and Development: A Longitudinal Study of the Guatemalan Earthquake. Athens, GA: Guatemalan Earthquake Study, University of Georgia.

Bates, F., Fogleman, C., Parenton, V., Pittman, R., & Tracy, G. (1963). *The Social and*

Psychological Consequences of a Natural Disaster. National Research Council disaster study 18. Washington, D.C.: National Academy of Science.

Baum, A., & Davidson, L. (1985). A suggested framework for studying factors that contribute to trauma in disaster. In B. Sowder (Ed.), *Disasters and Mental Health: Selected Contemporary Perspectives* (pp. 29–40). DHHS Publication No. (ADM) 85–1421. Washington, D.C.

Baum, A., Fleming, R., & Davidson, L. (1983). Natural disaster and technological catastrophe. *Environment and Behavior.* 15(3): 333–354.

Berren, M., Beigel, A., & Ghertner, S. (1980). A typology for the classification of disasters. *Community Mental Health Journal*, 16: 103–120.

Blaufarb, H., & Levine, J. (1972). Crisis intervention in an earthquake. *Social Work*, 17: 16–19.

Bolin, R. (1986a). Impact and recovery: A comparison of black and white disaster victims. *Mass Emergencies and Disasters*, 4(1): 35–50.

Bolin, R. (1986b). A quick response study of the 1986 California floods. Report to the Natural Hazards Information Center, University of Colorado, Boulder.

Bolin, R. (1985a). Disaster characteristics and psychosocial impacts. In B. Sowder (Ed.), *Disasters and Mental Health: Selected Contemporary Perspectives* (pp. 3–28). DHHS Publication No. 85–1421. Washington, D.C.

Bolin, R. (1985b). Disasters and social support. In B. Sowder (Ed.), *Disasters and Mental Health: Selected Contemporary Perspectives* (pp. 150–158). DHHS Publication No. (ADM) 85–1421. Washington, D.C.

Bolin, R. (1983). Social support and psychosocial stress in disaster. Paper presented at the Western Social Science Association Meetings, Albuquerque, NM. April.

Bolin, R. (1982). *Long-Term Family Recovery from Disaster.* Boulder: Institute of Behavioral Science, University of Colorado.

Bolin, R. (1976). Family recovery from natural disaster: A preliminary model. *Mass Emergencies*, 1: 267–277.

Bolin, R., & Bolton, P. (1986). *Race, Religion, and Ethnicity in Disaster Recovery.* Boulder: Institute of Behavioral Science, University of Colorado.

Bolton, P. (1979). Family recovery following disaster: The case of Managua, Nicaragua. Unpublished Ph.D. Dissertation, University of Colorado, Boulder.

Boyd, S. (1981). Psychological reactions of disaster victims. *South African Medical Journal*, 60: 744–748.

Britton, N. (1981). *Darwin's Cyclone Max: An Exploratory Investigation of a Natural Hazard Sequence on the Development of a Disaster Subculture.* Townsville, Queensland, Australia: Centre for Disaster Studies, James Cook University of North Queensland.

Bromet, E., & Dunn, L. (1981). Mental health of mothers nine months after the Three Mile Island accident. *The Urban and Social Change Review*, 14: 12–15.

Church, J. (1974). The Buffalo Creek disaster: Extent and range of emotional and/or behavioral problems. *Omega*, 5: 61–63.

Covello, V. (1983). The perception of technological risk: A literature review. *Technological Forecasting and Social Change*, 23: 285–297.

Davis, I. (1975). Disaster housing: A case study of Managua. *Architectural Design*, Jan.: 42–47.

Dohrenwend, B., Dohrenwend, B., Kasl, S., & Warheit, G. (1979). *Report of the Task Force on Behavioral Effects of the President's Commission on the Accident at Three Mile Island.* Washington, D.C.

Drabek, T. (1986). *Human System Responses to Disaster.* New York: Springer-Verlag.

Drabek, T., & Boggs, K. (1968). Families in disaster: Reactions and relatives. *Journal of Marriage and the Family*, 30 (August): 443–451.

Drabek, T., & Key, W. (1984). *Conquering Disaster: Family Recovery and Long-Term Consequence.* New York: Irvington.

Dudasik, S. (1980). Victimization in natural disaster. *Disasters*, 4(3): 329–338.

Dudley, E. (1986). In the aftermath of Chernobyl: Contamination, upheaval and loss. *Nucleus*, 8(3): 3–5.

Dynes, R., & Quarantelli, E. (1976). The family and community context of individual reactions to disaster. In H. Parad, H. Resnik, & L. Parad (Eds.), *Emergency and Disaster Management: A Mental Health Sourcebook* (pp. 231–245). Bowie, MD: Charles Press.

Erikson, K. (1976). *Everything in its Path*. New York: Simon & Schuster.

Figley, C. (Ed.) (1985). *Trauma and Its Wake*. New York: Brunner-Mazel.

Folkman, S. (1984). Personal control and stress and coping processes: A theoretical analysis. *Journal of Personality and Social Psychology*, 46: 839–852.

Frederick, C. (1977). Current thinking about crisis or psychological intervention in United States disasters. *Mass Emergencies*, 2: 43–50.

Fried, M. (1963). Grieving for a lost home. In J. Duhl (Ed.), *The Urban Condition: People and Policy in the Metropolis*. New York: Basic Books, pp. 151–171.

Fritz, C. (1961). Disasters. In R. Merton & R. Nisbet (Eds.), *Contemporary Social Problems*. New York: Harcourt, pp. 651–694.

Garrison, J. (1985). Mental health implication of disaster relocation in the United States. *Journal of Mass Emergencies and Disasters*, 3(2): 49–66.

Gleser, G., Green, B., & Winget, C. (1981). *Prolonged Psychosocial Effects of Disaster: A Study of Buffalo Creek*. New York: Academic Press.

Goldsteen, R., & Schorr, J. (1982). The long-term impact of manmade disaster. *Disasters*, 6: 50–59.

Golec, J. (1983). A contextual approach to the social psychological study of disaster recovery. *Journal of Mass Emergencies and Disasters*, 1 (August): 255–276.

Green, B. (1982). Assessing psychological impairment following disaster: Consideration of actual and methodological dimensions. *Journal of Nervous and Mental Disease*, 170: 544–552.

Green, B. (1985). Conceptual and methodological issues in assessing the psychological impact of disaster. In B. Sowder (Ed.), *Mental Health and Disaster: Selected Contemporary Perspectives*. DHHS Publication No. 85–1421. Washington, D.C.

Green, B., Wilson, J., & Lindy, J. (1985). Conceptualizing post-traumatic stress disorder. In C. Figley (Ed.), *Trauma and Its Wake*. New York: Brunner/Mazel, pp. 53–72.

Greenson, R., & Mintz, T. (1972). California earthquake 1971: Some psychoanalytic observations. *International Journal of Psychoanalytic Psychotherapy*, 1(5): 7–23.

Haas, J., & Drabek, T. (1973). *Complex Organizations*. New York: Macmillan.

Haas, J., Kates, R., & Bowden, M. (1977). *Reconstruction Following Disaster*. Cambridge, MA: M.I.T. University Press.

Hannigan, J., & Kueneman, R. (1978). Anticipating flood emergencies: A case study of Canadian disaster subculture. In E. Quarantelli (Ed.), *Disasters: Theory and Research*. Beverly Hills: Sage, pp. 129–146.

Hartsough, D. (1982). Planning for disaster: A new community outreach program for mental health centers. *Journal of Community Psychology*, 10(3): 255–264.

Hocking, F. (1965). Human reactions to extreme environmental stress. *Medical Journal of Australia*, 2: 477–482.

Holmes, T., & Rahe, R. (1967). The social readjustment scale. *Journal of Psychosomatic Research*, 11: 213–218.

Houts, P., Miller, R., Tokuhata, G., & Ham, K. (1980). *Health Related Behavioral Impact of the Three Mile Island Nuclear Incident, Part I*. Harrisburg, PA: Pennsylvania Dept. of Health.

Hufnagel, R., & Perry, R. (1982). Collective behavior: Implications for disaster planning. Paper presented at Pacific Sociological Association Meeting, San Diego.

Instituut voor Sociaal Onderzoek van het Nederlandse Volk Amsterdam. (1955). *Studies in the Holland Flood Disaster 1953*. National Academy of Science-National Research Council, Volumes I–IV: Washington, D.C.: National Academy of Sciences.

Kahn, R., & Antonucci, T. (1980). Convoys over the life course: Attachment roles and social support. In P. Baltes & P. Brim (Eds.), *Life Span and Development*. Boston: Lexington, pp. 381–412.

Kasperson, R., & Pijawka, D. (1985). Societal response to hazards and major hazard events: Comparing natural and technological hazards. *Public Administration Review,* 45: 7–18.

Kessler, R. (1979). A strategy for studying differential vulnerability to the psychological consequences of stress. *Journal of Health and Social Behavior,* 20: 100–108.

Kinston, W., & Rosser, R. (1974). Disaster: Effects on mental and physical state. *Journal of Psychosomatic Research,* 18: 437–456.

Kliman, A. (1976). The Corning Flood Project. Psychological first aid following a natural disaster. In J. Parad, J. Resnik, & L. Parad, (Eds.), *Emergency and Disaster Management: A Mental Health Sourcebook* (pp. 325–335). Bowie, MD: The Charles Press.

Knaus, R. (1975). Crisis intervention in a disaster area: The Pennsylvania flood in Wilkes-Barre. *Journal of the American Osteopathic Association,* 75: 297–301.

Kuhn, T. (1970). *The Structure of Scientific Revolutions.* Chicago: University of Chicago Press.

Lazarus, R. (1966). *Psychological Stress and the Coping Process.* New York: McGraw-Hill.

Lazarus, R., & Cohen, J. (1977). Environmental stress. In I. Altman & J. Wohlwill (Eds.), *Human Behavior and Environment: Current Theory and Research.* New York: Plenum, pp. 89–127.

Leik, R. K., Leik, S. A., Ekker, K., & Gifford, G. A. (1982). *Under the Threat of Mount St. Helens: A Study of Chronic Family Stress.* Family Study Center, Minneapolis: University of Minnesota.

Leivesley, S. (1977). Toowoomba: Victims and helpers in an Australian hailstorm disaster. *Disasters,* 1(4): 315–322.

Levine, A. (1982). *Love Canal: Science, Politics and People.* Toronto: Lexington.

Lifton, R. J., & Olson, E. (1976). The human meaning of total disaster. *Psychiatry,* 39: 1–18.

Lindy, J. D., Grace, M. C., & Green, B. L. (1981). Survivors: Outreach to a reluctant population. *American Journal of Orthopsychiatry,* 5: 468–478.

Lindy, J. D., Grace, M. C., & Green, B. L. (1984). Building a conceptual bridge between civilian trauma and war trauma. In B. van der Kolk (Ed.), *Post-Traumatic Stress Disorder: Psychological and Biological Sequelae.* Washington, D.C.: American Psychiatric Press, pp. 43–57.

Lindy, J. D., & Grace, M. (1985). The recovery environment: Continuing stressor versus a healing psychosocial space. In B. Sowder (Ed.), *Disasters and Mental Health: Selected Contemporary Perspectives* (pp. 137–149). DHHS Publication No. (ADM) 85-1421. Washington, D.C.

Lindy, J. D., & Titchener, J. (1983). Acts of God and man: Long-term character change of survivors of disasters and the law. *Behavioral Science and the Law,* 1(3): 16–21.

Logue, J., Hansen, H., & Struening, E. (1979). A study of health and mental health status following a major natural disaster. In R. Simmons (Ed.), *Research in Community and Mental Health* (pp. 217–274). Greenwich, CT: JAI Press.

Logue, J., Holger, H., & Struening, E. (1981). Some indications of the long-term effects of a natural disaster. *Public Health Reports,* 96: 67–79.

Loizos, P. (1977). A struggle for meaning: Reactions to disaster amongst Cypriot refugees. *Disasters,* 1(3): 231–239.

Melick, M. (1978). Life change and illness: Illness behaviors of males in the recovery period of a natural disaster. *Journal of Health and Social Behavior,* 19: 335–342.

Mileti, D. (1980). Human adjustment to the risk of environmental extremes. *Sociology and Social Research,* 64(3): 328–347.

Mileti, D., Drabek, T. E., & Haas, J. E. (1975). *Human Systems In Extreme Environments.* Boulder, CO: Institute of Behavioral Science, University of Colorado.

Miller, J. A., Turner, J. G., & Kimball, E. (1981). Big Thompson flood victims: One year later. *Family Relations,* 30: 111–116.

Milne, G. (1977). Cyclone Tracy: Some consequences of the evacuation for adult victims. *Australian Psychologist,* 12(1): 39–54.

Milne, G. (1979). Cyclone Tracy: Psychological and social consequences. In J. I. Reid (Ed.),

Planning for People in Natural Disaster. Townsville, Queensland, Australia: James Cook University of N. Queensland, pp. 116–123.

Ollendick, D., & Hoffman, M. (1982). Assessment of psychological reactions in disaster victims. *Journal of Community Psychology,* 4: 64–67.

Parker, G. (1975). Psychological disturbance in Darwin evacuees following cyclone Tracy. *Medical Journal of Australia,* 1(24): 650–652.

Parker, G. (1977). Cyclone Tracy and Darwin evacuees: On the restoration of the species. *British Journal of Psychiatry,* 130: 548–555.

Pearlin, L. I., & Schooler, E. (1978). The structure of coping. *Journal of Health and Social Behavior,* 16: 2–21.

Pelanda, C. (1982). Disaster and order: Theoretical problems in disaster research. Paper presented at World Congress of Sociology, Mexico City, D.F.

Perry, R. W., & Lindell, M. K. (1978). The psychological consequences of natural disaster: A review of research on American communities. *Mass Emergencies,* 3: 105–115.

Perry, R., Lindell, M., & Greene, M. (1980). The implications of natural hazard evacuation warning studies for crisis relocation planning. Seattle: Battelle Human Affairs Research Center.

Perry, H., & Perry, S. (1959). The School House Disasters. National Academy of Sciences/ National Research Council Disaster Study #11. Washington, D.C.: National Academy of Sciences.

Quarantelli, E. (1979). *The Consequences of Disasters for Mental Health: Conflicting Views.* Monograph #62. Columbus, OH: Disaster Research Center, The Ohio State University, 1979.

Quarantelli, E. (1982). *Sheltering and Housing after Major Community Disaster: Case Studies and General Conclusions.* Columbus, OH: Disaster Research Center, Ohio State University.

Quarantelli, E. (1985a). Social support systems: Some behavioral patterns in the context of mass evacuation activities. In B. Sowder (Ed.), *Disasters and Mental Health: Selected Contemporary Perspectives* (pp. 122–136). DHHS Publication No. (ADM) 85–1421. Washington, D.C.

Quarantelli, E. (1985b). An assessment of conflicting views on mental health: The consequences of traumatic events. In C. Figley (Ed.), *Trauma and Its Wake: The Study and Treatment of Post-Traumatic Stress Disorder.* New York: Brunner-Mazel, pp. 173–215.

Quarantelli, E. (1985c). What is a disaster? The need for clarification in definition and conceptualization in research. In B. Sowder (Ed.), *Disasters and Mental Health: Selected Contemporary Perspectives* (pp. 41–73). DHHS Publication No. (ADM) 85–1421. Washington, D.C.

Quarantelli, E., & Dynes, R. (1985). Community responses to disaster. In B. Sowder (Ed.), *Disasters and Mental Health: Selected Contemporary Perspectives* (pp. 158–168). DHHS Publication No. (ADM) 85–1421. Washington, D.C.

Reisner, M. (1986). *Cadillac Desert.* New York: Viking.

Selye, H. (1976). *The Stress of Life.* New York: McGraw-Hill.

Singer, T. (1982). An introduction to disaster: Some considerations of a psychological nature. *Aviation, Space and Environmental Medicine,* 53: 245–250.

Slovic, P., Fischhoff, B., & Lichtenstein, S. (1979). Rating the risks. *Environment,* 14–20.

Smith, E. (1984). Chronology of disaster in Eastern Missouri. Report for the National Institute of Mental Health, Contract No.83md525181.

Solomon, S. (1985). Enhancing social support for disaster victims. In B. Sowder (Ed.), *Disasters and Mental Health: Selected Contemporary Perspectives* (pp. 107–121). DHHS Publication No. (ADM) 14–8521. Washington, D.C.

Sorensen, J., Soderstrom, J., Coperhaver, E., Carnes, S., & Bolin, R. (1987). *The Impacts of Hazardous Technology: The Psychosocial Effects of Restarting TMI-1.* Albany, NY: SUNY Press.

Sowder, B. (1985). Some mental health impacts of loss and injury: A look outside the disaster field. In B. Sowder (Ed.), *Disasters and Mental Health: Selected Contemporary Perspectives.* DHHS Publication No. (ADM) 14–8521. pp. 74–106. Washington, D.C.

Taylor, V., Ross, G. A., & Quarantelli, E. (1976). *Delivery of Mental Health Services in Disasters: The Xenia Tornado and Some Applications.* Columbus, OH: The Disaster Research Center, Book and Monograph Series, Vol. II, The Ohio State University.

Tierney, K. (1986). Disasters and mental health: A critical look at knowledge and practice. Paper presented at the Italy-United States Conference on Disasters, Newark, Delaware, Disaster Research Center.

Tierney, K. J., & Baisden, B. (1979). *Crisis Intervention Programs for Disaster Victims: A Source Book and Manual for Small Communities.* DHEW Publication No. (ADM) 79–675. Washington, D.C.

Titchener, J., & Kapp, F. (1976). Family and character change at Buffalo Creek. *American Journal of Psychiatry,* 133: 295–299.

Trainer, P., & Bolin, R. (1976). Persistent effects of disasters on daily activities. *Mass Emergencies,* 1(October): 279–290.

Turner, R. H., Nigg, J. M., & Paz, D. (1986). *Waiting for Disaster.* Berkeley: University of California Press.

Wallace, A. (1956). *Tornado in Worcester.* National Academy of Sciences/National Research Council Disaster Study #3. Washington, D.C.: National Academy of Sciences.

Walsh, E. (1984). Local community vs. national industry: The TMI and Santa Barbara protests compared. *Mass Emergencies and Disasters,* 2(1): 147–164.

Warheit, G. (1985). A propositional paradigm for estimating the impact of disasters on mental health. *Mass Emergencies and Disasters,* 3(2): 29–48.

Weller, J., & Wenger, D. (1973). Disaster subcultures: The cultural residues of community disasters. Paper presented at the North Central Sociological Society Meetings. Cincinnati, Ohio.

Western, J. S., & Milne, G. (1979). Some social effects of a natural hazard: Darwin residents and Cyclone Tracy. In R. L. Heathcote & B. G. Thom (Eds.), *Natural Hazards in Australia.* Canberra: Australian Academy of Science, pp. 488–502.

White, G., & Haas, E. (1975). *Assessment of Research on Natural Hazards.* Boulder: Institute of Behavioral Science, University of Colorado.

Withey, S. (1976). Accommodation to threat. *Mass Emergencies,* 1: 125–130.

Wolfenstein, M. (1957). Casual attribution and personal control. In J. Harvey, W. Ickers, & R. Kidd (Eds.), *New Directions in Attribution Research.* Hillsdale, NJ: Erlbaum, pp. 56–67.

Zusman, J. (1976). Meeting mental health needs in a disaster: A public health view. In J. Parad, H. L. P. Reznik, & L. G. Parad (Eds.), *Emergency and Disaster Management: A Mental Health Sourcebook.* Bowie, MD: Charles Press, pp. 159–167.

3

Response to Technological Accidents

ELIZABETH M. SMITH, CAROL S. NORTH,
and PAUL C. PRICE

Although a great deal has been written about disasters, there has been surprisingly little systematic study of the mental health consequences of disasters. Data on technological disasters are particularly sparse. We know even less about the consequences of human-made events than we do about those associated with natural hazards.

Studies of technological disasters are not only of theoretical significance, but of great practical importance as well. As our technology expands, we can expect an increase in the frequency of these human-made accidents. The 1984 toxic gas leak in Bhopal, India, which claimed over 2,000 lives, and the 1986 nuclear accident at Chernobyl in the Soviet Union are dramatic examples of failures in our expanding sophisticated technology. It is precisely this growing threat that has stimulated so much recent interest in disasters of a technological nature.

While events such as Bhopal and Chernobyl seem to be clear-cut examples of technological accidents, other events are less clear. The boundaries of the category of technological disaster are fuzzy. There is a lack of consensus in the literature on what constitutes a technological disaster. In fact, the terms "human-made" and "technological" have been used interchangeably, as have the terms "accident," "catastrophe," and "disaster." Events as diverse as nuclear accidents, toxic chemical spills, shipwrecks, plane crashes, explosions, structural failures, fires, dam breaks, transportation accidents, acts of terrorism, kidnapping, and war-related incidents have been included in the general category of technological disasters. Other kinds of disasters could presumably be added to the list ad infinitum as new and more bizarre disasters are manufactured. These examples illustrate the heterogeneity of the character of the existing spectrum of technological disasters.

Classification strategies are needed to organize the literature, specifically strategies which will be scientifically meaningful and constructive for purposes of applying research in this area. It is impossible to draw conclusions about the psychological effects of specific classes of disasters if one cannot determine how a particular disaster would fit into the classification scheme.

In this chapter an attempt is made to delineate technological accidents as a subcategory of human-made disasters. Studies of technological accidents which include information on mental health effects will be reviewed in an effort to establish the extent of psychological disturbance resulting from exposure to these events, specific characteristics of both the events and the individuals that put them at high risk, and the types of responses observed. Methodological difficulties associated with these studies will also be discussed, as will implications for future research.

Issues of Definition and Classification

Even the more basic term "disaster" has not been adequately defined. There are almost as many definitions of disaster as there are researchers of the subject. Solomon (in press) notes that the most immediate problem associated with the conduct of disaster research in general is the lack of agreement about what constitutes a disaster. In addition to being vague, definitions of disaster as "a collective stress situation" (e.g., Barton 1969; Kinston & Rosser, 1974) are problematic because they are based on the concept of stress for which a consensus of definition is also lacking. The problem of defining and conceptualizing the general phenomena to be called "disaster" has been discussed by a number of experts in the field and is beyond the scope of this chapter. The reader is referred to Quarantelli (1985) for a more detailed discussion.

In an effort to identify the critical elements of disaster that make it a stressful experience, a variety of taxonomies have been proposed. Barton (1969) employed a four-fold model of classifying disasters by the following characteristics: scope of impact, speed of onset, duration of impact, and social preparedness. Berren and associates (1980) proposed a five-factor typology which examines disasters in terms of type of disaster agent, duration of disaster, degree of personal impact, potential for reoccurrence, and control over future impact. Quarantelli (1985) cited eight dimensions to be considered in developing a typology of disaster: preparation of the involved population, social centrality of the affected population, length of involvement of the affected population in the crisis, rapidity of involvement by the population in crisis, predictability of involvement in a crisis, unfamiliarity of the crisis, depth of involvement of the population in the disaster, and recurrency of involvement.

Warheit (1985 and this volume) has developed one of the most comprehensive schemes to classify factors of variability across the different disaster situations to be studied. Patterning his scheme along a stress paradigm, he divided potential risk factors into those related to the event, to the community, and to the individual. Event-related factors included suddenness of impact, salient response required, unavoidability of event, high risk to life/property, persistence over time, fluctuations of intensity, and pervasiveness of impact. Community-related factors included lack of prior experience with the event, lack or loss of relevant community resources, community dissensus/conflict, ambiguous/conflicting definitions, and long-term disruption. Individual characteristics included preexisting predisposing factors, loss of interpersonal support networks, cultural-structural integration, lack of prior experience with similar situations, lack of relevant resources, and loss of coping resources.

Inspection of these models reveals that there are a variety of possible dimensions that might help predict which disasters are likely to have the most negative psychological effects.

Some researchers have suggested that whether a disaster has natural versus human-made causation is an important factor in determining the extent of its psychological consequences (Berren et al., 1980; Baum et al., 1983a; Logue et al., 1981; Gleser et al., 1981; Beigel & Berren, 1985; Frederick, 1980). Technological disasters have been considered more likely to produce distinct psychological outcomes (Berren et al., 1980; Logue et al., 1981; Gleser et al., 1981; Lindy, 1985), and long-term psychological impairment and to require more long-term treatment (Baum et al., 1983a). It has also been suggested that technological disasters, because of their potentially unique characteristics, may warrant very different psychiatric intervention and treatment techniques than do natural disasters (Baum et al., 1983a; Gleser et al., 1981). Quarantelli (1985), on the other hand, has rejected the idea that the psychological effects of disaster are agent-specific and calls the distinction between natural and technological disasters "unrewarding."

Baum and his coworkers (1983a) attempted to delineate the specific characteristics which would separate technological disasters from natural ones. These characteristics include duration of impact, unexpectedness, perceptions of control, and absence of an identifiable low point (1983a, 1983c, 1985).

Unfortunately, these characteristics apply neither universally nor specifically to technological hazards. Although technological disasters generally tend to have negative effects which may occur at a nonspecific point in time (such as birth defects related to thalidomide), and which may continue for very long periods (years or even decades as with the dioxin disaster), some natural disasters such as droughts can behave this way, too. A tornado might be just as unexpected as a 757-jumbo jet crash; a drought might develop just as insidiously as a toxic waste leak. And it seems likely that many of those affected by 1972 Hurricane Agnes (natural disaster) perceived their loss of control as much as the victims of the 1972 Buffalo Creek dam break and flood (technological disaster).

A number of authors (Beigel & Berren, 1985; Lindy, 1985; Quarantelli, 1985) have identified problems in trying to classify a disaster as natural or technological, pointing out that the distinction between the two may be misleading. A given disaster may have both natural and human-made attributes simultaneously. An example of an airplane crash due to engine failure would be purely technological, while an airplane crash resulting from ice hampering the working parts in a storm, even though it contains important natural elements, would also be classified as technological. While most people would tend to classify the 1985 Mexico City earthquake disaster as natural, portions of it might be considered to have clearly technological characteristics, as in the collapse of the hospital where so many died. A different hospital with an effective antiearthquake structural architecture might have avoided collapse of the building altogether, or at least minimized the damage and fatalities. Thus, it can be seen that various components of clearly natural disasters can have important technological aspects.

Perceived causation by natural vs. human-made factors may vary among different individuals affected by the disaster. For instance, after the dam break and flood of Buffalo Creek of West Virginia, there was much controversy over the cause of the disaster. Spokesmen for the mining company owning the dam called the event an act of God because of the unusually heavy rains which appeared to have precipitated the dam break, while the victim residents of the valley saw it as negligence on the part of the mining company (Erikson, 1976b) for failing either to realize the danger or to correct the problem prior to the disaster. Instead of trying to determine exactly how much of the blame was God's and how much

Man's, it might seem more useful to categorically term this disaster "technological" because of the key part played by the human-made element, the insufficient dam.

From the above example, it can also be seen that within the category of human-made disasters the *manner* of the human causation of the disaster also requires consideration. Along these lines, Beigel and Berren (1985) classified human-made disaster acts as: 1) acts of omission (negligence) and 2) intentional acts of commission, such as terrorism or mass kidnappings like the Chowchilla school-bus kidnapping (Terr, 1981).

It can be seen, then, that human-made disasters may be accidental, purposeful, or part of a middle gray area of negligence, and these boundaries may be difficult to separate from one another. Disasters having apparent components of negligence, such as the earlier-mentioned Buffalo Creek dam break, can be equally as severe as both natural and intentionally committed human-made disasters (Beigel & Berren, 1985).

Probably the best definition of technological catastrophes has been set forth by Baum and coworkers (1983a) as "events that are human-made in that they are accidents, failures, or mishaps involving the technology and manipulation of the natural environment that we have created to enhance our standard of living." It is from that definition that this chapter will launch its review of the existing literature on the subject. In keeping within the confines of this definition, intentional (purposeful) disasters such as acts of kidnapping, other terrorism, and war-related events are considered beyond the scope of this chapter which will examine only technological *accidents* for effects on mental health.

The dispute over how the subject of disaster should be subdivided and categorized cannot be settled without a consensus of well-designed studies which test the hypothesis that differences in psychological outcome variables are correlated with characteristics of the causal agents. The following review of the available literature on technological accidents will determine to what extent this has been accomplished.

REVIEW OF LITERATURE ON
TECHNOLOGICAL ACCIDENTS

In this section will be selectively reviewed published research on technological accidents believed to be representative of the various events which have been studied (see Table 1). Readers interested in the broader body of disaster studies are referred to several excellent reviews (Kinston & Rosser, 1974; Logue et al., 1981; Melick, 1985), as well as the annotated bibliography on disaster and mental health (Ahearn & Cohen, 1983).

TABLE 1

Summary of Mental Health Effects of Selected Studies of Technological Accidents

Authors & Year of Publication	Event	Methods	Results
Adler, 1943	Coconut Grove nightclub fire, Boston, Massachusetts, Nov., 1942. 491 killed and many more injured.	Systematic neuropsychiatric examinations of 46 survivors. Initial exam done 2–3 weeks after the fire. Follow-up exams done 9 months later. No controls.	46% had no psychiatric complications. 54% showed symptoms of nervousness and anxiety for at least 3 months. 28% still suffered the same effects 9 months later. In those who did not develop psychiatric complications, prolonged unconsciousness seemed to be a factor. Gender, loss of friends/relatives, and severity of burns did not predict outcome.
Baum et al., 1983b	Nuclear accident at Three Mile Island (TMI) March–April, 1979. No fatalities.	Behavioral (proofreading and embedded figures tasks), self-report [SCL-90 and Beck Depression Inventory (BDI)] and physiological (catecholamine levels in urine) measures of stress were taken for 121 subjects approximately 1½ years after the accident; 38 of the subjects lived within 5 miles of TMI, 32 lived within 5 miles of an undamaged nuclear plant, 24 lived within 5 miles of a coal-fired power plant, and the remainder lived in an area 20 miles from any power plant.	TMI residents reported significantly greater emotional stress, more global symptoms and somatic complaints, and higher levels of anxiety and alienation than each of the 3 control groups. TMI residents tended to have higher BDI scores, though this finding did not reach significance. Task performance was somewhat lower in the TMI group. Although urinary catecholamine levels were somewhat higher in the TMI group, they were considered to fall in the normal range.

(continued)

57

TABLE 1 (continued)

Authors & Year of Publication	Event	Methods	Results
Boman, 1979	Granville commuter train derailment and collision, Sydney, Australia, January 18, 1977. 83 killed, many more suffered severe injuries.	Descriptive study: Clinical observations of an unknown number of survivors over the 18 month period after the collision.	Immediate responses included feelings of numbness, unreality, and detached calm. A significant frequency of symptoms, often the result of ineffective family support or pre-accident neuroses, was noted.
Bromet et al., 1984	Nuclear accident at Three Mile Island	150 children living near TMI, between the ages of 8 and 16 years, and 99 controls were interviewed approximately 3½ years after the accident. The Child Behavior Checklist was used to assess social competence and behavior problems. Fearfulness and self-esteem were also rated.	No significant differences were found between the TMI and comparison group children.

TABLE 1 (continued)

Authors & Year of Publication	Event	Methods	Results
Bromet et al., 1980	Nuclear accident at Three Mile Island	Interviews, including the SCL-90, Schedule for Affective Disorder and Schizophrenia—Lifetime Version (SADS-L), and Social Support Interview Schedule were given to 328 mothers of preschool children in the TMI area, 189 workers at the nuclear plant, and 177 clients of local mental health centers at 9 months after the accident. Controls from a site with a nuclear power plant that did not have an accident were similarly interviewed. Follow-up interviews were conducted at approximately 12 months after the accident.	TMI mothers had excess anxiety and depression during the year after the accident. The most symptomatic were those with a previous psychiatric history, those living within 5 miles of the plant, and those with less adequate social support. There was only a small difference between TMI and control workers, although TMI workers reported feeling more rewarded by their jobs. TMI mental health clients did not show significantly higher symptom levels than did controls.

(continued)

TABLE 1 (continued)

Authors & Year of Publication	Event	Methods	Results
Cleary & Houts, 1984	Nuclear accident at Three Mile Island	Telephone interviews with 403 TMI residents living within 5 miles of the plant 3 and 9 months after the accident, and telephone surveys of 1506 people residing within 55 miles of the plant at 3 months after.	Those living closer to the plant perceived more threat, were more upset, and reported more psychological symptoms. Women were more likely to have such problems than were men. Single people and older people were less likely to perceive a threat or to be upset. Those who tried to cope actively with the situation (took protective action, were active in organizations, sought out others) were more likely to be upset at 9 months.
Davidson et al., 1982	Nuclear accident at Three Mile Island	The stress levels of 44 subjects from within a 5-mile radius of TMI and 31 controls from Frederick, Maryland, were determined 1½ years after the accident using behavioral, self-report and physiological measures. Each subject's perceived control over his or her environment was also determined.	TMI residents reported more control-related problems than did controls, did poorer than controls on the embedded figures task, and reported greater symptom distress and physiological arousal. TMI residents with less perceived control over their environment reported greater symptom distress, poorer task performance, and higher levels of physiological arousal.

TABLE 1 *(continued)*

Authors & Year of Publication	Event	Methods	Results
Dohrenwend et al., 1981	Nuclear accident at Three Mile Island	Telephone surveys were conducted between 2 weeks and 5 months after the accident with a probability sample of 484 male and female heads of household within a 20-mile radius of TMI; 425 mothers of newborns, from two locations; 632 7th, 9th, and 11th graders in the area; and a convenience sample of 198 clients of community mental health centers.	The accident produced a substantial immediate impact, with 26% of victims interviewed the month following the accident showing severe demoralization. Women were more upset than men, younger people more than older people, and people with preschool children were more upset than those without. The accident had a lasting impact on the population in terms of their distrust of authorities with respect to nuclear power.
Friedman & Linn, 1957	Collision of the *Andrea Doria* with the Swedish liner *Stockholm* off the coast of Nantucket Island, Massachusetts, July, 1956, in which 52 were reported killed or missing.	Descriptive study: psychiatric observations by the authors who were passengers on the *Ile de France* which participated in rescue operations.	Survivors were passive and compliant initially, but after the initial shock they found a great need to tell and retell their stories, reliving the trauma. Many looked for a scapegoat.

(continued)

61

TABLE 1 (continued)

Authors & Year of Publication	Event	Methods	Results
Gatchel et al., 1985	Nuclear accident at Three Mile Island	50 residents within 5 miles of TMI and 31 controls living at least 15 miles from any power plant were tested for stress. Behavioral, self-report, and physiological measures were taken at 4 times: 3–5 days before, during, 3–5 days after, and 6 weeks after the venting of remaining radioactive gases approximately 15 months after the accident.	TMI residents showed consistently poorer performance on behavioral tasks, reported significantly more symptoms of depression and anxiety, and exhibited greater somatic distress than did controls.
Gleser et al., 1981	Dam Break and Flood at Buffalo Creek, W. Virginia, February, 1972, in which 125 were killed and 4000 left homeless.	Study of 654 survivor plaintiffs filing suit against the owners of the dam 2–5 years postdisaster. Multiple measures were used, including a symptom checklist of family description indicators and Psychiatric Evaluation Form. Selection of comparison group of nonlitigants not specified.	Approximately one-third continued to suffer disabling psychiatric symptoms 4–5 years later. Over 75% reported sleep disturbance 2 years after the disaster. 30% reported increased alcohol consumption.

TABLE 1 (continued)

Authors & Year of Publication	Event	Methods	Results
Green et al., 1983	Beverly Hills Supper Club fire near Cincinnati, Ohio, in May, 1977. 165 fatalities.	147 subjects, 30 of whom were rescue workers or relatives of victims and were not at the fire when it broke out, were interviewed using the Psychiatric Evaluation Form and the SCL-90 one year after the disaster. 88 were reinterviewed 2 years postfire.	The "not at fire" group received significantly higher bereavement score and reported significantly higher levels of subjective stressfulness of the event a year later. Two years later, the severity of this group's symptoms had decreased significantly, while the "at fire" group experienced a significant increase in its scores on the hostility subscale of the SCL-90.
Henderson & Bostock, 1977	Shipwreck of the *Southern Star*, a small cargo vessel, off the coast of Tasmania, October, 1973. 7 of 10 crew members survived after drifting for 9 days.	Descriptive study: joint psychiatric interviews by the authors on each of 7 survivors within 1–5 days of rescue. Follow-up interviews done 12–24 months later. No controls.	Coping behavior employed by the men during the ordeal included attachment ideation, the drive to survive, and modeling, as well as prayer and hope. Follow-up findings indicated that five of the men had developed substantial psychiatric disorders.

(continued)

63

TABLE 1 (continued)

Authors & Year of Publication	Event	Methods	Results
Hoiberg & McCaughey, 1984	Maritime collision of USS Belknap and USS Kennedy during maneuvers in the Mediterranean Sea, November, 1975. 7 on the Belknap were killed, and 46 suffered injuries, burns, or smoke inhalation.	329 Belknap survivors and 387 controls from the USS Yarnell, which had had a similar mission, were compared using data extracted from the Naval Health Research Center's medical inpatient and career history computer files covering the 3 years prior to the collision and the 3 years after.	Significantly more experimental subjects were hospitalized or separated from service because of neuroses after the collision.
Kasl et al., 1981	Nuclear accident at Three Mile Island	Structured telephone interviews were conducted with 324 TMI workers and with 298 Peach Bottom nuclear plant controls approximately 6 months after the accident. The Demoralization Scale with a modification of psychiatric impairment was included.	TMI workers differed from controls in their reported exposure to radiation at the time of the accident and in their feeling that their health had thus been endangered. They had lower job satisfaction and reported more uncertainty about their occupational futures. TMI workers also reported greater frequency of anger, extreme worry, extreme upset, and various psychophysiological symptoms after the accident.

TABLE 1 (continued)

Authors & Year of Publication	Event	Methods	Results
Leopold & Dillon, 1963	Maritime collision of the gasoline tanker *Mission San Francisco* with a freighter in the Delaware River near Newcastle, Delaware, March, 1957. 10 of 45 crew members of the tanker were killed.	Descriptive study: 27 survivors examined between 1–13 days following the accident. Four years later 25 of them were reexamined along with 9 new subjects.	Immediate effects on survivors included mood and affect disturbance, sleep difficulties, and somatic reactions. Reexamination showed appreciable deterioration in 71% of the survivors. Only 22% were free of psychiatric symptoms.
Lifton & Olson, 1976	Dam break and flood at Buffalo Creek.	A total of 43 clinical interviews were done on 22 survivors between April, 1973, and August, 1974. No controls.	All experienced some or all of the following manifestations of the "general constellation of the survivor syndrome"; 1) the death imprint, death anxiety; 2) death guilt; 3) psychic numbing; 4) impaired human relationships; and 5) a struggle to give significance and meaning to the disaster experience.

(continued)

65

TABLE 1 (continued)

Authors & Year of Publication	Event	Methods	Results
Lopez-Ibor et al., 1985	Widespread distribution and use of industrial-quality rape-seed oil for cooking in Madrid, Spain, and surrounding areas beginning in the spring of 1981. As of January, 1985, over 20,000 cases had been reported and 349 had died.	Computerized records of 2926 adult victims who had been referred to psychiatrists were studied.	Authors identified a "reactive disaster syndrome," consistently characterized by the expression of anxiety, depression, sadness, and loss of concentration. Factors which correlated well with psychological symptoms or referral to a psychiatrist included being female, having a low socioeconomic and educational level, and having a past history of nervous disturbances.
Perlberg, 1979	Collision of two jumbo jets on Santa Cruz de Tenerife Island, Canary Islands, March, 1977. 580 were killed.	Review of a study by Catanese, where 8 survivors were interviewed 5 months after the accident. MMPI, TAT and Rorschach tests were included. No controls.	All suffered from 75% to 100% of the symptoms of traumatic neurosis: decrease in various ego functions, spells of uncontrollable emotions, sleeplessness, dreams or mental repetitions of the event, and psychoneurotic secondary complications.

TABLE 1 (continued)

Authors & Year of Publication	Event	Methods	Results
Robins et al., 1986	A series of events including floods, tornadoes, discovery of dioxin contamination, and discovery of radioactive waste in the water supply which occurred in a semirural area near St. Louis, Missouri, in 1982. There were no deaths or serious injuries and most were able to return to their homes.	365 individuals originally interviewed as part of the ECA study just prior to the disasters were reinterviewed 1 year later using the Diagnostic Interview Schedule/Disaster Supplement (DIS/DS). Surprisingly, only 44 of these subjects were exposed to one or more of these disasters. The remainder served as controls.	No significant mental health effects were found. The relative mildness of the disasters may have contributed to the negative findings.

(continued)

TABLE 1 *(continued)*

Authors & Year of Publication	Event	Methods	Results
Smith et al., 1986	Floods and/or dioxin exposure which occurred in a semi-rural area near St. Louis, Missouri, in 1982. 5 were killed and thousands left homeless by the flood. The majority of dioxin victims were permanently relocated.	501 individuals residing in the area during the disasters were interviewed one year later using the DIS/DS. 173 were directly affected (floods, N=75; dioxin, N=29; flood and dioxin, N=69). 139 were indirectly affected through exposure of friends or relatives, and 189 had no exposure.	The majority of disaster victims did not develop psychiatric disability. Degree of exposure predicted degree of psychiatric impairment, and those doubly exposed (flood and dioxin) were most impaired. Type of disaster (flood vs. dioxin) did not affect the pattern of mental health consequences. Aside from post-traumatic stress disorder, new psychiatric problems were not an outcome. Disaster contributed to persistence or recurrence of preexisting psychiatric disorders but not to the development of new ones.
Taylor & Frazer, 1982	Mount Erebus air-crash, Antartica, November, 1979. All 257 on board were killed on impact.	180 workers who handled or identified bodies were interviewed immediately after the event and 3 and 20 months later. Clinical interviews, structured questionnaires including the Hopkins Symptom Checklist, and other materials were used. No controls.	Approximately one-third were in high-stress groups: 21% after 3 months and 23% at 20 months. Membership in the high-stress groups changed over time. Only 9% had no signs or symptoms by combined self-report and interview data.

TABLE 1 (continued)

Authors & Year of Publication	Event	Methods	Results
Titchener & Kapp, 1976	Dam break and flood at Buffalo Creek.	"Psychoanalytically oriented interviews" were done on 654 survivor plaintiffs filing suit against the owners of the dam approximately 2 years after the disaster. No controls.	90% still had symptoms such as anxiety, depression, changes in character and lifestyle, maladjustments, and developmental problems in children. 80% received a diagnosis of "traumatic neurosis."
Wilkinson, 1983	Collapse of skywalks at the Hyatt Regency Hotel, Kansas City, Missouri, July, 1981. 114 were killed and over 200 were seriously injured.	102 subjects—27 victims, 27 observers, and 48 rescuers—were given a questionnaire based on DSM-III post-traumatic stress disorder between 1 week and 5 months after the collapse.	88% of the subjects suffered repeated recall of the event, 83% reported sadness, 57% fatigue, and 54% recurrent feelings of anxiety or depression. There were only slight differences between the groups.

The mental health effects of a variety of technological accidents have been studied, including transportation accidents, fires and explosions, structural collapse, a nuclear accident, and exposure to toxic substances. In recent years, the two most widely studied events have been the dam collapse and flood of Buffalo Creek and the nuclear accident at Three Mile Island. It is surprising that there have been no systematic studies of the mental health effects of exposure to toxic wastes for residents of Love Canal. A fascinating sociological account of the residents' experiences (Levine, 1983), as well as anecdotal information on the residents' mental health (Hess & Wandersman, 1985; Stone & Levine, 1985) suggests that the Love Canal experience was a stressful one. Unfortunately, however, systematic data on the mental health consequences are lacking.

We were also unable to locate published studies of the mental health consequences of the Chernobyl nuclear accident or the toxic gas leak in Bhopal. As a result, we know far less about these toxic types of technological accidents than we do about the more traditional accidents.

Because disaster research has proceeded without definitional consensus, it is difficult to organize research findings (see Perry & Lindell, 1978; Hartsough, 1985; Green, 1985). Not only is there wide variability in the events studied, but there is also a great deal of variation in type of information reported and the format used in reporting it.

Rates of Psychiatric Impairment

Reported rates of psychiatric disturbance following a technological disaster vary as greatly as the number of disasters studied. Studies of the Buffalo Creek disaster suggest that virtually everyone was affected (Lifton & Olson, 1976). After two years, 90% still had symptoms, and 80% received a diagnosis of "traumatic neurosis." Titchener and Kapp (1976) and Gleser and coworkers (1981) found that 75% still had nightmares associated with the disaster two years later, and by four to five years later over one-third continued to suffer from disabling psychiatric symptoms.

A short term (five month) follow-up of survivors of a jet collision (Perlberg, 1979) found that all the subjects suffered from most or all of the symptoms of traumatic neurosis. Two studies of ship accidents reported psychiatric symptoms in 70–75% of those studied. Leopold and Dillon (1963) conducted a four-year interview study of survivors of a marine explosion and found that approximately three-fourths continued to have psychiatric symptoms. Henderson and Bostock (1977) in another interview study of survivors of a shipwreck found that 70% had developed psychiatric problems one to two years later.

Taylor and Frazer (1982), using psychoanalytically oriented interviews, found that following the Mount Erebus aircrash, 81% of body handlers reported symptoms, and 91% showed signs or symptoms of distress. At least 88% of survivors and rescue workers of the Hyatt Regency Hotel skywalk collapse showed psychiatric symptoms following the disaster (Wilkinson, 1983).

Two studies of survivors of nightclub fires, conducted nearly 40 years apart, found surprisingly similar results. Adler (1943) reported that a little over one-fourth (28%) of the survivors of the Coconut Grove fire had symptoms of nervousness and anxiety nine months later. Green and associates (1983) found evidence of emotional problems in approximately one-third of victims studied up to 15 months after the Beverly Hills Supper Club fire.

By contrast, Bromet and her colleagues (1981, 1982), in a study of a high-risk population of mothers of young children living near Three Mile Island, found that only 14% received a psychiatric diagnosis during the year after the accident.

Smith and associates (1986) found similarly low rates of psychopathology one year after a series of disasters. Eighteen percent of residents exposed to dioxin and severe floods (a double disaster) and 14% of those exposed only to dioxin received a psychiatric diagnosis.

While the wide variability in the proportion of impaired survivors could be interpreted to mean that there are real differences between the various types of disasters in terms of their psychological impact, Green (1985) points out that the discrepancy in rates may not be a "true" difference. She points out that large differences between studies in terms of disaster impact, especially in regard to rates of survivor impairment, may be attributable to how, when, and on whom the data were collected rather than on the type of event. As illustrated above, studies providing information on rates of symptoms yield much higher rates of psychopathology than those studies reporting data on psychiatric syndromes or diagnoses. This will be discussed in further detail below.

Types of Mental Health Responses

A wide range of psychological symptoms and emotional responses to technological disasters has been reported. General fears, anxieties, and tensions are frequently mentioned as common emotional responses (Adler, 1943; Boman, 1979; Cleary & Houts, 1984). Guilt is a well-known outcome in disasters that claim lives (Lifton & Olson, 1976; Titchener & Kapp, 1976; Boman, 1979). Grief reactions are commonly reported among disaster survivors (Gleser et al., 1981; Green, 1982; Adler, 1943; Boman, 1979). Erikson (1976b) described the phenomenon of "death imprint" as remembrances associated with "death, dying, and massive destruction," and Lifton and Olson (1976) also included "death imprint" as part of a descriptive constellation of survivor manifestations.

The disaster literature contains a wide spectrum of other assorted emotional responses, including repeated recall of the event (Wilkinson, 1983; Perlberg, 1979), reliving the trauma (Friedman & Linn, 1957), psychic numbing (Boman, 1979; Rangell, 1976; Lifton & Olson, 1976), searching for a scapegoat (Friedman & Linn, 1957) or for meaning (Lifton & Olson, 1976), demoralization (Dohrenwend et al., 1981), somatic symptoms (Gatchel et al., 1985, Baum et al., 1983b, Leopold & Dillon, 1963), hostility (Green et al., 1983), distrust for authorities (Dohrenwend et al., 1981), alienation (Baum et al., 1983b, 1983c), and increased alcohol consumption (Gleser et al., 1981). Sleep disturbances have been mentioned by multiple observers (Gleser et al., 1981; Leopold & Dillon, 1963; Perlberg, 1979), and specifically recurrent dreams or nightmares (Perlberg, 1979).

While some researchers have focused on individual symptoms, others have examined disaster victims for psychiatric syndromes or diagnoses. "Neuroses" related to disasters have been described by Boman (1979) and Hoiberg and McCaughy (1984). Perlberg (1979) and Titchener and Kapp (1976) described "traumatic neuroses" following disasters; others have used the term "traumatic neurotic syndrome." Lopez-Ibor et al. (1985) identified a "reactive disaster syndrome," and Lifton and Olson (1976) described a "general constellation of the survivor syndrome." Another term, "the Buffalo Creek syndrome," has been coined by those who studied this catastrophe (e.g., Titchener and Kapp, 1976).

While the majority of authors examined disaster victims for individual symptoms such as "the expression of anxiety, depression, and sadness" (Lopez-Ibor et al., 1985), a few have reported rates of specific DSM-III (American Psychiatric Association, 1980) diagnoses of anxiety disorders and major depression (Bromet et al., 1980; Smith et al., 1986) and post-traumatic stress disorder (Smith et al., 1986).

In reviewing the literature, Solomon (in press) concluded that among DSM-III diagnoses, post-traumatic stress disorder is the psychiatric disorder of greatest relevance to the experience of disaster. A study by Shore and coworkers (1986) of the Mt. St. Helens volcano eruption found that three disorders showed an increased postdisaster prevalence in high exposure samples compared to controls. These disorders, termed the "Mt. St. Helen disorders," included single-episode depression, generalized anxiety disorder, and post-traumatic stress disorder. Interestingly, Smith and associates

(1986) found elevated postdisaster onset rates for the same three disorders in victims of dioxin contamination. This suggests that psychiatric outcome, at least as measured by specific psychiatric diagnosis, may not differ between type of disaster, i.e., technological versus natural disasters.

Certain individual symptoms described in the literature such as sadness, sleeplessness, inability to concentrate, guilt, and grief might well be subsumed under a well-recognized diagnostic category such as DSM-III major depression. Other symptoms such as fear, reliving the trauma, repeated recall of the event, and nightmares may actually represent individual symptoms of post-traumatic stress disorder. Advantages of examining emotional responses to technological disaster in terms of psychiatric diagnosis might include simplification and more organized reporting of disaster outcome, as well as improved comparison across studies.

Ignoring psychiatric diagnosis to evaluate purely by global symptom ratings seems destined to produce excess false positives. When translated into intervention measures, this could result in waste of precious resources in the postdisaster period at a time when resources are scarce to begin with.

Bromet and Schulberg (in press) concluded that the distinction between transient psychiatric symptoms and more severe clinically diagnosable psychiatric syndromes has crucial implications for evaluation of mental health effects of disaster. This distinction could seriously affect reported results on four measures: 1) *severity*, as a psychiatrically diagnosable condition might point to greater severity than symptoms alone; 2) *prevalence*, as symptoms would be expected to occur more frequently than diagnoses; 3) *endurance of psychiatric sequelae*, in that symptoms could be expected to be more transient and diagnosable syndromes more persistent; and 4) *intervention*, in that symptoms might disappear without treatment, but diagnosable syndromes might tend to linger unless treated.

While focusing on these clinically diagnosable psychiatric syndromes, it will conversely be important to avoid overlooking the more common psychiatric symptoms of distress that cannot be attributed to a specific psychiatric diagnosis. Just as ignoring psychiatric diagnosis would be a serious oversight, so would it be to forget individual symptoms, which could result in overlooking significantly distressed individuals within an otherwise essentially normal population. Attention to individual symptoms might be a key element not only in providing immediate intervention to reduce human suffering, but also in preventing further psychiatric morbidity in individuals at high risk for developing full-blown psychiatric disorders.

Examination of potential benefits of studying both symptoms and diagnosable psychiatric syndromes would suggest that each would yield distinct yet important data with regard to mental health effects of disasters. Future research must examine both. Recent research on technological accidents has begun to head in this direction, e.g., the studies of the Three Mile Island nuclear accident by Bromet and associates (1980, 1982) and dioxin exposure in Missouri (Smith et al., 1986).

Instruments of Assessment

Even after clarifying the issue of whether to collect data regarding psychiatric symptoms vs. clinically diagnosable psychiatric disorder has been settled, there yet remains the matter of choosing an instrument of measure of whichever form of mental health response that is to be measured. A glance at the existing literature on disaster (see Table 1) reveals the use of a variety of instruments of measure of the mental health effects of techno-logical disaster. Many studies have utilized homemade scales, general observation, open and nonstructured interviews, and retrospective medi-cal record review. This failure to use comparable instruments for measur-ing impairment makes it impossible to compare results across studies to derive any collective meaning from the available literature.

An important minority of disaster researchers, however, have employed standardized research instruments such as the Diagnostic Interview Schedule/Disaster Supplement (DIS/DS) (Robins & Smith, 1983), and the schedule of Affective Disorders and Schizophrenia-Lifetime Version (SADS-L) (Endicott & Spitzer, 1978). Some of the studies reviewed (e.g. Bromet et al., 1980; Collins et al., 1983; Gleser et al., 1981; Green et al., 1983) used standardized symptom checklists such as the SCL-90 (Derogatis, 1977), or standardized scales such as the Beck Depression Inventory (BDI) (Beck, 1978) and the Psychiatric Evaluation Form (PEF) (Spitzer et al., 1968).

Hartsough (1985) has emphasized the importance of exercising fore-sight in choosing a standardized instrument of measure for conducting disaster research. Condemning the use of homemade questionnaires or inventories, he stated that these "may be the path of least resistance at the time a study is planned, but after the data are in, what can they tell us about a disaster population in comparison with others?"

Several investigators have concluded that, in general, adverse mental health consequences are found in much higher rates in studies using in-depth, open format interviews or self-report than with standardized structured research instruments (Dohrenwend, 1975; Melick, 1985). Our own analysis of the available literature would certainly support this conclusion.

Appropriate application of standardized instruments is fraught with other problems. First, correlation of one instrument such as the SCL-90 with another such as the SADS-L within the same study population may yield unacceptably low values (Bromet & Schulberg, in press), suggesting that in order to make cross-study comparisons the same instrument might have to be used on both populations. Yet another difficulty with using standardized instruments is that their intrinsic specificity and sensitivity may be undesirably low even with a single-study population (Bromet & Schulberg, in press). Finally, Hartsough (1985) has pointed out that a major disadvantage of structured interviews and questionnaires is addressed by the use of several instruments or methods of gaining data.

Timing of Assessments

Not only are study results seriously affected by type of psychiatric response observed and type of instrument of measure used, but timing of assessment is also crucial in obtaining valid data. Melick et al. (1982) termed this timing of study measures the "phasic perspective." Hartsough (1985) pointed out that both the nature and intensity of psychological sequelae appear to vary with the point in time at which they are measured. For example, in their study of the *Andrea Doria* survivors, Friedman and Linn (1957) observed an initial state of "psychic shock" characterized by helpless dependency and emotional regression which later transformed into a recovery phase marked by compulsive retelling of the experience and psychological reliving of the trauma.

Adler (1943) observed that the initial 63% rate of nervousness and anxiety following the Boston Cocoanut Grove Night Club fire dropped to one-half over the next six months. Bromet and associates (1980) noted that point prevalence of anxiety and depression varied fourfold from month to month following the Three Mile Island incident, with the largest peak directly following the event and a secondary peak occurring late that same year.

In the studies reviewed, timing of observations or assessments varied from immediately after the disaster (Friedman & Linn, 1957) to five years later (Gleser et al., 1981). The majority of assessments occurred within one year. There have been few long-term studies and even fewer studies providing assessments at multiple points in time. Only rarely have studies had the advantage of comparing data obtained predisaster with postdisaster assessments. Often, even modestly helpful predisaster information such as prior psychiatric records have been destroyed by the disaster, or may be marred by incompleteness, inexact diagnostic criteria, and selective bias of the population sample having such records. A later section of this chapter will give a more detailed description of a study (Robins et al., 1986; Smith et al., 1986) which, although limited by certain difficulties, attempted to take advantage of an unusual and fortuitous opportunity to obtain data with the same instrument of assessment both shortly before and following a series of both natural and technological disasters.

Sample Size and Source

The existing technological disaster literature contains considerable variation in the number of subjects studied, ranging from N=7 (Henderson & Bostock, 1977) to N=2926 (Lopez-Ibor et al., 1985). Methods of subject selection also vary widely. While Henderson and Bostock (1977) were able to interview all seven survivors of the *Southern Star* shipwreck, Perlberg (1979) reported on only eight of the 64 survivors of a jumbo jet collision since a large number of those located and contacted refused to participate. Other studies provide no information on numbers studied, e.g., Boman (1979) and Friedman and Linn (1957).

In choosing a sample population for study, it is often difficult to determine what constitutes an affected population vs. an unaffected population. Furthermore, there are varying degrees of exposure, ranging from injured victims and their close relatives and friends to rescue workers and body handlers to observers, the nearby population, and the general community. Bolin (1985) categorized victims as either primary, i.e., those directly exposed to disaster injury or destruction, or secondary, i.e., those indirectly affected, as bereaved relatives of primary victims. Some studies have included disaster victims of only one degree of exposure, such as Adler's study (1943) of survivors of a nightclub fire and Taylor and Frazer's study (1982) of body handlers following an aircrash with no survivors. Wilkinson's study (1983) of a structural collapse in a hotel compared reactions of victims, observers, and rescuers. Researchers of the Three Mile Island nuclear accident reported that the degree of psychiatric response varied in proportion to the distance a particular subject lived from the nuclear plant. As expected, those with the highest degree of exposure, i.e., those living closest to the plant, suffered the greatest degree of psychological distress (Cleary & Houts, 1984).

Although traditional descriptive studies of disaster have generally not employed control subjects (e.g., Adler, 1943; Boman, 1979; Friedman & Linn, 1957; Henderson & Bostock, 1977; Leopold & Dillon, 1963; Lifton & Olson, 1976), several carefully designed, systematic, data-oriented studies have done so (e.g., Baum et al., 1983b; Bromet et al., 1980, 1984;

Davidson et al., 1982; Gatchel et al., 1985; Robins et al., 1986; Smith et al., 1986). When control subjects are not utilized for comparison, it is not possible to conclude that any differences found in individual outcome are specifically associated with the disaster.

Unfortunately, identifying an appropriate control group can be fraught with difficulties. In trying to choose controls as similar as possible to disaster victims in all respects except for the experience of the disaster, individuals with minimal or indirect exposure to the disaster may be included in the control group. Melick (1985) observed that non-victim control groups have been found to experience stress as a result of disaster. Shippee and coworkers (1982) found that individuals not overtly affected by a disaster may be as fearful and as much in need of service as persons who clearly suffered direct physical and psychological distress. Robins and coworkers (1986) and Smith and coworkers (1986) found that in their populations individuals only indirectly exposed to disasters (e.g., only vicariously via experiences of relatives or friends) had certain adverse psychological experiences not shared by those never exposed.

Sampling bias can be difficult to avoid in disaster populations. For example, it has been observed that individuals at risk to suffer a disaster may be a different group to begin with (Smith et al., 1986). It follows, then, that survivors of a disaster might well represent an intrinsically biased sample compared to otherwise comparable populations. For example, it has been suggested that the victims of the Times Beach dioxin exposure and flooding may have been a population of lower socioeconomic level or of unique psychological characteristics which led them to build their houses on a flood plain to begin with. Such potential for sampling bias would make it even more crucial to include a comparable control group. Bromet and associates (1980) and Baum and associates (1983b) attended to this problem by choosing a population living near a similar but undamaged nuclear plant to compare with their Three Mile Island populations; they were thus able to attribute increased psychiatric sequelae to the nuclear accident itself. Hoiberg and McCaughey (1984) compared their maritime ship collision survivors to controls from another ship with a similar mission. The survivors were shown to have a higher postdisaster incidence of neuroses.

The Buffalo Creek dam break and flood studies (Gleser et al., 1981; Lifton & Olson, 1976; Titchener & Kapp, 1976) all encountered a unique problem of sampling bias in that they studied plaintiffs in litigation against the dam owners. This may have contributed to the high rates of reported psychopathology.

Risk Factors for Mental Health Effects

The existing literature suggests that information regarding risk factors of disaster situations may be loosely divided into three categories: individual factors, situational factors, and agent-related factors.

The category with the greatest collection of data on risk factors appears to be the one on individual factors. Cleary and Houts (1984) discovered that being single seemed to protect individuals from psychological distress relative to their married counterparts, while Dohrenwend et al. (1981) found that having a preschool child was a predisposing factor. Individuals with less adequate social support (Bromet et al., 1980) and persons with lower levels of education and socioeconomic status (Lopez-Ibor et al., 1985) have also been found to be at higher risk. Cleary and Houts (1984) and Dohrenwend and associates (1981) found that younger victims experienced fewer psychological effects than older victims. Women were found to be at higher risk than men for psychiatric sequelae in three studies (Cleary & Houts, 1984; Dohrenwend et al., 1981; Green & Gleser, 1983; Lopez-Ibor et al., 1985).

However, even some of the above individual risk factors are still in debate. Bromet and Schulberg (in press) reviewed the general disaster literature and concluded that methodological inconsistencies and design variation have generated inconsistent findings regarding personal risk factors, especially in studies of effects of disaster in children. In one-third of such studies reviewed, girls were more adversely affected than boys; in one-third, boys were more adversely affected than girls; and in the remaining one-third, no gender-specific associations were found. Similarly, one-third of the studies reviewed found older children to be more distressed than younger children; one-third found younger children to be more distressed than older children; and the remaining one-third found no age-specific associations. Bromet and Schulberg concluded that the only risk factor consistently found to affect response to disaster is having a psychiatric diagnosis prior to its occurrence. Several studies in the current literature review (Bromet et al., 1980, 1982; Lopez-Ibor et al., 1985; Smith et al., 1986) support the finding of preexisting psychiatric history as being a clear risk factor (Warheit 1985), and to our knowledge no studies have reported contradictory findings.

Adler's study of victims of fire (1943) cited one factor which appeared to have a protective effect against psychiatric sequelae, that being the occurrence of prolonged unconsciousness.

Of situational risk factors, degree of the victim's involvement with the disaster agent appears to be the most relevant and most studied characteristic.

Two studies of Three Mile Island (Bromet et al., 1980; Cleary & Houts, 1984) both found that those living closest to the nuclear plant were at highest risk for mental health effects. Green and coworkers (1983) found that those in direct physical contact with the Beverly Hills Night Club fire had elevated rates of bereavement and general stress, in contrast to those only indirectly affected (family members of victims and rescue workers who were not physically involved with the fire itself) who instead had elevated hostility levels. Adler's study (1943) of a different night club fire, however, failed to show any correlation of degree of burn or smoke inhalation injury with psychological outcome. The same study found that among the physically injured victims, additional bereavement over loved ones lost in the fire did not predict risk for post-traumatic personality changes.

Less is known about specific characteristics of disaster agents themselves in regard to risk for mental health effects. This is largely because it is so technically difficult to compare one kind of disaster to another, given the large number of crucial variables that could affect outcome—variables such as suddenness, predictability, severity, and others as suggested by Warheit (1985) and others earlier in this chapter.

Chamberlin (1980) reviewed disaster literature in general, including some technological disasters such as the Buffalo Creek Dam break and flood, and concluded that "the severity and totality of the stress (the disaster) supercedes the intrapsychic predisposition as a determinant of neurotic stress response." Although basing his conclusions largely on studies of war-related stress, Hocking (1970) proposed that at the far end of the continuum of stressful situations predisposing psychological factors become irrelevant since all individuals break down under such an extreme degree of stress. He also proposed that "preexisting personality characteristics may do no more than determine how long an individual can withstand prolonged extreme stress." Lifton and Olson (1976) have examined Hocking's ideas in regard to technological disasters with their study of the Buffalo Creek Dam break and flood, an especially severe disaster in terms of fatalities, physical injury, loss of personal property, and sheer horror and grotesqueness; they concurred with Hocking's viewpoint. The severity of the Buffalo Creek Dam disaster may well account for the uniformly high rates of psychopathology in its victims as found in three studies (Lifton & Olson, 1976; Gleser et al., 1981; Titchener & Kapp, 1976). Perhaps because of its extreme degree of severity, the Buffalo Creek Dam disaster may not be representative of technological disasters in general.

Bolin (1985) has suggested that some technological accidents have a high potential for terror or horror. Events such as the Buffalo Creek Dam collapse or the Regency Hotel skywalk collapse produced sickening descriptions of experiences such as churning black slag and huge walls of water sweeping away everything in sight and depositing mud-covered corpses in black sludge along the way (Green & Gleser, 1983; Titchener & Kapp, 1976); "bodies literally exploding," amputated limbs strewn around, a man's stomach protruding through his mouth, a body cut neatly in half just below the thorax, people crushed beyond recognition, and victims pinned under piles of steel with water and blood flowing all around and creating "a penetrating odor that seemed to last forever" (Wilkinson, 1983).

Bolin (1985) writes that horror, or exposure to death, goes beyond sheer terror in producing mental health effects. In reference to the Buffalo Creek Dam disaster, Erikson (1976b) and Lifton and Olson (1976) have described the phenomenon of "death imprint" or "death anxiety" as a psychological response to the horror-filled event.

Other aspects of technological disasters that various authors have suggested as contributing to mental health effects include the degree of immediate intensity of the disaster agent (Bolin, 1985), its duration and frequency, the degree of suddenness and unexpectedness of the event (Mileti et al., 1975; Erikson, 1976b; Bolin, 1982), and impact ratio, which is the ratio of loss to available resources (Bolin, 1985).

Additionally, perceptions of the victims about the disaster agent may modify the impact of the disaster on the individual (Bromet & Schulberg, in press). Bolin (1985) writes that " . . . the reality of a hazard often has little to do with how individuals perceive it" (Van Arsdol et al., 1964), and that "threat as a disaster characteristic is conceptually bound to the notion of risk perception by potential victims." If a victim does not perceive himself as victimized, then it follows that his mental health sequelae would be less. Baum and associates (1983c) hypothesized that it is the issue of the victims' perceptions of loss of control that makes technological disasters more distressing than natural disasters. Victims are likely to perceive a *loss* of control in technological disasters where they view the technology as something which *should* have been under control. In natural disasters, the victims perceive a *lack* of control of something that never was in control. The victims' perception of loss and subsequent assignment of blame are thought to contribute heavily to their psychological distress.

Frederick (1980) believes that one important reason for the difference in psychological outcome of technological vs. natural disasters lies with assignment of blame to the victim for having at least partly precipitated the disaster. However, no supporting data are provided to substantiate this belief. In fact, findings of the 1986 study by Smith and associates did not bear out Frederick's hypothesis. Smith and coworkers discovered that victims of flooding (natural disaster) suffered the additional burden of blame assigned to them by one-third of non-victims (unpublished data). Reasons cited by those who blamed the victims included the victims having built flimsy houses, having built on a flood plain, not carrying insurance, and ignoring warnings. In contrast, only 4% of non-victims blamed the victims of dioxin contamination (technological disaster) for their misfortune. Thus, blaming the victim is a phenomenon that is neither unique to technological disasters nor even necessarily descriptive of them.

Baum (1983a) noted that in technological disasters victims may blame specific individuals or agencies for the disaster, resulting in more focused anger. This focus of blame and anger has been suggested to be a factor differentiating technological disasters from natural ones. Unpublished data of the dioxin/flooding study by Smith et al. support this idea. Ninety-two percent of victims of dioxin contamination blamed others, including the involved businesses and their personnel for improper disposal of waste products, and government agencies for inadequate regulation of disposal activities. Sixty-two percent of flood victims blamed others, primarily the government, for poor flood control.

Characteristics of the disaster agent thought to contribute to mental health sequelae, then, include overall severity, terror or horror, immediate intensity, duration and frequency, suddenness or unexpectedness, impact ratio, and the victims' perceptions of the disaster. But, in fact, all of these factors might be subsumed under the general concept of severity of the disaster. Great intensity and long duration may be two distinct characteristics contributing to the disaster's overall severity. Likewise, unexpectedness and terror and horror would also be ways in which a disaster might be more severe. And certainly, victim perception of the disaster would contribute to the severity of the disaster (in the victim's mind where the psychological effects of the disaster are presumably generated).

As in research on stress and life events, it might be feasible and advantageous to develop an instrument of assessment analogous to the Paykel Life Events Scale (Paykel, 1974) to create a standardized weighted rating system of the overall severity of a particular disaster agent. Then, different disasters could be compared systematically across studies. Bromet and Schulberg (in press) note that part of the reason for the extreme difficulty in identifying consistent predictors of psychiatric disorder following disasters is the problem of the disasters themselves being quite different in severity. It is possible that once the degree of severity is controlled, differences in psychological outcome between technological and natural disasters may vanish.

A look at the literature will reveal that the majority of natural disasters previously studied have been short-term events with a recognizable low point (such as hurricanes and floods), and most technological disaster research has tended to focus on chronic events whose long-term consequences have been uncertain, such as gradual toxic exposures to chemicals or radiation (Solomon, in press).

Solomon has also recognized that certain elements associated with technological disasters rather than the intrinsic nature of the disaster agent itself may confound the psychological consequences. In other words, selected natural disasters with similar qualities might place the same hazards as a technological disaster might upon the affected population. For example, a long-term natural disaster agent such as a drought or a famine, when examined against an equivalent technological agent such as a slowly developing toxic contamination, might erase the entire difference in outcome. Thus, the previously proposed differences in mental health effects of the two different kinds of disaster might be explained on the basis of the bias in various contributors to the overall severity of the disaster agent rather than on the intrinsic basis of a possibly arbitrary division between technological vs. natural disasters themselves.

A remaining difference potentially setting technological disasters apart from other disasters is the phenomenon of having no knowledge that a disaster has occurred until afterwards. In fact, the impact of disaster may be felt by its victims more directly as the impact of *learning* the news that a disaster has occurred (Beigel & Berren, 1985). For example, victims of the dioxin contamination accident had been exposed to the harmful chemical for as long as 10 years before they learned of the catastrophe (Smith et al., 1986). Beigel and Berren have further noted that the time frame of negligence-related technological disasters such as toxic spills has another unusual twist, that being a long period of anticipatory concern on the part of the future victims, termed the "ticking time bomb effect." It has now been nine years since the 1979 Three Mile Island accident, and throughout all that time the residents of the area have had to merely wonder and worry about potential health hazards. (Research studies [Upton, 1981] have finally shown that the only health effect associated with Three Mile Island was psychological, with no significant impact on any aspect of physical health.) As observed by Beigel and Berren (1985), it might be years or even generations before measurable physical consequences occur from such technological disasters. This "ticking time bomb effect" is not known by these authors to have ever arisen out of a natural disaster, and the case is the same for the phenomenon of not knowing that a disaster has occurred until afterwards. These characteristics might well be the only ones uniquely intrinsic to technological disasters. But using these characteristics to describe a unique subset of disasters as technological is problematic in that they seem to apply *only* to a few specific technological events, including toxic spills of hazardous chemicals or radiation, and do not apply to other technological accidents such as airplane crashes.

The previously-mentioned study by Smith and coworkers (1986) is unique in its attempt to compare both technological and natural disasters in one study. This study examined mental health effects of a technological disaster (dioxin contamination) and a natural disaster (flooding) which both occurred together within the Times Beach population, and separately in other areas. Few significant differences were found in rates or types of psychiatric symptoms or syndromes associated with either disaster agent. It is possible that the relative mildness of both disasters served to dampen any apparent differences. Victims more severely affected, however, i.e., victims of double disaster (both dioxin and flooding), did experience higher rates of psychopathology than those exposed to only one disaster.

In order to help untangle the confound surrounding the technological-vs.-natural separation of disasters, Baum and his coworkers are currently involved in a study comparing several disasters having different combinations of characteristics with respect to the disaster agent. In the end, it is hoped that Baum's study will help clarify whether it is some factor related specifically to the human-made component of technological disasters, such as chronicity, which makes them seem different, or whether there is no difference aside from variation in severity.

EPIDEMIOLOGICAL STUDY OF DIOXIN AND FLOODING

In this section we will describe an epidemiological study conducted by one of the authors (Smith) of the effects of various disasters on mental health. The study was designed to minimize some of the methodological problems discussed earlier by utilizing careful sampling techniques and standardized assessment instruments and by the inclusion of a control group. The series of events described below provided the unique opportunity to compare reactions to technological as well as natural disasters.

Beginning in the fall of 1982, a series of disasters occurred in the St. Louis area. In October, the Environmental Defense Fund announced 14 confirmed and 41 suspected dioxin sites in Missouri. The majority of these sites were in a semirural area near St. Louis. Oil mixed with dioxin had been sprayed on roads in these areas to control dust as long as 10 years before and was still present in levels well above those considered safe. Around the same time, some wells which supplied drinking water in the area were found to have unacceptable levels of radiation, presumably caused by seepage from a uranium plant's waste which had been buried in the 1960s.

In December, a time of year in which floods are rare, a series of devastating floods swept through the area. The floods caused five deaths and necessitated the evacuation of 25,000 persons from their homes. Property damages were estimated at $150 million. Although for many of the victims the evacuation was only temporary, for residents of one flooded community, Times Beach, it proved to be permanent.

Three weeks after the flood and two days before Christmas, as residents of Times Beach were returning to their homes to clean up and repair the flood damage, a second disaster occurred. The Center for Disease Control (CDC) issued a health advisory warning residents to stay out of Times Beach because of high levels of dioxin found in soil samples taken prior to the flood.

Residents were scattered over a wide area as they moved into temporary housing. They had left behind most of their personal belongings, for what had not been destroyed by the flood was believed to be tainted by dioxin. Because the community had voted to take itself out of the federal flood insurance program, residents had no prospect of reimbursement for damages.

In mid-February, the State and Federal governments agreed to purchase Times Beach, the first time the Federal government had ever initiated a "buy-out" of an entire community. The buy-out moved slowly and was met with protests by residents, who believed the appraisals of their property were too low and that payment was too slow in coming. One year after the disasters, the majority of the residents were still in temporary housing, and only a few had received payment for their property.

The arrival of spring brought more disasters to the already devastated communities. Flood waters again covered the area, additional dioxin sites were discovered, and a series of tornadoes left a path of destruction. Coincident with these dramatic occurrences, the involved areas suffered massive layoffs in many local plants. The unemployment rate in the area rose to a record high of 10.3%. A more complete chronology of these disasters has been reported by Smith (1984).

These disasters occurred just as Washington University was completing interviews for Wave 2 of the Epidemiologic Catchment Area (ECA) project. The ECA project was designed to estimate the prevalence and incidence of specific psychiatric disorders in the general population (Eaton & Kesler, 1985). The project was carried out at five sites—New Haven, Baltimore, North Carolina, Los Angeles, and St. Louis—and included approximately 21,000 individuals. Respondents participated in two in-person interviews that were separated in time by about one year. Also, an additional interview was conducted by telephone midway between the times of the two in-person interviews. The in-person interviews assessed psychiatric disorders according to DMS-III criteria using the Diagnostic Interview Schedule (DIS) developed by Robins and associates (1981).

To our knowledge, this was the first time that an area affected by disaster had ever, by chance, also been the site of a careful evaluation of psychiatric status just before the disaster occurred. It offered a remarkable opportunity: to return to respondents who were affected by disaster in order to learn whether exposure to floods or tornadoes, or notification of long-standing exposure to dioxin or radioactive well water, had affected their psychiatric status. This effect could be judged by comparing changes in their mental health status with changes in the mental health of a control group.

Conveniently, the fact that only some areas of the research site were affected provided another unique advantage—a control group from a similar area, similarly evaluated for psychiatric disorders prior to the disasters. As a result of this happenstance, baseline information existed on psychiatric status shortly before these events for persons who were exposed to these disasters and for unexposed individuals living in similar areas.

Subjects and Methods

To identify ECA sample members likely to have experienced these disasters, the assistance of a variety of governmental agencies was sought to ascertain areas that had been exposed to the disasters in the counties that constituted our interviewing area. Respondents were then labeled as presumed exposed cases if their residence at the time of their second in-person ECA interview was within one of the officially designated disaster areas.

Out of a total of 743 individuals interviewed for the ECA study in a three-county area made up of rural sections and small towns, 252 ECA respondents who were believed to have lived in areas exposed to one or more disasters were identified. All of those respondents were selected, plus a control sample of 200 ECA subjects selected at random from those believed not to have been exposed.

Because of this study's interest in dioxin exposure and the small yield of persons exposed to dioxin in the ECA sample, 100 non-ECA households were selected at random from the five confirmed dioxin sites in the St. Louis area. Eighty of these 100 households were drawn from the 800 Times Beach households where flooding had also occurred. The remaining 20 households were selected from the approximately 200 non-ECA households in the four dioxin sites where no flooding had occurred.

A comparison group of 100 unexposed non-ECA households was randomly selected from households located in the ECA study area thought to be comparable to the dioxin-exposed sample in socioeconomic status. These households had originally been listed for possible inclusion in the ECA project, but random selection of neighborhoods had left them out of that survey and thus they had not been interviewed for the ECA project.

Data were collected over an 8-month period beginning approximately one year after the onset of the disasters. The interviews required approximately 90 minutes and were administered in the subjects' homes by professional interviewers. A total of 547 individuals were interviewed. The refusal rate was 8% for the sample. It was highest (10%) among those in the ECA sample who had been interviewed previously.

In collaboration with NIMH's Emergency/Disaster Research Program, an instrument was developed to assess victims' experiences and responses to a range of natural and technological emergencies (Robins & Smith, 1983). This instrument, the Diagnostic Interview Schedule/Disaster Supplement (DIS/DS), was designed to provide a comprehensive picture of the emergency experience and to be applicable across a wide range of emergencies. The instrument assesses the type of event, type and extent of loss, individual and family risk factors, use of formal and informal support systems, behavioral response to the traumatic event, and 15 DSM-III diagnoses selected for their potential relevance to the disaster experience. Diagnoses with low prevalence rates in the ECA survey (for example, schizophrenia and obsessive-compulsive disorder) were excluded.

Respondents were asked whether they had ever experienced each symptom of the relevant diagnoses. Psychiatric symptoms were scored as positive if they met criteria for clinical significance and were not explained entirely by physical illness or substance ingestion. Questions were added to ascertain onset and recency for each positive symptom. Thus, information was available as to the presence or absence of each symptom during the interval between the disaster and the interview, and prior to the disaster. The post-disaster interview also repeated a number of other measures that might be sensitive to changes in mental health. These included use of health services and psychoactive drugs, health and disability status, role function, social support, and changes in employment and marital status.

In addition to these questions, all of which were repeated from the ECA interview, the disaster section explored the disaster experience and its meaning for the respondents. It elicited information on exposure of respondents as well as of friends and relatives, personal beliefs regarding the effects of exposure, and evidence for symptoms of post-traumatic stress in other members of the household. All respondents were asked to evaluate news coverage of the disasters, whether they believed victims had been stigmatized, on whom they blamed the disasters, and whether other stressful life events had occurred in the past year.

The comprehensiveness of the DIS/DS served to enhance its utility across a range of disaster events, thereby permitting the kind of standardized assessment needed for cross-study comparison of results.

Selected Findings

All subjects were 20 years or older, and almost all were white. Fifty-five percent were female, and more than two-thirds were married. Two-thirds had at least a high school education, and median income was in the range of $20,000–$30,000.

For purposes of analysis, subjects were classified into the following three groups: directly exposed, indirectly exposed (through friends or relatives), and not exposed. The directly-exposed group was further subdivided according to type of disaster agent, i.e., those exposed only to dioxin, only to flood, or to both dioxin and flood. The numbers of individuals exposed to radioactive well water and tornadoes were so small that they were not included in this analysis. Although one of the strengths of the study was the opportunity to obtain information following disaster on persons previously interviewed, the number of individuals reporting disaster exposure on reinterview was only 44, much lower than that expected on the basis of prior information from various public agencies. It was not clear why there were so few cases of self-identified exposure to disaster (especially radioactive well water and dioxin) in this sample.

Subjects exposed to dioxin only were significantly younger than any of the other exposed or nonexposed groups. Compared to controls, the disaster victims had less often completed high school and had lower incomes. This held true for each type of disaster agent. The Times Beach sample (both flood and dioxin exposure—i.e., double disaster) had the lowest income and education, and the highest proportion of divorced or separated individuals.

Essentially all the Times Beach subjects and more than 90% of the flood-only victims reported significant property damage or loss as a result of the disaster, far more than the dioxin-only victims. Times Beach victims had an excess of postdisaster disruption of living arrangements, with an average of three moves during the year following the disaster, compared to two for dioxin-only victims and one for flood-only victims.

The great majority (87%) of the Times Beach group believed that the disaster experience had caused them great harm, compared to less than one-third of the two single-disaster groups.

The doubly-exposed Times Beach group reported higher levels of upset (91%) than did those who had directly experienced only dioxin (45%) or floods (55%). One year after the disasters, only one-third of all victims reported that they had fully recovered from the disaster experience. Flood-only victims were twice as likely to report full recovery (55%) than were the groups exposed to dioxin alone (24%) or to dioxin-with-flood (25%).

In determining the effects of disaster on mental health, demonstration of more psychiatric symptoms in victims than in controls is by itself not sufficient to conclude that the disaster experience caused the symptoms. Such an effect cannot be determined without showing that the disaster accounted for a greater increase in symptoms than would have been expected during that year.

Nonexposed and indirectly exposed groups had equal percentages of subjects with psychiatric symptoms (71% and 72%) during the year after the disasters, but those directly exposed had significantly more symptoms (87%) in general, and more symptom complaints per subject. The doubly-exposed group had somewhat more subjects with symptoms (90%) than either the dioxin group (83%) or flood group (85%) alone, and more symptoms per subject.

Victims of all combinations of disaster agents showed significantly higher proportions with symptoms of six disorders: depression, somatization, phobia, generalized anxiety, post-traumatic stress disorder (PTSD), and alcohol abuse. Dioxin victims (with or without flooding) had a higher proportion of subjects reporting symptoms of somatization disorder than did victims of flooding only. This suggests that victims of toxic exposure might feel more uncertain about potential health effects and would explain the higher frequency of symptoms.

The increase of psychiatric symptoms in disaster victims over controls might suggest a powerful effect of disaster on subsequent mental health, but the results do not consider whether these are new symptoms or whether they were preexisting symptoms in the victim population. To clarify this, it was necessary to determine the proportion of symptoms in each category that had occurred for the first time after the disaster. When this was accomplished, differences were much less dramatic. Only two significant differences were found. All of the direct exposure groups had more new symptoms of depression and PTSD than did the nonexposed group; the indirect exposure group had an increase in new PTSD symptoms over those not exposed.

Of interest, new depressive symptoms in the direct exposure groups were concentrated in those with preexisting depressive symptoms. This pattern was not seen in the indirectly exposed and nonexposed groups, which exceeded the direct exposure groups in the frequency of a *first* depressive symptom. These results suggest that the disaster exacerbated preexisting depression rather than creating depression de novo in previously depression-free individuals.

The pattern for PTSD was somewhat different. The rate of new PTSD symptoms was eight times greater for the disaster victims and four times greater for the indirectly exposed subjects than for the nonexposed controls. All groups had equal rates of prior PTSD symptoms, and new postdisaster PTSD symptoms developed in individuals independent of prior history. Thus it was reasonable to conclude that the disasters produced new PTSD symptoms in subjects both with and without a previous history of these symptoms.

To learn whether exposure to disaster led to the development of new psychiatric disorders, postdisaster rates of new-onset psychiatric disorders were calculated. There were new cases of only four disorders: depression, alcoholism, generalized anxiety, and PTSD. Only PTSD showed significantly elevated rates compared to controls.

Since the preponderance of psychiatric disorders could not be explained on the basis of newly developed cases following the disaster, other explanations were sought. It turned out that the possibility of persistence of symptoms of a preexisting disorder following disaster did not adequately explain the problem, since symptoms were found to cluster *immediately* after the disaster and dissipate by the one-year mark.

Important differences were found in certain predisaster characteristics of the disaster victims. They were younger, more often separated or divorced, poorer, less educated, and more likely to have preexisting psychiatric symptoms. Given their predisposing characteristics, the disaster victims started out with a higher risk of developing physical and mental health problems. This initial status, especially in psychiatric history, overwhelmed the contribution of disaster exposure in predicting outcome.

In other words, their risk might have been the same had no disaster ever occurred. Such findings greatly diminish the apparent impact of the disaster events themselves.

This study found little evidence that either type of disaster agent caused the onset of mental disorders, caused remitted disorders to relapse, preserved symptoms of disorders, or caused new symptoms (with the exception of PTSD). The higher rates of psychiatric symptoms in disaster victims appeared to be due primarily to a proliferation of prior symptoms rather than to the development of symptoms or disorders totally new to them. The only disorder which apparently arose de novo out of the disaster was PTSD, but even for this disorder there were surprisingly low rates. Closer examination of the victim groups revealed a dose-response relationship for PTSD. Doubly-exposed victims (both dioxin and flooding) had the highest proportion (31%) with PTSD symptoms, compared to 24% of dioxin-only victims and 16% of flood-only victims. Despite the frequency of PTSD symptoms, the proportion of those actually meeting criteria for a diagnosis was low (around 5%).

It has been suggested that part of the reason for the apparent low impact of disaster on mental health is that the disasters studied were relatively mild in nature. However, this was not the case for the Times Beach residents who not only experienced severe flooding and dioxin exposure, but were also forced to relocate due to the contamination. Even in this group, which started out with the highest risk profile and experienced the worst disasters, the majority survived the experience without developing psychiatric disabilities.

Even though the incidence of new cases of psychiatric disorder following disaster was relatively low, this is not to say that the degree of suffering following the disasters was insignificant. In fact, 90% of the double-exposure group experienced psychiatric symptoms during the year after the disaster, compared to 71% of controls. The dioxin-only and flood-only victims had similarly high rates (83% and 85% respectively).

In this study which contained the unique combination of both technological and natural disasters, it might be tempting to speculate about unique mental health effects on the basis of comparison of outcomes specific to the two kinds of disasters. The observation that the flood (natural disaster) victims reported full recovery from the disaster twice as often as the dioxin (technological disaster) group might suggest that technological disasters have far worse mental health consequences. However, the objective data on psychopathology from DIS interviews (reported above) do not confirm this finding. Results of this study suggest that the type of disaster agent is not as important as its severity in producing mental health effects.

IMPLICATIONS FOR FUTURE RESEARCH

This chapter has attempted to summarize what we now know about the mental health effects of technological accidents. If the findings seem uncertain, that truly reflects the state of our knowledge. While it seems clear that psychiatric sequelae are to be expected among significant proportions of the affected populations, it is not clear whether the consequences of technological accidents differ from those associated with natural hazards. We cannot confirm or refute the notion that technological disasters have greater psychological consequences or that the effects endure for a longer period of time. Until there are more systematic studies of technological accidents, this question cannot be answered, nor can the relevance of this question be determined.

Studies of technological accidents share many of the methodological limitations found in research on natural disasters. There is a great need for well designed studies which utilize standardized instruments and data collection techniques, scientific sample selection, and control or comparison groups. Such studies would permit cross-study comparison and replication and generalization of findings. Longitudinal studies which include various types of natural and human-made disasters, such as the research being undertaken by Baum and associates, could assist in determining similarities and/or differences in mental health consequences.

Those doing research also need to think in terms of intervention strategies when they design their studies. Careful studies of factors that might mediate the impact of disaster are needed (e.g., Fleming et al., 1982; Collins et al., 1983). Bromet and Schulberg (in press) suggest that it is time to undertake experimental epidemiologic studies with identified high risk groups with the dual purpose of testing causal models of acute and chronic distress patterns as well as evaluating the effectiveness of different types of intervention processes.

It may not be possible to protect individuals from disaster, but identification of risk factors will assist mental health practitioners in targeting their interventions toward those in greatest need of assistance.

REFERENCES

Adler, A. (1943). Neuropsychiatric complications in victims of Boston's Cocoanut Grove Disaster. *Journal of the American Medical Association, 123*: 1098–1101.

Ahearn, F. L., & Cohen, R. E. (1983). *Disasters and Mental Health: An Annotated Bibliography.* Washington, D.C., DHHS Publication No. (ADM) 84–1311.

American Psychiatric Association. (1980). *Diagnostic and Statistical Manual of Mental Disorders, Third Edition.* Washington, D.C.: American Psychiatric Association.

Barton, A. H. (1969). *Communities in Disaster: A Sociological Analysis of Collective Stress Situations.* Garden City, NY: Doubleday.

Baum, A., & Davidson, L. M. (1985). A suggested framework for studying factors that contribute to trauma in disaster. In B. J. Sowder (Ed.), *Disasters and Mental Health: Selected Contemporary Perspectives* (pp. 29–40). Washington, D.C., DHHS Publication No. (ADM) 85-1421.

Baum, A., Fleming, R., & Davidson, L. M. (1983a). Natural disaster and technological catastrophe. *Environment and Behavior,* 15: 333–354.

Baum, A., Gatchel, R. J., & Schaeffer, M. A. (1983b). Emotional, behavioral, and physiological effects of chronic stress at Three Mile Island. *Journal of Consulting and Clinical Psychology,* 51: 565–572.

Baum, A., Fleming, R., & Singer, J. E. (1983c). Coping with victimization by technological disaster. *Journal of Social Issues,* 39(2): 117–138.

Beck, A. T. (1978). Depression inventory. Philadelphia: Center for Cognitive Therapy.

Beigel, A., & Berren, M. (1985). Human-Induced Disasters. *Psychiatric Annals,* 15(3): 143–150.

Berren, M. R., Beigel, A., & Ghertner, S. (1980). A typology for the classification of disasters. *Community Mental Health Journal,* 16: 103–111.

Bolin, R. (1985). Disaster characteristics and psychosocial impacts. In B. J. Sowder (Ed.), *Disasters and Mental Health: Selected Contemporary Perspectives* (pp. 3–28). Washington, D.C., DHHS Publication No. (ADM) 85-1421.

Boman, B. (1979). Behavioural observations on the Granville train disaster and the significance of stress for psychiatry. *Social Science and Medicine,* 13: 463–471.

Bromet, E. J., & Dunn, L. D. (1981). Mental health of mothers nine months after the Three Mile Island accident. *The Urban and Social Change Review,* 14: 12–15.

Bromet, E. J., Hough, L., & Connell, M. (1984). Mental health of children near the Three Mile Island reactor. *Journal of Preventive Psychiatry,* 2: 275–301.

Bromet, E. J., Parkinson, D. K., Schulberg, H. C., et al. (1980). *Three Mile Island: Mental Health Findings.* Pittsburgh: Western Psychiatric Institute and Clinic and the University of Pittsburgh.

Bromet, E. J., Parkinson, D. K., Schulberg, H. C., et al. (1982). Mental health of residents near the Three Mile Island reactor: A comparative study of selected groups. *Journal of Preventive Psychiatry,* 1: 225–276.

Bromet, E. J., & Schulberg, H. C. (1986). The Three Mile Island disaster: A search for high-risk groups. In J. H. Shore (Ed.), *Disaster Stress Studies: New Methods and Findings* (pp. 1–20). Washington, D.C.: American Psychiatric Press.

Bromet, E. J., & Schulberg, H. C. (in press). Epidemiologic findings from disaster research. In R. E. Hales & A. J. Frances (Eds.), *Psychiatric Update: American Psychiatric Association Annual Review, Volume VII.* Washington, D.C.: American Psychiatric Press.

Chamberlin, B. C. (1980). The psychological aftermath of disaster. *Journal of Clinical Psychiatry,* 41(7): 238–244.

Cleary, P. D., & Houts, P. S. (1984). The psychologic impact of the Three Mile Island incident. *Journal of Human Stress,* 10: 28–34.

Collins, D. L., Baum, A., & Singer, J. E. (1983). Coping with chronic stress at Three Mile Island. *Journal of Applied Social Psychology,* 128: 280–289.

Davidson, L. M., Baum, A., & Collins, D. L. (1982). Stress and control-related problems at Three Mile Island. *Journal of Applied Social Psychology,* 12: 349–359.

Derogatis, L. (1977). The SCL-90 Manual I: Scoring, administration and procedures for the SCL-90. Baltimore, Johns Hopkins University School of Medicine, Clinical Psychometrics Unit.

Dohrenwend, B. P. (1975). Sociocultural and social-psychological factors in the genesis of mental disorders. *Journal of Health and Social Behavior,* 16: 365–392.

Dohrenwend, B. P., Dohrenwend, B. S., Warheit, G. J., et al. (1981). Stress in the community: A report to the President's Commission on the Accident at Three Mile Island. *Annals of the New York Academy of Sciences,* 365: 159–174.

Eaton, W. W., & Kessler, L. (Eds.) (1985). *Epidemiologic Field Methods in Psychiatry: The NIMH Epidemiologic Catchment Area Program.* New York: Academic Press.

Endicott, J., & Spitzer, R. (1978). A diagnostic interview. The Schedule for Affective Disorders and Schizophrenia. *Archives of General Psychiatry,* 33: 766–771.

Erikson, K. T. (1976a). *Everything in its Path.* New York: Simon & Schuster.

Erikson, K. T. (1976b). Loss of communality at Buffalo Creek. *American Journal of Psychiatry,* 133: 302–305.

Fleming, I., & Baum, A. (1985). The role of prevention in technological catastrophe. In A. Wandersman & R. Hess (Eds.), *Beyond the Individual: Environmental Approaches and Prevention* (pp. 139–152). New York: Hawthorne Press.

Fleming, R., Baum, A., Gisriel, M. M., et al. (1982). Mediating influences of social support on stress at Three Mile Island. *Journal of Human Stress,* Sept.: 14–22.

Frederick, C. J. (1980). Effects of natural vs. human-induced violence upon victims. *Evaluation and Change,* Special Issue, 71–75.

Friedman, P., & Linn, L. (1957). Some psychiatric notes on the *Andrea Doria* disaster. *American Journal of Psychiatry,* 114: 426–432.

Gatchel, R. J., Schaeffer, M. A., & Baum, A. (1985). A psychophysiological field study of stress at Three Mile Island. *Psychophysiology,* 22: 175–181.

Gleser, G., Green, B., & Winget, C. (1981). *Prolonged psychosocial effects of disaster: A study of Buffalo Creek.* New York: Academic Press.

Green, B. L. (1982). Assessing levels of psychosocial impairment following disaster: Consideration of actual and methodological dimension. *The Journal of Nervous and Mental Disease,* 17: 544–552.

Green, B. L. (1985). Conceptual and methodological issues in assessing the psychological impact of disaster. In B. J. Sowder (Ed.), *Disasters and Mental Health: Selected Contemporary Perspectives* (pp. 179–195). Washington, D.C., DHHS Publication No. (ADM) 85-1421.

Green, B. L., & Gleser, G. C. (1983). Stress and long-term psychopathology in survivors of the Buffalo Creek disaster. In D. F. Ricks & B. S. Dohrenwend (Eds.), *Origins of Psychopathology: Problems in Research and Public Policy.* New York: Cambridge University Press.

Green, B. L., Grace, M. C., Lindy, J. D., et al. (1983). Levels of functional impairment following a civilian disaster: The Beverly Hills Supper Club fire. *Journal of Consulting and Clinical Psychology,* 51: 573–580.

Hartsough, D. M. (1985). Measurement of the psychological effects of disaster. In J. Laube & S. Murphy (Eds.), *Perspectives on Disaster Recovery* (pp. 22–60). Norwalk, CT: Appleton-Century-Crofts.

Henderson, S., & Bostock, T. (1977). Coping behavior after shipwreck. *British Journal of Psychiatry,* 131: 15–20.

Hess, R. E., & Wandersman, A. (1985). What can we learn from Love Canal? A conversation with Lois Gibbs and Richard Valinsky. In A. Wandersman & R. Hess (Eds.), *Beyond the Individual: Environmental Approaches and Prevention.* New York: Hawthorne Press.

Hocking, F. (1970). Psychiatric aspects of extreme environmental stress. *Diseases of the Nervous System,* 31: 542–545.

Hoiberg, A., & McCaughey, B. G. (1984). The traumatic aftereffects of collision at sea. *American Journal of Psychiatry,* 141: 70–73.

Kasl, S. V., Chisholm, R. F., & Eskenazi, B. (1981). The impact of the accident at Three Mile Island on the behavior and well-being of nuclear workers. *American Journal of Public Health,* 71: 472–495.

Kinston, W., & Rosser, R. (1974). Disaster: Effects on mental and physical state. *Journal of Psychosomatic Research,* 18: 437–456.

Leopold, R. L., & Dillon, H. (1963). Psycho-anatomy of a disaster: A long-term study of post-traumatic neuroses in survivors of a marine explosion. *American Journal of Psychiatry,* 19: 913–921.

Levine, A. G. (1983). *Love Canal: Science, Politics and People.* Lexington, MA: Lexington Books.

Lifton, R. J., & Olson, E. (1976). The human meaning of total disaster: The Buffalo Creek experience. *Psychiatry,* 39: 1–18.

Lindy, J. D. (1985). The trauma membrane and other clinical concepts derived from psychotherapeutic work with survivors of natural disasters. *Psychiatric Annals,* 15(3): 153–160.

Logue, J. N., Melick, M. E., & Hansen, H. (1981). Research issues and directions in the epidemiology of health effects of disasters. *Epidemiologic Reviews,* 3: 140–162.

Lopez-Ibor Jr., J. J., Canas, S. F., & Rodriguez-Gamazo, M. (1985). Psychopathological aspects of the toxic oil syndrome catastrophe. *British Journal of Psychiatry,* 147: 352–365.

Melick, M. E. (1985). The health of postdisaster populations: A review of literature and case study. In J. Laube & S. Murphy (Eds.), *Perspectives on Disaster Recovery* (pp. 179–209). Norwalk, CT: Appleton-Century-Crofts.

Melick, M. E., Logue, J. N., Frederick, C. (1982). Stress and Disaster. In L. Goldberger & S. Breznitz (Eds.), *Handbook of Stress.* New York: The Free Press.

Mileti, D. S., Drabek, T. E., & Haas, J. E. (1975). *Human Systems in Extreme Environments: A Sociological Perspective.* Monograph No. 21, Boulder, CO: Institute of Behavioral Science, University of Colorado.

Paykel, E. S. (1974). Life stress and psychiatric disorder: Applications of the clinical approach. In B. S. Dohrenwend & B. P. Dohrenwend (Eds.), *Stressful Life Events: Their Nature and Effects.* New York: John Wiley & Sons.

Perlberg, M. (1979). Trauma at Tenerife: The psychic aftershocks of a jet disaster. *Human Behavior,* 8: 49–50.

Perry, R. W., & Lindell, M. K. (1978). The psychological consequences of natural disaster: A review of research on American communities. *International Journal of Mass Emergencies,* 3(2/3): 105–115.

Quarantelli, E. L. (1985). What is disaster? The need for clarification in definition and conceptualization in research. In B. J. Sowder (Ed.), *Disasters and Mental Health: Selected Contemporary Perspectives* (pp. 41–73). Washington, D.C., DHHS Publication No. (ADM) 85-1421.

Rangell, L. (1976). Discussion of the Buffalo Creek disaster: The course of psychic trauma. *American Journal of Psychiatry,* 133: 313–316.

Robins, L. N., Fischbach, R. L., Smith, E. M., et al. (1986). Impact of disaster on previously assessed mental health. In J. H. Shore (Ed.), *Disaster Stress Studies: New Methods and Findings* (pp. 22–48). Washington, D.C.: American Psychiatric Press.

Robins, L. N., Helzer, J. E., Croughan, J. L., et al. (1981). *Diagnostic Interview Schedule (Version 3).* Rockville, MD: National Institute of Mental Health.

Robins, L. N., & Smith, E. M. (1983). The Diagnostic Interview Schedule/Disaster Supplement. St. Louis, MO: Washington University School of Medicine.

Shippee, G., Bradford, R., & Gregory, W. (1982). Community perceptions of natural disasters and post-disaster mental health services. *Journal of Community Psychology,* 10: 23–28.

Shore, J. H., Tatum, E. L., Vollmer, W. M. (1986). The Mount St. Helens stress response syndrome. In J. H. Shore (Ed.), *Disaster Stress Studies: New Methods and Findings.* Washington, D.C.: American Psychiatric Press.

Smith, E. M. (1984). *Chronology of Disasters in Eastern Missouri.* Rockville, MD: National Institute of Mental Health, Mimeo.

Smith, E. M., Robins, L. N., Przybeck, T. R., et al. (1986). Psychosocial consequences of a disaster. In J. H. Shore (Ed.), *Disaster Stress Studies: New Methods and Findings* (pp. 50–76). Washington, D.C.: American Psychiatric Press.

Solomon, S. D. (in press). Evaluation and research issues in assessing disaster's effects. In R. Gist & B. Lubin (Eds.), *Psychosocial Aspects of Disaster.* New York: Wiley & Sons.

Spitzer, R. L., Endicott, J., Mesnikoff, A. M., et al. (1968). The Psychiatric Evaluation Form. New York: Biometrics Research.

Stone, R. A., & Levine, A. G. (1985). Reactions to collective stress: Correlates of active citizen participation at Love Canal. In A. Wandersman & R. Hess (Eds.), *Beyond the Individual: Environmental Approaches and Prevention* (pp. 153–177). New York: Hawthorne Press.

Taylor, A. J. W., & Frazer, A. G. (1982). The stress of post-disaster body handling and victim identification work. *Journal of Human Stress*, 8: 4–12.

Terr, L. C. (1981). Psychic trauma in children: Observations following the Chowchilla school-bus kidnapping. *American Journal of Psychiatry*, 138: 14–19.

Titchener, J. L., & Kapp, F. T. (1976). Family and character change at Buffalo Creek. *American Journal of Psychiatry*, 133: 295–299.

Upton, A. C. (1981). Health impact of the Three Mile Island accident. *Annals of the New York Academy of Sciences*, 365: 63–75.

Van Arsdol, M. G., Sabagh, J., Alexander, F. (1964). Reality and the perception of environmental hazards. *Journal of Health and Human Behavior*, 5: 144–155.

Warheit, B. J. (1985). A propositional paradigm for estimating the impact of disasters on mental health. In B. J. Sowder (Ed.), *Disasters and Mental Health: Selected Contemporary Perspectives* (pp. 196–214). Washington, D.C., DHHS Publication No. (ADM) 85-1421.

Wilkinson, C. B. (1983). Aftermath of a disaster: the collapse of the Hyatt Regency Hotel skywalks. *American Journal of Psychiatry*, 140: 1134–1139.

4

Human Response to War and War-Related Events in the Contemporary World

ROBERT S. LAUFER

The focus of this chapter is on the issue of psychosocial responses to war. However, even interpreting the task somewhat narrowly within the psychosocial tradition of the volume and the series of which it is a part, we are still confronted with a formidable problem. There is rather limited research in this area, with the notable exceptions of research on veterans of war and victims of genocide (Holocaust survivors and Cambodian refugees). Furthermore, the title includes "war-related events," which complicates the issue. There are three questions that must be addressed prior to examining the existing evidence in this area. First, how can war be classified as a catastrophic stressor? Second, what distinguishes war from other forms of catastrophic trauma that come under the label of traumatic stress and are clinically conceptualized as Post-Traumatic Stress Disorder? Third, what distinguishes war from war-related events?

There is also a general point of some note which the reader should keep in mind throughout this chapter. Both of the World Wars, the Korean conflict, and the Vietnam War created a concern about social support systems to sustain combat and the individual/psychological limits of

The research on which this chapter is based was, in part, supported by NIMH grant R01 MH26832-06 and Veterans Administration contracts V101(134)P-610 and V101(134)P-130. The author wishes to express his appreciation to Dr. Ellen Frey-Wouters for her careful reading of the drafts of this chapter, suggestions for revisions, and editorial contributions.

exposure to the stress of war, as well as postwar adjustment (Futterman & Pumpian-Midlin, 1951; Havighurst et al., 1951; Brill & Beebe, 1956). Yet, in each instance except the Vietnam War, the issue faded soon after the cessation of hostilities. Although research on postwar adjustment after 1972, when American Soldiers were no longer significantly involved in the war, grew, it was not until almost a decade after the Vietnam War (1980) that the effects of catastrophic war stress were incorporated into the diagnostic nomenclature of American psychiatry, the *Diagnostic and Statistical Manual of Mental Disorders (DSM-III)* (APA, 1980), as Post-Traumatic Stress Disorder (PTSD). The dominant focus in both World War I and World War II was on the effects of war stress *during* rather than *after* the conflict (Stouffer et al., 1949).

As I proceed with the discussion, it should be noted that skepticism about the long-term impact of exposure to war stress exists within and outside the mental health professions. Why? The resistance, in my view, is grounded in the commitment of psychological/psychiatric theory to the impact of childhood trauma and developmental patterns (predispositional factors) in the shaping of adult lives.

The literature on the effects of war on postwar adult development is derived largely from studies of early adult exposure to the catastrophic stress of war. Thus, it should be clear to the reader that the development of contemporary perspectives on the effects of war on the adult lifeline has generated a major clash with established clinical theory on this subject.

The perspective of this chapter, based on evidence accumulated over the last two decades on the Holocaust, World War II, Korea, and Vietnam, as well as research in the immediate aftermath of World War II, indicates that war stress plays a decisive role in postwar adult development, but that predisposing factors play a significant role in particular patterns of psychosocial response in individuals exposed to warfare.

A CONCEPTUALIZATION OF THE NATURE OF WAR TRAUMA AND THE AFTERMATH OF WAR

War as a Catastrophic Stressor

As we read the evidence, war transcended the category of severe stress within the range of normal human experience and became catastrophic trauma outside the range of normal human experience during the Civil

War (Linderman, 1987). However, it was not until World War I that this transformation was generally recognized in the civilian world.

Combat in this period had become a form of terror before which normal men could legitimately experience fear, rage, and powerlessness, while mastery of that fear and perseverance in the face of overwhelming fear were perceived as heroism. It was acknowledged that even the strongest men could not long endure the sights, sounds, smells, and physical demands of war. The weaponry of war provided carnage sufficient to daunt the bravest and made death or mutilation an impersonal event meted out by chance. It transformed men by immunizing them against death and normal emotions, encouraged savagery and barbarism against all forms of life, and countenanced the destruction of the inanimate as well. In the aftermath of World War I, the dominant view among those who fought the battles — victors and vanquished alike — was that in war there are only victims. Finally, especially in the writings of postwar British writers, the gulf between the combat soldier's and civilian's imagery of war, between the prewar civilian and the postwar veteran self, and between the veteran and his civilian social network, intimate and more general, was unbridgeable because the experience of war had produced irreparable change in the soldier's personae and because the experience was not communicable (Fussel, 1979; Wohl, 1979).

   1. The Civil War: The transition from heroic to impersonal warfare. It is worth noting that by the turn of the century evidence of the catastrophic character of warfare was evident in the American Civil War. Indeed, though history was rewritten to suit civilian perceptions of the war in the 1880s and 1890s, by 1865 the glamour of war had been demolished by exposure of the combatants to mass warfare (Linderman, 1987). The key point that Linderman makes can be summarized in his analysis of the changing mentality of soldiers who went off to war in 1861–1862 and those who lived to complete the war by 1864–1865. Linderman labels the early years of the civil war "Courage's War," and exemplifies this concept with a quote from a Southern soldier's description of the soldierly ethos: "In a thousand ways he is tried . . . every quality is put to the test. If he shows the least cowardice he is undone. His courage must never fail. He must be manly and independent" (Linderman, 1987, p. 7). The ethos of warfare by 1864–65 has materially changed as Linderman shows:

> The changing nature of combat weakened drastically the original soldier's conviction that at the center of war stood the confident individual. On the contrary, this war had demonstrated its power to

punish all soldiers far more severely than any personal deficiency could possibly penalize the single soldier. In short, private concerns regarding one's courage or cowardice began to yield to the collective experience, and soldiers became more concerned with survival than any private triumph of values. (Linderman, 1987, p. 234)

What brought about the change in perspective reflected in the above quotes? The answer is technological change in the tools of warfare, which destroyed the possibility of viewing warfare as centered in the moral purpose of the individual soldier. The structure of battle and its execution created an environment in which the outcome of battle moved beyond the soldier's influence and the experience of battle outside the realm of his imagination. The carnage and the pattern of slaughter no longer conformed to the idea that courage rather than chance affected the likelihood of survival. Second, the nature of that war severed the link between the warrior and civilian society.

In reality, the soldier had nowhere to turn save to his friends in the ranks, for the experience of combat had isolated him from the patterns of civilian life . . . . (Linderman, 1987, p. 236)

Thus, combat soldiers had to turn to one another rather than their familial social networks or noncombat military peers for the social and emotional support necessary to cope with the rigors of combat.

. . . . Civil War soldiers discussed much more frequently comradeship's emotional affiliations. To them it was a refuge in a day when previously important links with others within and beyond the armies was weakening or disappearing. (Linderman, 1987, p. 236)

It is useful to remember that the American Civil War depended almost entirely on civilian soldiers whose primary identity was civilian before and after the war. The civilian society to which the veteran would return became in stages a source of disillusionment and a place of isolation. For, as Linderman clearly demonstrates, the combat veterans of the Civil War could only talk to each other; their experiences cut them off from friends and family to whom they could not imagine describing the nature of war, nor had they made the effort to comprehend the nature of death, dying, and mutilation on the field of battle. The response was silence for nearly 20 years. It was not, as Linderman so brilliantly demonstrates, until combat veterans in their latter years could accept heroic descriptions of the Civil War — originally anathema to the returning veterans, but central to the civilian world's perception of the war—that the war became a literary event.

In the immediate aftermath of the Civil War there appeared a great chasm between the returning soldier and his civilian environment which reflected the repugnance with which soldiers viewed their war years and the desire, especially in the North, to view the war in heroic terms.

> The Wisconsin officer Michael Fitch described how he and his comrades turned their faces from war. Sherman's soldiers, he claimed, were unmoved even by the Grand Review marking the end of the war. They did not bestir themselves to watch the Army of the Potomac parade through the streets of the capital; they were indifferent to the cheers greeting their own maneuvers. "To them this magnificent display [200,000 soldiers, marching sixty abreast] which so impressed the thousands who had not been in the war, was merely the last ordered duty in a long, arduous and deadly struggle in which they had triumphed and from which they were only too glad to get away." Once at home, they wished only to forget the war. . . . "At the muster out . . . the nerves of the soldiery had not recovered [the] tremor of the battle charge.". . . Stephen Weld was "reluctant to reminisce about his army days" and was unwilling to publish his war journals. . . . Only with comrades-in-arms would Abner Small sometimes discuss old campaigns. (Linderman, 1987, pp. 269–270)

It was not until the 1880s that the temper of Civil War veterans began to undergo a change in attitude toward the war.

> About the year 1880 American interest in martial matters began to revive. Civil War books became popular. The circulation of the *Century* nearly doubled when, between 1884 and 1887, that magazine ran its series "Battles and Leaders of the Civil War." Militias in almost every state found new support and began programs of expansion. (Linderman, 1987, p. 275)

> As the Civil War was incorporated in public ritual and the reputation of soldiering rose, participation in war became an important mark of merit. Honor attached itself less to courageous or cowardly conduct, battles won or lost, causes preserved or destroyed, than to one's simple presence in the war. Survival, too, by whatever circumstances actually achieved, became a source of pride. Veterans experiencing some return of confidence told themselves that it could not have been mere chance, that they must have possessed certain worthy attributes or acted in certain meritorious ways that accounted for their survival. As community ritual magnified the war, the war

began to magnify all those who had fought and lived. (Linderman, 1987, p. 277)

As accounts of World War I and II and Vietnam have come to demonstrate, the pattern of recoil from the war by its veterans in the early stages of the postwar period is common.

2. *The persistence of "heroic" imagery of war: Changing patterns, mortality, and colonial wars.* The historical revisionism of the nature of the Civil War which was eventually embraced by veterans in the 1880s recreated a heroic image of the soldier. The failure of veterans to articulate the nature of the war to their civilian compatriots certainly played a role in the eventual triumph of the civilian version of the war. As Linderman (1987) demonstrates, historical revisionism infected even such hardened generals as Sherman and those who ministered to the war's disabled in military hospital wards. For whatever reasons, soldiers found some measure of gratification long after the fact of coming together, Northerners and Southerners, to celebrate their survival in reunions and veterans organizations from the middle 1880s onward.

As the battlefields had long ago returned to nature the gruesome reality of death, such futile charges as Pickett's at Gettysburg were recreated in heroic imagery. In Western Europe this same period was a time of colonial wars, but, with exception of the short German-French War of 1867, was the period of the 100 years' peace on the continent. The silence of the battlefields at industrial centers of the United States and Western Europe was matched by a time of expansion. Warfare, as Cannadine (1982) and Linderman (1987) both argue, came to be viewed in terms of sporting contests in the early years of the 20th century. The question we should ask, is how could this view of war develop, especially in the United States after the Civil War?

In these years the West participated in an industrial revolution at home and a colonial policy abroad. In the United States, there was the expansion of the nation and the destruction of the Native American population. Those wars, including the Spanish-American War in the United States, which involved a small number of civilian volunteers, were wars fought by professional soldiers. Even the Anglo-Boer War of the late 19th century did not involve a mobilization of the domestic English population. The basic point is that the colonial wars were fought by professional armies at a sufficient distance from the homeland, and with relatively limited human costs, so that the heroic imagery of war could be resurrected, especially among the elites of these societies.

There is, however, a second part of the puzzle which is equally important. There was a profound change in the relationship of civilians to death. Changes brought about by the industrial revolution created a society in which dying became increasingly associated with old age rather than a constant scourge haunting every moment of life. As Cannadine (1982) points out, there was ". . . a spectacular fall in the death rate . . . , from 22 per thousand in the 1870's to 13 per thousand by 1910. And the simultaneous fall in fertility meant that not only were fewer children being born, but also that an even smaller proportion were dying in infancy" (p. 193). In addition, life expectancy rose from 40 for males in the middle of the 19th century to 52 by 1910. Thus, as Cannadine points out, ". . . death became ever more commonly associated with old age . . . for parents to grieve for the loss of some of their offspring, and the children to possess a vivid sense of impending death at an early age, [was] by Edwardian times . . . exceedingly rare" (Cannadine, 1982, p. 193).

Why should those changes in infant mortality and life expectancy have any significance for the perception of war? I would argue that a social order that begins to conceive of the normal aging process as uninterrupted by early morbidity or mortality by definition moves in the direction of experiencing war as out of the range of normal human experience. War, after all, is defined by early morbidity and mortality. As the early and middle stages of the lifeline came slowly but surely to be characterized by the absence of morbidity and mortality, normative civil society was beginning to define itself imperceptibly but inevitably as a system in which the experiences of war and the warrior were redundant. The rigid demarcation of civil society from war would take place over time and require exposure to destructive potential of industrial warfare. However, it is also true that in the industrial transformations of the 20th century, especially where the process has gone the furthest—the Western world— the technology which systematically reduced the role of the individual in war also systematically diminished the individual's potential to experience the rituals of pain and suffering of the earlier epochs of humankind.

The duality of enhanced life giving and destroying power of technology which began systematically to alter the human lifeline in the latter part of the 19th century has created a civilian social order which in the normal course of its functioning is entirely divorced from the experience of war. As these societies still have a propensity to engage in war, the individuals who enter war on behalf of their civilian compatriots, those civilians exposed to the routinized traumatization of war, are thereby created different, for the duration of their lives, from their fellow citizens.

The transformation of modern warfare from the domain of what DSM-III-R labels as severe stress to catastrophic stress appears rooted in these aspects of social change in industrial society which began to take shape in the late 19th and early 20th century and became gruesomely evident during World War I.

3. *The world wars and mass death.* The experience of veterans of the 20th century with technological warfare would bury forever the traditional idea of war as an opportunity for individual expressions of manly courage. Although men entered World War I with this conception of war, trench warfare destroyed the idea of heroic warfare forever (Cannadine, 1982; Fussel, 1979; Wohl, 1979).

World War II was fundamentally different from the outset. It is worth remembering that there were only 20 years between the great wars. Memories of World War I had contributed to both the growth of pacifism and, in the United States, isolationism. Entry into World War II was resisted by governments and civilians in the West until it was forced on nations by Germany and Japan. England and France waited until the invasion of Poland in 1939 and the United States refused to enter the war until attacked by the Japanese; the Soviet Union first entered into a pact with the Nazis to carve up Poland and then waited until Germany invaded Russian soil. Thus, one could argue that the human costs of World War I played a central role in the refusal of nations to use military force to deal with the Nazi threat until the guns of the enemy left them no alternative but to defend themselves or capitulate. And, in the case of a number of European nations, the defense failed and was followed by the German occupation. We can see that, by this point, nations held no illusion of grandeur or heroism of war.

World War II opened without the idea of heroism to be claimed on the battlefield in most Western nations, Germany excepted. The human toll of the war, counted in the tens of millions, proved a grisly monument to the enhanced power of technological destruction and individual powerlessness in battle. Nonetheless, this war came to be glamorized. The glamour of World War II, however, was different from that of the Civil War. At the core of the glamorization of World War II was the justification for fighting the war. The evidence of the Nazi death camps, the very early postwar film clips of mass graves, and the surviving human wreckage that the camps inadvertently failed to destroy left the world aghast. The Nuremburg War Crimes Trials which attempted, in a small way, to punish those who organized the Holocaust, forged an image of absolute evil which could justify the costs of the war. This, it seems, was not true in either the Civil War or World War I.

While all of the above is true, it should be pointed out that it was the visual media of film, far more than the literature of World War II, that was instrumental in glamorizing the war and sanitizing it. From 1945 to the present, the serious literary and scholarly works about World War II retain a sense of the massive destruction of the war culminating in the use of the atomic bomb in Hiroshima and Nagasaki. This war has had an enduring impact on mankind in general and particularly on its survivors. Those who fought that war did not, it appears from the literature, come out unscathed. Indeed, from the moment the war ended up to the present there is consistent evidence that World War II left profound scars on the frontline veterans (Gray, 1959; Jones, 1951, 1962, 1979; Manchester, 1979; Mowatt, 1979; Terkel, 1984). Thus, two images of World War II have coexisted over the years: a sanitized version and the more fundamental picture of the horrors of that war, ending in the ultimate technological destruction in Hiroshima and Nagasaki, which remains controversial even today (Lifton, 1967).

The imagery of war as wanton destruction, combined with random terror, and the merging of the civilian population with the combatants which justified depredations against civilians in particular cases and made them the targets of military strategy in general began during the Civil War. This imagery did not take firm root in general consciousness until World War I; and it was decisively ingrained in public consciousness during and after World War II. Similarly, while the systemic differentiation of the civilian soldier from his civilian roots was already evident in 1864–65, it was not until World War I that we see civilian and soldier/veteran recognition that the experience of the combat soldier was a decisive factor in the veteran's postwar lifeline. And, only after World War II did systematic scholarly evidence develop to support this view. However, it would take the Vietnam war to focus scholarly, policy, and public attention on the relationship between exposure to war stress and postwar adult development. In addition, the aging of the World War II veteran population in the United States and former members of European resistance movements has recently drawn attention to effects of war in late adulthood. The concern over Vietnam veterans has spurred researchers to pay new attention to World War II veterans. The evidence is mounting that war-stressed veterans of World War II and former members of European resistance movements continue to experience social and mental health problems. Thus, World War II and Vietnam now both drive the effort to understand the relationship between exposure to war stress and adult development.

War as "Routinized Traumatization"

War is distinguished from other catastrophic trauma because it involves the systematic destruction of human beings as the means for achieving the policy objective of collective dominance of one social system over another or among groups within social systems (in the contemporary world we label these social systems *nations*). Further, the effort to impose dominance through resort to warfare or to rebel against authority takes place over time, that is, it is a process. This second component of warfare is the basis for our assertion that the key characteristic of war trauma is "routinized traumatization" and that post-traumatic stress related to war reflects "routinized traumatization." DSM-III-R Axis IV (APA, 1987, p. 11) has adopted this conceptualization and now differentiates between catastrophic events and processes such as war.

1. *"Voluntary" participation in war and routinized traumatization.* When we think of warfare, the initial images that come to mind involve soldiers, either regulars or guerrillas, who in some sense "voluntarily" agree to participate in "legitimated" killing of some defined "enemy" and concurrently agree in principle and practice to sacrifice their own lives and those of others like themselves (i.e., comrades in arms). The ideological basis for the contemporary call to arms is usually phrased in the terminology of nationalism or patriotism to the nation state. The rhetoric of nationalism is the primary mechanism for exacting "voluntary participation" in killing and dying by those who rally to the flag; or, conversely, in intrastate conflicts (civil wars) the opposition recruits "volunteers" by asserting the age-old challenge to "legitimate authority"—"Quo Warranto" —against the current rulers. Thus, victims of a regime (what we shall refer to as "involuntary participants" in war-related events) are often transformed into voluntary participants in war.

2. *Involuntary participation in war-related events and routinized traumatization.* From my perspective, war-related events are those that expose individuals involuntarily to routinized traumatization by those who voluntarily, in the service of their society, engage in killing other human beings. Thus, I would argue that war-related events represent that class of events in which individuals and/or groups are involuntarily caught up in the destruction of warfare. How can we differentiate those who are involuntarily victimized by the routinized traumatization of warfare? The answer is clearly civilian noncombatants. There are, however, different categories of involuntary participants in routinized traumatization.

The most important group in this category are "targeted civilian populations." At various times and for varied reasons, societies decide to target certain civilian groups for destruction. Two recent examples are Jews in the Holocaust by the Nazis; and Cambodians who were thought to be infected by the modern world (such as inhabitants of cities, those trained in professions, and indeed anyone who was perceived to have been in any way Westernized), by the Khymer Rouge, i.e., victims of genocide. Targeted groups of civilians are then individuals who are in no way related to warfare per se, but are perceived to possess a characteristic which is deemed by elites inimical to the welfare of the larger social order, and in some sense the view is supported in a general way by the rest of the civilian population.

A second group of involuntary civilian victims are those perceived by one side of the struggle for societal domination to either harbor, or support the efforts of, the combatants. As modern interstate and intra-state warfare (guerrilla warfare) both are dependent upon the production of the weapons of war, food, and financial support of the civilian population, civilians are routine targets of warfare. This is especially true now because the range and destructiveness of modern weapons make it virtually imprac-tical to employ these weapons at targets such as factories without assum-ing that the civilian population will also be exposed to destruction. In the Vietnam War the protective hamlet and free-fire-zone policies were specif-ically designed to remove civilians from combatants they might otherwise have harbored. This type of civilian population is involuntarily exposed to routinized traumatization because they are in fact or thought to be in a broad sense voluntarily supportive of the war around them.

However, I will consider those civilians who pursue their ordinary lives as involuntary participants even if, in a broader sense, they provide some measure of support for voluntary participants. Especially in civil wars, these civilians are often forced to provide succor to both sides and are therefore twice victimized. In interstate war, we know by now that the appeals to nationalism and demands for cooperation with the national war effort makes resistance to war both potentially and actually a risky proposition, which exposes civilians to ostracism or, under certain cir-cumstances, to reprisals from the governing elites. Acknowledging that in this context participation in the war effort is somewhere between volun-tary and involuntary, I would argue that as long as individuals remain civilians not centrally engaged in the organization or prosecution of the war, they remain involuntary participants.

Let me add immediately that while those who bear arms are equally exposed to the call of patriotism and the threat of state violence, once they take up arms they must be considered voluntary participants in war. As I shall discuss, this scenario is based on the fact that in modern warfare the source of military personnel is derived largely from the civilian popu-lation and that war plays only a minor role in the life cycle of the soldiers.

A third group of civilians who under special circumstances may be exposed to the trauma of war (although not necessarily routinized traumatization) are those who are victimized by accidental situations of which they are not a part. For example, civilians who, because they are in the vicinity of a military action which one side or the other regards as threatening their control over the civilian population, occasionally or routinely engage in indiscriminate retaliation. The Nazis executed civilians in areas where the resistance movement had staged an attack. The victims may have been utterly indifferent to the war until the moment of attack. The survivors of such events may never again be exposed to any aspect of war.

A fourth group comprises civilians who are incidentally and temporarily caught in the crossfire of contending parties. Whether or not this group becomes victimized routinely is determined by how long the contending parties remain in the area, or whether the area has military value so that each side moves through the area several times.

Finally, there are those civilians who are driven deliberately or as a by-product of the war from their homes and forced to seek shelter elsewhere, that is, refugees. The level of force required to uproot individuals and groups from their traditional residence in practice usually means that they have been routinely and repetitively exposed to war and/or that their movement is forced in such a way as to qualify as a form of routinized trauma.

All of the above groups are involuntarily exposed to the trauma of war. However, there are adequate data only on some of these groups, such as Holocaust survivors and Cambodian refugees—that is, the civilian populations targeted for genocide. Comparatively little is known about postwar adult development of the other civilian populations described above. The key point to be made is that while exposure to a single incident may be the basis of long-term postwar trauma, in general it is those who are exposed to the process of war and traumatized repetitively and routinely who are likely to carry the burden of post-traumatic stress through their postwar lives.

The above discussion forms a basis for the contention that the framework of DSM-III-R, which differentiates event from process, provides the essential perspective for understanding human responses to war and war-related events; in other words, this class of catastrophic stressors reflects a traumatic process.

Age of Exposure to Warfare

The preceding discussion leads inexorably to another fundamental problem of dealing with aftereffects of war on postwar adult development.

The populations affected by war cover the range of age groups in any society. However, those involved "voluntarily" in war come from a smaller group of age cohorts. Even more important, research on the effects of war on "voluntary" and "involuntary" participants in war is available on age cohorts predominantly between the ages of 18 to their early thirties at the time of exposure to war trauma. This, it turns out, is also true, with some extension of the age parameters, for the survivors of genocide. Recently, research on these populations has been extended into the relationship of the war experience to late adulthood.

It should be clear that in this chapter we have to rely on the data that are available on existing populations who survived "normative traumatization." As in all developing fields, one has to make to do with available evidence and attempt to extrapolate within reasonable bounds from those data.

The Psychosocial Aftermath of War

The above discussion hinges on recognition of a historical transformation which gives meaning to the endeavor to answer the question of the effects of war on individuals within the context of DSM-III and DSM-III-R, of PTSD and Axis IV conceptions of stress (i.e., the PTSD diagnosis is predicated on the presence of exposure to extreme catastrophic stress). The symptoms associated with the diagnosis cannot be used to classify an individual in this diagnostic category if the stressor is absent.

It must be emphasized that in the contemporary context there has also been an important transition in the soldier. In a world where war was part of the normal pattern of systemic interaction, the soldier/warrior population was composed of a caste or class of individuals defined through their lifeline as soldiers; soldiering is what they did with their lives. That group represents an infinitesimal part of the modern army, which is populated by the amateur/draftee/civilian on temporary duty, whose life is temporarily on hold. Indeed, the military in America, which operates a volunteer force, presents itself as an interregnum for those who lack resources or status. Actual participation in warfare is not advertised as an attraction of military service.

As discussed before and argued elsewhere (Laufer, in press a, b), only comparatively recently in human history is it possible to talk about warfare as out of the range of normal human experience. Although warfare was not less gruesome or frightening in the past, war was not outside the range of ordinary human experience, and those engaged in warfare were most often involved in war throughout a significant portion of their adult lives.

In the contemporary world, in spite of the wars that have debased this century and marked it as the century of technological destruction, war has become an anachronism. In the West in particular, but increasingly in the rest of the world as well, slowly but inexorably the systemic basis for a developmental role through the life course for those we have called warriors is being extinguished. Our task is to attempt to understand, in the contemporary context, the impact of war on postwar adult development where the experience of war reflects neither a developmental evolution/transition within a society from childhood to adult to old age (i.e., where there is no ritually structured warrior identity) and where there is no role for the warrior identity in the aftermath of war. The same, of course, is true of "targeted civilian" survivors. These men and women reenter a civilian world in which the traumatizing environment is viewed as aberrant by themselves and their civilian peers.

Further, the adult must proceed to develop his/her lifeline in a civilian environment that largely ignores the experience of warfare as developmentally relevant to the individual or socially relevant to the institutions in which the survivor must function. Adult roles, relationships, and institutional settings have neither a functional need nor a ritual place for the war experience. Indeed, only in societies where the relationship between war and civilian life is rigidly demarcated is it possible to talk of warfare as out of the range of normal experience. Post-Traumatic Stress Disorder is a relevant diagnosis only in societies where war has become incidental to societal functioning and individual reality.

This is not to say that those exposed to warfare in prior historical settings were not subjected to severe stress; rather, it would have been implausible to talk about the stress in the current terminology of DSM-III-R. It is the contemporary assumption of war as archaic that makes the issue of its impact on survivors so critical.

I have focused on the theoretical and historical background to this presentation, on the issues of voluntary and involuntary participation in routinized traumatization, and on the emergence of war as outside the range of normal human experience because it is my contention that the voluntary participants in war (the soldier/veterans) and the involuntary victims of war in the modern world are both fundamentally civilians. It is from this perspective that I explore the impact of war on postwar adult development.

The problem addressed in this chapter, then, is the dissociated location of warfare in human development at this historical moment. The approach proposed as the background to the examination of the existing evidence on human responses to war and war-related events is rooted in the view that the central issue of postwar adult development is how civilians respond to the experience of routinized traumatization. As will be discussed below, the boundary between combatant and noncombatant is no longer a stable basis for distinguishing responses to war in the postwar period, as the lifeline of both combatant and noncombatant develops within the framework of civilian society. This particular insight requires us also to recognize that war and war-related environments are social systems which in our time are distinct from and antagonistic to civilian society.

Victimization: Victims and Victimizers

My approach to the impact of "routinized traumatization" is dependent upon the above discussion because it appears to me from the data that voluntary participants in warfare (soldiers) and involuntary victims of warfare (civilians), especially targeted civilian populations, share a common destiny in the postwar period. The experience of massive psychic trauma in the postwar world appears to have similar consequences for those who engage in victimization and their victims. The above argument must immediately be qualified by clarifying that the specific content of the traumatic recollections is fundamentally different for those who are victims and those who victimize. However, it is imperative to understand that, psychopathic victimizers aside, in a civilian world those who wield the weapons of destruction are also victims of the nationalist myth that induces their participation in human destruction, as legalized murderers of their age peers who compose the military opposition and of civilians who are exposed to routinized traumatization.

1. *Participants in genocide.* The issue of participation in genocide, the destruction of a targeted civilian population, such as those in the Holocaust and Cambodia, poses a different problem. Here we are confronted with systematic physical and psychological destruction of a civilian population by armed groups who in the context of a war need not experience combat or the stress of war (except, of course, as they participate in governmentally sanctioned and sanctified murder). Executioners, sadists, or even nonideological but cooperative participants cannot be placed in a comparable position to the victims. Thus, while I have argued that combatants on either side and civilians victimized by war share, in some sense, a common fate, it is necessary to make a clear distinction between targeted civilian populations and those killers who hunt their prey in the service of extermination of a particular group of civilians.

Participation in mass murder and sadism certainly alters the personae of the participants. Yet, as Lifton (1986) shows, the agents of state-organized extermination seem able to live simultaneously in the extermination system and the surrounding civil society. The experience of mass murder certainly alters the self systems of the participants—and does so permanently. However, what differentiates this population from other groups discussed so far is that they returned to a different civil society after the end of the war, where sanction for their prior behavior was withdrawn. In Cambodia, while a civil war continues, the participants in genocide have as yet not returned to a civilian social order. Thus, for participants in genocide it is not that they return to their civil society, but that the civil society which sanctioned their voluntary participation in murderous and/or sadistic behavior is destroyed. The issue of the destruction of one civilian social order, and its replacement with another antagonistic civil social system in which the prior conduct is criminalized and some groups of the actors are publicly stigmatized, prosecuted, incarcerated, and executed, poses a quite different set of issues than those addressed in this chapter.

2. *Garrison states.* A second exception of a different order to my conceptual approach to war trauma, is that the co-equal fate of the aggressor and victim applies only to those societies where warfare occurs as a solitary event within a limited chronological time frame for participants who are essentially civilians, but not in a garrison state. In the latter societies, there is a developmentally relevant role for those who enter into warfare through the life course. The experience of warfare can be integrated through the life course. The victim and aggressor experience post-trauma development quite differently. For example, the Northern Irish, the Israelis, and the Palestinians do not in fact fit this conceptualization. In these societies, warfare and the warrior are connected developmentally over the lifeline; and the mature warrior is central to key social institutions, personal relationships, and social roles not centered on warfare. It is nonetheless worth noting that these societies are viewed as aberrant, and within these societies the principle objective is to reach a situation in which the warrior is no longer central to civilian identity and institutions. Moreover, each of these societies has a rather high rate of emigration to places that are defined by civilian societies. It appears that given the choice, individuals within these societies seek after civilian rather than military social systems.

3. *Summary of the conceptual focus.* The focus of my analysis of the existing studies is then clearly defined. I will examine the impact of war on civilians in and out of uniform. Further, while the exploration occurs

within psychosocial parameters, the larger context in which psychosocial development occurs is the nation-state and the ideology of nationalism (Piven, 1986). What the data indicate is that the nationalist myth is no longer capable of defending even those who voluntarily participate in the routinized trauma of war. For example, as will be demonstrated in the following discussion, the common assumption that World War II veterans were immunized by the public support for their role in the "good war" (Gray, 1959; Terkel, 1984) will not stand the scrutiny of the accumulated scientific evidence.

The point to be developed in the remaining portion of the chapter is that the evidence indicates a fundamental contradiction between self/ ego/identity systems of civilian social systems and the warfare society (Laufer, in press, b).

COMMONALITIES IN POSTWAR DEVELOPMENT AMONG SURVIVORS OF ROUTINIZED TRAUMATIZATION

The evidence on veterans and civilians (essentially, targeted civilian populations under the Nazis [Jews] and Cambodian refugee survivors) who have been exposed to the stress of war shows some remarkable commonalities among civilians with the post-trauma experiences of soldiers and former members of World War II resistance movements.

Readjustment

1. *Public recognition of survivors: Veterans.* The argument after Vietnam, which was captured in Polner's *No Victory Parades* (1971), suggested that the failure to recognize the sacrifices of Vietnam veterans was a decisive factor in postwar adjustment problems. It became part of the myth about why Vietnam veterans were different from other veterans. Yet, more careful scrutiny of returning veterans from the Civil War onward, including World War II, shows that the theme of resentment against the civilian population repeats itself with regularity. Soldiers at the front share more of an understanding of the nature of war with their enemies than with the civilian population, especially when that population is not directly affected by the war (as in the United States during all four wars in this century, or Great Britain in World War I and to a lesser extent in World War II). Soldiers at the front feel hostility toward civilians safe at home, and victory parades do not in any significant way reduce that hostility.

2. *Communicating the experience of war.* The second problem that was overlooked in the Vietnam literature is that among Holocaust survivors and war veterans from the World Wars, Korea, and even the Civil War, there was a period of silence immediately following the end of the war or genocide experience. That pattern is so common that it tends to get overlooked. It is nonetheless significant. As the violence ends, it appears that those victimized need a respite before they can bear witness to the experience. In the early stages, it appears that the problem of communicating the experience to those who are innocent of the enormity of the carnage and suffering is beyond the capacity of the victims/survivors/soldiers. It is not only the abstract public, but even intimates such as wives, parents, children, or friends, who are excluded. The striking similarity of this response among veterans going back to the Civil War should mark this characteristic of the war-stressed as part of the "setting-the-self-aside" process.

If one examines reports of veterans from each of these wars, Holocaust survivors, and former members of the French and Dutch Resistance during World War II, what is evident is that the establishment of boundaries where only the initiated may enter is the first step in a lifelong separation of the "survivor" from all others he/she will encounter or to whom he/she will relate (Dane, 1984; Epstein, 1979; Morgan, 1987). Thus, the phenomenon of the war-stressed Vietnam veteran population confiding only in each other repeats the pattern of previous groups of survivors. Moreover, there is also evidence that except for those who will, after a time, publicly articulate their experience through the creation of cultural artifacts, including scientific works, the verbalization of the trauma remains by and large hidden and/or muted.

The problem which the recent literature fails to sufficiently appreciate is that language is inadequate for the imagery and the emotions of the experience. Furthermore, there is a profound problem of "signification failure" almost inevitably coming from the listener to or recipient of such messages. By "signification failure," I mean to convey two ideas: 1) that the object of the message has a limited response range, i.e., there can really only be a largely cognitive response to a phenomenological/emotive message; and 2) the listener's inability to grasp intrasubjectively the imagery associated with verbal presentation limits the possible range of response, i.e., in a fundamental sense the experience cannot be discussed, only conveyed.

The search for partners with whom the survivor can discuss the experience thus leads to a search for significant others who share the experience. Where we find male and female survivors of war and war-related events, there appears to be a tendency of the survivors to become marital partners.

In addition, there is some evidence that when both partners are survivors, intergenerational parent-child relationships around the parental experience are likely to be less stressful (Bergmann & Jucovy, 1982).

There is another element here, too: fear of being misunderstood. The survivor fears at one and the same time that the listener will not appreciate the survivor's suffering and that the survivor will be seen as presenting a case for special treatment or heroic recognition or, at worst, exposing a spoiled identity. This issue could be pursued further, but the key point is that those who actually experienced the trauma of war, voluntarily or involuntarily, and survived have for more than 100 years resisted the incursion of all outsiders into their private hell. Survivors who have allowed outsiders to enter have too often found their worst fears realized. By and large, however, as Linderman (1987) points out with Civil War veterans and applies to all those who followed, survivors have accurately read civilians' desire not to be told the real story.

3. Delayed public communication of war trauma. It is interesting that in most wars it is only after nearly a decade or more has passed that a limited group of the survivors begin to feel comfortable about telling their tale in public. And, a good part of the initial story presented through literature and later the visual arts required a sanitized version of war which civilians could grasp or point to in their own terms. Further, the mass media and elite culture diverge on their portrayal of war. In the latter, we find the baser part of the story, while in the former, war is made less gruesome. Here the Vietnam war has altered the pattern because even in the mass media the imagery of war has been overwhelmingly grotesque. Yet, here too, *Rambo* and its relatives have made at least a partially successful effort to glamorize and sanitize warfare.

4. Silence and delayed response to war stress. The silence from the survivors of war initially tends to hide the psychosocial costs from public view and from the survivors themselves. Readjustment problems are most evident among those who are physically in need of recovery. And, indeed, it is physical recovery that dominates the early stages of the post-traumatic experience. There is some evidence that in the immediate readjustment period there is little recognition of the long-term costs of the trauma even among the survivors. This can be accounted for by the need to attempt to establish postwar life patterns before they can be seen to be marred or haunted by the transformation of the survivor. In addition, there is a tendency among veterans, POWs, and even Holocaust survivors (though in the latter case, it is less feasible) to pretend it is possible to resume life in civilian society where it was left off (Laufer et al., 1981; McCubbin et al., 1976). The effort is an attempt to exorcise the past; it takes time until the survivor is in one way or another able to acknowledge that the present can only be lived by the self that has emerged from the war experience (i.e., that the survivor can never return to the former self) and that the future can be mastered only by creating a self system which acknowledges and must constantly cope with the trauma-rooted self, even as the postwar civilian self is created.

It also takes time to recognize that the dreams and nightmares are part of the self and that they recede often to return under subsequent stress. Divorce requires marriage, unemployment or job failure requires reentry into the job market, and parental failures require children. Most important, survivors require time at the end of war to recognize that "survivor" is a lifetime identity which must, nonetheless, be shed in everyday life. The tension between those two realities are common across types of survivors and across time (Archibald & Tuddenham, 1965; Bergmann & Jucovy, 1982; Brill & Beebe, 1956; Brenner, 1980; Havighurst et al., 1951; Kinzie, in press; Krystal, 1968; Laufer, Joyce, & Gallops, 1985; Laufer et al., 1981; Op den Velde, 1985).

War Stress and the Lifeline: Psychosocial Consequences

In the years after return from the maelstrom of war there is a tendency in the recent veteran literature to continue to treat social and psychological patterns of behavior that are found to be related to war stress in terms of readjustment. I wish to explicitly dissociate the following discussion from that perspective. Readjustment as a concept requires a relatively limited time frame if it is to have any substantive meaning. An alternative approach is to see the period after the initial return, conceived of as a short period of years after the end of exposure to catastrophic traumatization, as the readjustment period. Subsequently, I would argue, we are dealing with the issue of war stress and the lifeline during early, middle, and late adulthood.

A life course or aging perspective on the relationship between war stress and psychosocial development is, perhaps, a more useful approach because it allows us to determine the relationship of war trauma to the stages of the life course. The evidence indicates a need to differentiate between the effects of war stress on aging per se and the way in which the different stages of the life course are impacted by the war experience. Finally, there is a need to understand that aspects of the war experience, for the general population, more often play an episodic (Dane, 1984) than chronic role in the life course of survivors.

As noted earlier, prior to 1980, Post-Traumatic Stress Disorder was not part of diagnostic terminology. Since that time the psychopathology of war survivors has been heavily focused on this disorder. Thus, in comparing populations over time, it is necessary to examine the extent to which the symptom picture described in the PTSD diagnosis in either DSM-III or DSM-III-R is consistent with the symptom picture found in populations studied prior to inclusion of the disorder in the psychiatric nomenclature. This means that the comparisons of rates of PTSD or patterns of PTSD in war-stressed populations studied before and after the introduction of the diagnostic category will be inexact. Nonetheless, the examination of the evidence from survivors of war or war-related events is brought into clearer focus by comparing current findings with prior studies on comparable populations. Although this is certainly a significant problem, it should be kept in mind that the symptom picture of PTSD in DSM-III and DSM-III-R differ substantially. There are important differences on each of the four criteria for the diagnosis (APA, 1980, 1987):

> *Criterion A:* DSM-III requires the existence of a recognizable stressor that would evoke significant symptoms of distress in almost everyone. In DSM-III-R the person has to have experienced an event outside the range of usual human experience (examples are provided). However, the differentiation on Axis IV between "acute events" and "enduring circumstances" is of equal consequence, as DSM-III only used events in the Axis IV description of stressors, including catastrophic stress. "Enduring circumstances" clearly includes war and raises important questions as to how the trauma is to be measured. Specifically, it is no longer necessary to focus on a particular event in enduring catastrophic circumstances. Rather, it is now more appropriate to conceptualize the traumatizing process and develop measures of the traumatizing process.
>
> *Criterion B:* In DSM-III, there were three categories of symptoms while in DSM-III-R there is a fourth class of symptoms, i.e., intense psychological distress at exposure to events that symbolize or resemble an aspect of the traumatic event, including anniversaries of the trauma.
>
> *Criterion C:* In DSM-III the category was labeled numbing of responsiveness, while in DSM-III-R it is described as persistent avoidance of stimuli associated with trauma. More important, in DSM-III there were three symptom categories and the patient/respondent needed to report one symptom to be scored positive on this dimension. In DSM-III-R there are seven symptom categories and

the respondent must report three of these types of symptoms to score positive on this criterion.

Criterion D: In DSM-III this was a miscellaneous category with six symptoms, of which the respondent had to report two to score positive on this criterion. In DSM-III-R the criterion is focused on symptoms of increased hyperarousal. The number of symptoms and the scoring procedure are unchanged. However, survivor guilt, which was included in DSM-III in Criterion D, has been dropped out of the diagnosis altogether.

The "chronic" and "acute" differentiation in DSM-III has also been altered in DSM-III-R.

In summary, then, the approach to the stressor has changed significantly between DSM-III and DSM-III-R and the symptom picture has been drastically revised. The most important change, in my view, is the heavy emphasis on avoidance of stimuli associated with the trauma in DSM-III-R over DSM-III. There is, however, insufficient empirical evidence that the avoidance phenomenon plays the disproportionate role in the disorder indicated by the new diagnostic criteria. Thus, it seems highly likely that the new diagnosis will generate considerable controversy and demands for further changes in DSM-IV.

Whatever the criticism of the DSM-III diagnosis, it cannot be argued that the changes made in the symptom requirements in DSM-III-R were based on solid epidemiological and clinical studies. Therefore, the need to use best approximations of the PTSD symptom configuration in longitudinal research ought not to be considered an insurmountable barrier in comparing the effects of war in current and prior traumatized populations.

1. Early adult development: Psychopathology and behavioral impairment. The survivor population for which we have adequate data is generally in their early twenties to early thirties. Thus, the immediate postwar period usually occurs during the early years of adult development. The evidence suggests that there is a pattern of delayed onset of problems among war survivors. The research findings also indicate that problems survivors experience include significant war-related psychiatric symptoms, psychopathology, and impaired social functioning.

A review of the literature on the Holocaust (Bergmann & Jucovy, 1982; Brenner, 1980; Harel, Kahana, & Kahana, in press; Krystal, 1968) indicates rather clearly that those symptoms we associate with PTSD are present in this population. Similarly, research findings from World War II provide persuasive evidence that symptom patterns associated with PTSD are disproportionately common in World War II combat veterans (Archibald & Tuddenham, 1965; Brill & Beebe, 1956; Futterman & Pumpian-Midlin, 1951; Havighurst et al., 1951). Recent research on Cambodian refugees (Kinzie, in press) also shows that this population suffers relatively high rates of PTSD symptoms and disorder. Finally, an examination of the literature from World War I and the Civil War (Burke, 1973; Cannadine, 1982; Fussel, 1979; Laufer, in press, a; Linderman, 1987) suggests that the response of combatants during these wars was similar to more recent conflicts, from which there is more accurate scientific evidence.

The Vietnam literature, of course, provides rather specific data on the presence of PTSD symptomatology and disorder in the war-stressed Vietnam veteran population (Brett & Mungine, 1985; Brende & Parson, 1985; Card, 1983; Green & Lindy, 1985; Hendin & Haas, 1984; Laufer, Brett, & Gallops, 1985; Laufer, Joyce, & Gallops, 1985; Laufer et al., 1981; Polk et al., 1982; Wilson & Krauss, 1985). Among those studies that examined general populations, the epidemiological evidence indicates, in general, that about 20% of the war-stressed population showed evidence of PTSD in their late twenties and early thirties.

Furthermore, a number of the above studies also showed that symptomatology and disorder other than PTSD are also associated with war stress. Two examples stand out. First, in further analyses of the *Legacies of Vietnam* (Laufer et al., 1981) data, Laufer, Gallops, and Frey-Wouters (1984) found a relationship between war stress and the guilt, angry feelings, demoralization, active and passive expression of hostility scales on the Psychiatric Epidemiological Research Interview (PERI). In addition, Lindy, Grace, and Green (1984) and Green and Lindy (1985) found a strong relationship between the overall 90 Symptom Checklist scale score (SCL-90) and war stress. Moreover, they found evidence that the SCL-90 scores of combat veterans 13 years after exposure was higher than civilian survivors of the Buffalo Creek disaster two years after that disaster and survivors of the Beverly Hills Supper Club Fire one year after the fire. Furthermore, they found hostility an issue in combat veterans. On the hostility subscale of the SCL-90, the Vietnam sample was significantly higher than the Beverly Hills Supper Club sample.

In clinical diagnoses of the war-stressed Vietnam veteran population, Hough and Gongla (1982) and Green and Lindy (1985) have found evidence that PTSD is commonly associated with other psychopathology, including depression, and phobic, alcohol, and substance disorders.

The pattern of findings that war stress is associated with long-term deficits has been buttressed by findings that indicate a pervasive pattern of impaired social functioning in this population. The evidence is, at the moment, strongest with regard to the Vietnam veteran population in a broad range of areas. However, among POWs (McCubbin et al., 1976), Holocaust survivors (Bergmann & Jucovy, 1982; Krystal, 1968; Matussek, 1971), Cambodian refugees (Kinzie, in press), World War II veterans (Havighurst et al., 1951), former members of the Dutch Resistance (Erasmus Universiteit, 1986), and even among Civil War veterans (Linderman, 1987) there is evidence that the war experience is a source of stress in marital and familial relations. There is clear evidence that the war experience plays a disruptive role in marital relationships and that there is a second-generation family problem as well. The interaction between war-stressed parents and their children is a significant and problematic factor in the lives of war-stressed adults. This point is worth noting because it indicates that the ramifications of exposure to war do not end even with the death of the survivors. Thus, it is important to emphasize that there are systemic costs of war trauma experienced by individuals; that is, damage to personality systems have implications for social structure over time.

The Vietnam literature is consistent on the issue of marital strife in the lives of Vietnam veterans. Harris (1980) and Laufer and Gallops (1985) found there was a strong relationship between war stress and divorce. Furthermore, in analyses of the *Legacies of Vietnam* data, Laufer, Gallops, and Frey-Wouters (1984) and Yager, Laufer, and Gallops (1984) found a persistent relationship between combat exposure and postservice arrest and convictions. In addition, there is also evidence of second-generation effects which negatively influence family processes and parental relationship (Haley, 1985; Marrs, 1985).

Finally, on career deficits the evidence is less clear. Some of the early data showed a relationship between presence in Vietnam, especially among black veterans, and career problems (Card, 1983; Polk et al., 1982; Rothbart, Sloan, & Joyce, 1981). However, in the Rothbart et al. study (which was part of *Legacies of Vietnam*), there is no relationship between Duncan occupational prestige scale and income. But there is an indication that age of entry plays a significant mediating role in the impact of the war on veterans' careers. In the *Legacies* data set, recent analysis shows evidence consistent with Polk et al. (1982) that veterans exposed to war who enter military service at a very early age and without or with only a high school education are more likely to achieve significant educational gains in the postservice period than those who have some college education or a college degree. The implication of the finding is that in some way the war experience is more likely to stunt educational advancement of those who would be likely to benefit most from it. On the other hand, those who most need additional education are likely to receive such training. The absence of statistically significant findings on occupational attainment may well reflect educational/occupational losses of the older, more-educated veterans and the gains of the younger, less-educated veterans. Thus, in the early studies conducted during the formative adult years there does not seem to be a clear relationship between exposure to war stress and the early career of the Vietnam veteran population.

Finally, a finding in the *Legacies of Vietnam* indicates that the correlation between psychopathology and impaired social functioning is rather low. This suggests that war stress affects a broad range of the war-stressed population. The finding is of importance because it suggests that predisposing factors may influence the type of war-related disruption of adult development rather than be the cause of such disruption. Furthermore, it indicates that the lives of a large proportion of the war-stressed population are affected or altered in some manner, rather than that a small group of war-stressed veterans are severely disabled. The small, severely disabled group is also present, however, and becomes the focal group for institutional inpatient services. However, in the general population the issue is one of more widespread disruption of the early stages of adult development which debilitates but does not incapacitate the survivors.

2. War stress and the mid-life years. Studies on these populations in mid-life, especially during their forties, are lacking and, in some sense, this lacuna presents the largest gap in our knowledge. Archibald and Tuddenham (1965) studied World War II veterans, and their data do indicate a special constellation of symptoms which are consistent with the PTSD disorder. Recently, research on Vietnam veterans (Laufer, Joyce, & Gallops, 1985; Kulka, Schlanger, & Chromy, 1986) shows that the relationship between war stress and PTSD persists in the mid-life period. A current study being conducted by Kulka, Schlanger, et al., at the Research Triangle on Social and Psychological Functioning, focused on PTSD, will provide findings on this stage of the life course over the next two years.

Laufer, Joyce, and Gallops (1985) and Begans (1985) have found a consistent relationship between war stress and divorce among veterans in mid-life. What is of interest here is that these studies find no evidence that the increased rates of divorce in the Vietnam War age cohorts overall, between early adulthood and mid-life, in any way alter the relationship between war stress and divorce rates. This strongly indicates that second-generation problems are likely to emerge in the war-stressed Vietnam population.

Findings in the area of occupational attainment among Vietnam veterans indicate that over time, as men enter their late thirties and early forties, war-stressed veterans are significantly more likely to experience serious employment problems (Laufer, Joyce, & Gallops, 1985). Specifically, there is evidence that the proportion of Vietnam veterans who experienced high levels of combat are significantly more likely to become labor market dropouts and have lower earnings and occupational prestige; there is also evidence that there is more downward occupational mobility in this population as they age, i.e., moving from positions in the primary to secondary sector labor market.

On the other hand, there is as yet no comparable evidence of downward mobility among World War II veterans. However, in World War II age is clearly a major determinant of upward career mobility. The age range of World War II veterans is far broader than among Vietnam veterans. The average age of World War II veterans was 26 versus 20.5 years for Vietnam veterans. Even that does not adequately capture age differences among civilian soldiers in the two wars. Furthermore, the economies of the United States in the 1940s and early 1950s was far more expansive than in the late 1960s through the late 1970s.

There is some clinical evidence that Holocaust survivors used work as a means of avoiding psychological trauma. Thus, it is also possible that work and achievement are means of coping with mental health problems. Finally, Linderman (1987) suggests that Civil War soldiers were resentful of economic opportunities lost during their years of military service. He cites an interesting if marginally significant point that none of the great fortunes made during the post-Civil War period belonged to veterans of that war; and that the veterans were fully aware of this fact and expressed resentment against those plutocrats who evaded military service. Thus, the impact of war stress on economic achievement remains to be determined.

Green (1986) also provides some indication of the impact of war stress on coping patterns. She found, among Vietnam veterans at the border of early and middle adulthood, that those who had successfully coped with PTSD were more likely to have used Emotional Expressive and Sublimation/Comparison coping patterns than veterans who had no history of PTSD or those who remained PTSD positive. Indeed, in the posttreatment phase of a subset of the sample, Green found that those who reported getting the most out of the experience employed both of the above coping strategies. On the other hand, those who reported themselves sicker were more likely to use Event Processing, Time-out, Denial, and Turning to Religion and Philosophy coping patterns. Thus, there is some evidence that coping patterns make a significant difference in war-stressed veterans' ability to achieve better mental health.

Current research by the author on veterans with a history of employment and mental health problems in an employment training program
will provide more detailed data on the relationship between reported
Vietnam coping patterns and current coping patterns as measured by the
Lazarus Community Coping Measure. The research will also shed more
light on the relationship between war stress and current coping patterns,
PTSD, and current coping and work orientation as measured by the Work
Attitudes and Work Values Inventories. The relationship between coping
patterns in mid-life and early adult trauma is of considerable significance
because it provides us with an insight into the dynamics of war stress in
adult functioning.

Finally, we have only recently begun to acquire data on mortality
patterns among Vietnam veterans as they approach mid-life. The evidence
so far is chilling in that it suggests that among other consequences of early
adult exposure to the stress of war, veterans are more likely to die earlier
than their age peers (Andersen, 1986; Hearst, Newman, & Halley, 1986).

3. *Late adulthood.* The full implications of the encounter with war
stress for the adult lifeline emerge with the aging process, late adulthood.
Here we have some data, but they are still clearly inadequate. What we do
have suggests that aging per se may not be affected, but that the later
stages of the life cycle may be seriously affected by exposure to the stress of
war in the early adult years.

If PTSD and other psychological problems are a common response to
war stress in early and middle adulthood, it is worth asking whether the
symptomatology persists over time. Here the evidence is less clear because
few longitudinal studies were designed to answer this question. However,
Elder and Clipp (in press) found that World War II veterans currently in
their fifties and sixties from the Oakland-Berkeley Longitudinal Study do
continue to show evidence of symptoms consistent with the PTSD diagnosis.
Additional data from the analysis of the Elder and Clipp data (1987a,
1987b) also indicate that the effects of war stress on mental health persist.
A recent clinical study by Van Dyke, Zilberg, and McKinnon (1985) shows
that the onset of late adulthood can also trigger new incidence of PTSD.
From a case study, essentially they argued that the loss of occupational
function can serve to trigger psychopathology related to long-suppressed
traumatic war experiences in early adulthood. Finally, there is evidence
that reunions in later life among former comrades can trigger long-
suppressed emotional distress in a cathartic fashion (Elder, personal
communication). However, newspaper accounts of reunions in the Philip-
pines and Normandy both indicate that such reunions can also activate

mental distress that contributes to persistent symptomatology in late adulthood. Thus, there is some evidence that indicates that World War II soldiers are susceptible to new incidence of delayed or post-traumatic stress which has both positive and negative mental health implications.

The work of Harel, Kahana, and Kahana (in press) on Israeli Holocaust survivors and controls, as well as that of clinical researchers on Holocaust survivors, indicates that the trauma takes on new forms as the individual ages (Bergmann & Jucovy, 1982; Brenner, 1980; Danieli, 1981, 1985). In late adulthood the encounter with adversity may provide some mechanisms for effective coping with travails of aging. Nonetheless, as Harel and associates point out, survivors have a higher reported incidence of life crises and are more likely to worry about their children's Jewish identification than controls; they were also found to have slightly lower levels of locus of control. On the other hand, the researchers found the survivors to be more task-oriented and pressed for time than the controls, and they scored higher on instrumental, emotional coping, and acceptance of fate. Moreover, they were found to be more likely to have "slightly higher levels of communication with their children." However, it should also be pointed out that survivors had lower morale than a comparable group of controls. Finally, there were no sociodemographic differences among the groups (Harel, Kahana, & Kahana, in press).

Thus, while the Holocaust survivors do not present a simple picture, it is clear that in the late adult years there are important differences between them and their peers. The impact of the trauma has complex implications, not all of which are inimical to coping with advancing age. Indeed, some of the findings by Harel et al. are consistent with Elder's (1985) analysis of a sample of the Oakland and Berkeley females who experienced economic deprivation during the Depression. In each study there is some support for the assertion that exposure to trauma in early adulthood serves as a learning experience for coping with stress of late adulthood. However, among Holocaust survivors there is also evidence that the trauma continues to have negative mental health implications in later life.

Research on survivors of the Dutch Resistance during World War II also indicates that in their fifties and early sixties there is a reemergence of mental health and coping problems associated with exposure to war stress. There is a hint in this literature that the empty-nest phenomenon may in fact activate the reawakening of the unresolved elements of the trauma of early adulthood. The summation aspect of old age may also create a sense of unfulfilled expectations raised during the war years, exacerbate any feeling of unappreciated sacrifices or lack of recognition, and strengthen feelings of parental failure (Dane, 1984, 1985).

The above discussion indicates that the evidence on the relationship between war stress and late adulthood is as yet inadequate. A number of studies of the relationship between exposure to war stress in the early adult years and late adult development are currently underway. For example, Elder and Clipp are completing their longitudinal study of Oakland and Berkeley cohorts of the Depression who served in World War II and Korea. Elder, Clipp, and Laufer are currently reanalyzing the Terman Gifted Men Study, which has prospective data from 12 waves of questionnaires from 1922 to 1986 among men who served in World War II; and Wilson, Kahana, Kahana, and Harel are involved in a study of survivors of Pearl Harbor. In addition, Harel, Kahana, and Kahana are currently completing their analysis of aging and exposure to the Holocaust. Finally, Op den Velde, Falger, Frey-Wouters, Laufer, and Elder are conducting a study of former members of the Dutch Resistance during World War II. Thus, in the coming years there will be significant additional data on the effects of war stress on late adulthood. In those studies that are retrospective, we will be able to get at the issue of current PTSD and obtain some indication of the PTSD history over the life course. In longitudinal studies— the few where there are adequate data on military history—we will have information on life course patterns and symptom configurations which are compatible with PTSD, but evidence on the diagnostic category will not be available. These studies will also provide a wealth of detail on the relationship between war stress in early adulthood and morbidity and mortality, an area where good data are needed to provide an insight into the physical toll of the war experience, as well as the relationship between early exposure to war stress and the long-term relationship between physical and mental health.

CONCLUSION

The central points I have tried to make in exploring the issue of the mental health consequences of war and war-related events is that in social systems where war has become an aberration and affects civilian "voluntary" and "involuntary" participants (soldiers and noncombatants), both groups share a common fate. Entry into the world of war separates the survivors from their peers, who have no direct contact with that world. The catastrophic traumatization that occurs cannot be undone. The experience is, in my view, the decisive trauma in the lifeline and overrides childhood trauma, although the particular patterns of response draw on the predisposing history.

A second point is that war and war-related events have always been a very stressful experience. However, modern warfare is different from earlier forms of warfare. The essential difference between modern warfare and earlier warfare is that war has become an essentially technological endeavor whose outcome is largely outside the control of the warrior. The heroic image of the soldier described by Linderman is no longer credible. Furthermore, technology has changed the scope of war so that it can only be conceptualized as total—that is, the boundaries between civilians and warriors have relatively little meaning in modern wars compared to premodern wars.

Although warfare has become ever more destructive and unlimited, civilian experience with mortality has become, especially in Western societies, ever more associated with old age and natural causes. As death recedes from consciousness, even though the modern world is poised on the edge of destruction, everyday life in these societies is ever more removed from the experience of war. In the process, the boundaries of warfare and civilian life are sharply demarcated.

The process of demarcation between war and civil society creates an environment in which those who go to war experience a world radically at odds with their civilian lives and ego systems. The self systems constructed to function in the warfare society have no basic place in the civil society to which survivors return. Thus, the self created in war and war-related events is an anachronism in the postwar period. Thus, I would argue that war has come to be an experience out of the range of normal human experience.

Those who survive war must cope with that trauma in its variegated forms through their life course: during the readjustment period; and in early, middle, and late adulthood. How the trauma plays itself out in these stages of the life course is then a central problem in societies that have significant numbers of survivors. We are only now beginning to appreciate the dimensions of the problem and the societal significance of postwar trauma among war's survivors.

The literature indicates that depression, anxiety, and phobic symptomatology and disorder, substance abuse as well as divorce, intergenerational conflict, antisocial behavior, and career deficits are all related to exposure to war stress among veteran, POW, and targeted civilian populations. Further, there is some evidence that in these populations the largest proportion of the incidence of psychopathology occurs in early adult development, although there is also evidence that there is some incidence of psychopathology even during late adulthood. Thus, it appears that disruptive symptomatology and psychopathology are a persistent part of the life course of war's victims.

There are relatively little data—and indeed one cannot expect to get precise data—on patterns of onset of PTSD. We know that the rates of PTSD in studies over the last decade among the war-stressed population of Vietnam veterans remain relatively constant, in the 20% range. This finding suggests that onset of PTSD for the vast majority of the affected population occurs within the first five to 10 years after leaving the war environment. However, it also appears that the individuals who suffer from PTSD are by and large not chronically affected by the disorder. We make this argument based on constancy of the proportion in cross-sectional data and evidence from longitudinal studies that such constancy often indicates a shifting population of affected individuals (Elder, 1985).

Let me conclude this chapter by acknowledging that the problem I have been exploring, the mental health consequences of war and war-related experiences, is not simply a problem for individuals; it is a societal issue. The dimensions of the impact of war on the lifeline at the level of personality and microsocial institutions has to date obscured its impact on social systems (nations) and the interactions between these systems. What we have not begun to address is the pattern of interaction between individual trauma and international relations on which the decisions to make war rest and, indeed, on which hinges the survival of mankind.

The final and related point is that part of the interest in the mental health consequences of war have come from a perception, by elites, that by understanding the dynamics of war-related social and psychological pathology at the individual and microsystem level, it is possible to find a way to prevent post-traumatic stress. That search, I would argue, is the modern-day equivalent of the search for the eternal fountain of youth. The evidence points in another direction. We have it in our power to make war; we can ameliorate some of the post-war mental health problems among survivors, but we cannot eliminate them. Nor, it should be pointed out, is it possible for the mental health professions to protect survivors from lifelong, though generally episodic, experiences of intrapsychic, interpersonal, familial, and/or occupational war-related distress.

REFERENCES

American Psychiatric Association (1980). *Diagnostic and Statistical Manual of Mental Disorders, Third Edition.* Washington, D.C.: American Psychiatric Association.

American Psychiatric Association (1987). *Diagnostic and Statistical Manual of Mental Disorders, Third Edition, Revised.* Washington, D.C.: American Psychiatric Association.

Andersen, H. A. (1986). *Wisconsin Vietnam Veteran Mortality Study: Final Report.* Madison, Wisconsin Division of Health.

Archibald, H. C., & Tuddenham, R. D. (1965). Persistent stress reaction after combat: A 20-year follow-up. *Archives of General Psychiatry,* 12: 475–481.

Begans, P. (1985). *ABC News/Washington Post Poll: Survey 0186 & 0187.* New York: ABC News Polling Unit.

Bergmann, M. S., & Jucovy, M. E. (Eds.) (1982). *Generations of the Holocaust.* New York: Basic Books.

Brende, J. O., & Parson, E. A. (1985). *Vietnam Veterans: The Road to Recovery.* New York: Plenum.

Brenner, R. B. (1980). *The Faith and Doubt of Holocaust Survivors.* New York: The Free Press.

Brett, E. A., & Mungine, W. (1985). Imagery and combat stress in Vietnam Veterans. *Journal of Nervous and Mental Disease,* 173: 309–311.

Brill, N. Q., & Beebe, G. W. (1956). *A Follow-Up Study of War Neuroses.* Washington, D.C.: Veterans Administration Monograph.

Burke, K. (1973). War response and contradiction. In *The Philosophy of Literary Form: Studies in Symbolic Action* (3rd ed.). Berkeley: University of California Press.

Cannadine, D. (1982). War and death, grief and mourning in modern Britian. *Mirrors of Mortality: Studies in the Social History of Death.* New York: St. Martin's Press.

Card, J. J. (1983). *Lives After Vietnam: The Personal Impact of Military Service.* Lexington, MA: Lexington Press.

Dane, J. (Ed.) (1984). *Keerzijde van de Bevrijding.* Deventer: van Loghum Slaterus.

Dane, J. (Ed.) (1985). *Praktijk van de Hulpverlening aan Oorlogsen en Andere Geweldsslachtoffers.* Lisse: Swets & Zeitlinger.

Danieli, Y. (1981). On the achievement of integration of aging survivors of the Nazi Holocaust. *Journal of Geriatric Psychiatry,* 14: 191–210.

Danieli, Y. (1985). The treatment and prevention of long-term effects of intergenerational transmission of victimization: A lesson from Holocaust survivors and their children. In C. R. Figley (Ed.), *Trauma and Its Wake.* New York: Brunner/Mazel.

Elder, G. (1985). *Life Course Dynamics.* Ithaca, NY: Cornell University Press.

Elder, G., & Clipp, E. (1987a). *Combat experience in men's lives: The trauma and resilience of survivors.* Unpublished paper, Chapel Hill, North Carolina.

Elder, G., & Clipp, E. (1987b). *War camaraderie and enduring friendship: Influences across forty years in men's lives.* Unpublished paper, Chapel Hill, North Carolina.

Elder, G., & Clipp, E. (in press). Combat experience, comradeship and psychological health. In B. Kahana, B. Harel, & J. P. Wilson (Eds.), *Human Adaptation to Extreme Stress: From the Holocaust to Vietnam.* New York: Plenum.

Elder, G., Laufer, R. S., & Clipp, E. (1986). Military service in adult development. *NIMH Merit Grant 1986–1989.*

Epstein, H. (1979). *Children of the Holocaust.* New York: Putnam.

Erasmus Universiteit, Institute Psychiatrie (1986). Literatuuronderzoek: Medische causaliteit bij oorlogsgetroffenen 1940–1945. Unpublished manuscript, Rotterdam.

Fussel, P. (1979). *The Great War and Modern Memory.* New York: Oxford.

Futterman, S., & Pumpian-Midlin, E. (1951). Traumatic war neurosis five years later. *American Journal of Psychiatry,* 108: 401–405.

Gray, J. G. (1959). *The Warriors.* New York: Harper & Row.

Green, B. L. (1986). *Chronic coping with stress.* Society for Traumatic Stress Studies, Denver, Colorado.

Green, B. L., & Lindy, J. D. (1985). Prediction of delayed stress after Vietnam: A summary of preliminary study findings. *NIMH Final Report.* Cincinnati: University of Cincinnati.

Haley, S. A. (1985). The Vietnam veteran and his pre-school child: Child rearing as delayed stress in combat veterans. In W. Kelly (Ed.), *Post-Traumatic Stress Disorder and the Veteran Patient.* New York: Brunner/Mazel.

Harel, Z., Kahana, B., & Kahana, E. (in press). Predictors of psychosocial well-being among Holocaust survivors and immigrants in Israel. In B. Kahana, B. Harel, & J. P. Wilson

(Eds.), *Human Adaptation to Extreme Stress: From the Holocaust to Vietnam*. New York: Plenum.

Harris, L. (1980). *Myths and Realities: A Study of Attitudes Toward Vietnam Veterans*. Washington, D.C.: U.S. Government Printing Office.

Havighurst, R. J., Baughman, J. W., Eaton, W. H., & Burgess, E. W. (1951). *The American Veteran Back Home*. New York: Longsman, Green & Co.

Hearst, N., Newman, T. B., & Hulley, S. B. (1986). Delayed effects of the military draft on mortality. *The New England Journal of Medicine*, 314: 620–624.

Hendin, H. & Haas, A. P. (1984). *Wounds of War: The Psychological Aftermath of Combat in Vietnam*. New York: Basic Books.

Hough, R., & Gongla, P. (1982). Post-Traumatic Stress Disorder Structured Interview. Unpublished study, Brentwood, Los Angeles.

Hugenholtz, P. T. (1984). De Factoren bij de Instandhouding van de psychosociale Problematiek van Oorlogsgetroffenen. In J. Dane (Ed.), *Keerzijde van de Bevrijding*. Deventer: van Loghum Slaterus.

Jones, J. (1951). *From Here to Eternity*. New York: Dell.

Jones, J. (1962). *The Thin Red Line*. New York: Dell.

Jones, J. (1979). *Whistle*. New York: Dell.

Kinzie, J. D. (in press). The psychiatric effects of massive trauma in Cambodians. In B. Kahana, B. Harel, & J. P. Wilson (Eds.), *Human Adaptation to Extreme Stress: From the Holocaust to Vietnam*. New York: Plenum.

Krystal, H. (1968). *Massive Psychic Trauma*. New York: International Universities Press.

Kulka, R. A., Schlanger, W. E., & Chromy, J. R. (1986). The National Vietnam Veterans Readjustment Study: Objectives, design and initial implementation. Paper prepared for a Joint Briefing of the Staffs of the Committees on Veterans' Affairs of the U.S. Senate and House of Representatives. Research Triangle Park, North Carolina.

Laufer, R. S. (in press, a). The aftermath of war: Adult socialization and political development. In R. S. Sigel (Ed.), *Handbook of Adult Political Socialization: Theory and Research*. Chicago: University of Chicago Press.

Laufer, R. S. (in press, b). The serial self: War trauma, identity and adult development. In B. Kahana, B. Harel, & J. P. Wilson (Eds.), *Human Adaptation to Extreme Stress: From the Holocaust to Vietnam*. New York: Plenum.

Laufer, R. S., Brett, E. A., & Gallops, M. S. (1985). Patterns of symptomatology associated with post-traumatic stress disorder among Vietnam veterans exposed to war trauma. *American Journal of Psychiatry*, 141: 1304–1311.

Laufer, R. S., & Gallops, M. S. (1985). Life-course effects of Vietnam combat and abusive violence. *Journal of Marriage and the Family*, 47: 839–853.

Laufer, R. S., Gallops, M. S. & Frey-Wouters, E. (1984). War stress and trauma: The Vietnam veteran experience. *Journal of Health and Social Behavior*, 25: 65–85.

Laufer, R. S., Joyce, K., & Gallops, M. S. (1985). *Opportunities for Intervention: Employment Needs of Vietnam Veterans in New York City*. New York: New York City Vietnam Veterans Memorial Commission.

Laufer, R. S., Yager, T., Frey-Wouters, E., & Donnellan, J. (1981). Post-war trauma: Social and psychological problems of Vietnam veterans in the aftermath of the Vietnam War. In A. Egendorf, C. Kadushin, R. S. Laufer, G. Rothbart, & L. Sloan (Eds.), *Legacies of Vietnam, Vol. III*. Washington, D.C.: U.S. Government Printing Office.

Lifton, R. J. (1967). *Death in Life: Survivors of Hiroshima*. New York: Random House.

Lifton, R. J. (1986). *The Doctors of Auschwitz*. New York: Basic Books.

Linderman, G. F. (1987). *Embattled Courage: The Experience of Combat in the American Civil War*. New York: The Free Press.

Lindy, J. D., Grace, M., & Green, B. L.(1984). Building a conceptual bridge between civilian trauma and war trauma: Preliminary psychological findings from a clinical sample of Vietnam veterans. In B. van der Kolk (Ed.), *New Perspectives on Post-Traumatic Stress*, Washington, D.C.: American Psychiatric Press.

Manchester, W. (1979). *Goodbye Darkness*. Boston: Little, Brown.

Marrs, R. (1985). Why the pain won't stop and what the family can do to help. In W. Kelly (Ed.), *Post-Traumatic Stress Disorder and the Veteran Patient*. New York: Brunner/Mazel.

Matussek, P. (1971). *Internment in Concentration Camps and Its Consequences*. New York: Springer-Verlag.

McCubbin, H. I., Dahl, B. D., Lester, G. R., Benson, D., & Robertson, M. L. (1976). Coping repertoires of families adapting to prolonged war-induced separations. *Journal of Marriage and the Family*, 38: 461–476.

Morgan, T. (1987). Voices from the Barbie trial. *New York Times Magazine*, August 2, 1987.

Mowatt, F. (1979). *And No Birds Sang*. Toronto: Stewart & Granger.

Op den Velde, W. (1985). Postraumatische Stres-Stoornis als Laat Gevolgvan Verzetsdeelname. *Ned. T. Geneesk*, 129: 834–838.

Piven, F. F. (1986). Introduction. In E. Frey-Wouters, & R. S. Laufer, *Legacy of a War: The American Soldier in Vietnam*. Armonk, NY: M. E. Sharpe.

Polk, K., Cordray, S., et al. (1982). *Cohort Careers and the Vietnam Experience*. Unpublished manuscript. Eugene, OR: University of Oregon.

Polner, M. (1971). *No Victory Parades: The Return of the Vietnam Veteran*. New York: Holt, Rinehart, & Winston.

Rothbart, G., Sloan, L., & Joyce, K. (1981). Educational and work careers: Men in the Vietnam generation. In A. Egendorf et al. (Eds.), *Legacies of Vietnam, Vol. II*. Washington, D.C.: U.S. Government Printing Office.

Stouffer, S. A., Lumsdine, M. H., Williams, R. M., Smith, B., Janis, I. D., Starr, A., & Cottrell, L. S. (1949). *The American Soldier: Combat and Its Aftermath, Vol. 2*. Princeton: Princeton University Press.

Terkel, S. (1984). *The Good War*. New York: Pantheon.

Van Dyke, C., Zilberg, N. J., & McKinnon, J. A. (1985). Post-traumatic stress disorder: A thirty year delay in a World War II veteran. *American Journal of Psychiatry*, 142: 1070–1073.

Wilson, J. P., & Krauss, G. E. (1985). Predicting post-traumatic stress syndromes among Vietnam veterans. In W. Kelly (Ed.), *Post-Traumatic Stress Disorder and the Veteran Patient*. New York: Brunner/Mazel.

Wohl, R. (1979). *The Generation of 1914*. Cambridge: Harvard University Press.

Yager, T., Laufer, R. S., & Gallops, M. S. (1984). Some problems associated with war experience in men of the Vietnam generation. *Archives of General Psychiatry*, 41: 327–333.

PART II

Social and Clinical Intervention Programs

5

American Red Cross Disaster Services

ARMOND T. MASCELLI

The American Red Cross for the past 106 years has provided assistance to disaster victims in the United States and supported disaster relief operations in numerous foreign countries. As a Congressionally chartered, but independent, privately funded, volunteer organization, the American Red Cross (ARC) has grown since its establishment in 1881, and now provides a wide variety of community centered services and programs. Yet, Disaster Services continues to be a central and vital component of the organization. On the national and local community scenes, the Red Cross during its 1986 reporting year responded to 43,658 disaster incidents and expended $122,669,696 for its domestic and foreign disaster preparedness and relief activities (ARC Annual Report 1986).

The primary focus of past Red Cross preparedness and relief actions has centered on disasters caused by the forces of nature. However, increased attention has recently turned to the growing frequency of man-made or technological emergencies and disasters. Moreover, while ever careful to preserve its humanitarian ideals and values, the American Red Cross, as the steward of donated funds, must constantly seek to enhance the effectiveness and efficiency of its disaster and other program activities. Sound and appropriate business practices are being adopted, increased emphasis is being placed on human resource development, computer and other technological tools are being installed at rapid pace—all with the aim of ensuring the continued availability of reliable and high quality disaster relief services.

A brief review of the American Red Cross mission, values, service delivery structure and programs will form a framework upon which the Disaster Service program can be discussed in detail.

MISSION AND VALUES

The American Red Cross defines its mission as: "to improve the quality of human life; to enhance self-reliance and concern for others; and to help people avoid, prepare for and cope with emergencies. It does this through services that are governed and directed by volunteers and are consistent with its Congressional charter and the principles of the International Red Cross" (ARC Strategic Plan 1986). The services, management, and direction and objectives of the American Red Cross are guided by a set of five organizational values:

> *Humanitarianism:* a commitment to people and their well-being, and a dedication to people caring for those who suffer.
> *Impartiality:* the provision of services equitably and impartially to those in need regardless of their citizenship, race, religion, age, sex, or political affiliation.
> *Service Excellence:* a commitment to rendering the highest quality of service and management as stewards of the human and financial resources contributed by the American people.
> *Volunteerism:* a maintenance of the organization as a community-based, voluntary organization governed, supported, and principally staffed by volunteers who work with paid staff in all programs and services.
> *Internationalism:* a recognition that human suffering knows no borders, and that the American Red Cross is a part of the worldwide Red Cross movement through cooperation with the International Committee of the Red Cross and membership in the League Of Red Cross and Red Crescent Societies.

SERVICE DELIVERY STRUCTURE

The American Red Cross was established by Clara Barton as a volunteer association in 1881. Ms. Barton first gained national recognition for the nursing and other services she organized and provided to Union and Confederate soldiers during the Civil War. During a trip to Europe she was introduced to the Red Cross movement that was growing as a result of the impetus of Swiss businessman Henry Durant. The Red Cross movement called for the establishment of international agreements for the protection of the sick and wounded during wartime without respect to nationality, and for the formation of volunteer national societies to give aid on a neutral basis (Gilbo, 1981).

The American Red Cross received a charter from the United States Congress in 1905. The charter requires cooperation with the U.S. government in matters pertaining to the Geneva Conventions for the protection of war victims and requires that the Red Cross serve as a communication between members of the armed forces and their families at home, that the Red Cross provide aid to the sick and wounded in time of war, and that the Red Cross carry on a program of voluntary relief for victims of disaster (U.S. Congress, 1905).

The American Red Cross is a not-for-profit, nonsectarian and politically nonpartisan organization. It is not a government agency supported by appropriated funds, although the U.S. Supreme Court has confirmed its legal status as a Federal instrumentality in view of its duties to the government and people. All powers of direction and management of the organization are lodged in an all-volunteer 50-member Board of Governors. The President of the United States appoints 8 of the governors, 30 are elected by chapters at an annual convention, and 12 are elected by the Board itself as members-at-large.

In addition to providing overall direction, volunteers are also recruited and trained by Red Cross to provide most of its direct service to people. Money required to fund the Red Cross comes from the American public. Funding sources include local United Way organizations, the Combined Federal Campaign, independent Red Cross membership enrollment, special disaster campaigns, and restricted or special gifts from individuals and other contributors.

The organization's service delivery structure consists of a national headquarters in Washington, D.C.; three operations headquarters; 57 Blood Service Regions; field stations on U.S. military bases; and over 2,800 community based chapters. The national headquarters is responsible for formulating corporate goals and policies; developing new services, and improving or, if appropriate, eliminating existing ones; managing communication and relationships with national, multinational, and foreign organizations and governmental entities; monitoring compliance with resource management policies and procedures by national sector units. The operations headquarters are responsible for assessing the performance of chapters and other field units; providing technical assistance to chapters and other field units; directing service operations or fund raising activities that cannot be effectively done by chapters and other field units. Blood Service Regions are responsible for the recruitment, collection, processing, and distribution of blood and blood products.

Chapters are the primary service delivery units of the American Red Cross. Each chapter is responsible for providing Red Cross services and programs within a given geographic area. Chapters are governed by a volunteer board of directors that reside within the chapter's service territory.

In anticipation of or following a major disaster, Red Cross may establish a temporary disaster relief service delivery structure dedicated to providing uniform emergency Red Cross relief and services within the affected disaster area. The relief operation works closely and coordinates its activities with the chapters located in and near the disaster affected region.

PROGRAMS AND SERVICES

In addition to fulfilling its Congressional charter obligations, the American Red Cross has, over the years, steadily developed a wide variety of programs and services it can offer to the American public. The Congressionally mandated services to disaster victims and to the armed forces are required of all Red Cross chapters. The other Red Cross programs and services can be provided by a chapter if there is both the need and support for such activities within the chapter's service territory.

The current inventory of American Red Cross services to the general public can be grouped into five basic categories or Lines Of Service (ARC Strategic Plan 1986):

Disaster Services Line Of Service—the provision of assistance to individuals and families who have experienced an emergency that requires a rapid response to meet an urgent need. Disaster services are directed at such client groups as:

1. domestic victims of local disasters and major national disasters;
2. international disaster and conflict victims;
3. military personnel and their dependents during periods of conflict;
4. relatives of disaster victims, victims of conflict, and military personnel during periods of conflict.

Social Support Line Of Service—involves assistance to alleviate chronic, identifiable community or individual problems. Client groups receiving such services include the housebound and disabled elderly, at-risk youth, military personnel or their families who need special assistance, homeless individuals and their families. Some of the services that can be provided by a Red Cross chapter include: transportation services for the elderly and disabled; homemaker and chore services for the elderly and other special need populations; financial counseling, support group assistance, and referral services for military and civilian families; food, clothing, and shelter assistance for the homeless; youth leadership development centers and youth exchange programs.

Tissue Line Of Service—the provision of processed bone and other tissues needed for surgical procedures. At the present time, Red Cross is primarily involved in the provision of processed bone that is used in a bone graft procedure to repair or replace a patient's bone structure. The users of this Line Of Service are physicians (neurosurgeons, orthopedic surgeons, dentists, maxillofacial surgeons), members of their surgical teams, and hospitals. The key activities for this Line Of Service are donor recruitment, bone collection, processing, and distribution.

Blood Line Of Service—involves actions to assure that a safe, adequate supply of whole blood, blood components, and plasma derivatives are available for surgery and blood therapy in the Red Cross Blood Regions that geographically serve more than half the United States, and about half of the hospitals in the country. Specific Red Cross activities that support the delivery of blood and plasma products include the recruiting of volunteer blood donors, the collection, processing and testing of donated blood, and the distribution of blood and blood products. Red Cross Blood Regions also provide diagnostic and other blood-related services such as paternity testing and blood type compatibility testing. A component of this Line Of Service includes a Rare Donor Registry, A Donor Deferral Registry and Blood Resource Management System maintained at the Red Cross national headquarters.

Health And Safety Line Of Service—centers on actions designed to enhance and maintain an optimum state of health of an individual or group, prevent illness or injury, and allow persons to make informed personal health decisions. The focus of these actions is the community, work site, military installations, and schools. Major categories of health and safety activities are:

1. health and safety courses such as home and family health courses, water and boating safety skill development courses, first aid, cardio pulmonary rescusitation (CPR), and back injury prevention courses;
2. vocational training, including homemaker and home health aid training, swimming instructor and lifeguard training;

3. health and safety assistance and screening and counseling activities, including health fairs, immunization services, and the provision of first aid stations;
4. health and safety information and advertising campaign activities including Acquired Immune Deficiency Syndrome (AIDS) public education, and campaigns to recruit health and safety course participants.

DISASTER SERVICES

The American Red Cross Disaster Services program of today is in large part the product of the organization's long experience in preparing for and responding to a wide variety of emergencies and disasters.

History and Service Evolution

The American Red Cross had formally been established by Clara Barton for only one month when it responded to its first disaster—the Michigan Forest Fires of August, 1881. Ms. Barton directed the relief activities and donated $3,000 of her own funds to the $80,000 Red Cross relief fund (Knowledge Systems, 1984). Ms. Barton believed that the victims of disaster were of as much concern as the victims of war. Major disasters that would have a significant impact on Red Cross Disaster Services followed in relatively close order.

In responding to the Ohio Valley Floods of 1882, Red Cross conducted its first national fund appeal. During its response to the Ohio and Mississippi Floods of 1884, Red Cross hired its first paid field agent, Dr. Julian Hubell. The American Red Cross provided temporary housing to homeless victims following the Johnston, Pennsylvania, flood of 1889, where 2,145 died, and the organization responded to the Galveston, Texas, Hurricane of 1900 where between 5,000 and 6,000 were killed and 8,000 left homeless. The American Red Cross also provided relief supplies to Russia during that country's drought and famine of 1892, and Clara Barton led relief activities following the Armenian Massacre in 1896 (Knowledge Systems, 1984).

During the early years, Red Cross relief efforts generally centered on a few individuals (primarily volunteers) bringing in-kind relief items to disaster-affected areas. The Red Cross workers recruited local volunteers and organized a system for distributing materials to needy victims. The assistance items were either purchased by Red Cross or donated to the organization by manufacturers and merchants and included food, clothing, shoes, lumber, medical supplies, building and farm tools, seed, and animal feed.

At the time, disaster relief, as with welfare and social services in general, were considered the responsibility of local communities. Poverty was also viewed by many as the result of personal weakness or failure and government assistance, according to the adherents of Social Darwinism, was not only inappropriate but detrimental to society (Federico, 1973). Disaster-affected individuals, families, and businesses were viewed as having primary responsibility for their own disaster recovery and the role of local government was to act only when disaster aid from churches, private citizens, friends, neighbors, and family members had been depleted. Federal government involvement was infrequent, and limited to the temporary provisions of Congressional action taken for a specific major disaster incident.

Red Cross accepted the principle that disaster victims have the primary responsibility for their ultimate recovery. The organization, by experience, however, could not hold that the disaster-caused needs of individuals and families were the result of personal failing or weakness. Many victims required assistance and guidance to avoid unnecessary suffering and to facilitate their recovery efforts. Ms. Barton also did not accept the premise that government should be free from caring for its citizens following a disaster. She frequently petitioned government officials for action following disasters. As a result, Red Cross developed and has maintained the practice of disaster victim advocacy before the U.S. Congress and individual Federal agencies.

Red Cross disaster assistance was originally intended to address disaster-caused basic and immediate human needs. The organization, however, was soon called upon to also routinely provide recovery and rehabilitation types of aid. Also, during the early years, Red Cross as an "outside organization" (not of the disaster-impacted area) did not become involved with long-standing, pre-disaster community problems. Instead, the organization concentrated on disaster-caused issues and needs. Deeper community involvement by Red Cross would later follow with the growth and expansion of Red Cross chapters.

While the relief efforts of the new organization received nationwide praise and support, the Red Cross did encounter some problems in following its disaster relief and humanitarian ideals. When a severe hurricane struck Sea Island, Georgia, in 1893, no other relief organization was willing to go to the aid of the disaster victims, the great majority of whom were black. The limited financial resources of the affected region, plus the general apathy of the rest of the nation, kept Red Cross workers on the job for nearly a year. Following the Johnstown Flood of 1889, the *New York World* criticized the Red Cross, claiming that the organization had "introduced pauperism" by giving out provisions and clothing to the more "shiftless class" (Knowledge Systems, 1984).

In 1905 the disaster response and relief efforts of the American Red Cross were formally recognized by a Congressional charter which required it: "to continue and carry on a system of national and international relief in times of peace and apply same in mitigating the suffering caused by pestilence, famine, fire, floods and other great national calamities, and to devise and carry on measures for preventing the same" (U.S. Congress Act of 1905). The following year, Red Cross was asked by President Theodore Roosevelt to take charge of relief efforts following the San Francisco Earthquake. During the relief operation, the organization initiated a program of providing disaster-recovery loans to individuals and businesses. It was an attempt to provide disaster victims with needed assistance that could not easily be accomplished with in-kind assistance items. The loan program proved very difficult to administer. Moreover, many individuals both within and outside Red Cross, questioned the propriety of the organization providing loans as a form of disaster assistance. The practice of providing loans to disaster victims was never again attempted by the Red Cross.

In 1913 following the Ohio Valley Floods, Red Cross issued cash grants and merchant purchase orders that allowed victims to directly purchase furniture and pay for repair work on their homes. Eventually, the issuance of cash grants and disbursing orders to disaster victims for relief items became the primary assistance mechanism for Red Cross to disaster victims. Because of logistical difficulties, heavy manpower requirements, growing administrative and handling costs, and the benefits of assisting with the recovery of the disaster area's local economy, the distribution of in-kind disaster assistance declined in favor of the direct purchase or disbursing order approach. Gradually, in-kind assistance by Red Cross was limited to the bulk distribution of needed items that were either not available or could not be purchased for a reasonable cost in or near the disaster-affected area.

While the role and importance of volunteers would remain a corner-stone of the Disaster Services program, Red Cross proceeded to gradually increase its number of paid professional disaster personnel. To augment Red Cross volunteer and paid staff, the national director of Disaster Services in 1908 secured a cooperative agreement with other private agencies to provide social workers on a temporary basis to serve as Red

Cross disaster relief caseworkers. With the provision of direct financial assistance to disaster victims came more of an emphasis on the casework process for determining needs, formulating a practical recovery plan, evaluating available personal and community resources, and determining the amount and type of Red Cross assistance.

By 1918 the Red Cross had grown to 3,742 chapters established by communities throughout the United States. During that year an influenza epidemic struck the nation and eventually claimed 545,000 American lives. The Red Cross chapters became involved in a nationwide response to the epidemic. They helped recruit 18,000 nurses and provided equipment and supplies to local hospitals and convalescent homes (Knowledge Systems, 1984). The epidemic was the greatest disaster to affect the United States. It was significant for Red Cross as after the epidemic the chapters proceeded with a greater involvement in providing disaster relief services within their service jurisdictions.

Before the epidemic, Red Cross disaster relief operations were generally conducted following major disaster incidents and were administered by the organization's national headquarters. In the years that followed, Red Cross chapters began forming disaster preparedness committees and extended their programs by responding to limited and local emergencies. When large disasters occurred that required relief operations administered by the national headquarters, the local chapters, in addition to providing volunteer and paid staff support, formed advisory committees, composed of local citizens, to advise and guide the disaster relief operation. The chapter role as a service provider continued to grow within the Red Cross as the national headquarters became increasingly involved with policy development, planning, organizational capacity building, and providing technical assistance, support and guidance to the chapters.

The Great Depression brought a decline in the Red Cross organization and a reduction in its disaster relief efforts. A suggested Congressional grant of funds to the organization was rejected by Red Cross as contrary to its principles of independence and reliance on private philanthropy. At President Herbert Hoover's request, however, the Red Cross agreed to distribute excess government food and supplies as disaster relief in the midwest (American Red Cross, 1931). During World War II the American Red Cross regained its financial standing and immediately proceeded to rebuild its disaster relief program. For the next 25 years, Red Cross was the primary source of immediate disaster relief in the United States. During this period, the Red Cross increasingly called upon its chapters to plan for and respond to emergencies and disasters occurring within their respective service territories.

The first comprehensive Federal disaster relief legislation was passed by Congress as the Disaster Relief Act of 1950. An expansion of Federal disaster relief programs followed after the Alaska Earthquake of 1964. Congress passed PL 91-79 one month after Hurricane Camille in 1969 to further increase Federal aid to state and local governments and to individual disaster victims. The Disaster Relief Act of 1974 outlines current provision of Federal assistance for disaster planning, response, and recovery.

Each of these acts recognized the role and responsibilities of the American Red Cross in time of disaster. Moreover, the legislation also outlined and established lines of communication and areas of cooperation between Red Cross and the Federal government in the areas of disaster planning, preparedness, response and relief. The American Red Cross continues to maintain a strong relationship with such disaster-related Federal agencies as the National Oceanic and Atmospheric Administration, The Federal Emergency Management Agency, and the State Department's Office Of Foreign Disaster Assistance.

The principle effect of the Federal legislation on the Red Cross Disaster Services program was a reduction of Red Cross rehabilitation assistance and greater attention to victim emergency needs. The Disaster Relief Act of 1974, for example, provided a grant program that could issue up to $5,000 to disaster-affected families with serious and necessary needs following a disaster. In 1976, following the East Mississippi tornadoes and Typhoon Pamela, Red Cross resumed its program of rehabilitation aid under the title of Additional Assistance. Red Cross took this action for a number of reasons: The grant program was available only following the larger disasters; numerous disasters and emergencies occur in the United States for which the grant is not available; for those disasters where the grant program is activated, cases arose where the recovery needs of some disaster victims exceeded the grant limit; the grant program in many states took several weeks, if not months, to process applications. This delay hindered the recovery efforts of disaster victims. It aggravated existing problems, and often created new problems for the families.

In reviving its rehabilitation or Additional Assistance to disaster victims, the Red Cross developed standard operating procedures with the Federal government to identify disaster victims with needs beyond the grant limit, and to prevent the duplication of Federal and Red Cross assistance. Since 1976, a number of successful actions have been taken by the Federal government to improve the speed of the grant program. Red Cross continues, however, to provide Additional Assistance to disaster victims following both major and limited disaster incidents.

Basic Program Policies

Seven policy statements issued by American Red Cross Board Of Governors in July 1977 provide the current foundation for the services and relief provided by the organization's Disaster Services program. The policies are designed to provide a uniform, nationwide program capable of appropriately responding to the wide range and varieties that occur in the United States (ARC 3003, 1984):

1. The American Red Cross will maintain its status as an independent voluntary body dedicated to performing the disaster preparedness and relief obligations entrusted to it by the Congress of the United States, and will coordinate with all private and government bodies and agencies now existing or hereafter created for disaster preparedness and relief. The Red Cross at all levels will give priority to planning for and providing assistance in disasters of any size regardless of the number of families involved.

2. The Red Cross will provide a program of both emergency mass care and assistance to individuals with urgent and verified disaster-caused needs. Such care and assistance will be given on the basis of uniform guidelines and procedures. In preparing to provide such assistance the Red Cross chapter should budget for recurrent local disasters and utilize available community resources, public and private, on a preplanned basis. An active chapter must be prepared to provide assistance and must be capable of doing so whenever there is a disaster caused human need. Nationally, the Red Cross will provide necessary operational direction and support, including supplies and financial resources, when required to augment the resources of the community and chapter.

3. When government and other recovery assistance is available, Red Cross assistance will be limited to that required to meet emergency needs, and Red Cross will serve as an advocate to assist disaster victims in obtaining such assistance. When government or other recovery assistance is not available, Red Cross will assist with additional essential recovery needs.

4. The Red Cross will seek to promote and enhance the role of the Federal, State, and local governments in providing extended recovery programs that are adequate for meeting the needs of disaster victims, and will encourage participation in the National Flood Insurance Program, as well as the adoption of State and local

hazard mitigation programs such as land use regulations, improved building codes, and adequate construction standards.

5. Chapters will actively seek disaster fund contributions whenever a disaster occurs within their jurisdiction, without waiting for a request from the national sector.

6. The Red Cross may act upon behalf of local or national government disaster assistance programs on a purchase-of-service or other mutually acceptable reimbursement basis. Agreements therefore must cover only those activities appropriate to Red Cross organizational responsibilities and must be approved in advance by the Red Cross President.

7. Where suffering and want result from civil disorders and fundamental human needs are not being met, the Red Cross will participate in community action to supplement the effort of responsible civil authorities in extending emergency service and relief to the victims of such disturbances. However, when in the view of the Red Cross, fundamental human needs are not being meet and there is no indication that either the community or responsible authorities are aware of these needs or are making an adequate effort to meet them, the Red Cross chapter, with the support and approval of the national organization, will inform all appropriate authorities of the emergency needs and of recommended Red Cross proposals, and the Red Cross will carry out such proposals to the greatest extent possible.

Mass Care

Before an anticipated disaster and immediately following a disaster's onset, Red Cross will provide feeding for disaster victims and emergency workers. Mass care feeding is initially provided to all those who present themselves at a Red Cross fixed feeding site, or at a mobile feeding unit. Mass feeding activities are gradually terminated when restaurants and supermarkets resume business and the utilities to habitable homes are restored. Those disaster victims with severely damaged and destroyed homes and individuals placed in transient facilities or staying with friends or relatives are provided a standard food allowance based on number of family members and availability of cooking facilities.

If needed, mass shelters are established at pre-designated sites, in or near the disaster impacted area, such as schools and other large buildings. Shelters are intended to provide a temporary haven for disaster evacuees and those people with damaged and destroyed homes. Red Cross considers mass shelters to be necessary but nevertheless a generally unfavorable environment for disaster victims, especially children and the elderly (Drabek & Key, 1984). Most of the people who go to a shelter are soon able to return home or find lodging at the homes of friends or relatives. Red Cross also assists shelter residents with locating alternative accommodations.

Red Cross mass care assistance also includes the bulk distribution of disaster-related relief supplies. This can include cots and blankets for use at the shelters. Clean-up kits (containing mop, broom, shovel, disinfectant and soap) are provided following a flood to people attempting to clean their homes. Comfort kits can also be provided (containing personal hygiene items such as soap, shaving cream, razor). Other items may be distributed to victims to meet particular needs following specific disasters if they are needed in mass quantities and are not available at the disaster site.

Disaster Welfare Inquiry Services are also provided, when required. In this activity Red Cross seeks and provides information on individuals confirmed to have been killed or hospitalized as a result of the disaster. The information is provided only to immediate family members residing outside the disaster area. The service is in high demand following disasters with a great number of casualities and it is of particular importance to U.S. servicemen stationed overseas where information on developments in the U.S. may be vague, and the serviceman's presence may be required for funeral and other arrangements.

Emergency Assistance to Families

While the emergency needs of disaster victims are often met by the provision of mass care services, there are often emergency needs that can be more effectively and adequately addressed on an individual basis. Red Cross provides such assistance to individuals and families through an interview process where verified disaster-caused victim needs are matched with available community and Red Cross resources (ARC 3045, 1983). The interview usually takes place in a Red Cross service center established in the disaster-affected area, or it may be conducted at a Red Cross shelter, or at the victim's home. The Emergency Assistance Interview accomplishes the following tasks:

Assesses the disaster-caused emergency needs of the family;
Assists the family in identifying available personal resources;
Informs the family of available community resources or recovery resources available through government and other private agencies;

Assists the family in formulating a plan to proceed with its recovery
efforts;

Provides financial assistance for family emergency needs until other
assistance is made available from other sources.

Eligibility requirements center on verification that the individual or
family resided in the affected region, and that some disaster loss occurred
which cannot be met without assistance. The client is asked to produce
some form of identification confirming residence. Verification of home
damage is produced by the Red Cross damage assessment that was conducted
on individual homes immediately following a disaster. If the degree of
home damage and claimed client need do not conform with the Red Cross
damage assessment information, a home visit is immediately made to the
client's home to resolve the issue.

On the average, the interview takes about one hour and the interviewer,
depending on need, discusses financial assistance for the following items:
food; clothing; transportation; rent; minor repairs to make homes habitable;
utility deposits; household accessories; essential furniture; medical and
health needs; cleaning supplies; and personal occupational supplies and
equipment.

While the interview is designed to determine the immediate material
needs of a disaster victim or disaster-affected family, and to provide
information on available aid, the session is also intended to be conducted
in an empathetic manner. Victims should have an opportunity to express
and vent their feelings, and to reflect on their problems and possible
solutions. When confronted with individuals showing severe stress and
emotional reactions, the interviewer seeks the assistance and guidance of
a nurse. The nurse then secures the assistance of an appropriate mental
health professional or crisis intervention agency.

Additional Assistance

When recovery is beyond the personal resources available to an individual or family, Red Cross attempts to work with the family to address
those needs. The objective of Red Cross additional assistance is to bridge
the gap between what the family is able to accomplish for itself and what it
actually needs to resume its normal family life in the home and community.
In doing so, the Red Cross considers the emotional, physical, and material
needs created or aggravated by the disaster and limits its assistance to
those items that are essential to the family's recovery. Red Cross meets
additional assistance needs through the casework process that identifies
disaster-caused problems for consideration and provides for assistance

when other resources are inadequate. Individuals or families may be considered for additional assistance when they have disaster-caused needs and (ARC 3046):

1. Government assistance is not available;
2. Government assistance is available, but the family or individual does not qualify;
3. Personal, family, government and other resources, although they may be available, are insufficient to effect the necessary recovery.

The need for additional assistance may follow a large or a small disaster and is most likely to occur when extensive damage, material loss, or debilitating injury has occurred. More experienced Red Cross workers are assigned to provide additional assistance to families. They must have in-depth understanding and skill in analyzing and responding to disaster problems. Once all the disaster-caused needs are identified, a case recovery plan is formulated which outlines how the family will proceed with and participate in its recovery. The plan will consider the age, health, and resources of all the family members, government disaster relief assistance, and available community resources. Red Cross additional assistance is based on disaster-caused need and not loss. The intent is to assist with the family's recovery and not to completely replace losses. The types of Red Cross assistance provided directly to the family include (ARC 3046):

A. Providing for continued maintenance needs such as food, clothing, rent, and transportation;
B. Assisting the family in applying for available government assistance and acting as an advocate for the family before appropriate government agencies.
C. Providing financial assistance for the repair or rebuilding of a home, or mobile home; the purchase of household furnishings, and occupational supplies and equipment; the payment of funeral and burial costs for disaster-related fatalities; the payment of medical care arising from a disaster-caused injury or related illness; assistance with refinancing predisaster indebtedness, and the payment of predisaster debts to allow family qualification for more extensive government recovery assistance.

When a Disaster Occurs

When a disaster threatens or suddenly strikes, the local Red Cross chapter proceeds to notify its paid and volunteer staff, opens shelters, if needed, provides feeding for victims and workers, assembles damage assessment teams, and assigns a liaison to the appropriate government agencies — usually at a city or county emergency operations center. If the necessary Red Cross response is anticipated to exceed the chapter's resources, surrounding Red Cross chapters will be contacted in accordance with joint mutual aid agreements and asked to provide personnel, vehicles, supplies, and other resource assistance. Chapters, when confronted with a disaster that may exceed their resources and capacity, concentrate on providing emergency services such as mass feeding and sheltering and request immediate assistance from either surrounding chapters or the national sector.

When a disaster does occur, ARC chapters are expected to provide immediate emergency or mass care services to evacuees, disaster victims and their families, and emergency workers who are involved in the disaster. These services include feeding, establishing first aid stations and supplementing available local health services, sheltering evacuees and victims, assisting at morgues, distributing cleanup supplies providing emergency transportation, giving social services to the hospitalized and their families, securing blood and blood products, and handling disaster welfare inquiries (ARC 3027).

American Red Cross chapters vary in size and program capacity. The larger chapters are located in urban areas, while the smaller chapters are in the less populated and rural regions of the United States. The larger chapters employ a professional staff and usually provide a wide variety of traditional Red Cross and community specific programs and services. Most of the smaller chapters have either a part-time paid staff or a totally volunteer staff, and tend to provide the basic programs and more traditional services of the American Red Cross. Chapters are expected to meet the disaster needs that routinely occur within their service territory. Chapters recruit and train interested volunteers and establish formal and working relationships with disaster response government agencies and private agencies, associations, and organizations involved in disaster response.

The jurisdictional operations headquarters will also be alerted to the threatening or approaching disaster. That office will monitor and evaluate reports from chapters and other sources, and attempt to relate variety and scope of anticipated victim needs with the resources and capabilities of the affected and surrounding chapters. If needed, and in consultation with the affected chapters, the operations headquarters can commit national sector personnel, supplies, and equipment to the relief operation, along with personnel and other resources from non-affected chapters throughout the operations headquarters jurisdiction. If the resources within an operations headquarters are insufficient, additional support can be requested from the other two operations headquarters and national headquarters. When a disaster affects several chapters or when the number of disaster victims is substantial, Red Cross may establish a disaster relief operation structure and headquarters within the disaster-affected disaster area to provide uniform and standardized disaster relief assistance and services throughout the area. The relief operation headquarters works closely with the local chapters in providing assistance and allows the chapters to maintain other ongoing responsibilities such as recruiting and collecting blood.

Training System

The American Red Cross maintains a nationwide inventory of specially trained volunteer and paid staff available for disaster assignment. This is necessary for several reasons:

1. The high frequency of emergencies and disasters that routinely occur in the United States;
2. The manpower-intensive process of providing mass care and individual assistance to disaster victims;
3. The somewhat unique skills and specialized knowledge base required by effective disaster-response personnel;
4. The often physically demanding and stressful environment-of-disaster relief;
5. The limited offering of formal emergency management and associated disaster response training by colleges, universities and graduate schools.

In order to assure a consistent response in time of disaster, the Red Cross maintains a national uniform approach to disaster training. The responsibility for the initial response to any disaster rests with the local chapters. Additional Red Cross personnel, however, will be assigned to the disaster area from other chapters, operations headquarters, and national headquarters if the scope of the disaster exceeds the affected chapter's available personnel resources. In such cases, it is essential that Red Cross personnel from various units of the organization and from different regions of the country immediately relate to and work with one another. The Disaster Training System provides the "glue," or the standard operating procedures and values that allow people from diverse locations and backgrounds to suddenly come together and immediately work toward a common set of objectives within the chaotic and stressful environment of a disaster site. Moreover, the training courses are important components of the general Red Cross human resource development system which facilitates the professional and general development of both paid and volunteer staff.

The Disaster Services training courses fall into two basic categories: general preparedness training courses and relief operation courses. The general preparedness training courses are divided into three groups. The Basic Courses provide fundamental information about Red Cross and its Disaster Services program. Functional Courses prepare the participants for a specific job on a future disaster relief operation. Administrative/Supervisory Courses are designed to prepare the participants for either highly specialized disaster relief operation positions, or for the supervision or administration of a disaster operation function. The Basic and Functional Courses are frequently offered by Red Cross chapters to new Red Cross volunteers and seasoned Red Cross volunteers with no disaster experience. The Administrative/Supervisory Courses are restricted to experienced volunteer and paid Red Cross staff and are presented by certified instructors expert in the course subject matter. Red Cross Preparedness training is also provided to the personnel of other volunteer agencies and organizations which have a cooperative disaster-response agreement with the Red Cross. Some of the general preparedness courses developed and offered by the Red Cross include (ARC 3065):

Shelter Management	Emergency Assistance to Families
Disaster Feeding Operation	Supervision in Disaster
How to Conduct a Disaster Damage Assessment	Providing Health Services in Disaster
How to Estimate the Repair of Disaster Damage	Administering a Small Disaster Operation
Providing Disaster Health Services in Radiation Accidents	Additional Assistance to Families

The second basic category of Red Cross disaster training (Operational Training) involves the courses presented during actual disaster relief operations. These courses are specially prepared condensed versions of selected general preparedness training courses. They are designed to meet the specific training needs of an individual disaster relief operation. The course participants are primarily new Red Cross volunteers recruited from the disaster-affected area. Disaster-trained and experienced Red Cross paid and volunteer staff may take this training as refresher and update sessions. Since there is a need for timely and uniform assistance in the disaster area, a high motivation to learn by the participants, and the opportunity for immediate application of skills learned, this training is routinely provided by Red Cross following most major disasters.

A somewhat different type of instruction session is the relief operation orientation that is provided by all major Red Cross relief operations. All volunteer and paid staff assigned to the relief operation are required to attend the generally one-hour session that provides information on:

- the type, date and time of the disaster;
- the degree, type and extent of damage;
- the geography and culture of the disaster affected area;
- personal safety guidance;
- personal health guidance;
- stress management.

Cooperative Agreements

Working closely with other voluntary organizations has long been a part of Red Cross disaster relief operations. Often, church buildings are used as shelters and union halls are used as a hurricane watch district offices. In some communities, Red Cross has a formal agreement by which it coordinates the disaster preparedness and response efforts of many private agencies and organizations. Chapter disaster plans should include voluntary agencies within its service territory. Red Cross operations headquarters and chapters also work to ensure that arrangements are made with other voluntary agencies for mutual support and cooperation in disaster preparedness and response.

Generally, a national agreement or statement of understanding is signed by the Red Cross national headquarters and the national counterpart of the agency or organization. This document is then used by the regional and local units of both organizations to develop local relationships, plans, and operating procedures. Agreements with other private and volunteer organizations usually involve four areas:

Manpower—A variety of skills and experience can be found in the membership and staff of volunteer agencies, service clubs, and community action groups. Some people in these organizations are routinely or professionally engaged in the delivery of health and social services, counseling, recreation, child care, and food preparation. Some are bilingual and can serve as interpreters, if

needed. Many of the religious groups that have cooperative agreements with Red Cross have specialized cadres to provide mass
feeding services, pastorial counseling, care for the children of
disaster victims, including monitoring for signs of emotional
disturbance, and assistance with the repair and rebuilding of
homes for the elderly and the disabled.

Equipment & Supplies — Several agencies and religious groups have
vehicles, warehouse space, mass feeding supplies, cots and blankets,
and other items that can be used on a disaster relief operations.
With proper planning, such resources are quickly made available
to supplement or support Red Cross activities.

Facilities — Many religious groups have schools, recreation halls and
other buildings that can be used as shelters, service centers, and
aid stations. Labor unions also have similar resources and routinely
made them available to Red Cross.

Special Programs — Some church and service groups have their own
disaster assistance programs, or programs that can become resources
to disaster victims. For example, in many communities the Lions
Clubs have an Eye Glass Fund; the Mennonite Disaster Service
and the Church of the Brethren can provide skilled labor for the
repair and rebuilding of homes for elderly and disabled disaster
victims; the Church of the Brethren also has a child care program;
the Southern Baptists have mass feeding vehicles; the Seventh-day
Adventists have an excellent clothing program; the Christian
Reform World Relief Committee has trained disaster caseworkers;
the American Radio Relay League and the Radio Emergency
Associated Citizens Teams International, Inc. (REACT) have communications equipment and personnel trained to use that equipment; the Society of St. Vincent de Paul often provides household
appliances and furniture. Additionally, many communities have
"food closets" for fire victims.

FUTURE ISSUES AND DIRECTIONS FOR RED
CROSS DISASTER SERVICES

In a rapidly changing environment, the longevity of any social service
program relies in great part on its ability to accurately identify current and
future human needs; to determine its role and technical competence in
relation to those needs; and to meet or assist in meeting those needs in the
most effective and efficient fashion possible. Red Cross Disaster Services

believes that several of its current and future challenges are also shared by many government agencies and volunteer organizations active in disaster planning, preparedness, relief, and mitigation. Some of the challenges are outlined below:

I. The Allocation of Limited Resources and Service Accountability

The American Red Cross and other social service providers must be constantly concerned about both the public policy and intraorganizational debate over the allocation of limited resources. Should limited resources be directed at new programs and services—because of a new and increasing public concern—or will sufficient resources continue to be applied to long-standing programs? Should highly visible and easily provided services be funded at the expense of more substantial yet low-keyed activities? Should long-standing programs continue to be offered without a constant evaluation as to their relevance, effectiveness, and efficiency? Moreover, in considering the movement into new service areas and the revision of existing programs, can the appropriate expertise be secured or developed? Every social service agency and organization has the common responsibility of rendering services that will generate positive rather than negative affects on its client population.

The resource allocation debate has long existed within the disaster relief field and will probably grow with the increased competition for both private and government funds. Should more attention and resources be dedicated to disaster mitigation activities, directed at reducing the frequency and severity of disasters? Should efforts be geared more toward preventing problems as opposed to dealing with problems after they occur? Disaster relief produces an almost immediate and dramatic affect or "payback" in results, while disaster mitigation efforts usually require several years before realization of a somewhat less apparent and dramatic payback.

Related to the issue of resource allocation is that of measuring both the quality of services and results achieved by programs. The problems of measuring and documenting quality of social services are fairly well known, yet the issue of accountability cannot be ignored by responsible agencies. Services must be based on documented need, not subjective perception (Drabek & Key, 1984). In addition, the value and the effectiveness of the services must also be measured. An accurate knowledge of the service users and their needs must be maintained (Bolin, 1982).

In the United States, government agencies and not-for-profit organizations have long been advised to adopt business and management techniques and approaches (Macleod, 1971). The simple desire to do good and the undocumented claims of service value are not sufficient to justify the substantial acquisition and expenditure of public and private funds. Social service agencies must be better able to ensure that appropriate services are developed, that the services do what they are intended to do, and that the services are provided as efficiently as possible. The "service side" and "business side" of an organization need not be in conflict with one another if there is an acceptance of the organization's values and a joint understanding and support of its goals.

Red Cross Disaster Services is proceeding along three basic tracks in its attempts to enhance accountability and improve the efficiency of its service delivery system:

1. The use of computers on major disaster relief operations to enhance the quality and reduce the time required for data collection, analysis and reporting (Congressional Research Service, 1984); and to facilitate the process of dedicating more relief operation personnel to providing service as opposed to handling paperwork.

2. The development of procedures with Federal disaster assistance agencies to simplify the process of disaster victims applying for Federal disaster assistance, and to reduce delays in disbursing Federal disaster relief.

3. The development and use of decision support systems and decision analysis techniques to support decision-making in disaster planning and response activities, to enhance training and development activities, and to reinforce analysis techniques used for the postoperation analysis of disaster relief efforts (Gass & Chapman, 1985).

4. The development and implementation of a Disaster Operations Assessment System designed to judge the performance of major disaster relief operations from the perspective of Red Cross personnel, disaster victims, local officials, and allied private and government disaster-response agency representatives. This system is currently in the field test stage. It is intended to identify trends and to provide data supporting the formal establishment of disaster relief operation service and performance standards (Knowledge Systems, 1984).

II. Hazardous Materials and Technological Disasters

In the middle 1970s, the Red Cross nationally noticed a sharp rise in the number of hazardous materials incidents that required the emergency sheltering of local residents. Subsequent research suggested the potential magnitude of hazardous materials mishaps in the United States and the likelihood that local emergency management officials and Red Cross Chapters would continue to be called upon to respond to hazardous materials accidents. For example, in 1982 it is estimated that 1.5 billion tons of hazardous materials were transported by land, sea, and air in the United States. Truck transport, by a fleet of 467,000 trucks, accounted for more than half of the hazardous materials shipments (Office Of Technological Assessment, 1986).

The growing awareness of hazardous material transportation problems was reinforced by "fixed site incidents" such as Love Canal and Three Mile Island. In Times Beach, Missouri flood waters spread the hazardous chemical dioxin throughout the flooded area, thus generating fear of a possible health hazard for both returning residents and disaster relief workers. Hazardous materials, technological disasters, or man-made disasters (Weinburg, 1986) often present a set of challenges not always encountered with natural disasters:

1. Many technological disasters are rapid in onset, with little or no advanced warning. They can occur at fixed sites that use, store, manufacture or produce as a by-product hazardous substances; they can occur anywhere along rail lines and rivers; and they can occur on any street, road, or highway used by motor haulers. Hazardous materials incidents demand immediate, knowledgeable action by local officials, by the first responders, and by the general population. Local first responders must be able to control or contain the material at the incident site. Appropriate official warnings must be issued rapidly to the local residents, along with any required health protection guidance. When needed, evacuation orders must be promptly given and evacuation assistance provided, if needed. These critical decisions must, in many cases, be made in minutes, not hours.

2. Technological disasters often require special training and expertise that is not always readily available to local governments and first responders. Accidents involving various types of hazardous materials must be approached in specific ways to prevent injury to the first responders and to avoid actions that exacerbate the situation. Many local governments and their agencies have limited training resources. The Office Of Technology Assessment in its report to the U.S. Congress stated that it is people problems—inadequately trained personnel and poor coordination and communication—rather than technological shortcomings that cause accidents, injuries, and environmental damage.

Moreover State programs affecting hazardous materials transportation are characterized by a multiplicity and diversity of regulations and areas of jurisdiction. Responsibilities are divided among State utility commissions and transportation, health, environmental, and emergency response agencies. Great variations among state laws and regulations exist as well. Finally, there are no nationally accepted standards for establishing an acceptable level of emergency response skills or for certifying instructor qualifications (Office Of Technological Assessment, 1986).

3. It is difficult for many communities to secure sufficient data to conduct an appropriate risk analysis, which is a basic element of any emergency or disaster preparedness and response plan. In most cases, the risk analysis is based more on assumption than fact. Information is difficult to secure on the number and type of hazardous material disasters that occur in the United States each year. Many agencies keep records and collect information, but the process is geared to their individual responsibilities and needs. Information on the type and amounts of hazardous materials that pass through a given community is also difficult to obtain (Research And Special Programs, 1986).

4. In many cases it is difficult to prove scientifically that a specific illness or birth defect is the result of a specific exposure to a specific substance (Weinburg, 1986). This is particularly true when the illness surfaces several years after the incident. There is a great deal of public fear and distrust over hazardous materials incidents. In part, this fear is the result of uncertainty regarding hazardous materials and their potential health-threatening characteristics. In some cases, this fear may be reinforced during hazardous material accidents when public officials appear unsure of the danger the incident presents for the general public. The fear generated during and after an incident may require special attention not normally provided or available after a natural disaster.

The success or failure of Red Cross to plan for and respond to such disasters will depend in large part on its work with local emergency management officials, community leaders, and concerned citizens to jointly deal with these challenges. On the local level, Red Cross chapters have been working with local government to prepare for and respond to such disasters. On the national scene, American Red Cross has been working with the Environmental Protection Agency, the Federal Emergency Management Agency, the Department Of Transportation, the Chemical Manufacturers Association, and others. Clearly, more needs to be accomplished and more interested organizations need to become involved. The topic of technological disasters is a complex and serious one that is further compounded by an abundance of political, economic, and emotional overtones.

III. Timely Mental Health Services for Disaster Victims and Stress-Management Assistance to Disaster Relief Workers

In the past, Red Cross, like most disaster and emergency response agencies and organizations, focused its attention on providing emergency material assistance to disaster victims. While the emotional impact of a disaster on residents was somewhat acknowledged, little clear direction, both within and outside Red Cross, has been provided. The provision of crisis intervention and allied counseling services was believed to be beyond the capabilities of most Red Cross disaster-response workers. In some communities, local mental health officials have shown a keen interest in and capacity for providing such services to disaster victims immediately after a disaster's impact (Cohen & Ahearn, 1980). This has been supported by the availability of Federal funds to States under Section 413 of the 1974 Disaster Relief Act. Yet, the rapid provision of crisis intervention and counseling services to disaster victims has not been consistent.

Red Cross has yet to decide how it will proceed regarding crisis intervention and counseling services as an element of its Disaster Services program. If the services are needed and they are not being provided by others, then Red Cross would seriously consider offering the services after developing the appropriate personnel resources. If, however, the services are provided routinely by a competent organization following a disaster, then Red Cross would cooperate with and support that organization to the fullest extent possible.

The effects of stress on disaster relief workers has also been acknowledged in the past by Red Cross, but little has been done to directly address the issue. Stress was considered more or less an accepted part of disaster relief work that should be handled in a variety of individual and personal ways. In response to the writing of Jeffery Mitchell (Mitchell, 1985) and others, a greater appreciation and understanding of stress and its negative effects have steadily grown within Red Cross (Eby, 1985).

As a result the organization has initiated a series of actions designed to reduce stress (particulary system-generated stress), and provide the opportunity for individuals to develop effective strategies and techniques for better managing and coping with stress:

1. Personal stress management education is now available to disaster-response volunteers and paid staff. The sessions cover personal recognition of stress and strategies and techniques for coping with stress.
2. Stress recognition and intervention training is now included in Disaster Services supervision training. All supervisors have the

responsibility of monitoring stress reactions experienced by individuals assigned to their unit.

3. Stress monitoring is conducted throughout the disaster relief operations by Disaster Health Services. Information, counseling, and advice are also provided by Disaster Health Services on coping with and adapting to stress.
4. The implementation of internal processes and procedures to address worker stress:
   (a) An orientation conducted on each major disaster relief operation, for both paid and volunteer staff, which includes a component on stress awareness and management.
   (b) A debriefing session conducted by a supervisor when each paid and volunteer worker completes a disaster assignment.
   (c) An outprocessing session conducted by the staffing office of a relief operation to discuss any issues or concerns that may not have been resolved at the debriefing session.

While the above actions have been implemented, Red Cross will continue to pay greater attention to worker stress and to more appropriately address the issue of stress and its impact on disaster relief workers.

Clearly, more work needs to be done in this area. The successful coping with stress by each Red Cross disaster relief worker will have a positive impact on the provision of services and assistance to disaster victims.

REFERENCES

ARC 3003 (1984). Administrative regulations. *Disaster Services Regulations and Procedures.* Washington, D.C.: American Red Cross.

ARC 3027 (1980). Chapter preparedness and disaster operations. *Disaster Services Regulations and Procedures.* Washington, D.C.: American Red Cross.

ARC 3045 (1983). Family service—Emergency assistance to families. *Disaster Services Regulations and Procedures.* Washington, D.C.: American Red Cross.

ARC 3046 (1985). Family service—Additional assistance to families. *Disaster Services Regulations and Procedures.* Washington, D.C.: American Red Cross.

ARC 3065 (1981). Disaster training system. *Disaster Services Regulations and Procedures.* Washington, D.C.: American Red Cross.

American Red Cross (1986). *American Red Cross Strategic Plan: FY 1987–1991.* Washington, D.C.: American Red Cross.

American Red Cross (1931). *Relief Work in the Drought of 1930–31: Official Report of Operations.* Washington, D.C.: American Red Cross.

Bolin, R. (1982). *Long-Term Family Recovery From Disaster: Family Recovery Project Final Report.* Washington, D.C.: National Science Foundation.

Cohen, R., & Ahearn, F. (1980). *Handbook for Mental Health Care of Disaster Victims.* Baltimore: Johns Hopkins University Press.

Congressional Research Service, Library Of Congress (1984). *Information Technology for Emergency Management.* Washington, D.C.: U.S. Government Printing Office.

Drabek, T., & Key, W. (1984). *Conquering Disaster: Family Recovery and Long-Term Consequences.* New York: Irvington.

Eby, D. (1985). A disaster worker's response. In *Role Stressors and Supports for Emergency Workers* (pp. 119–125). Washington, D.C., DHHS Publication No. (ADM) 85-1408.

Environmental Protection Agency (1985). *Chemical Emergency Preparedness Program: Interim Guidance.* Washington, D.C.: Environmental Protection Agency.

Federico, R. (1973). *The Social Welfare Institution.* Lexington, MA: D. C. Heath & Company.

Gass, & Chapman, (Eds.) (1985). *Theory and Application of Expert Systems in Emergency Management Operations.* NBS Special Publication 717 Department Of Commerce. Washington, D.C.: U.S. Bureau Of Standards.

Gilbo, P. (1981). *The American Red Cross: The First Century.* New York: Harper & Row.

Kates, R. (Ed.) (1977). *Managing Technological Hazards: Research Needs and Opportunity.* Boulder, CO: University of Colorado.

Knowledge Systems (1984). History of disaster services. In *Study Of Disaster Services Of The American Red Cross.* Syracuse, NY: Knowledge Systems and Research, Inc.

Macleod, R. (1971). Program Budgeting Works in NonProfit Institutions (pp. 123–133). *Harvard Business Review,* No. 71510. Cambridge, MA: Harvard University Press.

Mitchell, J. (1985). Healing the helper. In *Role Stressor And Support For Emergency Workers* (pp. 105–118). Washington, D.C., DHHS Publication No. (ADM) 85-1408.

Office Of Technological Assessment (1986). *Transportation of Hazardous Materials.* Office Of Technological Assessment, Congress Of The United States. Washington, D.C.: Congress of the United States.

Research & Special Programs (1986). *Report to the Congress on Hazardous Materials Training, Planning and Preparedness.* Washington, D.C.: U.S. Department of Transportation.

U.S. Congress (1905). *U.S. Congress Act Of January 5, 1905,* as amended, 36 USC. Washington, D.C.: Congress of the United States.

U.S. Congress (1974). *Disaster Relief Act Amendments of 1974.* PL 93-288. Washington, D.C.: Congress of the United States.

Weinburg, A. (1986). Science and its limits. In *Hazards: Technology And Fairness* (pp. 9–23). Washington, D.C.: National Academy Press.

6

Clinical Intervention After Natural and Technological Disasters

JAMES L. TITCHENER

The sight of a ruined community, with houses, churches, trees, stores, and everything wrecked, is apparently often consciously or unconsciously interpreted as a destruction of the whole world. (Wallace, 1956)

From research and clinical experiences in many disasters, mental health professionals do know what the needs of disaster victims are; they do not know precisely how to meet these needs. This chapter offers ways of addressing the massive public health consequences of the devastation to communities and individuals of unleashed water, fire, wind, lava, and quake. A psychodynamic approach to stress resolution is presented, using a holistic view that victims' reactions to disaster transform personality and character.

These reactions are preshaped in each case by repressed memories of infantile trauma and by the transforming effects after disaster of unconscious fantasies about what has happened. The elements in this approach include: 1) specifics of community event or catastrophe; 2) specifics of individual traumatic experience; 3) likelihood of matching traumatic reaction with earlier reaction to helplessness and unresolved conflict; and 4) the influence of unconscious fantasy as an obstacle to crisis resolution.

The approach involves working from the outside in, beginning with interventions at the community or system level and proceeding steadily inward toward the core of individual transformation and how it might be modified. There is little in the literature that can be cause for optimism. We seem capable only of showing the immensity of the suffering from catastrophe and the possibly lifelong scars and chronicity of the effects; we have very few examples of actual instances of reversal of pathogenic consequences. However, the publication of this book is an encouragement to continue the struggle.

What is the basis for the view presented here? First, there was our research on the human experience of surgical illness and surgery, followed by studies of the long-term psychological effects of physical injury. Next came our studies of survivors of the Buffalo Creek dam break of 1972 and of the Beverly Hill Supper Club fire on Memorial Day, 1976, where 165 persons perished out of an estimated 3,500 present on the night of the fire. Our Cincinnati Trauma Study Center teams also worked in a consultative capacity with four areas devastated by tornados: Zanesville, Ohio, in 1974; two cities in Iowa in 1977; and Wichita Falls, Texas, in 1978. Finally, we worked with victims of the panic-crush at a rock concert of the "Who" in Cincinnati in 1980, which resulted in 11 deaths, bereaved parents and families, and problems in many attendees who had feared for their lives and felt responsible for the crush in the crowd that night.

In addition to personal experience, the chapter draws upon reports and data from research on the volcanic eruption of Mount Saint Helens in 1984, the earthquake in Mexico City in 1985, and various bushfires in Australia occurring in 1985. Each of these events has its own character, structure, and progression, as well as vast differences in the aftermaths that the community, the families, and individuals had to cope with when the acute disaster was over. Compare the racing fires in the Australian bush with the high, railroad-train speed of the wall of black water crashing down the Buffalo Creek Valley in West Virginia. No two disasters are alike; they all have different meanings and varying potentials for stimulating unconscious fantasy. In order to prevent mental health problems and initiate intelligent intervention, a wise assessment and imaginative, informed analysis of every disaster must be made at the outset and revised as necessary in order to provide an effective response.

PREPAREDNESS AND PUBLIC POLICY FOR NATURAL DISASTERS

Some disasters are almost entirely psychosocial, exacerbated by impulsive and poorly considered political action or by the media (e.g., Love

Canal and Three Mile Island). Some disasters are not entirely psychosocial events, but principally so, like the Beverly Hills Supper Club Fire and the collapse of a hotel mezzanine in Kansas City. Most of the money won in a suit by the Buffalo Creek inhabitants was for "psychic impairment." It is hard to think of a disaster that would *not* be principally psychosocial. The massively fatal Bhopal chemical leak comes to mind, and one could argue that sheer death would overshadow the psychological factors. But that is absurd; emotional effects reached as far as West Virginia, because Union Carbide had similar plants there.

What is meant by "principally psychosocial"? It is not my intention to minimize the other elements: losses of loved ones, injury, mutilation, illness, and property damage. The intent is to point out that psychosocial aspects are *always* there interacting with the other troubles, making them worse or being made worse by them. It is time, then, that a psychiatric professional should be working at the highest levels of planning and policy making for disaster preparedness and at the highest levels of directing the community response and reintegration when a disaster has occurred. The psychiatrist needs to have an entirely different role than ever before, not working as a consultant or adviser but having directorial responsibility and voting powers in decision making. Mental health teams have usually been included in organizations for disaster preparedness, with a psychiatric coordinator and a disaster assessment apparatus listed, *on paper*, in the organization manual. However, there have been many occasions when the mental health coordinator was not called when a mock disaster was staged, and there seems to be a degree of lip service with regard to psychosocial factors.

There is an exemplary study showing the need for the new direction advocated here. Erikson's (1976) research of Buffalo Creek is a report of hundreds of hours of interviewing by one sociologist in the Valley, of his observations of the physical effects of the massive dam break on the geography and manmade structures there, and of the history of Appalachian social and political institutions and how they responded. A great deal can be discovered about disaster from Erikson's work, but certain findings and principles will be described briefly. Erikson's report begins with a detailed and vivid account of mountain culture and its history with comment from observers of that culture, both past and present. One of his important findings concerns the organization of mountain culture, with its special attention to the sense of connectedness. The mountaineers are fiercely democratic in their relationships, resulting in a decided lack of stabilizing, ongoing social institutions. There were no social institutions or political organizations in Buffalo Creek to orient and regulate relations with others. There are still few community structures on which urban life depends, except possibly for the construction of a firehouse donated by the law firm representing the inhabitants in a suit arising from the disaster. But Erikson found one social institution that is usually less clearly delineated than church, police, agencies, or medical clinics; it was the institution of neighborhoods. Erikson describes the *necessity* for the mountaineer of a neighbor and a neighborhood, with their physical representation being the front porch.

It is said that if you were thirsty, you could walk into a neighbor's house and from his refrigerator take a can of beer or juice. Along the road in the Valley there are signs telling you that you are entering "Braeholm" or "Lorado," but these places have no existence in any formal sense. They are simply where "I and my neighbours live." Erikson calls this a "thin fabric" of organization absolutely essential for the maintenance of a sense of connectedness and for combating feelings of isolation in mountain culture.

This disaster shattered the feelings of being connected to others, and feelings of hopeless isolation were a strong feature of the clinical pictures that emerged. Four thousand were left homeless, and many would never be able to return home because of total devastation. The latter were forced to live for months in federally owned mobile homes. Huge trailer parks were set up in various locations and families were assigned in a random fashion to a selected trailer in a certain park. The destroyed neighborhoods were not reestablished, as they might have been, so the only social institution underlying connectedness was rendered dysfunctional and individual isolation worsened. One woman said, "It has changed from the community of paradise to Death Valley."

The Buffalo Creek disaster is a striking example of what can go wrong when psychosocial considerations are not included in public policy making following disaster. It reinforces the position stated earlier that mental health professionals must be included at the highest level of decision making.

THE MEDIA AND DISASTER

Those who have been on the site of a disaster right after its occurrence will never forget its emotional atmosphere, though there may be differences from one event to another. Erikson (1976) said that disaster "refers to a sharp and furious eruption of some kind that splinters the silence for one terrible moment and then goes away. It is extraordinary—a freak of nature, a perversion of the natural processes of life" (p. 254).

The atmosphere of these times is extremely tense. Information—most or all of it conflictual—springs from everywhere. Rumor leads to anxious and outrageous conclusion and then vanishes to be replaced by its opposite. Confusion and chaos reign.

Palacios et al. (1986) report on the traumatic effects of mass communication in the 1985 Mexico City earthquake. Their study is important because it shows the traumatic effects of the media on the masses in this century's most serious earthquake. It also demonstrates how the media can function therapeutically instead of traumatically. In that quake almost 20,000 persons perished and approximately 300,000 persons were directly affected. Yet these psychoanalysts' thesis is: "The main traumatic agent was the mass communications media. It can be said beyond doubt that such a psychological catastrophe could not have occurred in earlier centuries" (Palacios et al., 1986, p. 279).

The authors' analysis of the massive trauma created by the media begins with the weakening of the ego's synthetic capacity through the physical stress and repetitive mourning processes as time and losses continued. Second, they turn to Mexico's chronic financial and social instability as further strains on ego organization when the quake came to the Valley. Finally, the authors point to the impact of the sudden shattering of the dependability of mother earth, as seen in the overflow of traumatic stimuli from radio and television "too rapid to be effectively neutralized" (Palacios et al., 1986, p. 280).

This is a familiar psychological sequence seen nearly every day in microcosm, and in macrocosm with every disaster. "The media" is a human enterprise, too, reacting to the chaos and terror like everybody else. Commercial television stations "flooded their audience with untold images of agony and death, the most poignant and gruesome often being transmitted several times over a short period" (Palacios et al., 1986, p. 282). Television and radio have an even greater significance in Mexico than in the United States because of the less modern telephone system which was all but shut down by the quake. Initial reports and a barrage of reports for the next 72 hours spoke continually of tragedy and terror, with more to come. Everybody in rural and urban areas in the Valley of Mexico heard and saw all of it. The authors note the reports detailed the mutilation, death, and devastation, and that it all happened suddenly, unpredictably. But radio and television reports did not offer the compensatory information that 99.8% of the city was unscathed (300,000 directly affected out of 20,000,000 inhabitants).

These psychoanalytic observers of the consequences of the media-handling of events, in the days and weeks following, found in many inhabitants a profound reactivation of both normal and pathological mourning processes, i.e., previously forgotten reactions to loss: "What the combined force of the earthquake itself plus the lengthy exposure to sensational, biased reporting succeeded in doing was to pry open long forgotten psychological graves" (Palacios et al., 1986, p. 283). Thus the images from the media not only overwhelmed, disorganized, and threatened but also touched unconscious fantasy and repressed conflicts from the past, adding more to ego weakening.

The Mexican psychoanalysts asked themselves the question, If the media were so powerful in ego-weakening, destructive ways, couldn't the same power be used in an ego-strengthening, productive way? They found that media could indeed be used productively.

Radio spots were broadcast with messages that countered the sensationalism and panic-oriented style of the prior approach. Communicating was advised; the stress response syndromes were described and training courses for all sorts of personnel and crisis intervention groups were announced.

A panel of four psychoanalysts appeared on television before an estimated audience of 20 million people. They stressed five points in everyday, nontechnical language: 1) expression of thought and feeling is necessary (get the "bottled up" persons in groups with expressive persons); 2) minimal use of tranquilizers is indicated, to be used for rest only; 3) rescue workers should be on line only a few hours at a time; 4) debriefing, cognitive and affective, should be conducted periodically for all emergency personnel; 5) awareness of heroic performances by emergency personnel, and of the underlying unconscious guilt motivating some of the enthusiasm, energy, and self-sacrifice, should be addressed immediately.

The mental health personnel involved in preparedness and direction of official disaster responses should be alert to how the radio, television, and print media are responding. It is important to remember that the media are geared to the numbers of people they reach, not to how they reach them or to the quality of the information provided. It has been said that broadcast networks do not sell news programs for advertisers, they sell audiences; and newspapers sell readers to their advertising buyers. National and regional workshops on this topic could and should be launched to persuade and educate the mediapeople about their public role following disaster and about mental health responses in the disaster recovery effort.

COPING AND CRISIS INTERVENTION

The psychosocial definitions of the word "cope" are varied and controversial, yet the concept is essential to any understanding of stress on group and individual levels, essential to thinking about adaptive and pathogenic responses to disaster, and fundamental to the theory and practice of crisis intervention. Coping may be looked at in three ways: as ego process, that is, as a defense mechanism; as a collection of personality traits; or as situationally defined by special demands, such as illness.

Coping seen as a defense mechanism entails a hierarchical arrangement from the more adaptive defenses to the more primitive defenses. In disaster research and practice we debate whether denial, projection, and other defenses are adaptive or primitive, or are on the progressive or pathogenic ends of the continuum. It will take future research to ascertain the answer. When looked at as a defense system, coping is seen as a means of tension reduction rather than as a means of problem solving. Folkman and Lazarus (1980) maintain that both the tension-reduction and problem-solving sides of coping activity need to be considered.

Coping patterns are also seen as traits. This notion implies a stability of patterns, not easy to demonstrate. Finally, the situational approach to coping focuses on the behavior patterns that appear with regard to events such as illness, loss, or disaster.

In my view it is most useful for crisis intervention to depend on all three approaches: 1) to consider a hierarchy of defenses from shades of denial, through projection to isolation, from primitive and pathogenic defenses to protective and readily adaptive ones; 2) to view a stability of defensive and adaptive patterns forming traits in individuals and whole cultures (compare the Mexicans and the West Virginians); and 3) to look at different modes of coping according to different situations (compare fire with flood with earthquake). Each situation requires a slightly different repertoire of coping techniques.

Lazarus (Lazarus, Kanner, & Folkman, 1980; Lazarus & Launier, 1978) defines two processes mediating the relationship between the person and a stressful environment: appraisal and coping. There are three types of stress appraisal: harm–loss, the situation in which something bad has already happened; threat, in which the harm–loss is anticipated; and challenge, which is sudden opportunity for mastery or gain. These types are parallel to the psychodynamic differentiation between depression, in which the problem has already occurred, and anxiety, in which it seems that it will.

Coping involves "the cognitive and behavioral efforts made to master, tolerate, or reduce external and internal demands and conflicts among them . . . (serving) two main functions: the management or alteration of the person-environment relationship that is the source of stress . . . and the regulation of stressful emotions" (Folkman & Lazarus, 1980).

Ego-disorganization results in part from overly rapid and excessive stimulation creating a permeable stimulus barrier, followed quickly by activation of repressed fantasy, traumatic memories, unresolved grief, rage, and guilt. All of this, from the harm-loss and threat of a disaster, will block, impair, or overwhelm individual and group appraisal and coping. Crisis intervention is considered to be the most efficient way of on-site restoration, repair, or strengthening of coping processes.

The issue of crisis intervention can be approached in two ways: 1) by concluding that every disaster response team should be ready to do it; and 2) by describing how it has been done. The first approach will be touched upon briefly. The crisis intervention team should consist of a coordinator and at least two backup coordinators to assure there is one in town at all times. A disaster assessment group should include professionals ready to evaluate from the field the nature of the catastrophe, what can be expected from it, and how much and what sorts of interventions are required.

Three points can be made at the outset in describing crisis intervention: It takes courage to do it; one will not want to do it more than once in a lifetime (well, maybe three times at most, since we benefit from experience); it can be easily avoided.

Most administrators will never plead with psychiatrists, psychologists, or social caseworkers to set up a crisis intervention team with potential for effective functioning. Tokenism is more the rule. When there is a disaster, the administrators usually believe psychological treatment is unnecessary; ineffective; an effete, distracting luxury; and, worse, harmful. The latter is the strongest and least conscious feeling. It is a defensive position of the administrator or disaster response leader motivated by unconscious fear and guilt, colluding with similar defenses in the victim.

In the large-scale fire disaster to which the Department of Psychiatry, University of Cincinnati, provided crisis intervention, we were told by authorities that we need not come, that our help would be unnecessary, that the clergy would do all that we could do, and, "We'll call you if you can be of help."

The fire at the Beverly Hills Supper Club started in the early evening in some electrical circuits, smoldered a while, and then burst for freedom near midnight to flare furiously on the walls, decorations, and furniture of this sprawling, ornate, and luxurious nightclub. More than 3,000 patrons were in the club that night, scattered among the several rooms, enjoying wedding dinners, fashion shows, faculty reunions, and alumni parties. The fire raced toward the central performing area where 1,800 were gathered. People had little time to escape through the exits and windows. There was panic; the exits soon jammed and 165 persons perished with few casualties of lesser kind. The killer was smoke inhalation and the toxic fumes from the burning of decorations and upholstery. This was a modern-day version of Coconut Grove (Lindemann, 1944).

The psychiatric resident on call in the Emergency Room of the University Hospital was told to expect hundreds of casualties and called one of us to inquire what he might do with such numbers of "traumatic neuroses" (Lindy & Titchener, 1983). A group of about 10 professionals, most with some disaster experience, gathered after midnight to consider what was happening. With Coconut Grove and other disasters to haunt us, we expected, from what we were hearing on the radio and on television, an overwhelming number of burn casualties and those with other injuries, as well as distraught families, to arrive in ambulances at our hospital. The phenomenon of media panic described by the Mexican psychoanalysts was taking place several years before they wrote about it, though this media effect was less extensive and short-lived. By early morning we had a few burn and inhalation casualties and we were working with them and the families who had joined them at the hospital.

We realized then that there were many deaths, few physical injuries, and a large number of people who had been through a harrowing experience, including a vivid, unforgettable vision of human chaos, panic, and grotesque death. The ambulances were used for the dead: "Stacked like cordwood," so many said. Our discussion at the hospital was intense as we sorted through the information we were getting. Finally, we saw that the need for psychiatric services was at the place where the bodies were being transported.

The temporary morgue was located in a large armory in Kentucky where there was sufficient floor space to lay out 165 corpses. They were all there by 4:00 p.m. on Sunday morning May 30, 1976; the location was publicized. A family could come there and find one of their own by first checking at a desk where the already-identified dead were listed. Then they were taken to the armory floor to confirm the identification or search through all of the bodies to find someone presumed dead or missing and thought to have been at the Club.

No one who was there will ever forget it. It was like some gruesome dormitory with 165 shrouded sleepers under bright lights, large fans whirring, and softly murmuring clusters of people circulating and pausing at each sleeper to raise the shroud. The soft voices were the rule, once in a while broken by an outcry when a discovery was made.

Early in the morning two of us went to this armory, and within an hour phoned back a recommended plan for the next four days. We would have teams of six to eight mental health professionals working four-hour shifts with families and individuals arriving to identify their dead loved ones on the armory floor and at the desk where the dreaded list was steadily being compiled. The FBI and corps of dentists were at work by the second day on the technical side of identifying bodies. A surviving fingerprint or a bit of jaw would sometimes solve a problem of naming a corpse.

Our teams worked on the armory floor, at the official desk, walking up and down the rows with family and friends, and in any rooms they could find for privacy in the neighboring buildings, and, the next morning, under trees and on the lawn of this spacious facility. Our style, as one of my colleagues put it, was to be "aggressively hanging around." Since then, in many conversations and conferences on this topic, I have never heard the actual process of crisis intervention more accurately described. Almost anyone can do crisis intervention if someone wants you to do it. It takes a dedicated, skillful professional to do it in reality when no one wants you to do it. Everyone—victims, systems, government, authority, and emergency worker—wished urgently to avoid the emotional issues and they earnestly believed to do otherwise was harmful and dangerous.

This contagious attitude even struck us. The same worker who coined the above phrase was walking with a family on the armory floor. She was wearing sandals because it was a warm evening in late spring. Her bare toe brushed the toe of one of the shrouded bodies. In fear she leapt forward, landing on the back of a family member, crying out reflexively, "Can I help you?"

"I'm all right, why don't you help yourself, sister?", the man replied. Later she was of great help when the man broke down in tears at the desk after hearing his brother's body assigned a number for identification processing.

Various mixtures of terror, rage, and grief caused difficulties with coping. Everyone who came to the morgue had reason to fear loss. Many found they were right and so they experienced loss. Many of those who came had been at the Club and knew what had happened, and probably had been in some danger themselves, in addition to having accompanied the deceased person. By the next day there were already news stories indicating fault and blame for what had happened. It is difficult to decide whether such early speculation helps or hurts. It surely stirs up the anger, but anger would be there anyway, and to have a target focuses the feelings and provides release. Multiple suits were settled or won in the courts, mostly in favor of plaintiff-victims, in the next decade.

Disbelief and underreaction by people who were told, and who could see, the Club was on fire, was a major factor in the loss of life of so many, according to the fire insurance underwriter experts who did a thorough study of what happened at Beverly Hills. Part of the legend of Beverly Hills is that the famous busboy who came on stage to a microphone with first word of the fire was thought to be part of the act. The busboy story is legendary but also true.

Disbelief afflicted nearly all of the victims and bereaved in the four days at the temporary morgue. It seemed to them a nightmare, from which they would awaken soon, and that could not be happening. The earliest comments were, "You are struggling to believe what your eyes and ears are telling you, while the emotional side of you rejects what you hear and see," or words to that effect. It was a message stated more than once in several different ways.

Allied with disbelief was, "Why am I not crying or screaming when my (son, brother, sister, father, or other loved one) is lying there on the floor of this place? I must be a horrible, uncaring, and selfish person. Actually all I feel is dead. I wish to God I would feel *something!*"

An intervention was, "This (numbing) of feelings is a normal reaction. It will pass as you slowly absorb the loss of your (loved one) and the mourning process will naturally begin. Perhaps it would help for you to tell me what your (loved one) was like or what he(she) was to you. You will need to do a lot of that in the weeks to come."

Many of the bereaved asked, "I cannot stop trembling, though I feel nothing inside, why?"

A likely intervention was, "Do you think you might be trying to contain your anger and fear? Most of us worry about control of such feelings. You knew your son was playing in the orchestra. How did you first hear of the fire?"

Some persons had irrational feelings of responsibility from having suggested the club visit or for not resisting the idea strongly enough. We offered counterexplanations but did not argue, believing that further thought would be needed on such important and painful ideas. In later work with survivors we came upon much more burdensome, sometimes totally incapacitating, guilt feelings arising from some of the dramatic events the night of the fire (Green et al., 1983).

There were practical problems confronting everyone. Our work was short-term. We had to be resourceful for a high proportion of families who were paralyzed by the death of one of theirs. It is impossible to relate all that we did and said about this common phenomenon. Sometimes a family would go home for a while and return, and for other families additional family members were called in.

Fifty-five psychiatric faculty in teams of six or eight worked alone or in pairs over the four days the morgue was open. Most of the bodies were identified by Sunday evening, leaving a half dozen families tormented with uncertainty as the dentists, FBI, and radiologists worked. Each team was debriefed after its shift and participated in the briefing for the oncoming shift. We used Grand Rounds time for one final and massive debriefing.

PSYCHOPATHOLOGY AND DYNAMIC PSYCHOTHERAPY FOR THE CASUALTIES OF A DISASTER

There is still much to learn from long-term studies about the extent and frequency of individual psychopathology from a disaster. Findings with regard to Buffalo Creek (Gleser, Green, & Winget, 1981) and Mount St. Helens (Murphy, 1986) are too complex to summarize here. We can say that, depending on a range of factors, there is bound to be a certain amount of incapacity and disability lingering in the victims and some of it unfortunately becomes permanent (Titchener, 1986). In the remainder of this chapter the pathogenesis of stress response syndromes in the survivors of natural disasters and the methods advocated for treatment will be discussed. We not only find it possible to benefit individuals, and therefore families, in this activity, but we also learn more in depth about what goes on in the minds of the survivors. This clinical understanding helps us greatly with whatever else we do, including social planning for overall disaster response and crisis intervention programs.

Wichita Falls, Texas, has been a thriving industrial city, host to a major Air Force facility and a center for petroleum and cattle. In 1978 the most devastating tornado in U.S. history hit Wichita Falls with winds up to 254 mph.

Ms. J.C., 26 years old, a separated mother of two small children and in nurse's training, lived with a girl friend and her children. They listened to the warnings telling them that they were probably in the tornado's path. J.C. and her friend thought that their apartment building was unsafe and that their car would somehow be safer. So they set out with the children in their vehicle. Along the route to wherever they were headed they found they could flee no further because of the clogged traffic, and now the storm was near! They hurried out of the car and were encouraged to find a culvert under which they could hide. They could not and did not consider that the culvert was exactly aligned with the tornado's direction, so instead of protection they got concentration of the wind's force. Their situation was somewhat like being in the muzzle of a cannon about to be fired.

J.C.'s little son was killed instantly in her arms by a piece of wood flying through the culvert. Her friend survived the first blast but after a brief quiet came the second. During the second onslaught all she heard was a brief, soft outcry and her friend was dead when the silence returned, J.C. had compound fractures of the arm and shoulder holding her boy. Her daughter had minor injuries. J.C. was taken to the hospital where she was in training. We saw her there. The apartment they left was intact.

Terrible regret, remorse, guilt, emptiness, sadness, and terror were all evident in this expressive and insightful young woman. She would require help to work them through. It took a free-thinking friend to reveal her anger to her by raging for her, during a visit to her room, against the unfairness and injustice of what had happened.

Somewhat in contrast, a 40-year-old supervisor of electricians working the deep mines in Buffalo Creek, married father of three children, was an effective leader. He was innovative, respected, resourceful, spending himself heavily for others' welfare in the months of recovery after the flood. His family had lost their home to the flood but he stood in the road with a rifle when a Housing and Urban Development (HUD) trailer was trundling by, and directed it onto his own property where it remained when I visited him, the only one outside of the dismal trailer parks. A year later he was withdrawn, isolated, melancholic, and suffered severe headaches. He was drinking and smoking heavily. From being a prized and respected supervisor of electricians he had now been fired because of his anger, irritability, and absenteeism. It seemed when the heroism was over, so was he.

These cases are cited because each gives initial evidence of the seeds of future impairment. They are examples of survivors who would benefit and be spared permanent disability through a psychotherapy specifically designed for their conditions.

A theoretical point of view of the nature of the stress response syndromes is needed in order to design therapy. The theoretical approach utilized here is based on the work of Freud (1920), Horowitz (1976), Lifton (1967), Krystal (1975, 1978), on the thinking of a co-worker (Lindy, 1985, 1986), and on some of my own work (Titchener, 1986; Titchener & Ross, 1974).

Henry Krystal (1978) in a long and thoughtful review called "Trauma and Affect" reworks Freud and Breuer's original contributions to the concept of trauma and follows the development of the concept through decades of change (Breuer & Freud, 1893; Freud, 1919, 1920, 1926). There are two components necessary for a post-traumatic stress disorder (PTSD): The unbearable situation is the first component, consisting of fright, the infantile situation of helplessness, and the feeling of loss of control of self, affects, and situation. The situation is shattering of ego function and ego mediation with the environment. Bad as all that sounds, it is not the disorder we would be treating after disasters in individuals such as the two cases cited above. The second component is necessary for the reaction or condition to take form.

What we really treat and try to work through is not the unbearable situation, but what Krystal (after Freud) called "the dynamics of pathogenesis." This is the intrapsychic and pathogenic processing of the traumatic event: originating conflicts; mobilizing a steady accretion of defense systems to ward off conflict; beginning fears of recurrence of the unbearable situation, evoking several forms of regression including somatization, feelings of weakness, and conservation withdrawal.

The question can be asked: Why doesn't the pathology simply go away, disappear with time? After all, that is what most people once believed, and some still do—that the condition passes, only malingering continues. The medical expert witness for the defense in the suit of 700 inhabitants of Buffalo Creek Valley against the Pittson Mining Company responsible for the ill-fated dam said that the diagnosis of traumatic conditions had to be wrong since the problems would have cleared by the time of evaluation, that what were clinical findings must have been due to something else. If he had had his day in court, if the case had not been settled out of court, the judge or jury might have agreed with him. If he had won, both medical and legal history would have taken quite a different turn.

What causes the stress response syndrome? Horowitz (1976) says that after *outcry* (his word for an unbearable situation and ego disorganization), a process of *intrusion* (unbidden, forceful, distracting and depleting images, flashbacks), oscillates with *denial* (the reflexive attempt to drive the images out of mind). This cycling of intrusion and denial takes over, displacing and modifying many mental functions. This inner struggle between intrusive imagery, which is maintained by an "overactive memory storage" put there by the traumatic experience, and denial continues until some resolution is achieved or until it takes a firmer grip on the individual and he or she is in "frozen overcontrol" from the rigidifying accretion of unconscious defense mechanisms intended to reinforce the denial side of the inner war. The individual has unconsciously surrendered or, at best, has sought a negotiated peace with the traumatic memories in the form of intrusive images. Without intervention this surrender or negotiated peace is lifelong and generally is accompanied by isolation, withdrawal, and somatization.

The function of traumatic dreams is to achieve an adaptation to or moderation of the trauma through a reliving of the experience in vivid detail, with the goal of undoing its frightful aspects and regaining control of chaotic affects. Along with symptoms, especially the intrusive imagery, the dreams tell us the nature of affects accompanying traumatic memories. In these ways we know of the challenge to the ego's functioning. What is the source of the challenge?

We may turn to the cognitive aspect of an emotion, i.e, what it means to the individual having it, or as Krystal puts it, the "story" behind an affect. Each time an affect comes out too frequently from the overactive memory storage, becoming an intrusive image or thought, it represents a challenge and will provoke conflict because of what it means to the survivor.

For example, feelings of anger at the causes of the disaster carry with them the challenge of fears of loss of self-regulation and of retaliation from the environment. The feelings of increased vulnerability and the very secret "glad-it-was-not-me" feeling, which accompany nearly every bereavement, are among the cognitive challenges that excite the intrusion-denial cycles and require ever more depleting defensiveness until resolution comes about.

Some recent work by Weiss and Sampson (1986) pertains to the effects of unconscious "pathogenic beliefs." This concept is especially relevant to stress response syndromes of survivors of disaster. These grim and constricting beliefs are as unconscious as repressed wishes and fantasies, but quite separate and opposed to potentially gratifying thoughts. Some examples of pathogenic beliefs with relevance to disaster are: 1) "There is something wrong with surviving"; 2) "It is so awful I must deserve it" or "I must have done something wrong to make it happen"; and 3) "Anger will consume me and kill me or there will be retaliation, even for just thinking." These grim and constricting beliefs preexist the disaster, but are brought to life in their primitive and archaic forms by the affect charge and the regressive effects of the trauma and its ego disorganization.

Lifton (1967) describes psychic numbing and "death imprint" as changes in character structure and function which preserve the stress response syndrome and prevent resolution unless they are approached directly and resolved.

Returning once again to Krystal's work in our search for a treatment specific to the post-traumatic stress disorder (PTSD), we take up once more the "challenge of the affect experience." We have discussed the cognitive meaning of the affect; it may be totally objectionable (the feeling of triumph over the deceased), or it may be counter to grim and constricting beliefs preexisting the disaster but brought out partially by the stress (the loss is a deserved punishment), or it may just be terrifying (anger will consume or retaliation will occur). The second form of challenge is the "affect storm," a fear of losing control of emotions and of being plunged into the unbearable feeling of helplessness.

A couple lost a young child to the flood caused by the Buffalo Creek dam break; the mother had been visiting in another part of the Buffalo Creek Valley that morning. Both parents admitted to interviewers that they could not talk about anything emotional, let alone the child loss, because of the expectation of breakdown in the other person, which would be intolerable for the self, and, in their perceptions, would escalate the interaction of the two into an affect storm.

These challenges—the cognitive component of emotion and the fear of emotional dyscontrol—evoke defensive warding off. Each move toward defensive rigidity requires a further move in the same direction, because each increase of isolation and withdrawal decreases confidence in the ego's capacity to mediate and leads to even more aversive action. We have discussed elsewhere (Titchener & Kapp, 1976) the process of psychic conservatism in the declining stress response syndrome. Moving toward frozen overcontrol, the individual sacrifices recreation, socializing, sex, relationships, work, vocation, religion, and perhaps finally, marriage. The defense systems become arrayed to fend off *at any cost* any stimuli with the slightest chance of evoking either component of the affective challenge and thus the recurrence of new forms of the unbearable situation.

We have excellent opportunities for treating the stress response disorder arising from disasters as well as from other causes when the treatment is started early or any time up to two years after the disaster. The opportunity drops off sharply and the work becomes much more difficult as defense and resistance harden; the stress response disorders may be transformed from the easiest psychological conditions to treat to the impossible to treat.

At the present time psychiatry is enthused about brief focal psychotherapy. Gustafson (1984, 1986) reviews critically the main approaches, in addition to describing his own theories and methods. Luborsky's *Manual* (1984) is also pertinent.

This therapy, brief and focal, is what the stress response survivor of disaster should have, partly for tactical reasons but also for strategic ones—to keep the therapeutic nose to the grindstone. Most authors, including this one, advise 20 hours of such therapy. The therapeutic dyad should be able to work through in 20 hours the dynamics of pathogenesis—the focal issue posed by the traumatic experience of the disaster—or find that the ego disorganization exposed so many ancient conflicts that more than 20 hours will be needed, probably with someone other than the focal therapist.

We need a manual for the treatment of these conditions, particularly for the purpose of organizing and training a corps of therapists to respond after a disaster to a fairly large number of survivors. We would like them to employ a reasonably standardized sequence or algorithm so that we could determine what effects could be achieved by a focal and specific method of therapy for disaster disorders. Although we do not have a manual, we have three general theoretical approaches toward a unified and agreed-upon technique. The primary sources for a theory of psychotherapy for the stress response disorder may be found in the work of Mardi Horowitz and his associates (Horowitz, 1976, Horowitz et al., 1983), in the work of Jacob Lindy (1985, 1986), and my own thoughts in this chapter.

First, Horowitz contributes the ideas of information processing of the *content of the disorder*, and consequently of what needs to be changed for relief to occur. Second, Lindy emphasizes the relationship of therapist and patient, with the importance of a feeling of safety in the relationship for therapy to proceed. Lindy also describes more clearly and usefully than anyone the notion of discovering the links between details of the event and conflict in the present experience of the patient. Third, I make use of the other two conceptualizations in order to find a focus, immersing the therapeutic dyad in the trauma to find a way of waking up from the nightmare to find it really did happen.

Krupnick and Horowitz (1981) conceptualized a limited number of warded-off pathogenic themes in stress response syndromes and in cases of bereavement. Using the clinical experience of their research group they wrote out 20 such themes and ranked frequency of these warded-off themes during brief psychotherapy. They transcribed brief psychotherapy for 10 traumatized patients and 10 bereaved patients. They devised rules for rating the presence or absence of all 20 themes and went to work on the transcripts. Their results are useful almost every day in clinical work and in supervision.

Three warded-off themes stood out in each patient group and they can be easily kept in mind. In the therapy for the bereaved the warded-off themes were feelings of responsibility for the death, increased feeling of vulnerability, and sadness. A fourth theme was shared with the traumatized group—anger at the deceased for abandoning the self. Sadness is conscious in most, but not all, bereaved persons.

This research shows that most patients will not confront all of the loss nor the full meaning of it. Horowitz points to the principal task of grieving: correction of the cognitive discrepancy between the enduring internalized object representation and absence of the object in the outside world. "I am always expecting her to walk in the front door and take off her coat. I keep seeing her on the street, only to find it is someone else!"

Themes in the traumatized group were anger over the cause of the event and anger that it happened "to me" or "us" and not "to others," feeling responsible for what happened, fear of recurrence, and guilt over surviving when others did not. Note the opportunity for conflict in and amongst these warded-off themes: when feeling responsible that one did not do all that could have been done to save the deceased, the survivor may be angry at the lost object and at the same time "selfishly" concerned about his own mortality.

While doing evaluation and therapy, it helps greatly to have these themes in mind and to look for signs and derivatives of them to interpret to the patient because they are pathogenic and will remain so until clarified. The feeling of excessive responsibility, for example, is partly wishful and also has developmental roots in childhood trauma.

Lindy (1985, 1986) views the stress syndromes and its treatment as principally an intrapsychic or cognitive process. He contributes the idea of the *trauma membrane*, a structural and dynamic phenomenon. He states:

> Finally the patient has become particularly sensitive to people and relationships unfamiliar with the particular absurd meaning of the trauma, and who might serve to stimulate unwanted traumatic memories without a constructive context for healing. He has developed many ways to keep such people outside his "trauma membrane." Conversely, fellow survivors who truly know the absurd reality of what happened always have a special place of closeness within that "membrane." (1986, p. 200)

The above accurately describes the dynamic changes within relationships of the survivors of disaster. Also, it shows the main problem of treatment and the best way to solve it. The therapist must find a way to the boundary of the trauma membrane, then enter it, "and maintain that as *healing space* (italics mine), dosing or titrating traumatic memory and its processing" (Lindy, 1986, p. 201).

By his or her accepting scientific attitude—positive, friendly neturality—the therapist encourages the patient to open the trauma membrane, where he or she is trusted to carefully confront the absurd and unique experience of the trauma. (Why "absurd"? Because such things just cannot happen! The psychiatric casualty of a disaster catches that look of disbelief on everyone's face to whom he or she talks.) The therapist works on his or her own reactions to what is being related. The patient will always know when the subject is changed for the benefit of the *therapist*, not for the benefit of the psychotherapy, and then the trauma membrane will grow back at least for a while. However, we must also note the membrane comes back when there is too early or too much insistence on recovering traumatic details, though this error is in my experience far less frequent.

In addition to his emphasis on the therapeutic relationship, Lindy notes the process of *linking*, occurring naturally in the stress response syndrome, and of great value in psychotherapy. These are unconscious connections between a significant or highly significant detail of the trauma and a usually insignificant detail in the patient's present life. A Beverly Hills casualty reported having to leave a picnic the summer after the disaster, because someone was irritating her. "Was the irritation that bad?" She had had the same bugging from the person before, but this time it really enraged her, though the abrasiveness of the other was expectable. The clinician knew of the patient's experience at the Supper Club and had made it a part of him. He asked about the food at the picnic. The usual hot dogs and hamburgers. Did the cooking put out an odor? That was enough to bring back the patient's conviction of responsibility for deaths at the fire as she had smelled the smoke a few moments before. Perhaps worse, the cooking odor brought out the grotesqueness of death at Beverly Hills where human flesh was cooked. It was a while before she could attend barbecues, but the clinician demonstrated to the patient how the meaning of everyday events were reflecting the traumatic details in a pathogenic fashion. These links form a therapeutic thread to follow in the treatment of the psychiatric casualties of disasters.

Recently, a psychiatric resident in a seminar on the stress response syndrome and its treatment doubted strongly that the treating doctor could ever know what the victim had been through. It is probably neither wise nor helpful for the psychotherapist to have the victim's dreams, as I did after repeated trips to Buffalo Creek, but the story of the event and the individual experience of it must be imparted carefully and patiently, without any illusions. I use the word "imparted" advisedly as it covers the sharing aspect of communication. Once imparted by patient to doctor, the story resides there and is a part of the doctor. He or she uses his thorough familiarity (sometimes more than the patient remembers) to compare details of it as their meaning is reflected in reaction to current events.

Through this detailed and intimate knowledge of the patient's experience, the therapist can find in a few hours a few conflictful themes which can usually be expressed in one theme. The working through of this overall theme and its meaning in current living are what the therapist addresses in the remaining hours of brief and focal therapy with the disaster victim. As was stated earlier, if the individual's ego disorganization is such that more hours are needed, further work should probably be undertaken by another therapist.

REFERENCES

Breuer, J., & Freud, S. (1893). Studies on hysteria. *Standard Edition*, Vol. 2. London: Hogarth Press, 1955.

Erikson, K. T. (1976). *Everything in Its Path*. New York: Simon & Schuster.

Folkman, S., & Lazarus, R. S. (1980). An analysis of coping in a middle-aged community samples. *J. Health and Social Behavior*, 21: 219–239.

Freud, S. (1919). Introduction to psychoanalysis and the war neuroses. *Standard Edition*, Vol. 17: 205–210. London: Hogarth Press, 1955.

Freud, S. (1920). Beyond the pleasure principle. *Standard Edition*, Vol. 18: 1–64. London: Hogarth Press, 1955.

Freud, S. (1926). Inhibitions, symptoms, and anxiety. *Standard Edition*, Vol. 20: 75–176. London: Hogarth Press, 1959.

Gleser, G. C., Green, B. L., & Winget, C. N. (1981). *Prolonged Psychological Effects of Disaster: A Study of Buffalo Creek*. New York: Academic Press.

Green, B. L., Grace, M. C., Lindy, J. D., Titchener, J. L., & Lindy, J. G. (1983). Levels of functional impairment following a civilian disaster. The Beverly Hills Supper Club Fire. *J. Clin. & Consult. Psychology*, 51: 573–580.

Gustafson, J. P. (1984). An integration of brief dynamic psychotherapy. *Am. J. Psychiatry*, 141: 935–944.

Gustafson, J. P. (1986). *The Complex Secret of Brief Psychotherapy*. New York: W. W. Norton.

Horowitz, M. J. (1976). *Stress Response Syndromes*. New York: Jason Aronson.

Horowitz, M. J., Marmar, C., Weiss, D. S., DeWitt, K. N., & Rosenbaum, R. (1983). Brief psychotherapy of bereavement reactions. The relationship of process to outcome. *Arch. Gen. Psychiatry*, 41: 438–448.

Krupnick, J. L., & Horowitz, M. J. (1981). Stress response syndromes. Recurrent themes. *Arch. Gen. Psychiatry*, 38: 428–435.

Krystal, H. (1975). Affect tolerance. *The Annual of Psychoanalysis*, 3: 179–219.

Krystal, H. (1978). Trauma and affect. *Psychoanalytic Study of the Child*, 33: 81–116.

Lazarus, R. S., Kanner, A., & Folkman, S. (1980). Emotions: A cognitive-phenomenological analysis. In Plutchnik & Kellerman (Eds.), *Theories of Emotion*. New York: Basic Books.

Lazarus, R., & Launier, R. (1978). Stress-related transactions between person and environment. In L. Pervin & M. Lewis (Eds.), *Perspectives in Interactional Psychology*. New York: Plenum Press.

Lifton, R. J. (1967). *Death in Life: Survivors of Hiroshima*. New York: Random House.

Lindemann, E. (1944). Symptomatology of acute grief. *Am. J. Psychiatry*, 101: 141–148.

Lindemann, E., & Cobb, S. (1943). Neuropsychiatric observations after the Coconut Grove fire. *Annals of Surgery*, 117: 814–824.

Lindy, J. D. (1985). The trauma membrane and other clinical concepts derived from psychotherapeutic work with survivors of natural disasters. *Psychiatric Annals*, 15: 153–160.

Lindy, J. D. (1986). An outline for psychoanalytic psychotherapy of post-traumatic stress disorder. In C. R. Figley (Ed.), *Trauma and Its Wake, Vol. II*. New York: Brunner/Mazel.

Lindy, J. D., Green, B. L., Grace, M. C., & Titchener, J. L. (1983). Psychotherapy of survivors of the Beverly Hills fire. *Am. J. of Psychotherapy*, 27: 593–610.

Lindy, J., & Titchener, J. (1983). Acts of God and man: Long-term character change in survivors and the law. *Behavioral Sciences and the Law,* 1(3): 85–96.

Luborsky, L. (1984). *Principles of Psychoanalytic Psychotherapy: A Manual for Supportive and Expressive Treatment.* New York: Basic Books.

Murphy, S. A. (1986). Health and recovery status of victims one and three years following a natural disaster. In C. R. Figley (Ed.), *Trauma and Its Wake, Vol. II.* New York: Brunner/ Mazel.

Palacios, A., et al. (1986). The traumatic effect of mass communication in the Mexico City earthquake: Crisis intervention and preventive measures. *Int. Review of Psychoan.,* 13: 279–294.

Titchener, J. (1986). Post-traumatic decline: A consequence of unresolved destructive drives. In C. R. Figley (Ed.), *Trauma and its Wake, Vol. II.* New York: Brunner/Mazel.

Titchener, J. L., & Kapp, F. T. (1976). Family and character change at Buffalo Creek. *Am. J. of Psychiatry,* 133: 295–299.

Titchener, J. L., Kapp, F. T., & Winget, C. (1976). The Buffalo Creek syndrome: Symptoms and character change after a major disaster. In H. J. Parad, H. L. Resnik, & L. C. Parad (Eds.), *Emergency and Disaster Management: A Mental Health Sourcebook.* Bowie, MD: Charles Press.

Titchener, J. L., & Kapp, F. (1986). Post-traumatic decline: A consequence of unresolved destructive drives. In C. R. Figley (Ed.), *Trauma and Its Wake, Vol. II.* New York: Brunner/Mazel.

Titchener, J. L., & Ross, W. D. (1974). Acute or chronic stress as determinants of behavior, character and neurosis. In S. Arieti & E. Brody (Eds.), *American Handbook of Psychiatry.* 3: 39–60. New York: Basic Books.

Wallace, A. F. C. (1956). *Tornado in Worcester.* Disaster Study Number Three, Committee on Disaster Studies, National Academy of Sciences, National Research Council, p. 127.

Weiss, J., & Sampson, H. (1986). *The Psychoanalytic Process: Theory, Clinical Observation & Empirical Research.* New York: Guilford Press.

7

Clinical Interventions in Emergencies: Technological Accidents

H. ALLEN HANDFORD, ENOS D. MARTIN, and JOYCE D. KALES

Technological or man-made accidents are historically as old as humankind. Throughout history, as man has applied knowledge, skill and inventiveness in controlling his environment, the resultant technology has come to rival the forces of nature as a frequent source of human death and destruction. Mental health systems and the clinical interventions applicable to communities and individuals affected by technological accidents (and disasters) are still in their infancy.

The application of such interventions has been relatively minimal compared to the extent and frequency of disasters themselves. To understand this disparity, and how it may eventually be corrected, it is essential that we look at the complex nature of technological accidents, how mental health systems may function in such accidents, and how the mental and emotional problems of the people directly affected may be appropriately and effectively addressed.

The Industrial Revolution of the Nineteenth Century, coupled with the rise of large cities resulted in a marked increase in the hazards to which human communities were subject. The advent of technology in the Twentieth Century in the United States as well as in the other industrialized countries of the world has created an increased potential for community disasters giving rise to fears equal to or greater than those produced by natural disasters. The worst single recent technological disaster, the Bhopal, India, accident of 1984, claimed over 2000 dead and tens of thousands injured due to the release of a deadly toxic gas. The development of nuclear energy and the construction of operating nuclear power plants have greatly increased the risk of sudden cataclysmic technological disasters most recently seen in the nuclear accident at Chernobyl, near Kiev in the Soviet Union, in 1986.

Parallel to the increase in the potential for widespread destruction from technological accidents, the development of public agencies such as fire departments and paramedical rescue squads specifically designed to assist populations in coping with emergency situations has advanced significantly. As the emergency support network has grown, public health and welfare agencies, at first privately supported, and later publicly funded, have also begun to evolve approaches to public calamities. The major wars of this century, World Wars I and II, have given impetus to the development of these emergency systems, including those which deal with mental and emotional casualties.

Community mental health systems were established as a result of state and federal legislation in the 1960s. This development came as a result of theoretical advances in social psychiatry (Caplan, 1961) and pharmacologic advances in the treatment of mental disorders, coupled with political forces fueled by the civil rights movement. The latter focused on the rights of minorities, including the mentally ill and mentally retarded. There was a resultant shift in the locus of care of the mentally ill from large, often remotely located, state institutions to community-based mental health facilities. With their mandated crisis intervention services, these mental health centers represented a system not only capable of responding to the clinical needs of the mentally ill, but also to the mental and emotional problems of normal populations exposed to severe community stressors.

In this chapter we will describe various types of technological accidents and disasters. We will then review psychological effects of technological accidents, the theories which explain them, and the nature of the disaster-related mental disorders which are likely to require clinical interventions in technological accidents. We will also review the research with population samples affected by the Three Mile Island (TMI) nuclear plant accident, using that near disaster as a prototype for understanding the nature of modern technological accidents, particularly those involving nuclear energy. Then we will review the basic structure of mental health systems and their responses in times of general community crises. We will discuss the specific types of clinical interventions which may be used in technological accidents or emergencies. In concluding, we will consider the development of mental health disaster plans, public policy, and research needed to more effectively address mental health needs of individuals and communities experiencing technological accidents.

TYPES OF TECHNOLOGICAL ACCIDENTS AND DISASTERS

Specific Technological Disasters

Disasters occasioned by technological accidents or "man-made" disasters have been with us ever since man began to apply his abilities to alter the environment to improve the well-being of himself and his neighbors. The earliest technological disasters may well have been fire-related as ancient man mastered this natural phenomenon for his own use. Uncontrolled fires have occurred throughout history. One of the most notable ones in our era was the Coconut Grove fire in Boston, following which survivors and relatives of the victims were studied by psychiatrist Eric Lindemann and his coworkers (1944). This is one of the first reports of psychiatric assessment and the effects of intervention on the psychological functioning of the survivors in the aftermath of a disaster. Out of this study came the concept of "survivor guilt," the feeling of responsibility felt by those who escaped death in a disaster where others perished.

The immense hazards related to man's utilization of the powers of nature by technology are seen in the harnessing of nuclear energy and the disasters which have followed. The Hiroshima and Nagasaki atomic bombings of 1945 may quite accurately be termed technological disasters, in this case related to war. Man discovered atomic power and then used it deliberately to produce two of the worst human disasters in history in order to bring to an end a still greater disaster, World War II. The mental stress and psychological fallout among the Japanese people resulting from these disasters have been recorded in great detail by Lifton (1967) and others. In this situation, an actual cult of the damaged survivors (Hibakusha) has persisted. According to Lifton, these individuals have been subject to varying degrees of discrimination and rejection by their own society.

Two nuclear accidents which have followed these wartime events and are closer at hand for our study are the 1979 Three Mile Island and the 1986 Chernobyl nuclear plant accidents in the United States and the Soviet Union respectively. Although there was no direct loss of life at Three Mile Island, indirect consequences continue to this day. At Chernobyl there were 35 direct deaths and the exposure to radioactive fallout of tens of thousands of people throughout Europe and Scandinavia, as well as in the Ukraine area of the Soviet Union where the accident occurred.

Another significant type of technological accident has been the release of toxic chemicals or substances either into the environment of industrial plants or beyond that environment to surrounding communities. Recent examples of these disasters in the 1980s include Love Canal in Buffalo, New York, Times Beach, Missouri, and Bhopal, India.

Transportation accidents of varying degrees of magnitude have also been a reflection of our technology. Train wrecks were common transportation disasters of the 19th century and continue into the present century with human error often being the major cause despite greatly improved safety technology. Aircraft collisions and crashes have become the more prominent transportation accidents of the 20th century, a well-known early example being the Hindenburg dirigible explosion of 1936. Marine disasters are represented by the sinking of the Titanic in 1912 and the Andrea Doria in 1950. Despite the drama of these individual transportation disasters, the greatest disaster, apart from war, in the 20th century has been the 50,000 victims a year of the ongoing transportation disasters related to motor vehicle highway accidents in the U.S.

Health-related disasters have also occurred throughout history, but in the present century, medical disasters related to advances in technology have begun to appear. The current ongoing, worldwide medical disaster is AIDS, acquired immune deficiency syndrome. Although not directly a technological accident, AIDS became a technologically related disaster for the hemophilia population and other blood transfusion recipients as a result of a failure of blood and blood product safety control. Factor VIII, derived from the pooled plasma of thousands of unscreened donors, became available in the 1970s for the control of hemophilia-related hemorrhages. By 1979 the highly lethal AIDS virus had begun to enter the blood supply, and thousands of persons with hemophilia were exposed before heat treatment of factor product was developed and instituted in Factor VIII production.

Categories of Technological Disasters and Victims

There are basically two categories of technological disasters: those where the exposure of the population to life-threatening events is sudden and those where such exposure, although of equal or greater magnitude, occurs over an extended time period, sometimes decades. To oversimplify, we may call them either *sudden* or *slow* technological disasters. It is evident that the impact of technical accidents also varies in terms of the numbers of people affected and the degree to which they are affected as well.

In his very well researched book on destructive technological events, Perrow (1984) classifies these events into categories based on their "system characteristics," i.e., the multiple factors which usually act together to produce them. He makes a strong argument that these occurrences cannot be adequately understood or prevented simply on the basis of trying solely to identify single or primary causes. Instead, he refers to these events as complex systems which range from "incidents" which are defined as failures of parts only to "accidents" which involve the technological system as a whole. It is the latter, the "accidents," which can become "disasters" when they disrupt entire communities.

Perrow also addresses the matter of victims. He classifies them as "first party" (the operators of the system, the plant manager, airplane pilot, ship captain, etc.); "second party" (direct users of the system, e.g., passengers); "third party" (the innocent bystanders); "fourth party" (the later victims of radiation or toxic chemicals, unborn fetuses, and future generations). These classifications prove useful when we turn to addressing clinical interventions in technological accidents or disasters.

Natural Versus Technological Disasters

Very few natural disasters or large-scale accidents of any kind are free of technological factors. Even the so called "natural" hazards such as tornadoes, floods, and earthquakes may produce more casualties when technology in the form of early warning systems, geographic conditions, and evacuation plans are ignored or improperly applied.

In a thorough discussion of the similarities and differences between natural and technological disasters, Baum, Fleming and Davidson (1983) find that both are usually characterized by suddenness of occurrence, potential or actual power, and destructiveness, but may differ in predictability, presence of a low point (when the worst is over), and subsequent effects on the people involved. Technological accidents may have prolonged effects such as those caused by radiation or toxic waste contamination. These are very different from natural disasters where the problems often end after cleanup and reconstruction.

Summary

In summary, various types of technological accidents and disasters differ from natural disasters in that they may be either sudden or slow in occurrence, and may have prolonged toxic effects over extended time periods. Clinical interventions, therefore, must be adapted to the special nature of these events. Sudden occurrences with widespread death and destruction will require approaches quite different from those used in situations where casualties may be many, but are spread out over many months or years. The psychological aspects of human responses to technological accidents, and how they may determine the nature of clinical interventions for those affected by these events must be addressed before turning to the nature and mode of such interventions.

PSYCHOLOGICAL EFFECTS OF TECHNOLOGICAL ACCIDENTS

General Stress Reactions

Psychological reaction to stress, including fear, anxiety, or apprehension, is naturally present as a protective device in human beings in order that they may respond more effectively, i.e., with "fight or flight," to life-threatening occurrences. This knowledge goes back to the research of Selye (1976) and others who through experimental work over the past half century have elucidated the physiologic responses to stress. The fight or flight mechanisms go into effect as a consequence of the pituitary-adrenal axis response. Where stress is prolonged, physiological stress-related disorders have come to be recognized—for example, peptic ulcer, essential hypertension, and alteration of the immune system. This well-established physiological knowledge has given rise to the recent emphasis on stress reduction in the workplace and on relaxation therapies to reduce the potential for the development of physical and emotional disorders.

Psychological Effects of Technological Disasters

In assessing the psychological effects of technological disasters, considerable research has focused on the question of perception of locus of control. This research addresses the problem of whether or not individuals or populations are more affected psychologically by a disaster when they feel they have some control over the cause. It has been suggested that situations of stress which are under individual control are much better tolerated than those which are not (Pervin, 1963; Parker, Bruner, & Spencer 1980). Based on this reasoning, the threat of technological disaster should be less stressful than the threat of a natural disaster. Prevention of technological disaster is, by definition, more likely to be under human control. The technology is man-made and, therefore, the disasters related to technology are assumed to be, in part, preventable through technological expertise. When one carries this argument to its logical conclusion, human error is theoretically subject to correction or prevention. Therefore, communities might feel more comfortable with a supposedly well-constructed nuclear power plant in their midst than they would with recurrent floods or tornadoes in the same locality. Indeed, lifelong phobias related to severe storms, such as tornadoes which are very destructive and death dealing, are a common occurrence among those who have grown up in tornado-ridden areas.

Quite the contrary seems to be true when technology goes out of control, however. Then, the reaction to loss of control of what man has designed and should be able to operate safely seems to exceed that which occurs in response to natural disasters. Supporting this, Baum, Fleming and Davidson (1983), reporting on the psychological effects of natural versus technological disasters, compare the effects of accidents or breakdowns in human-made technology (such as at Three Mile Island) with those of natural disasters. As noted earlier, they find differences in areas such as power and predictability. Nuclear accidents may unleash tremendous power. Predictability is poor because the technology is designed not to fail. Their data suggest that technological catastrophes are more likely to have long-term effects, to affect people beyond the point of impact, and to pose different types of threats than natural disasters. On the other hand, natural disasters seem to trigger more social cohesion, with communities working together to overcome the adversities of nature.

If locus of control resides not in nature but in man, the stress related to technology gone out of control may, in contrast, be much higher than that related to natural disasters. This is especially true of the "third party victims," the innocent bystanders described by Perrow (1984). They have neither control nor warning of technological accidents. Here, research seems to suggest that human populations are made more anxious and are stressed to a greater degree when technological disasters occur because of the widespread belief that they could and should have been prevented. Furthermore, if the blame can be placed on other human beings, i.e., by the process of "scapegoating," first noted by Lindemann (1944) subsequent to the Coconut Grove Nightclub fire, then accusations of carelessness or inattention to technological detail become foremost. In their exaggerated form, they may take at times the shape of a paranoid belief that somehow the technological accident was deliberately produced.

Contrast this with the generally expressed feelings subsequent to a natural disaster. Those totally free of any human component, such as tornadoes, are often attributed to a mysterious fate or "God's Will." Even in those situations, however, it is human nature to try to place blame for the consequences of natural disasters. In the case of tornadoes, weather warning systems are blamed because they are not perfected to the point where potential victims can be given adequate alarm. In the case of floods, the failure to properly construct or maintain dams or waterways is seen as a fault of technology which combines with natural occurrences such as unusually heavy rainfall to produce disasters. It thus appears that it is a human tendency to blame others; this is a way to feel less stressed and more comfortable in the belief that somehow the disaster has been under human control or might have been prevented. Indeed, it is commonly thought that future disasters of a similar nature might well be prevented by improvement of technology, or by the further reduction of human error.

Methodological Issues in Disaster Research

In a detailed review of studies on the psychological effects of disaster, Green (1982) focuses on the methodological issues raised by previous disaster research. This author states that there has been no formal theory, "no framework to guide scientific inquiry" (p. 544).

She finds serious deficiencies in previous studies and strongly recommends that future disaster research studies take into consideration the specific type of disaster being addressed, and employ more uniform sampling, assessment, and data collection criteria. She proposes dividing disasters into "central," where an entire community along with its support systems is disrupted, "intermediate," where only part of a community is directly affected, and "peripheral," where victims are affected, but have come together by chance and return to intact communities. Such divisions help to more accurately define categories of disasters for research and intervention purposes.

Green's recommendations regarding uniformity of data collection are essential for placing research on the psychological effects of disasters on a strong scientific basis. Without such a systematic basis, the short- and long-term benefits of clinical interventions in technological accidents or disasters can never be scientifically measured.

Baum, Fleming and Davidson (1983) conclude from their studies that technological catastrophes are more likely than natural disasters to cause chronic stress and widespread effects. Based on this assumption, it becomes useful to assess the effects of a specific technological accident which has been more systematically studied, the Three Mile Island nuclear plant accident.

THE TMI NUCLEAR ACCIDENT AS A PROTOTYPE FOR TECHNOLOGICAL ACCIDENTS

Description of the Nuclear Plant Accident

Technological disasters with the most catastrophic potential in our age are related to nuclear events. In selecting a prototype of technological accidents, it seems appropriate to study the nuclear accident at Three Mile Island and the additional experience such as we know of it at Chernobyl. We will refer specifically to our research regarding the TMI accident (Handford et al., 1986). This occurrence, the worst in the history of nuclear power in the United States, may then serve as a model for understanding the impact of technological accidents on communities and ways in which the effects may be addressed.

"At approximately 3:58 a.m. on Wednesday, March 28, 1979, a series of malfunctions occurred in the cooling system of reactor unit 2 at the Three Mile Island Nuclear Power Plant (TMI) near Middletown, Pennsylvania. These malfunctions and the subsequent responses of plant personnel resulted in a partial meltdown of the reactor core, the overflow of thousands of gallons of radioactive water into an adjacent containment building, and the release into the atmosphere of a plume of radioactive steam approximately a half mile wide (Pennsylvania Department of Health, 1979). This event dominated the news and was described subsequently as the most serious accident in the United States' drive to harness atomic power for civilian purposes" (Burnham, 1979).

"Two days later the governor of Pennsylvania advised the evacuation of pregnant women and children under five years of age who lived within a five-mile radius of TMI. Many families hurriedly abandoned their homes and left the area. Despite costs estimated at $975 million (Bradley, 1983), there was no reported direct injury or loss of life or damage to property outside the plant" (Handford et al, 1986, p. 346).

Thus begins the report of our research team on the psychological effects on children and parents in the vicinity of the Three Mile Island nuclear accident. Before addressing the specific findings of our project, we will examine the nature of this nuclear accident and try to delineate the elements consistent with our descriptions of technological disasters.

The Three Mile Island Nuclear Plant is located on an island in the middle of the Susquehanna River adjacent to the metropolitan Harrisburg area of close to a million people. It is upstream from the populated areas of Lancaster and ultimately the Chesapeake Bay. Thus, this location presents the potential for immense nuclear radiation hazards should meltdown and radioactive steam and water contamination occur. With any nuclear plant, there is the potential for both airborne and waterborne nuclear radiation of the surrounding countryside and communities downstream, with serious potential consequences for generations after.

In the terminology of Perrow (1984), the TMI plant was a tightly coupled complex system. As such, it had a highly complicated array of control and safety subsystems, which out of control created the highest level of technological malfunction, a "system accident."

When the TMI accident occurred, it was several days before the surrounding community became fully aware of the potential danger. It was not until the third day of the accident that the governor advised the evacuation of pregnant women and children under five years of age to a shelter some 11 miles away at the Hersheypark Arena in Hershey. This order triggered a voluntary mass evacuation of a large proportion of the population in the area of metropolitan Harrisburg.

The elements of a disaster were present with the TMI accident although no loss of life or direct injury was reported. The surrounding community responded to a technological disruption which was viewed as acutely life-threatening. This response was partly government-directed, both at the local level where fire departments toured the streets warning people to evacuate and at the state level where the governor recommended evacuation of pregnant women and children at special risk. Perception of danger and threat was confirmed not only by the media—radio, television and newspapers—but by the government order which was interpreted by many as confirming the seriousness of the accident.

Once the immediate effects of the accident had subsided, the second element in the technological disaster prototype became more evident, namely the threat of long-term or delayed but permanent damage. Here damage was perceived as not only physical but also psychological and economic. There was concern not only with regard to immediate effects, but also with long-term genetic effects.

In surveying the stresses on the affected population, one may assess both the economic and physiological effects as two separate entities which combine to intensify the psychological effects of both acute and chronic stress. Economically, the population was concerned about loss of their homes and possessions. It was also very concerned about the loss of value of homes and land. In the rural areas, radiation damage to livestock was a concern. These fears were similar to the losses seen in natural occurrences such as floods, tornadoes, and hurricanes where economic loss may wipe out a lifetime of work and saving.

In a nuclear accident, physiological threat lies first in the immediate possibility of radiation exposure and radiation sickness related to fallout. Second is the possibility of long-term generation-to-generation effects of genetic damage. Both of these threats tend to increase the potential for psychological stress in the exposed population.

Research Data from the TMI Nuclear Plant Accident

In the psychological and sociological research subsequent to the TMI nuclear accident, Dohrenwend, Dohrenwend, Kasl and Warheit (1979) reported a marked increase in their Demoralization Scale one month after the accident. They also reported distrust for authority, perceived threats to physical health, and psychological and somatic stress. Bromet and her group at The University of Pittsburgh studied residual levels of anxiety and distress in mental patients (Bromet, Schulberg & Dunn, 1982) and subsequently pregnant mothers and mothers of children under five at the time of evacuation from the immediate area (Bromet & Dunn, 1981). Bromet found no difference between the effects on mental patients in an area located near a nuclear plant in the Pittsburgh environs and the reactions of mental patients in the TMI area. It is possible, however, that since both groups were living within proximity of a nuclear plant at the time of the TMI accident, anxiety might have been aroused in those living near an intact plant as a result of the accident at TMI. As for the pregnant mothers, they were found to have residual anxieties and depression, along with concerns about the future development of their children.

In their study of the TMI accident, Baum, Fleming and Singer (1983) made use of the Ways of Coping Inventory (Folkman & Lazarus, 1980), a self-report measure, to compare the responses of 38 people living within 5 miles of TMI with a control group of 32 people living near a safely operating nuclear plant more than 100 miles from TMI. Addressing coping with chronic stress, they assessed stress by making simultaneous measures of symptom reporting (Symptom CheckList-90 [SCL-90]; Derogatis, Lipman & Covi, 1973), Task Performance, and urinary cate-cholamines (epinephrine and norepinephrine). They found that both emotion-focused coping and self-blame were associated with less stress than problem-focused coping and denial. In addition, emotional regulation and assumption of responsibility for encountered difficulty were related to one another and to perceived control as well. Their conclusion was that a control-oriented coping style in which the perception of control is actively created and maintained can be effective in reducing distress associated with technological catastrophes.

In a related discussion of this study, Baum, Fleming and Davidson

(1983) outline what may be the most important difference between technological and natural disasters when it comes to predicting differences in psychological responses between populations exposed to one or the other. Because technological disasters are man-made, their prevention is considered to be determined by human control. Nuclear accidents such as the TMI disaster (and more recently Chernobyl), however, have given substantial evidence of being relatively uncontrollable. Faced with the task of reducing psychological and physiological stress in the face of nuclear catastrophe, individuals shift to some degree of self-blame or blame of other individuals, or focus on the control of their own emotions in order to regain feelings of control. Where these processes do not occur, chronic stress may be experienced, stress which goes beyond that experienced by the victims of recurrent natural disasters (e.g., floods or tornadoes).

Looking further at the research relative to TMI, Handford et al. (1986) at The Pennsylvania State University/Hershey Medical Center, using the Children's Manifest Anxiety Scale (CMAS) (Castenada, McCandless & Palermo, 1956), found residual levels of anxiety in the children of families living in the vicinity of TMI 18 months after the accident, anxiety which was unrecognized by their parents. These levels were significantly above norms for this standardized assessment measure, but significantly lower than similar findings in a psychiatrically disordered group of children. Psychiatrically disturbed members of this research sample were found at the extremes of anxiety reaction, at a very high level or extremely low level.

Also found was a significant relationship between parental disagreement as to whether to stay or to evacuate the area and the anxiety levels of the children. Children were more anxious if their parents were in disagreement as to what to do. This seems to confirm the impression that children are more affected by the reactions of their parents at times of disaster than by the disaster itself. Implied in their reaction to parental disagreement was the possibility that the children would be separated from one parent or the other, giving rise to separation anxiety in the face of the accident. During the accident, children were exposed to the distress and anxiety of their teachers since many were in school at the time when the evacuation of mothers and younger children was ordered. The retrieval of children from schools by their parents was unorganized and chaotic, leading to increased feelings of possible abandonment in these children.

Reported in the same study was the finding that a group of adult control subjects who had been assessed prior to the accident as part of an unrelated study had no significant levels of residual anxiety 18 months subsequent to the accident. This was true even though many individuals spoke of feeling physical or mental stress as a result of the accident.

Interestingly, in our study no individuals reported a full-blown post-traumatic stress disorder with flashbacks or memories of the event, suggesting that perhaps the TMI accident was not sufficiently traumatic to our study population to have produced this well recognized syndrome.

To summarize, the psychological effects of technological accidents such as TMI seem to be related to the matter of locus of control and the prevalence and seriousness of physical effects on third-party victims by the accident. The evidence seems to suggest that there is stress and trauma related to a nuclear plant accident. It is the kind of partially controlled accident which to a limited degree can be anticipated as a product of human error and where initially there may be little destruction or death. This is in contrast to disasters which have been noted to leave more severe long-lasting effects such as the Coconut Grove fire or the Buffalo Creek flood where technology was a secondary issue to the severe direct trauma of dealing with death and the totally destructive events themselves. As for the Chernobyl accident, information on psychological reactions has yet to be reported, but we may anticipate that they will be much greater than TMI because of greater destruction and fallout, and the permanent evacuation of entire communities to escape the threat of radioactive contamination.

MENTAL HEALTH CLINICAL SERVICES IN TECHNOLOGICAL ACCIDENTS

Functions of Mental Health Systems

In assessing mental health services which may be available in technological accidents or emergencies, it is important to understand the public mental health system and the services already in place as a result of federal and state legislation introduced in the 1960s (Foley, 1975). The community mental health system, federally funded centers and state and county funded mental health/mental retardation systems located throughout the country provide a kind of "safety net" specifically designed to provide intervention to individuals and to clearly delineated populations at times of personal crisis related to mental illness and mental deficiency. These systems have the potential to respond to technological accidents which have occurred in recent decades. It is appropriate to assess whether these systems are, in fact, sufficiently responsive to provide a network capable of assisting individuals and communities to cope with accidents and disasters related to technology.

Mental health intervention in technological accidents is appropriate from both conceptual and practical points of view (Cohen & Ahearn, 1980). The provision of mental health services to citizens of the United States has gradually evolved from the individual doctor-to-patient medical model of treatment to the more sociological system-to-system approach to care and treatment reflected in the growth of the mental health system itself. Simultaneous with this theoretical change has occurred a profound change in provision of mental health services. No longer is intervention with the mentally disordered and emotionally disturbed simply a matter of doctor/patient treatment. Intervention has become a network of services established in nearly every community of the United States to deal with individuals who are suffering from disturbances which are at least in part a community-wide rather than an individual or family oriented problem. As a result, it becomes logical to think of any situations which disrupt communities of people as being appropriate for the mental health intervention by a system designed specifically to address such population-wide distresses.

As a result of this conceptual development, public money has been appropriated through federal, state, and local legislation to provide services to individuals at all ages, particularly those who are unable to meet the costs themselves. Included are those who may be caught up in a disaster which, because of its destructiveness or economic deprivation, may result in large numbers of people being unable to secure adequate help or treatment by their own efforts.

Owing to the efforts of community mental health system pioneers (Caplan, 1961), such systems have developed, and have fortuitously paralleled the growth of contemporary industrial societies and technological systems. Trained community mental health personnel are potentially able to respond at times of individual, family, or community crisis. They thereby serve as the most readily available and potentially effective first line of aid and assistance in disaster situations (McGee & Heffron, 1976).

Responses of Mental Health Systems to Disaster

In reviewing the disaster literature, we find that one of the most effective uses of the public mental health system in responding to a major disaster occurred during extensive flooding in the Wilkes-Barre area of Pennsylvania subsequent to hurricane Agnes in 1972 (Okura, 1975; Poulshock & Cohen, 1975). In the face of a natural disaster which displaced between 70,000 and 75,000 people, temporary emergency mental health workers (college students) were sent into the field with experienced advisers. Nine teams of four persons each, some headed by psychiatrists, focused on serving up to nine evacuation centers each day. It is reported that these teams dealt with a large variety of people with psychiatric disorders, many requiring hospitalization, as well as providing verbal counseling for those adjusting to and learning to accept the reality of the disaster.

Similarly, in 1981, subsequent to the collapse of skywalks in the lobby of a Kansas City hotel which killed 114 people and injured another 200, seven bi-state metropolitan area community mental health centers responded. In a planned cooperative effort, these agencies opened their doors after hours to individuals and groups needing counseling as well as therapy (Wilkinson, 1983). Additional mental health personnel, including volunteers, were needed, however, to meet these needs.

The mental health system in many communities consists of a number of elements, any one or all of which might respond to a technological accident, depending on its magnitude. In the Three Mile Island accident, there was no clearly organized approach to possible mental health problems and consequences. There was no formal mental health component present at the evacuation site for mothers and children under five. If the disaster had been more extensive and displacement as well as death and injury had been present, the eventual response of the mental health system might have been similar to what it was in the Wilkes-Barre flood.

These examples illustrate that mental health systems, in order to effectively serve the victims of technological accidents or disasters, must be prepared to modify their usual procedures and provide "outreach" to the affected community. To accomplish this, mental health administrators and other personnel must establish collaborative working relationships with the private sector and volunteer agencies in advance of technological accidents. Otherwise, the affected populations may fail to make use of supportive mental health services. Such collaboration may also help to reduce the stigma which the public may ordinarily attach to utilizing the mental health system.

The specific services provided by the mental health system range from individual supportive counseling and the use of medications to relieve anxiety, depression, or psychosis to working with other social service agencies to arrange for secure shelter and feeding. Simply stated, these services can be coordinated with the services of other agencies to provide a system of support until individuals can reestablish their own safety and support network. In times of presidentially declared disaster, federal mental health disaster funds may be applied for and are infused into these systems to enable them to care for increased numbers of individuals (Frederick, 1977), primarily by employing additional staff and providing them with disaster-related training. Such training is highly concentrated, making use of mixed media, role-modeling, and reviews of how to deal with disaster-related human reactions, all based on the principles of crisis intervention which will be discussed later in greater detail.

Categories of Mental Health Services for Disasters

As we have indicated earlier, some technological accidents may resemble natural disasters in their sudden occurrence, while others are slow to occur. In sudden disasters, there is the progression of events which have been classically labelled Warning, Threat, Impact, and Recoil (Raphael, 1986). Interventions would be community-wide and address problems at each stage, using crisis intervention methods described below. In slow or long-term accidents where survivors are much more uncertain as to how or to what extent they were or might be affected, clinical interactions need to be highly individualized and designed to deal with more extended, chronic stress. Such treatment may appropriately be provided in conjunction with medical diagnosis and treatment of toxic conditions attributed to such accidents.

In reviewing the services which mental health professionals may provide to victims of technological accidents or disasters, it is useful to separate these services into two broad categories: 1) those provided to the community as a whole; 2) those provided to individuals. Category 1 would include administrative leadership efforts in close collaboration with emergency management officials and with the news media. With regard to the officials, mental health professionals would direct the crisis intervention training and triage work of mental health workers who would go into evacuation shelters, hospitals, morgues, and other areas where victims (and their families) might congregate and profit from clinical intervention.

With regard to the news media, mental health professionals would be of assistance in advising editors to avoid sensationalism and the display of shocking scenes of death or injury which might serve to intensify fear and anxiety, while reducing the ability of viewers to rationally respond to safety information and direction. In addition, such professionals could themselves appear in the media, providing calm, factual information regarding the essentially normal and transitory nature of most of the symptoms of disaster-related emotional trauma. Furthermore, they could provide advice based on the research findings from previous disasters. For example, from the TMI studies (Handford et al., 1986), one would advise that if at all possible, children not be separated from their parents (or if separated, be quickly reunited) for care or evacuation. Moreover, families should be helped to agree on the best options for safety such as the route and destination for evacuation through more specific advance public planning.

Another kind of public information would be specific telephone numbers ("crisis hot lines") and locations where mental health services might be obtained, either by telephone counseling or in person. In disaster situations where major communication systems have been rendered inoperable, such information might need to be delivered door-to-door or to evacuation shelters.

Once category 1 services are provided and individuals and families from the community directly affected by a technological accident or disaster are identified, informed as to availability and location of services, and relocated when necessary, category 2 services could begin to be delivered by those specially trained and supervised to do so. These services would be provided in evacuation shelters, hospitals, or other facilities where victims are commonly brought together.

Initially, contact is best made through the provision of direct, nonprofessional assistance in meeting basic human needs. Mental health workers in disasters are in a position to be most effective if they are directly involved in rescue or relocation operations. For example, a child psychiatrist, psychologist, or other mental health worker might make early contact by riding in an evacuation vehicle with children and their parents. There, devices for reducing anxiety by allowing for acceptable expression of feelings could be employed (questions could be answered, stories could be told, or songs sung about what everyone is experiencing). Similarly, in shelters, crayons and paper could be provided to allow for expression of fantasies about the technological accident, since these are often events not usually visible or easily explained by the victims.

Such efforts directed toward children should be accompanied by the provision to them and their parents of basic necessities such as comfortable bedding, ample food, water, and other nourishing liquids, as well as toilet and bathing facilities, and as much privacy as possible. Disaster victims are often especially sensitive to the presence of outsiders, particularly in the strange surroundings of evacuation centers. Therefore, it is essential that mental health personnel blend in with the affected groups, including staying with them during the ordeal.

Once basic needs are met and rapport is established, category 2 services to individuals would be provided in a more traditional crisis intervention fashion, such as described by Bellak and Small (1965) and Kales and Kales (1975). Initially, relevant information about the crisis and how it is affecting the individual is obtained through a brief interview. Symptoms are linked to the crisis experience. Allowing or encouraging the victim to ventilate about scenes of death and dying is quite therapeutic in reducing the anxiety related to many experiences. Only a very brief past history is relevant, usually to identify the presence or absence of previous major mental disorders. Then the postdisaster phenomena described by Horowitz (1985) are addressed step-by-step with the victim as they appear over time. He describes them as often occurring in the following order: 1) outcry (pangs of fear); 2) denial (numbness, unreality, partial or complete amnesia); 3) intrusiveness (hypervigilance, persistent recurrent thoughts, sleep and dream disturbances); 4) working through (adjustment with reduction of symptoms by frequent review of the traumatic event); 5) completion (refocusing on the present and future). Anxiety reduction through ventilation of painful memories and feelings, coupled by reassurance and redirection, are basic elements in the crisis intervention.

Horowitz emphasizes that previous conflicts, personality problems, and past symptoms may reemerge secondary to a disaster experience. When this occurs, the mental health professional may need to spend a more extended time period, in extreme cases up to a year or two, restabilizing the victim and restoring equilibrium once the acute phase of the disaster has passed.

The use of medication or psychiatric hospitalization, although available options, usually are not required for victims of disasters. In addition, only a very small percentage of victims would require individual services beyond the acute period. The exceptions appear to be in disasters where there are widespread death, destruction and permanent loss of community as described by Erikson (1976) after Buffalo Creek.

The basic goal of short-term, crisis-oriented intervention is to quickly restore the victim to his or her pre-accident state and enable preexistent support systems such as families, friends, and colleagues to again meet fundamental emotional needs. Insight-oriented psychotherapy is reserved for those with preexisting or more chronic problems and, in a large disaster, may need to wait while acute needs are being met. Wilkinson and Vera (1985) point out that there are no criteria for predicting who will need extended therapy beyond the initial intervention. In those people who do, dormant unresolved conflicts seem to have been stimulated by the disaster trauma.

During the acute phase as well as during the period of recovery, group therapy approaches may be particularly useful. Here, members of the group may share suffering in common. Similar experiences and emotions are relived, intellectual understanding of the technological accident is fostered, and coping mechanisms are exchanged and strengthened. Members of such support groups may continue to be of help to one another even after formal therapy sessions have ended.

Needs of Special Populations

In reviewing the services which a mental health system and its professionals may provide to populations affected by technological accidents, it is also appropriate to focus on special populations which may be uniquely affected by disasters and require highly specialized services to assist them with mental health problems that may arise.

The first population considered is that of on-site personnel who are immediately present and responsible for bringing such disasters under control. These would be the "first party victims" described by Perrow (1984). In industrial plants, these would be plant workers, maintenance personnel, or security personnel. They are the first to be exposed to the effects of the disaster and may be severely injured or lose their lives as a result of the initial events. They may be the first and in many cases the only ones exposed to scenes of death, disfigurement, or other severe injury (Taylor & Frazer, 1982). Similar to this group are members of rescue teams who move into the areas of technological accidents as soon as official alarm is received. Here again, these individuals may be directly exposed to the traumatic experiences and scenes that can accompany technological accidents.

In assessing the reactions that these individuals may have and planning the approach to helping them with traumatic experiences, one must appreciate the typical psychology involved. As Taylor describes it, direct experience with severe personal tragedy or human death or injury, particularly with macabre or distressing visual images, leaves individuals with lasting memories which may reappear periodically as "flashbacks" or as recurrent nightmares. These personal psychological experiences may continue for years after the events.

The value of mental health intervention with such workers is that when one approaches these traumatic experiences therapeutically from the standpoint of calmly reviewing visual or auditory images associated with death and destruction, these interventions may help the individual to associate intense images with more neutral or restful experiences. By a process often called "working through," the individual reaches the point where memories and conversation about these events become tolerable to the mind and are no longer the source of disabling anxiety or depression. Individual as well as group therapy approaches may be employed as previously described.

The best known examples of such experiences are those of the Vietnam veterans as well as veterans of other conflicts who directly observed and experienced the death or severe injury of their fellow fighting personnel. Such experiences were described in World War I as "shell shock." In World War II they were recognized as post-traumatic stress experiences and after a period of rest such victims were quickly returned to the front wherever possible. Subsequent to Vietnam, with the intense and widespread use of various drugs, the usual reactions were perhaps dampened and indeed psychologically buried only to reemerge as serious problems (Figley, 1978). In these cases, post-traumatic stress disorder (described on pp. 202–203) and psychiatric illness were often concurrent (Sierles et al., 1983). In this regard, on-site rescue workers and plant operators are comparable to soldiers in battle, those who must face death and destruction and then subsequently work through the disturbing memories they carry with them.

Another especially vulnerable population consists of the children who may be exposed to dramatic scenes of destruction, injury, and death. Here again, post-traumatic reactions may occur which can last over a considerable time period. Dissociative phenomena and severe neurosis later on in life have been described. For example, Pynoos and Eth (1986) have written of the reactions of children who have witnessed murder. It is our own experience that children who have witnessed such traumatic events may reexperience those events periodically, particularly when under stresses which bring them to mind. As a recent example, a two-year-old boy was slashed in both wrists by his psychotic mother. He seemed to adjust quite well in the year following this event. However, one day he was in the vicinity of an ambulance with a flashing light and had a panic reaction. This seemed directly related to the ambulance with a flashing light that arrived at the scene where his mother had tried to kill him.

Terr (1981) has reported that similarly traumatized children will repeat such occurrences endlessly in their play and that it is countertherapeutic to try to analyze the play; it is more helpful to intervene and put a halt to the play, introducing more positive play patterns. This technique is employed when the so-called working through process is not taking place, but instead the child is psychologically "stuck" on the traumatic event. If in the course of this therapeutic process there occur frequent and repetitive talking about and remembering of the traumatic event, the child is helped to refocus his attention and efforts on more age-appropriate thoughts and activities. Gradually, preoccupation with the traumatic event is relinquished. It is felt that initial attention to the details of the traumatic event is especially necessary because of clinical examples in which severely traumatic events were repressed or forgotten only to later reappear as disabling neurotic reactions, including psychological dissociation.

The geriatric population is another group of people who are especially vulnerable to the disruptions in the routine of daily life which may be produced by technological accidents (Poulshock & Cohen, 1975). The elderly, especially those who are chronically ill, are particularly sensitive to changes in environment. A common phenomenon when they are hospitalized is the so-called "sundowning effect." This is manifested by disorientation, especially as to time, place, and person, often at nightfall. Such disorientation often is accompanied by fearful agitation and, at times, paranoid thinking. These phenomena in the aged may be expected to occur commonly if they must be evacuated to public shelters. Just the simple matter of finding a toilet in the middle of the night in a shelter may be an insurmountable problem, at times leading to regressive bedwetting or urination and defecation in inappropriate places. Thus, the geriatric population needs special assistance, with the emphasis on orientation, repetitive reassurance of the helpful nature of the surroundings, and frequent reminders as to what has occurred, where they are, and what will be happening next.

In summary, there are special populations at higher risk than the general population in regard to the mental health effects of technological disasters. It therefore becomes appropriate in the planning processes to prepare to meet the special needs of these populations. All of the resources of the mental health system may be required, especially to deal with the strong residual traumatic effects on these individuals.

Specific Psychiatric Needs During Disasters

Among the many special needs which emerge in time of disaster and evacuation are the problems of the acutely or chronically mentally ill. Of these, persons with schizophrenia are considered the most vulnerable because of the often severe degree of their chronically disordered thinking. When disordered environment impinges on disordered thinking, the severity of the reaction may be even stronger. Such individuals may be found wandering in evacuation areas; many are receiving various psychotropic medications. The sudden withdrawal of these medications may result in the exacerbation of symptoms such as delusions or hallucinations. Therefore, it becomes essential that ample supplies of psychotrophic medications be readily available in the evacuation centers. Such medications include the neuroleptics, exemplified by Thorazine (chlorpromazine) or Haldol (haloperidol), for psychotic individuals and the antidepressants, exemplified by Tofranil (imipramine) or Elavil (amitriptyline), for chronically depressed patients. For bipolar (manic-depressive) patients, lithium should be stocked.

Benzodiazepine medications such as Librium (chlordiazepoxide) may be needed by alcoholics who are faced with acute withdrawal symptoms. Detoxification management of drug withdrawal, based on the substance of abuse, would also need to be individualized for drug-addicted patients.

Services comparable to inpatient psychiatric units may be required for those individuals who experience medication withdrawal or who, due to the effects of chronic psychosis, become agitated or hallucinate in the stress of disaster. These individuals may need a special secure setting staffed by mental health professionals separate from the mass care setting which might be utilized in the community for the majority of survivors.

Children and adolescents with preexistent mental disorders have their own unique needs. Mentally ill children are under treatment with medications similar to those used with adults and will have similar needs. Hyperactive children will require their stimulant medications, such as Ritalin (methylphenidate), to maintain calm behavior. Thus, with regard to the mental health system, it is not only people who function within the normal range in their day-to-day life who may need the services during a disaster, but also those who have already been identified as mentally or emotionally disordered and will need a continuation of their mental health services in evacuation situations.

It is well recognized that a disaster does not invariably produce mental and emotional disorders in the normal population other than short-term anxiety resulting from exposure to a life-threatening situation. The one exception to this would be the post-traumatic stress disorder described by Horowitz, Wilner and Kaltreider (1980). This may occur subsequent to a disaster depending on the degree of exposure of the individual to frightening or traumatic experiences or scenes. This disorder is described as follows in the *Diagnostic and Statistical Manual of Mental Disorders, Third Edition, Revised* (American Psychiatric Association, 1987, pp. 250–251):*

A. The person has experienced an event that is outside the range of usual human experience and that would be markedly distressing to almost anyone, e.g., serious threat to one's life or physical integrity; serious threat or harm to one's children, spouse, or other close relatives and friends; sudden destruction of one's home or community; or seeing another person who has recently been, or is being, seriously injured or killed as the result of an accident or physical violence.

B. The traumatic event is persistently reexperienced in at least one of the following ways:

(1) recurrent and intrusive distressing recollections of the event

---

*Reprinted with permission.

(in young children, repetitive play in which themes or aspects of the trauma are expressed)

(2) recurrent distressing dreams of the event

(3) sudden acting or feeling as if the traumatic event were recurring (includes a sense of reliving the experience, illusions, hallucinations, and dissociative [flashback] episodes, even those that occur upon awakening or when intoxicated)

(4) intense psychological distress at exposure to events that symbolize or resemble an aspect of the traumatic event, including anniversaries of the trauma

C. Persistent avoidance of stimuli associated with the trauma or numbing of general responsiveness (not present before the trauma), as indicated by at least three of the following:

(1) efforts to avoid thoughts or feelings associated with the trauma

(2) efforts to avoid activities or situations that arouse recollections of the trauma

(3) inability to recall an important aspect of the trauma (psychogenic amnesia)

(4) markedly diminished interest in significant activities (in young children, loss of recently acquired developmental skills such as toilet training or language skills)

(5) feeling of detachment or estrangement from others

(6) restricted range of affect, e.g., unable to have loving feelings

(7) sense of a foreshortened future, e.g., does not expect to have a career, marriage, or children, or a long life

D. Persistent symptoms of increased arousal (not present before the trauma), as indicated by at least two of the following:

(1) difficulty falling or staying asleep

(2) irritability or outbursts of anger

(3) difficulty concentrating

(4) hypervigilance

(5) exaggerated startle response

(6) physiologic reactivity upon exposure to events that symbolize or resemble an aspect of the traumatic event (e.g., a woman who was raped in an elevator breaks out in a sweat when entering any elevator)

E. Duration of the disturbance (symptoms in B, C, and D) of at least one month.

Specify delayed onset if the onset of symptoms was at least six months after the trauma.

Post-traumatic stress disorder is specifically trauma-related and is of considerable current interest in understanding a variety of psychiatric reactions to acute stress.

With regard to the clinical management of the post-traumatic stress syndrome, it should be noted that interventions which go beyond simple crisis intervention may be necessary to alleviate long-term duration of symptoms. It is a specific psychiatric disorder which may be produced by exposure to both technological and natural disasters and which may require more extended psychotherapeutic work with the victim.

CONCLUSIONS: MENTAL HEALTH PLANNING, PUBLIC POLICY, AND RESEARCH

We will attempt to draw conclusions and begin to make some judgments with respect to the optimal provision of clinical interventions to communities affected by technological accidents. In this regard, it is appropriate to take an overview of the planning that should occur, the public policy that is needed to make interventions possible, and the role of research in substantiating the efficacy of these measures.

Mental Health Planning

Insights gained from the TMI accident and other technological accidents suggest a number of directions for mental health planning to take. Disaster planners should help the general population become aware of the significance of the usual stages of human response to disaster and the variety of ways in which these stages are experienced in a technological disaster. In a natural disaster such as a flood, the specific events of the disaster are usually part of everyone's awareness. Each affected individual has personal memories of the day the dam broke or the tornado struck. In contrast, in a technological disaster such as that at TMI, people varied widely as to when they experienced the classic stages of disaster response, namely, warning, threat, impact, or recoil. Even during the time of greatest danger, some felt that there was only the *threat* of danger while others felt that they had faced the greatest impact and were already severely and irreparably damaged. These variations in perception led to tension and stress between persons in the same family and employees on the same job. These stresses in turn were associated with blaming and self-critical responses and with tensions in interpersonal relationships.

Mental health planners and workers need to consider the uncertainty and vagueness of perception that can lead to chronic anger and frustration often directed at "they" (e.g., the establishment or the government), because "somebody didn't do something" to prevent the disaster. In a sense, the victims of a technological accident are stuck in the initial phase of disaster with all of the attendant feelings of shock, anger, depression, and confusion. The vagueness of the object of anger and the lack of clarity concerning an appropriate response make it difficult for people to resolve their intense feelings and to reorganize their lives following the losses occasioned by a technological disaster.

Disaster planners need to promote public education regarding the significance of the findings on technological disasters. Some of this education can take place prior to disaster. For example, community mental health workers and administrators can be trained through disaster response seminars. These seminars should be offered frequently enough so that new personnel can be taught and mental health administrators kept aware of up-to-date findings. As Caplan (1981) points out in addressing the problem of mastery of stressful life circumstances, "persons may be helped prior to a stressful event by suitable education and training in generic skills that will enable the person to operate more effectively in any situation of frustration and confusion in which he is called to work out new responses to unexpected problems" (p. 415). Caplan gives as an example army battle training. While the whole population cannot be so prepared, key persons can be trained to anticipate the reactions and needs of the mental health care givers as well as the population being helped.

After a technological accident or disaster occurs, mental health planners can insure that the best of the disaster response knowledge is disseminated in the community. One-day seminars for community mental health workers, clergy, and other community leaders should be quickly scheduled as they were in the days immediately following the Kansas City Hyatt Hotel skywalk disaster (Wilkinson, 1983). Accurate mental health publicity should be conveyed to the media so that the public can be made aware of the basic nature of responses to disaster and the availability of resources to help deal with them. Knowledge of the availability of resources will communicate to the community that a caring and knowledgeable group of professionals is prepared to provide an empathic human response to a dehumanizing experience.

A second important principle that arises from disaster research is the importance of counteracting the dehumanization which may result from a major disaster. After any disaster, but in particular a man-made disaster, there is a tendency to feel weak, vulnerable, and lacking in personal significance. This can lead to an attitude of withdrawal and retreat from activity and human interaction such as occurred subsequent to the Buffalo Creek disaster. It is as though the person is saying, "I was hurt once,

I'll not risk getting involved in life again, so I won't be hurt anymore"
(Titchener & Kapp, 1976). Emphasis by industry during the post-disaster
period on the financial cost and haste to return to business as usual also
contributes to the sense of dehumanization.

Clergy and other community leaders have an important role to play in
interpreting the meaning of disastrous events. They provide leadership
and guidance in helping persons find ways to integrate the event and its
painful consequences into life's overall pattern of meaning. As Caplan
(1981) points out, persons may be helped to see how this event relates to
other difficult events in the history of humankind which have been
overcome. This perspective gives people the fortitude to cope with the
present situation. Thus, a person's drive is "buttressed by his memory that
his identification with certain values and the support and approbation he
receives from like-minded significant others help maintain his perseverance" (p. 415).

Clergy and other community leaders can also perform a valuable
function in alerting and motivating persons not affected by disaster to
reach out to those under great stress. When people undergo severe stress
and receive needed support, they fare better than those with less stress but
no support. As Caplan (1981) has said, various research studies "support
the thesis that high levels of social support protect against increased
vulnerability to illness of various kinds associated with high stress" (p. 419).
Thus, a well designed and executed mental health disaster plan has a very
important role to play in decreasing the overall morbidity associated with
technological disaster.

What does this mean then for mental health intervention in technological disasters? It suggests that the systems already in place to deal with
ongoing psychiatric and psychological stress, namely the mental health
systems of States and local communities, are best equipped to become
mobilized to help populations cope with the effects of both long-term and
sudden calamitous events. There must be available the following: highly
flexible services that can be provided at little or no cost to the recipient in
times of crisis; services which provide sufficient personnel trained to deal
with people in crisis; systems which have available medications for special
populations in need; systems which are prepared to provide services
through outreach in locations such as evacuation centers; professional
personnel who have access to partial or closed hospital settings as well as
to outpatient clinics.

Public Policy Recommendations

In anticipation of meeting these needs, public policymakers must assure
that these systems are supported by sufficient human and financial resources.

Continuing public mental health funding to meet the emergency as well as the day-to-day needs of the communities is essential. Like public utilities, the mental health systems are essential to the well-being of communities. All communities which may become evacuation points should have a mental health disaster intervention plan which addresses the needs of large numbers of evacuees in public shelters. At times of major disasters, communities may be called upon to serve many thousands of evacuees. Crisis intervention of this magnitude then becomes a matter of estimating numbers of potential evacuees and what resources need to be on hand to cope with these numbers. If 12 million people living in Manhattan suddenly must evacuate, 1,000 surrounding communities might be faced with the arrival of 12,000 evacuees each. Further dispersal obviously would be made to outlying communities, depending on the availability of transportation. Mental health disaster intervention becomes a very real necessity in the face of the disasters which are related to nuclear technology.

From our scant knowledge of Chernobyl, more than 100,000 people were evacuated to the nearest communities that were regarded as being safer. As testified to by the physicians who went to the Soviet Union to assist with bone marrow transplants for the immediate victims of radiation, medical facilities were for the most part outmoded and inadequate for medical intervention with the people affected. Our public mental health systems in the United States have generally been partitioned into service areas ranging in size from 10,000 to 200,000 individuals per area. However, at any given time, they may be serving only about 1% of this population. Deinstitutionalization of large numbers of the chronically mentally ill over the past decade has seriously stressed the capacities of current mental health systems, especially in urban areas, much as a large disaster might stress them under similar circumstances of mass relocation. These systems would bear the brunt of mental health clinical interventions in technological disasters. Consequently, a plan for augmenting current mental health systems for disaster intervention must be written into community disaster plans.

In anticipation of technological accidents or disasters, mental health system administrators must begin to collaborate with community emergency managers to develop written plans for appropriate clinical intervention. Such plans must identify personnel, alternate sites in case of widespread destruction or contamination, sources of necessary medications, and provisions for dealing with non-affected relatives and other potential members of support networks. Federal, state, and local financial resources should be made readily available, when necessary, in already established emergency fund accounts. Such a ready funding mechanism would relieve the necessity of expending valuable and urgently needed professional time on fund raising when the time is needed for direct intervention with affected populations.

Research Needs

To provide an adequate research basis to ultimately substantiate the value of such planning and intervention efforts, epidemiologic mental health data on the general population of each community should be established in advance to provide a baseline of statistical information upon which to begin plans for clinical interventions in technological accidents or disasters. Then, uniform data gathering subsequent to disasters through the use of standardized assessment instruments at clearly defined time intervals, e.g., one, six, 12, and 18 months subsequent to mental health intervention, would ensure research on the efficacy of mental health efforts and greatly advance our current limited knowledge. Human psychological reactions to disasters have been studied frequently, albeit imperfectly. Objective assessments of the efficacy of various types of clinical interventions are long overdue.

In conclusion, technological accidents and disasters are unavoidable in an industrialized civilization. As technological systems become more sophisticated and complex, and the potential for community crises increases, it becomes essential that public mental health systems be included in the advance planning process conducted by emergency management agencies at federal, state, and local levels. Only in this fashion will the mental and emotional traumata resulting from technological accidents be managed adequately and professionally.

REFERENCES

American Psychiatric Association (1987). *Diagnostic and Statistical Manual of Mental Disorders, Third Edition, Revised.* Washington D.C.: American Psychiatric Association.

Baum, A., Fleming, R., & Davidson, L. M. (1983). Natural disaster and technological catastrophe. *Environment & Behavior,* 15(3): 333–354.

Baum, A., Fleming, R., & Singer, J. E. (1983). Coping with victimization by technological disaster. *Journal of Social Issues,* 39(2): 117–138.

Bellak, L., & Small, L. (1965). *Emergency Psychotherapy and Brief Psychotherapy.* New York: Grune & Stratton.

Bradley, M. O. (1983). TMI cleanup: 5 more years. Harrisburg: *The Evening News.* February 1, pp. A1, A2.

Bromet, E., & Dunn, L. (1981). Mental health of mothers nine months after the Three Mile Island accident. *The Urban and Social Change Review,* 14(2): 12–15.

Bromet, E., Schulberg, H., & Dunn, L., (1982). Reactions of psychiatric patients to the Three Mile Island nuclear accident. *Archives of General Psychiatry,* 39: 725–730.

Burnham, D. (1979). Nuclear accident is laid to failure of several safety systems at plant. *The New York Times*, March 30, p. A1.

Caplan, G. (1961). *An Approach to Community Mental Health*. London: Tavistock Publications.

Caplan, G. (1981). Mastery of stress: Psychosocial aspects. *American Journal of Psychiatry*, 138(4): 413–420.

Castenada, A., McCandless, B., & Palermo, D. S. (1956). The children's form of the Manifest Anxiety Scale. *Child Development*, 27: 317–326.

Cohen, R. E., & Ahearn, F. L., Jr. (1980). *Handbook for the Mental Health Care of Disaster Victims*. Baltimore and London: The Johns Hopkins University Press.

Derogatis, L., Lipman, R., & Covi, L. (1973). The SCL-90: An outpatient psychiatric rating scale. *Psychopharmacology Bulletin*, 9: 12–28.

Dohrenwend, B. P., Dohrenwend, B. S., Kasl, S. V., & Warheit, G. J. (1979). *Technical Staff Analysis Report on Behavioral Effects to the President's Commission on the Accident at Three Mile Island*. Washington, D.C.: President's Commission on the Accident at Three Mile Island.

Erikson, K. (1976). *Everything in Its Path*. New York: Simon & Schuster.

Figley, C. R. (1978). *Stress Disorders Among Vietnam Veterans: Theory, Research and Treatment*. New York: Brunner/Mazel.

Foley, H. A. (1975). *Community Mental Health Legislation*. Lexington, MA: D. C. Heath and Company.

Folkman, S., & Lazarus, R. S. (1980). An analysis of coping in a middle-aged community sample. *Journal of Health and Social Behavior*, 21: 219–239.

Frederick, C. J. (1977). Psychological first aid: Emergency mental health and disaster assistance. *The Psychotherapy Bulletin*, 10: 15–30.

Green, B. L. (1982). Assessing levels of psychological impairment following disaster. *Journal of Nervous and Mental Disease*, 170(9): 544–552.

Handford, H. A., Mayes, S. D., Mattison, R. E., Humphrey, F. J., Bagnato, S., Bixler, E. O., & Kales, J. D. (1986). Child and parent reaction to the Three Mile Island nuclear accident. *Journal of the American Academy of Child Psychiatry*, 25(3): 346–356.

Horowitz, M. J. (1985). Disasters and psychological responses to stress. *Psychiatric Annals*, 15(3): 161–167.

Horowitz, M. J., Wilner, N., & Kaltreider, N. (1980). Signs and symptoms of post-traumatic stress disorder. *Archives of General Psychiatry*, 37: 85–92.

Kales, J. D., & Kales, A. (1975). Managing the individual and family in crisis. *American Family Physician*, 12(5): 109–115.

Lifton, R. J. (1967). *Death in Life: Survivors of Hiroshima*. New York: Random House.

Lindemann, E. (1944). Symptomatology and management of acute grief. *American Journal of Psychiatry*, 101: 101–148.

McGee, R. K., & Heffron, E. F. (1976). The role of crisis intervention services in disaster recovery. In H. J. Parad, H. L. P. Resnick, & L. G. Parad (Eds.), *Emergency and Disaster Management: A Mental Health Sourcebook* (pp. 309–323). Bowie, MD: Charles Press.

Okura, K. P. (1975). Mobilizing in response to a major disaster. *Community Mental Health Journal*, 11(2): 136–144.

Parker, S. D., Bruner, M. B., & Spencer, J. R. (1980). Natural disaster, perceived control, and attributions to fate. *Personality and Social Psychology Bulletin*, 6(3): 454–459.

Pennsylvania Department of Health. (1979). Evaluation of health impact of TMI accident, Attachment #3, Harrisburg, PA, April 18 (unpublished).

Perrow, C. (1984). *Normal Accidents: Living with High-risk Technologies*. New York: Basic Books.

Pervin, L. A. (1963). The need to predict and control under conditions of threat. *Journal of Personality*, 31: 570–587.

Poulshock, S. W., & Cohen, E. S. (1975). The elderly in the aftermath of a disaster. *Gerontologist*, 15(4): 357–361.

Pynoos, R. S., & Eth, S. (1986). Witness to violence: The child interview. *Journal of the American Academy of Child Psychiatry,* 25(3): 306–319.

Raphael, B. (1986). *When Disaster Strikes.* New York: Basic Books, pp. 6–9.

Selye, H. (1976). *The Stress of Life* (rev. ed.). New York: McGraw-Hill.

Sierles, F. S., Chen, J. J., McFarland, R. E., & Taylor, A. T. (1983). Post-traumatic stress disorder and concurrent psychiatric illness: A preliminary report. *American Journal of Psychiatry,* 140(9): 1177–1179.

Taylor, A. J. W., & Frazer, A. G. (1982). The stress of post-disaster body handling and victim identification work. *Journal of Human Stress,* 8: 4–12.

Terr, L. (1981). Forbidden games: Post-traumatic child's play. *Journal of the American Academy of Child Psychiatry,* 20(4): 741–759.

Titchener, J. L., & Kapp, F. T. (1976). Family character change at Buffalo Creek. *American Journal of Psychiatry,* 133(3): 295–299.

Wilkinson, C. B. (1983). Aftermath of a disaster: The collapse of the Hyatt Regency Hotel Skywalks. *American Journal of Psychiatry,* 40: 1134–1139.

Wilkinson, C. B., & Vera, E. (1985). The management and treatment of disaster victims. *Psychiatric Annals,* 15(3): 174–184.

8

Clinical Interventions in Emergencies: War-Related Events

JOE GELSOMINO and DAVID W. MACKEY

Proactive and reactive are common terms in the parlance of organizational management and associated strategies therein. Successful businesses-for-profit, among others, have recognized the need for long-range potential problem identification and analysis, planning, and response preparedness (Kepner & Tregoe, 1981; Naisbitt, 1984). Much can be learned from this forward thinking and applied to clinical intervention strategies which heretofore have been predominantly reactive.

The Veterans Administration's Vet Center program, originally established in 1979, was designed and structured to offer innovative, community-based psychosocial services for Vietnam Era Veterans in order to help veterans deal with psychological and social sequelae from the Vietnam War (Egendorf, Kadushin, Laufer, Rothbart, & Sloan, 1981). This approach was both a creative and reactive clinical intervention related to wartime events and experiences, and occurred several years after the last combatant left the shores of South Vietnam. Certainly, the controversial nature of the war contributed to this delayed response, but so did a lack of proactive contingency planning.

A comprehensive plan of clinical intervention to mitigate the frequency of mental health problems which occur as a result of war-related events is

The views expressed in this chapter are solely those of the authors and do not necessarily represent those of the Veterans Administration.

yet to be developed. Any such plan must include both proactive and reactive dimensions. This chapter attempts to advance the development of future strategic planning through examining past and present clinical interventions and processes, as well as the consequences of a lack thereof.

Although the phenomena associated with war trauma have been observed for generations in America's veterans (Modlin, 1986), corresponding clinical interventions are not well developed, nor are planning and coordination of efforts. As Milgram and Hobfoll (1986) eloquently point out,

> . . . it is unfortunate that humankind must devote precious energy and human resources to plan for war and/or defend against the threat of war. To fail to do so, however, is not to guarantee peace or to increase its likelihood. On the contrary, history has shown that when one side appears unarmed and defenseless, there is a strong temptation for the other side to resolve grievances or to advance perceived interests by attacking and/or exploiting the unarmed group. We are fully aware that these very assertions are self-fulfilling and that if other beliefs were widely held by the decision makers of the world, armies would become unnecessary and untenable.
>
> In the meantime, societies have an obligation to care for their physically and emotionally wounded. Soldiers and civilians need to be treated by the best state-of-the-art techniques that psychology and psychiatry can provide. It is unrealistic to think that the mental health professions can directly limit or eliminate war. As a group, we are not all of one political persuasion, party, or ideology, and would not cooperate as a single-minded special interest group or lobby. We may work, however, to treat war-related stress reactions and disorders more effectively. We may also make efforts to enhance the quality of life in people affected by life stressors in general and by war-related stress in particular. (p. 352)

While no rational individual or society desires war, to be unprepared for its eventuality is a disservice to those who must participate as well as a factor in the quantitative impact, chronicity, and severity quotient.

BACKGROUND

In order to develop comprehensive and responsive clinical intervention to the psychological aftermath of wartime events, it is useful to trace the evolution of one national response which was impeded by: 1) a negative societal reaction to the war itself; 2) a failure to separate the war from the individuals who took part in it; 3) lack of total commitment to those sent into battle; 4) large gaps in knowledge; and 5) nonexistence of a plan to address all of the above. In other words, review a worst case scenario.

It should be further noted that references to the clinical interventions incorporated in the Vet Center program are based on strategies implemented long after the war-related traumas and stressors. As will be seen, to clinically intervene at points in time when delayed and chronic features have become entrenched is far from optimal in terms of minimizing severity and complications. This delayed response will be contrasted with clinical interventions implemented during Israeli war experiences and resultant acute phases of PTSD (Milgram, 1986).

The incidence and severity of Post-traumatic Stress Disorder (PTSD) as found in Vietnam veterans would have been ameliorated had the nature of the origin and course of PTSD been better understood and responded to as an urgent/emergent situation in the 1960s and early in the 1970s. As Modlin (1986, p. 26) so aptly states, "good prognosis depends on early evaluation and diagnosis." This should be argument enough for rapid and thorough clinical interventions of an effective kind. With reference to post-traumatic deterioration and disablement, Titchener (1986) states, "early intervention is the best hope" (p. 17). Unfortunately, this has not been the case regarding the treatment of PTSD as found in combat veterans. The creation of the Vet Centers by Congress in 1979 was in part a result of the widespread realization among well-informed veterans, mental health professionals, and veteran's advocates that extant, traditional mental health programs were not adequately equipped to meet the broad range of psychosocial readjustment problems experienced by Vietnam veterans (Fuller, 1985).

Explanations for the past shortcomings of these mental health programs are manifold, and a few of the more prominent deficiencies warrant brief attention in the present discussion. Blank (1982) has noted a number of the difficulties which Vietnam returnees have experienced in their attempts to obtain treatment from conventional psychiatric treatment programs. One consequence of the previously-described deficiencies was that many Vietnam veterans, already distrustful and suspicious of government institutions as a result of their painful war and homecoming experiences, quickly learned that even when they took the initiative to seek professional assistance for their stress-related symptoms, the treatment received was likely to be inadequate and frequently counterproductive. The veterans' readjustment problems were, of course, also exacerbated by the fact that the military had conducted little or no significant psychological "debriefing" with them upon their return from the war zone. As a result of this unresponsive and perceived insensitivity to postwar needs, some veterans developed an understandable reluctance, if not outright refusal, to seek further help from conventional clinical sources.

Prior to its inclusion in the psychiatric nomenclature, Post-traumatic Stress Disorder (PTSD) was frequently an undiagnosed, partially diagnosed, or misdiagnosed condition. In 1980, the Diagnostic and Statistical Manual DSM–III (American Psychiatric Association, 1980) officially recognized PTSD as a diagnostic condition. Although improvement in the diagnosis and treatment of the disorder is evident, the need to accurately identify PTSD as a precondition for appropriate treatment continues to exist.

Historically, individuals who had experienced war-related trauma and presented PTSD symptoms may have been misdiagnosed, and treated with chemotherapy which was countertherapeutic and/or contraindicated by their actual condition (Blank, 1982; DeFazio, 1978; Domash & Sparr, 1982; Yost, 1980). In instances of partial diagnosis (e.g., anxiety reaction), treatment sometimes included a psychopharmacological approach that provided a substitute for or augmentation of the individual's self-medication with alcohol and/or "street" drugs. For these individuals, an appropriate clinical intervention for the underlying source of their emotional problems rarely occurred. Instead, a new, additional, or polydrug, dependency may have been fostered. In more innocuous situations, psychotherapy would just miss the mark (Figley, 1980; Lipton & Schaffer, 1986).

The pervasive lack of understanding among mental health professionals regarding war-related stress disorders resulted in numerous well-intended but misdirected clinical interventions. Blank (1982) observed that until the advent of DSM–III there was no official psychiatric diagnosis for trauma-induced stress disorders, given that the diagnostic category of gross stress reaction had been deleted from DSM II (American Psychiatric Association, 1968). Thus, prior to DSM–III, mental health professionals were deprived of an official diagnostic classification tool with which to specifically diagnose PTSD, even in those rare instances when the condition itself was accurately assessed and recognized.

Not unexpectedly, an obvious and often detrimental consequence of the misdiagnosis and partial diagnosis phenomena was the concomitant rendering of inadequate and inappropriate treatment to PTSD sufferers. Within the milieu of both inpatient and outpatient psychiatric facilities, well after the exposure to trauma, inappropriate treatment frequently occurred in the form of inaccurate or excessive use of psychotropic medications. In reaction to this, the individual who risked subjecting himself/herself to help often discontinued treatment and became hostile toward the "therapist" and/or the treatment facility. Concomitantly, some clinicians felt "de-skilled" and therefore tended to avoid clients who presented similar problems. The avoidance behaviors exhibited by these clinicians were often perceptible to clients, which sometimes resulted in the treatment facility gaining an unfavorable reputation.

In sum, the prolonged delay of clinical intervention, the unavailability of the diagnostic category, the therapists' lack of prior training in medical and graduate schools and/or irrational reactions, and overemphasis or circumscribed focus on premilitary development, in conjunction with the patients' reluctance to discuss emotionally painful content, have all combined to militate against the provision of accurate diagnosis and effective treatment (Blank, 1985; Horowitz, 1986; Lipkin, Blank, Parson, & Smith, 1982).

PRACTICAL AND THEORETICAL FOUNDATIONS

Various components of the "alternative" treatment approaches by the Vet Centers and other self-help-oriented programs have served to rectify some the aforementioned clinical shortcomings. Vet Center counseling staff, both mental health professionals and paraprofessionals, for example, have undergone extensive training in the recognition and clinical assessment of war-related stress reactions among Vietnam veterans. Additionally, well over half of the program's counseling staff are themselves Vietnam veterans who are successfully managing their own readjustment process, thereby serving as valuable role models for their clients. The resulting sensitivity of Vet Center staff to the presenting problems of their clients has helped to establish a key element of successful client-therapist relationships—*namely, that clients at Vet Centers tend to feel heard, acknowledged, and understood when they disclose the painful realities of their war-related trauma* (Blank, 1982; Bowen, Besecker, & Little, 1981; Little, Thacker, & Verenes, 1983). Thus, their experiences are seen as having been powerful and abnormal enough to engender a post-trauma reaction in virtually any person, irrespective of any premorbid personality characteristics.

The importance of this client perception of being heard and validated should not be understated. Effective therapeutic alliances cannot be successfully forged until sufficient agency and therapist credibility have been established. Such credibility can be promoted through clients' perceptions that the treating agency and its clinicians are capable of rendering accurate and sensitive assessments of their presenting problems. In other words, the "institutional attitude" encountered by clients will exert a major impact on their decisions about initiating and remaining engaged in treatment.

This assertion is consistent with the view of others such as Salasin (1980), who has noted Symonds' concepts of the "second injury," which refers to trauma victims' experience of not receiving the understanding and support that they need from community human service agencies. Classic examples of this "second injury" concept may be found not only in Vietnam veterans' past negative encounters with treatment facilities and mental health professionals, but also in the complaints that many rape victims have lodged with regard to the insenstitive treatment which they have experienced at times in dealings with police officers, courts, and medical examiners. Moreover, friends, relatives, and society in general may unwittingly offend the traumatized person which in turn can have a pejorative effect on the individual's condition and recovery process (Kadushin, 1985).

Due to 1) a lack of proactive clinical interventions, 2) negative feelings toward the war being misdirected toward the individual participants, and 3) a divided nation trying to come to grips with itself, the fallout from the Vietnam War continues to be significant (Kulka, Schlenger, & Chromy, 1986). However, there may be a "silver lining" in this long-lingering "cloud." As Parson (1986) stated, "only since the Vietnam War has adequate attention been given to the effects of combat stress on veterans" (p. 51). The Vet Center program has spearheaded a necessary alternative to clinical interventions which rigidly adhered to the more conventional "medical model" approach to the delivery of mental health services. The authors wish to underscore the importance of the treatment philosophy which serves as the theoretical foundation for the Vet Centers' community-based outpatient approach. It is believed, based upon a review of the literature as well as clinical experience, that this philosophy provides useful and fundamental explanations for the documented successes which this program has achieved in the outpatient treatment of PTSD, psycho-social crises, and life adjustment difficulties among Vietnam veterans. Moreover, this successful approach has important implications for proactive clinical interventions, as well as for treatment of PTSD in settings other than Vet Centers.

Several key aspects of the Vet Center program philosophy and theoretical underpinnings will be examined, along with observations on how these treatment concepts have been incorporated into the program's routine clinical operations. Periodic references will also be made with regard to implications for outpatient treatment with other survivors of traumatic experiences, such as victims of rape, criminal assaults, person-made disasters, and natural catastrophes.

Theoretical Bases for Approach

It is well documented in this volume and elsewhere (Figley, 1985; Figley, 1986; Quarantelli, 1985; Titchener, 1986) that singular, traumatic events over relatively short periods of time can necessitate clinical intervention for the emotional well-being of the affected — e.g., natural disasters, rape, severe auto accidents, etc. Combat and other war-related events have the potential for producing numerous traumas and stressors occurring repeatedly over a long period of time.

DeFazio (1978) theorized that "the Vietnam War, like other life threatening situations, involved the immersion in death in which individuals avoided psychosis or severe depression by 'psychically closing off,' e.g., retaining an acute awareness of events without experiencing the accompanying appropriate affect" (p. 35). Psychic numbing, intrusive-repetitive tendencies, and defensive denial in response to traumatic stress are the cornerstones of the traumatic stress process (Horowitz, 1976; Horowitz & Solomon, 1978). The opportunity to reattach emotions to the experiences in the safe and supportive environment provided by fellow survivors and others who care helps to forestall and circumscribe post-traumatic deterioration (Titchener, 1986). Concomitantly, the individual's ability to manage and extract value from the survivor experiences is developed. This has been a basic tenet from which the Vet Center Program and other effective interventions have evolved. It is a frame of reference which has been pivotal to the individual, group and family therapy provided throughout the Vet Center system.

Clinicians should bear in mind that combat veterans who are suffering with PTSD will sometimes direct their initial requests for professional or social service assistance for problems other than their psychological symptoms, such as unemployment, disability benefits, medical concerns, etc. While such presenting problems might not appear initially to involve PTSD, a closer examination of the client's background will sometimes reveal the existence of post-trauma stress symptoms which may be unrelated or contributing to the supposedly non-psychological problems initially presented. Moreover, socioeconomic and medical problems experienced by the individual might, in turn, serve to trigger, exacerbate, or mask the post-traumatic stress symptoms.

Once it is determined during the initial problem assessment phase that a client/patient is at risk for PTSD due to the stressors and traumas of combat, an extensive personal-social-military history becomes crucial. In fact, a personal and social history which includes an extensive military history, when conducted in a thorough and sensitive manner, can actually open numerous therapeutic doors as well as corroborate a tentative diagnosis (Figley & Leventman, 1980; Scurfield & Blank, 1985).

With PTSD, especially as found in Vietnam combat veterans, it is of great importance that the therapist be able to provide the facilitative conditions of genuineness, immediacy, responsiveness, and concreteness, among others (Carkhuff & Berenson, 1967). Most importantly, the therapist must possess and convey positive regard as a concomitant to being nonjudgmental. With regard to empathy, it is essential to be mindful of what Fuentes (1980) has referred to as "therapist transparency."

With this awareness, the therapist allows the combat veteran, who is the expert of his own experiences, to be the teacher of what those experiences were like. Therapist empathy can then occur in response to that which is learned from the client, and the therapeutic process is thereby facilitated. In contrast, the therapist's attitude and approach, if perceived as biased or negative, can have a countertherapeutic effect and result in patient dissatisfaction, isolation, and/or discontinuance of therapy (Blum, Kelly, Meyer, Carlson, & Hodson, 1984; Kolb, 1982).

In short, actively engaging veterans and other trauma survivors, and "walking" them emotionally through their experiences of stress-related and traumatic events, are the *sine qua non* to any treatment process and thorough clinical intervention. Reattaching the detached emotional response to the relevant experiences is also an essential aspect of therapy. Moreover, all approaches to treatment should consider the total person, including past and present functioning — in other words, utilize a "holistic" approach.

Psychological Debriefing

Clinical interventions with persons experiencing traumatic stress reactions are much more effective if they employ a theoretical framework in which the agency's clinicians view themselves not so much as treaters of pathology, but rather as facilitators and catalysts of a normal stress recovery and readjustment process. This philosophical orientation is viewed as being of particular clinical value in working with traumatized individuals whose life functioning, prior to the traumatic experience, was devoid of any significant psychiatric disorder — those individuals, in other words, who are already leading relatively "well-adjusted" lives.

Here it is emphasized that this category of persons experiencing PTSD should certainly be helped by therapists to achieve the realization that their post-trauma stress symptoms are indicators of a *normal and predictable* psychological healing process, and are *not* signs of "psychopathology." Indeed, DSM–III states in its diagnostic criteria for PTSD that the condition develops from exposure to traumatic stressors "which would evoke significant symptoms of distress in *almost everyone*" [emphasis ours], while DSM–III–R refers to a personal encounter with "an event that is outside the range of human experience and that would be markedly distressing to *almost anyone...*" [emphasis ours]. With reference to clinical research studies on PTSD among Vietnam veterans, Egendorf, (1982) asserts that "diagnosable conditions occur only among a minority of veterans," and that more attention should be devoted to the much larger number of veterans who are afflicted with what Egendorf calls a "subclinical malaise"—i.e., veterans who "are not suffering from a clear disorder but who could benefit greatly from some form of intervention."

The aforementioned conceptualizations of PTSD are emphasized in the theoretical model offered by Smith (1980) which is based upon extensive research and clinical experience with both Vietnam veterans and survivors of traumatic events other than combat. Smith's model recognizes that any person who survives a traumatic, life-threatening experience will undergo some form of normal and expectable psychological "stress recovery process." It might prove useful to view this recovery process as being an emotional parallel to the gradual natural biological healing which one undergoes in the aftermath of a serious physical injury such as a broken back.

The Role of Group Treatment and Support Networks with Other Survivors

The concept of the "normalcy" of the stress recovery process has important implications for the mode of treatment employed with Vietnam veterans and other survivors of trauma and catastrophy. Figley (1980) has emphasized that trauma victims should have the opportunity to engage in active contact and therapeutic dialogue with other survivors as an important means of promoting their healing process. Similarly, Blank (1979), Lifton (1973), Parson (1984), Smith (1985), and Williams (1980) have elaborated on the important role of "rap group" counseling models in the healing process of Vietnam combat veterans.

In practice, the "rap group" modality is a central part of the outpatient counseling services provided by Vet Centers, and is currently regarded by many clinicians as the treatment of choice for survivors who are experiencing PTSD or related symptoms. "Such participation for many offers for the first time the opportunity for sharing their distress with others they recognize as empathetic through similar experiences" (Kolb, 1986, p. 124). In addition to the demonstrated therapeutic value of group treatment models, they are also viewed as being more cost-effective as well as more efficient in terms of staff resource utilization.

Clinical intervention experiences with Vietnam veterans support the notion that veterans' (and other trauma survivors') understanding that their symptoms are "normal" can help to instill a sense of hope and optimism, and the view that the trauma, while presently a painful and disruptive force in one's life, can in time be psychologically integrated and managed (Brende & Parson, 1985). The healing power of group treatment in this recovery process needs to be underscored whether the treatment is rendered in an outpatient or an inpatient setting. However, it does appear that the goal of promoting a sense of normalcy among trauma survivors is more readily attainable when the level of severity in the client's symptomatology allows for treatment in a less restrictive environment which, unlike most inpatient psychiatric settings, permits the relatively well-functioning client to maintain daily living responsibilities in family and work.

Again, the acknowledgement and realization of one's capacity to maintain such functioning, even though that functioning might currently be at a less-than-optimal level, can furnish a valuable anchor in the stormy psychological aftermath of traumatic experience. Thus, we advise therapists to acknowledge and reinforce, when appropriate, all tangible indications that clients are indeed reassembling their lives in the wake of the personal fragmentation caused by their trauma. Treatment in the community on an outpatient basis, which takes into account the individual's total life functioning, should be viewed as the approach of choice. Keeping the affected individual "mainstreamed" can serve to limit life disruptions and minimize institutional impact. Inpatient institutionalization, if used prematurely, can potentially fuel the PTSD sufferer's worst fears of "being crazy." However, as a last resort and if the severity of the condition indicates, a specialized inpatient rehabilitation program may be needed for the most severely affected.

The above-stated approach, if it is to transcend the abstract and become a practical part of the foundation for effective clinical intervention, must be intuitively "felt" and actively applied by the clinicians who render treatment to traumatized persons. True understanding and insight into the essential nature of human trauma can perhaps be attained only by those clinicians who are willing to engage in serious self-reflection and processing of their own experience of despair and suffering. To accept the notion that *anyone* who experiences trauma can develop stress reactions is to acknowledge, at least in a tacit way, one's own personal vulnerability in this world—vulnerability not only to the frightening array of catastrophic events that one could possibly experience, ranging from individual criminal assault to nuclear warfare, but also to the painful psychological sequelae which are likely to ensue if one physically survives the traumatic event itself.

It thus seems plausible to hypothesize that at least some of the mental health professionals who vigorously deny the existence of PTSD, rigidly focusing instead on the role of premorbid personality variables, are in effect avoiding the disturbing realization of their own vulnerability to traumatic experience. This form of denial, along with other dimensions of therapist countertransference, should be routinely attended to during the training and clinical supervision of counselors who work with survivors of trauma.

The Role of Community Outreach in Clinical Intervention

As previously mentioned and consistent with Brende and Parson (1985) and Horowitz (1979), it has been noted throughout the Vet Center Program that certain traumatized individuals avoid seeking treatment altogether or present with secondary or camouflaged problems, e.g. information-seeking, employment opportunities, etc. In light of this, the range and depth of the Vet Centers' community outreach activities have been key components of their success in uncovering and treating stress disorders. Indeed, the nationwide Vet Center program itself was labeled "Operation Outreach" upon its inception in 1979. Based upon awareness of the conventional mental health community's limitations, the original Congressional and VA planners of the Vet Center program acted upon the recognized need to incorporate an outreach component designed to actively seek out and engage the large number of Vietnam veterans who needed treatment. Many veterans in need were disinclined to initiate treatment without prompting, due largely to the aforementioned historical factors which characterized their postwar experience—isolation, alienation from the community, inappropriate treatment approaches, and distrust of "the system," to name just a few.

Clinics and therapists intent on providing clinical treatment to Vietnam combat veterans suffering with PTSD should be mindful that other community social service agencies might have the first contact with those in need of their services (Egendorf et al., 1981). In light of this observation, it is essential to establish a solid interagency network for referral purposes.

Significant others and family members might also be the first point of contact for clinicians who provide outpatient treatment and crisis intervention services.

It seems appropriate here to examine some of the concrete, "nuts and bolts" outreach activities engaged in by Vet Centers. Outreach program counselors and administrators have routinely contacted and "networked" with a broad range of community health care and social service agencies. These, by virtue of their roles as human services providers, are excellent sources for reciprocal referral of veterans who are in need of readjustment counseling services. Such community programs include, but are certainly not limited to the following: other Veterans Administration (VA) and non-VA mental health, psychiatric, and substance abuse treatment programs (both inpatient and outpatient); public welfare agencies; crisis intervention centers (both "walk-in" and telephonic); employment and job placement services; spouse abuse centers; vocational rehabilitation programs; and veterans organizations.

Yet another client referral source which has recently gained considerable public attention is the criminal justice system. With regard to contacts developed through the legal system, Vet Center staff have conducted seminars for local police departments in order to train law enforcement officers in the recognition of behaviors which might be associated with war-related stress—more specifically, those aspects of postwar stress which might be a contributing factor in the crisis situations that police officers routinely encounter on a daily basis, such as public intoxication, domestic altercations, homelessness, vagrancy, and suicidal behaviors, as well as the less routine crises such as hostage and barricade situations. These behaviors may or may not represent manifestations of diagnosable PTSD, or may be indicative, of the "subclinical malaise" referred to by Egendorf (1982).

As for those veterans who have already "entered the system" via arrest and formal court proceedings, it should be noted that judicial authorities are frequently in search of counseling programs which can serve as a viable alternative to incarceration, particularly for defendants whose criminal records and behavioral profiles do not appear to warrant imprisonment. This is especially true in states and cities where the overcrowding of jail and prison facilities is a major sociopolitical problem. Similarly, probation and parole officials are inclined to actively seek out and employ structured counseling services for their clients, particularly those programs which offer alternatives to incarceration and real potential for lowering the risk of recidivism.

The clinical benefits emanating from Vet Centers' active "networking" efforts, such as those mentioned above, have been numerous and noteworthy.

One valuable outcome of these efforts has been the ongoing education and sensitization of mental health and human service professionals, a training process which has rendered these clinicians more capable of recognizing, understanding, and treating post-traumatic stress disorders among the clients whom they serve. Blank (1982) has pointed out, for example, that within inpatient psychiatric facilities there has historically existed a "dramatic failure to diagnose war-related stress disorders" (p. 915). He describes having personally observed "approximately 75 such cases" of inappropriate diagnoses over an eight-year period at one VA Medical Center, noting further that in 1980 "the phenomenon disappeared at that hospital due to the inception of Operation Outreach" (Blank, p. 915).

Largely as a result of their educational contacts with Vet Center staff and other well-informed consultants, some mental health professionals, as a routine component of their clinical assessment work-ups, are inquiring about their clients' military histories and are exploring the possible relevance of this data in greater detail when it is discovered that the client served in the Southeast Asia war zone. By extension, personal-social histories which unearth identifiable traumas should trigger greater exploration into the post-trauma stress recovery process. The relatively simple process of asking for such data from the client can be a critically important step towards obtaining meaningful clues about the etiology of presenting problems and symptomatology of a traumatic stress reaction.

An outpatient treatment program should also direct its outreach activities towards those community institutions which, while not being in the strict category of public human service agencies, nonetheless constitute important social support systems which psychologically troubled veterans might be utilizing. Examples are churches, synagogues, and similar religious organizations where veterans and/or their families might be seeking help in the form of pastoral counseling and spiritual guidance. Some communities have active cross-denominational ministers' alliances which regularly convene to address the collective spiritual and social service needs of their communities.

Vet Center staff have arranged educational seminars for such organizations, resulting in the valuable dissemination of information about readjustment counseling services to congregations and religious groups throughout the community. This can be an especially viable strategy for outreach to Black clients and other racial/ethnic minorities whose sociocultural experience and distrust for "the system" often render them more likely to seek assistance for "personal problems" from a well-respected and trusted person in their own communities, such as a member of the clergy.

The aforementioned suggestions on outreach to church groups provide impetus for some brief observations regarding the role of clergy in the multidisciplinary treatment of PTSD. It is the authors' observation that pastoral counseling, when provided by a properly trained clergy sensitive to the psychosocial stresses of postwar readjustment, can be especially useful and desirable for veterans who are philosophically inclined to accept such counseling. This may be particularly true when a significant portion of the veteran's problems consists of profound moral, spiritual, or existential issues.

Many clinicians, in the course of treating Vietnam veterans and other survivors of trauma, have often found their clients—and themselves as well—struggling with deep-seated and unresolved feelings of guilt, unworthiness, hatred, self-blame, remorse, grief, and loss, as well as the associated existential issues of forgiveness, atonement, self-acceptance, interpersonal connectedness, loving/being loved, and the sorting out of one's sense of personal meaning in the world. Both clients and therapists encounter powerful issues during the readjustment counseling process, and these offer vital paths to be explored in the course of individual and collective quests for personal and community healing from the aftermath of war or other forms of catastrophic human experience.

Marin (1981) has addressed many of these matters, arguing that the examination of moral issues constitutes a necessary, albeit painful element of any forthright analysis of the global human implications of the Vietnam War experience. In view of the above observations, clinicians are advised to remain open to the possible benefits of utilizing auxiliary counseling services when it appears that doing so might provide a valuable resource in the treatment process.

CRISIS INTERVENTION

As individuals, especially combat veterans, suffering with PTSD attempt to cope in the community, untreated conditions become increasingly vulnerable to crisis situations due to the deterioration of already ineffective coping processes interacting with the stressors of daily living. Where an individual has been suffering with PTSD for a long time and/or there is a delayed onset of symptoms, clinicians might become involved in the case at a point of crisis. Even when a client is already involved in the therapeutic process, the need for crisis intervention may arise.

The authors have observed that sometimes combat veterans who begin to deal with painful emotional content report feeling worse in the initial stages of treatment. This symptom intensification phenomenon has been likened to the fever which flares up when the body is fighting a physical infection. In some instances, this might result in increased self-medication or other ineffective coping attempts, thereby precipitating a crisis in the individual's life. In other instances, the individual may feel overwhelmed by his/her emotional state and see no recourse other than suicide. In all of the above situations, elements of PTSD exacerbated by stress from day-to-day life may require crisis intervention. Therefore, it is essential that strategies be developed and contingency plans formulated so that a safety net can be established for crisis-prone clients.

Crisis Intervention from an Outpatient Treatment Perspective

The major purpose of this section is to briefly identify some of the major types of crisis situations which are routinely encountered with Vietnam veterans, and to offer suggested guidelines for effective intervention. It is not our purpose here to provide an in-depth or exhaustive review of crisis intervention theory and procedures; such information is readily available elsewhere in the clinical literature (Linn, 1980; Resnick, 1980). The guidelines suggested here are offered more as a strategic framework for staff preparedness, because effective intervention and crisis management, particularly with life-threatening situations, can be accomplished only if those providing the intervention are adequately trained and equipped to respond to the crises which they encounter. It is thus crucial that clinical supervisors furnish staff training and development in crisis intervention policy and procedures.

Types of Crises Found Among Vietnam Veterans

The term "crisis," as used in this discussion, will be generally defined as an emergency situation wherein a client's behaviors and/or psychological state are such that he/she is considered to be a threat to self or others. Adcock (1982) has noted basic categories of such emergencies:

1. *Psychiatric Cases:* Those emergency situations involving persons who are suicidal, homicidal, assaultive, in a state of excessive chemical intoxication, or whose control of their violent impulses is not intact or functional.
2. *Perceived Emergencies/Crises:* Those life conditions or experiences perceived by the client to be presently unmanageable or overwhelming, such as extreme marital strife, loss of a loved one through death or separation, anxiety reactions, or financial destitution.

With regard to the first of these two categories, the authors have clinically observed a variety of psychiatric crises presented by Vietnam veterans who were experiencing more severe post-traumatic stress reactions. Some of the most difficult crisis situations involve reexperiencing of the trauma through recurrent and intrusive recollections of the original traumatic event, such as vivid nightmares of seeing close friends brutally killed in combat firefights (Ziarnowski & Broida, 1984). The traumatic reexperiencing also commonly manifests itself during the waking state through various forms of intrusive imagery of the traumatic episode.

The crisis-precipitating element of such traumatic reexperiencing is commonly associated with heightened states of anxiety and autonomic arousal triggered by intrusive imagery, resulting in the painful disruption of the individual's normal day-to-day life activities. Intrusive recollections experienced during the waking state are commonly referred to as "flashbacks," which can range from a momentary remembrance to relatively lengthy unconscious flashbacks (dissociative states). During the latter, one subjectively feels and sometimes symbolically reenacts or behaves as though the original traumatic event were actually reoccurring.

Such experiences can be evoked by a wide variety of environmental conditions or events which serve to trigger one's cognitive and affective memory of the trauma (Kolb, 1986). A few examples of environmental stimuli which have been known to commonly trigger such recollections are: Vietnam veterans seeing helicopters, which remind them of experiences such as landing in "hot L.Z.s" (landing zones) in the war zone or loading wounded and dying friends onto med-evac choppers; hot, humid weather that is strongly reminiscent of the fierce tropical climate which prevailed in Vietnam; odors; movies or televised news programs containing realistic and graphic representations of combat action.

Included in the category of "perceived emergencies" among Vietnam veterans are life experiences in the present-day postwar environment which evoke feeling states similar to those associated with past trauma. Such emotional stimuli might consist of the sudden, unexpected loss of a loved one, which triggers not only the predictable grief reactions over the current loss, but which also releases a flood of long-unresolved feelings connected with the tragic loss of friends through combat in Vietnam.

The life-threatening potential of these traumatic reexperiencing episodes frequently arises from the extremely painful and volatile emotional states which accompany the more graphic and intrusive imagery — overwhelming feelings of guilt, grief, abandonment, rejection, isolation, vulnerability, anger, and rage. Such affective states can overburden the already-fragile coping capacities of the psychologically troubled veterans, leading to a sense of losing control or to combat zone retaliation fantasies which can result in suicidal and/or homicidal ideation and feelings (Yost, 1980). Impulse control can, of course, become further impaired from chemical abuse, as is often the case with at-risk veterans who self-medicate their PTSD symptoms with alcohol or other drugs. This combination can be viewed as a statement or "scream" for help, with the precipitated crisis situation providing the vehicle for hoped-for relief and treatment.

Clinicians are advised to bear in mind that veterans who are experiencing highly-dissociative "flashback" states might unconsciously revert to behaviors formerly engaged in to protect themselves from enemy assault in the combat zone. These dissociative states have resulted, for example, in situations wherein a combat veteran has barricaded himself in a building with weapons, behaving as though he were defending his base-camp perimeter from a Viet Cong attack, when in actuality the "enemy" was the police SWAT Team which had been called to respond to the situation.

Crisis episodes of this extreme nature, if they are to be successfully resolved without a tragic ending, often require the well-coordinated teamwork of skillful counselors along with patient and sensitive law enforcement personnel who have been adequately trained to respond to these situations. The need for high quality crisis intervention training becomes especially crucial when dealing with significantly distressed war veterans whose capacity for violence has been intensified by the psychological and behavioral fallout from their combat experiences—war-zone situations wherein violence was experienced not as a remote abstraction, but rather as a concrete, necessary, and recurring reality of day-to-day survival.

Mental health workers are also urged to think not only in terms of crisis *intervention* techniques, but to also devote much attention to the area of crisis *prevention*. Within outpatient settings in particular, where a clinician's contact with a client is typically limited to one to three hours per week, it becomes especially critical to develop one's ability to perceive and therapeutically address those behavioral "early warning signals" which indicate possible escalation of the client's potential for violence and loss of impulse control.

Therapists are encouraged to acquaint themselves with an eclectic range of cognitive, behavioral, and affect-centered techniques which can be employed to reduce the risk of explosive behavior. Among those approaches which might be explored are Horowitz and Solomon's "hierarchical routes of behavior" (1978), as well as the techniques of Gestalt Therapy (Perls, 1969; Polster & Polster, 1974). Such techniques, when appropriately utilized in the proper therapeutic context, can help clients develop and expand their repertoire of anger management and stress reduction skills.

It is also strongly advised that outpatient therapists cultivate their skills in the area of family counseling, in view of the fact that community-based treatment programs are often called upon to intervene in domestic crises. Family interventions require that the therapist be able to effectively respond not only to the "identified client's" PTSD symptoms, but also to a wide range of intrafamily relationship dynamics which may both fuel and be fueled by the stress disorder. Families and significant others can play a major role in the amelioration of PTSD when they are appropriately integrated into the treatment process (Herndon & Law, 1986; Herndon, Law, & Gelsomino, 1987; Stanton & Figley, 1978).

The need for effective interagency networking should be highlighted as a critical program objective with regard to crisis intervention preparedness. It is particularly advisable for outpatient programs to develop viable and well-coordinated referral mechanisms for arranging client admissions into inpatient treatment facilities for crisis stabilization. Emergency inpatient care may be indicated when the crisis is of such severity and life-threatening potential that outpatient care alone cannot provide sufficient stabilization for the client.

Outpatient programs, particularly those with a small number of staff members (such as the 3 to 5 person Vet Center teams), are urged to take their limited personnel resources into account when planning their crisis intervention policy and procedures. Some Vet Centers, for example, have found it not advisable to routinely make their staff available for 24-hour crisis intervention duty, in order to avoid staff overload and burnout.

The high risk of job-related burnout among health care professionals is well-documented (Cherniss, 1980; Patrick, 1981), and should certainly be taken into account by clinicians who are exposed to the highly intense emotional demands involved in working with survivors of trauma. Routinely, all crisis interventions should be followed by an after-incident review which includes all parties involved. This crisis intervention "autopsy" should help to reinforce effective responses and eliminate/reduce inappropriate ones.

As a final recommendation, outpatient programs are advised to establish written guidelines on the management of life-threatening crisis situations. Such guidelines should address clinically-observed client needs and presenting problems, and should realistically reflect staff resources and capabilities. Furthermore, all newly-hired staff should, as an integral part of their job orientation, receive thorough training with regard to the agency's crisis intervention procedures, as well as ongoing updates.

EMPIRICAL FINDINGS

The relative dearth of scientific research and program evaluation in the area of war-related clinical interventions and stress does not appear to be due to happenstance. Milgram (1986) outlined a number of factors which inhibit and militate against scientific study of war-related stress. These include: 1) increased exposure to man inflicting death and pain on man; 2) a sense of aiding and abetting war activity through conducting research in the area; and 3) a belief that increased wherewithal in treating war-related stress will facilitate militarism.

In order to overcome these resistances, a high priority designation is necessary from within and without those agencies, departments, and branches of government responsible for the well-being of those at risk.

The clinical intervention which has come to be known as the Vet Center Program emerged after being stymied for nearly a decade within the Congress of the United States (Fuller, 1985). The design for this new treatment intervention and approach to war veterans grew out of specific needs and the experience of pioneers around the country who were attempting to comprehend as well as ameliorate the emotional pain and suffering they were encountering.

Not only was there a failure to recognize returning combat veterans as individuals at risk for PTSD, but psychological debriefing and "untraining" from combat readiness were virtually unheard of at that time. Psychological debriefing has been referred to earlier and is incorporated in the Vet Center Program. However, the "untraining" of the survival skills such as dehumanization, reliance on weapons, vigilance, "kill or be killed," which enhance one's ability to survive combat also need to be studied and addressed directly through or as an augmentation to clinical intervention.

As already discussed, the veterans of combat had their situation further compounded by negative reactions of a society misplacing and displacing its hostility. Moreover, as Smith (1986) pointed out, the United States neglected those it had committed to combat by failing to provide the necessary rites of reentry and ceremonies which are identifiable since primitive times and throughout history for the purpose of "cleansing" one's veterans of combat. "Following previous wars in America, remnants of those more 'primitive' rites and rituals have persisted in parades, medal

award ceremonies, uniforms and veterans' organizations. All these procedures symbolize the ritual of *sanction*, which tribes have traditionally
bestowed on their warriors" (Smith, 1986, p. 21). The complexity of
reactions to trauma and stress has been researched and "both traumatic
experience and type of psychological reaction to it directly affect the
presence and level of stress symptomatology" (Laufer, Frey-Wouters, &
Gallops, 1985, p. 88).

The Legacies of Vietnam Study (Egendorf et al., 1981) authorized by
Congress in 1977, documented and reported there was an extensive need
for clinical intervention with veterans from Vietnam. This corroborated
the 1978 issuance from the President's Commission on Mental Health and
studies conducted by Louis Harris and Associates in 1971 and 1980.
While estimates abound and appear quite considerable, "precise national
estimates of the *number* of Vietnam Veterans experiencing readjustment
problems and of the *severity* of those problems are not available. Prevailing data on the nature, scope, and etiology of such problems are subject to
substantial limitations" (Kulka, Schlenger, & Chromy, 1986, p. 2).

A study authorized in 1984 by the Veterans Administration and currently
underway hopefully will provide more definitive answers to incidence
and prevalence questions. Notwithstanding the unavailability of these
data, there appears to be general agreement by clinicians and scientists
alike that current clinical interventions are responding to a need of epidemic proportions (Blank, 1985; Egendorf, et al., 1981; Kulka, Schlenger,
& Chromy, 1986).

A study conducted in 1980 surveyed the consumer's perspective of
clinical and psychosocial services being delivered through Vet Centers in
the community (Bowen, Besecker, & Little, 1981). The feedback from this
study reflected a high level of client satisfaction with the clinical interventions provided to address their needs. Numerous anecdotes and unsolicited
oral and written testimony from veterans and their families corroborate
the results from the study.

Subsequently, an evaluation of the Vet Center operation was conducted
during 1983 to determine program effectiveness and assess its impact on
Vietnam veterans and their families (Little, Thacker, & Verenes, 1983).
This summative program evaluation found that the Vet Centers were
accomplishing their mission and clinical interventions were on target for
the most part in terms of assisting combat veterans and their families to
readjust to civilian life. This was being accomplished through a combination of strategic outreach, appropriate referral within established community networks, and the direct delivery of a full range of counseling services
oriented toward readjustment rather than psychopathology. Additional

systematic program evaluation and outcome studies need to be designed and conducted in order to build a data base for further refinement and development of clinical intervention models.

In a more systematic way and at earlier points in time relative to the war-related events, Milgram (1986) reported on empirical studies which have resulted from Israeli war encounters and experiences. These studies indicate that severity of combat with its related higher rate of casualties correlates with an increased incidence of traumatic stress reactions and other psychiatric diagnoses (Noy, Nardi, & Solomon, 1986). Similar results have been found for Vietnam veterans exposed to intense combat (Egendorf et al., 1981), thus yielding cross-cultural evidence of the relationship. This underscores a need for a more proactive and immediate clinical intervention for those most vulnerable.

Support for the concepts, principles, and benefits of immediate treatment in proximity to the combat area with the expectation of return to one's unit have been gleaned from Israeli war-related involvements (Milgram, 1986). Such data emerge from the context of a profound sense of community and commitment in and outside of the military, a data base for which a high price has been paid in terms of lost lives and traumatic stress, but one that is "based on the unique geopolitical situation in which Israel finds itself" (Milgram, 1986, p. xxxv).

During World War I and World War II, the overall military experience, immediacy of clinical interventions, and sense of a supportive nation were relatively consistent with and more closely approximated the Israeli experience than was the case during the Vietnam War (Lifton, 1978; Milgram, 1986; Stretch, 1986). Although exact figures are unavailable, it is inferred that the PTSD casualties from World War I and World War II would be proportionately lower than that found in Vietnam veterans, notwithstanding the lower psychiatric casualty rate during the Vietnam War (Milgram, 1986; Milgram & Hobfoll, 1986; Stretch, 1986.) Based on an estimate that more than 700,000 Vietnam combat veterans suffer from PTSD, the mental health needs of this group are substantial and pervasive. The findings of Milgram and other investigators (1986) strongly suggest that clinical interventions which incorporate the concepts of immediacy, proximity, expectancy, and sense of community can be effective in reducing some of the negative psychological impact of war-related events.

GAPS IN KNOWLEDGE

Thus far, we have highlighted the delayed clinical interventions now required by a previous lack of response to trauma effects in veterans from

Vietnam war events. As mentioned earlier and for reasons previously cited, this situation can be considered a worst case scenario requiring an array of strategies to deal with PTSD, both delayed and chronic. Comparatively and conversely, the Israeli experience with clinical interventions during and after wartime occurred for the most part under "best case" circumstances. These more responsive clinical interventions along with staunch national support have resulted in a relatively low incidence of PTSD (Milgram & Hobfoll, 1986). Furthermore, comparisons have been made between World War II and the 1973 Yom Kippur War on the one hand and World War I and the 1982 Israeli War in Lebanon on the other. The evidence from this comparative study suggests that front echelon clinical interventions are more efficacious than delayed clinical interventions (Milgram & Hobfoll, 1986). Further, crosscultural and interwar comparisons are useful tools for identifying and crystallizing state-of-the-art clinical interventions for war-related events.

In the military, individuals are exposed to rigorous basic and advanced training regimens. These include weaponry familiarization, quick-kill techniques, dehumanization of the enemy, etc. Such procedures are well developed. However, little has been done to facilitate necessary readjustment. The utility of providing continuity of care and/or readjustment needs to be programmed and subjected to comparative study.

Milgram and Hobfoll (1986) have pointed out that "ecological consistency" should be added to the Vet Center program and inpatient stress recovery units. They feel that this is an important dimension since it is within the military that the trauma occurred and therefore it is argued that approximating the military or providing this form of clinical intervention within the military would facilitate rehabilitation. This suggestion warrants further investigation through pilot programs which encompass the principle.

Stretch (1986) noted that the prevalence of PTSD in civilian veterans was greater than that for Vietnam veterans still on active duty, at least for those responding to his survey. He found the social supports in the military setting to be a factor in this difference. Further study of the interaction between certain personality types, social, and cultural setting and demographics would shed light necessary for the further refinement of clinical interventions subsequent to the trauma and stress of war as well as ecological consistency questions and issues.

Another area which needs to be further explored and studied deals with differential intervention. The Vet Center program utilizes numerous clinical and crisis interventions. Israel has used varied approaches at different times. Working toward a systematic approach of matching individual experiences and reactions to particular clinical interventions would appear to be a beneficial direction in which to travel lest we end up with a procrustean approach.

Lastly, Brende and Parson (1985), in discussing Mardi Horowitz's work at the Center for the Study of Neuroses in San Francisco, state that he

> undertook an interesting experiment testing "normal people" watching disturbing movies, and found that they too, for a period after, were plagued by intrusive images and memories. This finding substantiated what many mothers fear, that children who watch violent television programs before bedtime will have nightmares. It also suggested the significant finding that observers of a traumatic event are likely to have nearly as intense an emotional involvement in the event as the victim. (pp. 79–80)

By extrapolation, this has powerful implications. It raises many questions about the impact on those who watched the Vietnam War and other wars on television. What kinds of clinical interventions or preventive measures can facilitate the recovery and healing process for a nation which electronically participates in war-related events?

IMPLICATIONS FOR TRAINING, SERVICES, RESEARCH AND SOCIAL POLICY

At the outset of this chapter, it was stated that a number of factors have hindered the accurate diagnosis, effective clinical intervention, and appropriate treatment of PTSD. With the advent of DSM–III, the proliferation of articles and books on the condition, and the availability of expertise in the community for training purposes, the problems of misdiagnosis and failure to adequately treat or ensure treatment take on different meaning and raise new issues (e.g., malpractice, clinical privileges, competency). It is in the best interest of patients/clients and society, as well as of the health care professionals/paraprofessionals throughout the nation, to close the gap between available knowledge and actual treatment practices. This can be achieved through inclusion of such knowledge in formalized course work offered in graduate/medical schools as well as in continuing education requirements. As a result, the extant epidemic proportions of the PTSD condition can more fully and effectively be confronted and suffering lessened (Blank, 1982; Egendorf et al., 1981). Clearly, PTSD is not limited to combat veterans and is increasingly recognizable in the residual aftermath of disasters, catastrophes, and other life-threatening events

(Burgess & Holmstrom, 1976; Hoiberg & McCaughey, 1984; Powell & Penick, 1983; Quarantelli, 1985; Terr, 1983).

Largely as a result of knowledge gained in recent years through research and clinical experience with Vietnam veterans, allied health professionals and public policy planners have begun to devote considerable attention to the importance of acute care and early intervention with survivors of traumatic events such as rape, criminal assault, and natural disasters. Identifiably proactive and early clinical interventions are common threads throughout Milgram's (1986) work. When one reviews the clinical interventions which have been necessitated by the emergent nature of veterans suffering from the traumas and stressors of combat exposure years earlier, it becomes abundantly clear that a proactive stance is necessary to preclude the high incidence and severity levels of PTSD from recurring in any future conflicts that might arise.

Necessity and reactive creativity have resulted in a well-developed community-based set of clinical interventions and inpatient stress recovery units. Lessons from the Israeli experience underscore the importance of incorporating principles of expectancy, immediacy and proximity in clinical interventions in order to improve prognosis and course of recovery (Milgram, 1986). However, just as important is the need to be proactive in terms of strategic planning and preparedness as a social policy.

The aforementioned proactive posture, readiness of well-trained, mobile, mental health professionals and paraprofessionals who could respond on short notice, and cooperative efforts between the Department of Defense and Veterans Administration which focus on coordination and collaboration are essential ingredients of effective clinical intervention. Such an approach envisions continuity of care through maximizing the principles of immediacy, proximity, expectancy and sense of community throughout the military-related phase. These operations would then be closely linked with the community-based readjustment services described earlier in this chapter.

Thus, proactive preparation and responsiveness would be coupled with the capability to react and adapt to specific needs as they arise. As Starkey and Ashlock (1986) explicate, "for military personnel who have experienced combat or other military-related trauma, the ideal time for treatment from a clinical standpoint is while the person is still on active duty, possibly as part of the mustering out process" (p.44). To this clinical intervention would be added the joint and collaborative efforts expounded above between the military and Veterans affairs, as well as the essential continuum of care.

Research which includes evaluative and outcome studies should be inextricably interwoven into all aspects of clinical interventions associated with war-related events. This dimension would provide ongoing feedback over time to identify and facilitate needed adjustments to the approaches being utilized. Crosscultural and comparative studies should be designed and implemented whenever and wherever feasible, since no one would purposely orchestrate a war for experiment's sake.

In light of the foregoing and with a desire to minimize PTSD and elements thereof, implications for social policy emerge:

1. there needs to be a national commitment to those sent into combat;
2. the reasons for involvement need to be clear and have a sound moral basis;
3. a sense of community is needed within and without the military;
4. service to one's country needs to be equitable and all who serve should share the burden as equally as possible;
5. respect for and loyalty to the military needs to be cultivated;
6. drug and alcohol abuse should not be condoned at any level of the military;
7. capable mental health components should be trained, ready, and mobile in order to deal with whatever contingency might evolve; and
8. wars, responsibilities, and related issues must not become confused with the warriors required to respond (Berman, Price, & Gusman, 1982; Milgram & Hobfoll, 1986; Stretch, 1986).

Society has a responsibility to be proactive on behalf of those who put their lives on the line for their country. Only to the extent that clinical interventions reduce emotional pain and long-term suffering can mental health professionals and policymakers establish themselves in essential leadership roles.

BIBLIOGRAPHY

Adcock, J. (1982). *Crisis Intervention Handbook.* Unpublished manuscript, Jackson, Vet Center, Jackson, MS.

American Psychiatric Association (1968). *Diagnostic and Statistical Manual of Mental Disorders (2nd Edition).* Washington, D.C.: American Psychiatric Association.

American Psychiatric Association (1980). *Diagnostic and Statistical Manual of Mental Disorders (3rd Edition).* Washington, D.C.: American Psychiatric Association.

American Psychiatric Association (1987). *Diagnostic and Statistical Manual (3rd Edition — Revised).* Washington, D.C.: American Psychiatric Association.

Berman, S., Price, S., & Gusman, F. (1982). An inpatient program for Vietnam combat veterans in a Veterans Administration hospital. *Hospital and Community Psychiatry,* 33: 919–922.

Blank, A. S. (1979). *The Therapeutic Process in Rap Groups.* First Training Conference Papers of the Vietnam Veterans Operation Outreach. Unpublished manuscript. Washington, D.C., Veterans Administration Central office.

Blank, A. S. (1982). Apocalypse terminable and interminable: Operation outreach for Vietnam veterans. *Hospital & Community Psychiatry,* 33(11): 913–918.

Blank, A. S. (1985). Irrational reactions to post-traumatic stress disorder and Vietnam veterans. In S. Sonnenberg, A. Blank & J. Talbott. (Eds.), *The Trauma of War; Stress and Recovery in Vietnam Veterans* (pp. 69–98). Washington, D.C.: American Psychiatric Press.

Blum, M. D., Kelly, E. M., Meyer, M., Carlson, C. R., & Hodson, W. L. (1984). An assessment of the treatment needs of Vietnam-era veterans. *Hospital & Community Psychiatry,* 35(7): 691–696.

Bowen, R. M., Besecker, W. J., & Little, K. L. (1981). *Readjustment Counseling Program for Veterans of the Vietnam Era: Program Evaluation-Formative Phase.* Washington, D.C.: Veterans Administration.

Brende, J. O., & Parson, E. R. (1985). *Vietnam Veterans: The Road to Recovery.* New York: Plenum.

Burgess, A. W., & Holmstrom, L. L. (1976). Coping behavior of the rape victim. *American Journal of Psychiatry,* 133(4): 413–418.

Carkhuff, R., & Berenson, B. (1967). *Beyond Counseling and Therapy.* New York: Holt, Rinehart & Winston.

Cherniss, C. (1980). *Staff Burnout: Job Stress in the Human Services.* Beverly Hills, CA: Sage Publications.

DeFazio, V. J. (1978). Dynamic perspectives on the nature and effects of combat stress. In C. R. Figley (Ed.), *Stress Disorders Among Vietnam Veterans.* New York: Brunner/Mazel.

Domash, M. D., & Sparr, L. F. (1982). Post-traumatic stress disorder masquerading as paranoid schizophrenia: Case report. *Military Medicine,* 147: 772–774.

Egendorf, A. (1982). The postwar healing of Vietnam veterans: Recent research. *Hospital & Community Psychiatry,* 33(11): 901–908.

Egendorf, A., Kadushin, C., Laufer, R. S., Rothbart, G., & Sloan, L. (1981). *Legacies of Vietnam: Comparative Adjustment of Veterans and Their Peers.* Washington, D.C.: Veterans Administration, U.S. Government Printing Office.

Figley. C. R. (Ed.) (1978). *Stress Disorders Among Vietnam Veterans.* New York: Brunner/Mazel.

Figley, C. R. (1980). The glory and the gore! An introduction to Section I. In C. R. Figley & S. Leventman (Eds.), *Strangers at Home: Vietnam Veterans Since the War* (pp. 3–8). New York: Praeger.

Figley, C. R. (Ed.) (1985). *Trauma and Its Wake (Vol. I).* New York: Brunner/Mazel.

Figley, C. R. (Ed.) (1986). *Trauma and Its Wake (Vol II).* New York: Brunner/Mazel.

Figley, C. R., & Leventman, S. (Eds.) (1980). *Strangers at Home: Vietnam Veterans Since the War.* New York: Praeger.

Fuentes, R. (1980). Therapist transparency. In T. Williams (Ed.), *Post-Traumatic Stress Disorders of the Vietnam Veterans.* Cincinnati, OH: Disabled American Veterans.

Fuller, R. B. (1985). War veterans' post-traumatic stress disorder and the U.S. Congress. In W. Kelly (Ed.), *Post-Traumatic Stress Disorder and the War Veteran Patient* (pp. 3–11). New York: Brunner/Mazel.

Harris, L., & Associates (1971). *A Study of the Problems Facing Vietnam Era Veterans: Their Readjustment to Civilian Life.* Washington, D.C.: Louis Harris & Associates.

Harris, L., & Associates (1980). *Myths and Realities: A Study of Attitudes Toward Vietnam Era Veterans.* Washington, D.C.: Louis Harris & Associates.

Herndon, A. D., & Law, J. G. (1986). Post-traumatic stress and the family: A multimethod approach to counseling. In C. R. Figley (Ed.), *Trauma and Its Wake (Vol. II)* (pp. 264–279). New York: Brunner/Mazel.

Herndon, A. D., Law, J., & Gelsomino, J. (1987). *Post-Traumatic Stress Disorder: Family Coping Styles.* Submitted for Publication.

Hoiberg, A., & McCaughey, B. G. (1984). The traumatic aftereffects of collision at sea. *American Journal of Psychiatry,* 141(1): 70–73.

Horowitz, M. J. (1976). *Stress Response Syndromes.* New York: Aronson.

Horowitz, M. J. (1979). *States of Mind.* New York: Plenum.

Horowitz, M. J. (1986). Stress-response syndromes: A review of posttraumatic and adjustment disorders. *Hospital & Community Psychiatry,* 37(3): 241–249.

Horowitz, M., & Solomon, G. (1978). Delayed stress response syndromes in Vietnam veterans. In C. R. Figley (Ed.), *Stress Disorder Among Vietnam Veterans.* New York: Brunner/Mazel.

Kadushin, C. (1985). Social networks, helping networks, and Vietnam veterans. In S. Sonnenberg, A. Blank, & J. Talbott (Eds.), *The Trauma of War: Stress and Recovery in Vietnam Veterans* (pp. 57–68). Washington, D.C.: American Psychiatric Press.

Kepner, C. H., & Tregoe, B. B. (1981). *The New Rational Manager.* Princeton: Princeton Research Press.

Kolb, L. C. (1982). Healing the wounds of Vietnam. *Hospital & Community Psychiatry,* 33(11): 877.

Kolb, L. C. (1986). Treatment of chronic post-traumatic stress disorders. In *Current Psychiatric Therapies, Vol. 23,* (pp. 119–128). New York: Grune & Stratton.

Kulka, R. A., Schlenger, W. E., & Chromy, J. R. (1986). *The National Vietnam Veterans Readjustment Study (NVVRS): Objectives, Design and Initial Implementation.* Research Triangle Parks, Research Triangle Institute.

Laufer, R. S., Frey-Wouters, E., & Gallops, M. S. (1985). Traumatic stressors in the Vietnam War and post-traumatic stress disorder. In C. R. Figley (Ed.), *Trauma and Its Wake* (pp. 73–89). New York: Brunner/Mazel.

Lifton, R. J. (1973). *Home from the War.* New York: Simon & Schuster.

Lifton, R. J. (1978). Advocacy and corruption in the healing profession. In C. R. Figley (Ed.), *Stress Disorders Among Vietnam Veterans* (pp. 209–230). New York: Brunner/Mazel.

Linn, L. (1980). Other psychiatric emergencies. In H. I. Kaplan, A. M. Freedman, & B. J. Sadock (Eds.), *Comprehensive Textbook of Psychiatry, 3rd Edition.* Baltimore & London: Williams & Wilkins.

Lipkin, J. O., Blank, A. S., Parson, E. R., & Smith, J. R. (1982). Vietnam veterans and posttraumatic stress disorder. *Hospital & Community Psychiatry,* 33(11): 908–912.

Lipton, M. I., & Schaffer, W. R. (1986). Post-traumatic stress disorder in the older veteran. *Military Medicine,* 151: 522–524.

Little, K. L., Thacker, B. M., & Verenes, C. G. (1983). *An Evaluation of the Veterans Administration's Readjustment Counseling Program for Veterans of the Vietnam Era: Summative evaluation (Phase II).* Washington, D.C.: Veterans Administration.

Marin, P. (1981). Living in moral pain. *Psychology Today,* November (15), 68–80.

Milgram, N. A. (Ed.) (1986). *Stress and Coping in Time of War: Generalizations From the Israeli Experience.* New York: Brunner/Mazel.

Milgram, N. A., & Hobfoll, S. (1986). Generalizations from therory and practice in war-related stress. In N. Milgram (Ed.), *Stress and Coping in Time of War: Generalizations From the Israeli Experience* (pp. 316–352). New York: Brunner/Mazel.

Modlin, H. C. (1986). Posttraumatic stress disorder: No longer just for war veterans. *Postgraduate Medicine,* 79(3): 26–42.

Naisbitt, J. (1984). *Megatrends.* New York: Warner Books.

Noy, S., Nardi, C., & Solomon, Z. (1986). Battle and military unit characteristics and the prevalence of psychiatric casualties. In N. Milgram (Ed.), *Stress and Coping in Time of War: Generalizations From the Israeli Experience* (pp. 73–77). New York: Brunner/Mazel.

Parson, E. R. (1984). Role of psychodynamic group therapy in the treatment of the combat veteran. In H. Schwartz (Ed.), *Psychotherapy of the Combat Veteran.* New York: S. P. Medical and Scientific Books (Spectrum, Inc.).

Parson, E. R. (1986). The Vet Center system: Psychosocial services for Vietnam veterans. *VA Practitioner,* December, 51–54.

Patrick, P. (1981). *Health Care Worker Burn-Out: What It Is, What to Do About It*, Chicago: Blue Cross Assn.

Perls, F. S. (1969). *Gestalt Therapy Verbatim*. Lafayette, IN: Real People Press.

Polster, E., & Polster, M. (1974). *Gestalt Therapy Integrated: Contours of Theory and Practice*. New York: Vintage Books.

Powell, B. J., & Penick, E. C. (1983). Psychological distress following a natural disaster: A one-year follow-up of 98 flood victims. *Journal of Community Psychology,* 11: 269–276.

President's Commission on Mental Health. Report of the Special Working Group: Mental Health Problems of Vietnam Era Veterans. Washington, D.C., February 15, 1978.

Quarantelli, E. L. (1985). An assessment of conflicting views on mental health: The consequences of traumatic events. In C. Figley (Ed.), *Trauma and Its Wake* (pp. 173–215). New York: Brunner/Mazel.

Resnick, H. L. P. (1980). Suicide. In H. I Kaplan, A. M. Freedman, & B. J. Sadock (Eds.), *Comprehensive Textbook of Psychiatry, 3rd Edition*. Baltimore & London: Williams & Wilkins.

Salasin, S. (1980). Treating Vietnam veterans as survivors: An interview with Charles Figley. *Evaluation and Change* (Special Issue), 135–141.

Scurfield, R. M., & Blank, A. S. (1985). A guide to obtaining a military history from Vietnam veterans. In S. Sonnenberg, A. Blank, & J. Talbott (Eds.), *The Trauma of War: Stress and Recovery in Vietnam Veterans* (pp. 263–291). Washington, D.C.: American Psychiatric Press.

Smith, J. R. (1980). *Vietnam Veterans: Rap Groups and the Stress Recovery Process*. Unpublished manuscript, Duke University.

Smith, J. R. (1981). *Common Questions About Post-Combat Stress Reactions*. Unpublished manuscript, Duke University.

Smith, J. R. (1985). Rap groups and group therapy for Vietnam veterans. In S. Sonnenberg, A. Blank, & J. Talbott (Eds.), *The Trauma of War: Stress and Recovery in Vietnam Veterans,* (pp. 165–191). Washington, D.C.: American Psychiatric Press.

Smith, J. R. (1986). Sealing over and integration: Modes of resolution in the post-traumatic stress recovery process. In C. R. Figley (Ed.), *Trauma and Its Wake (Vol. II)* (pp. 20–38). New York: Brunner/Mazel.

Stanton. M., & Figley, C. (1978). Treating the Vietnam veteran within the family system. In C. R. Figley (Ed.), *Stress Disorders Among Vietnam Veterans*. New York: Brunner/Mazel.

Starkey, T. W., & Ashlock, L. E. (1986). Inpatient treatment of PTSD: Final results of the late, great Miami model. *VA Practitioner*, 3(11): 41–44.

Stretch, R. H. (1986). Post-traumatic stress disorder among Vietnam and Vietnam era veterans. In C. R. Figley (Ed.), *Trauma and Its Wake (Vol. II)* (pp. 156–192). New York: Brunner/Mazel.

Terr, L. C. (1983). Chowchilla revisited: The effects of psychic trauma four years after a school-bus kidnapping. *American Journal of Psychiatry*, 140(12): 1543–1550.

Titchener, J. L. (1986). Post-traumatic decline: A consequence of unresolved destructive drives. In C. R. Figley (Ed.), *Trauma and Its Wake (Vol. II)* (pp. 5–19). New York: Brunner/Mazel.

Williams, T. (Ed.) (1980). *Post-Traumatic Stress Disorders of the Vietnam Veteran*. Cincinnati, OH: Disabled American Veterans.

Yost, J. (1980). The psychopharmacological treatment of the delayed stress syndrome in Vietnam veterans. In T. Williams (Ed.), *Post-Traumatic Stress Disorders of the Vietnam Veteran*. Cincinnati, OH: Disabled American Veterans.

Ziarnowski, A. P., & Broida, D. C. (1984). Therapeutic implications of the nightmares of Vietnam combat veterans. *VA Practitioner,* July, 63–68.

9

Community Outreach
After Emergencies

JACK N. PEULER

The mental health and emotional needs of victims of natural disasters and environmental emergencies have only recently attracted the attention of service providers. Natural disasters, including earthquakes, fire, floods, tornadoes, and hurricanes, have been present with humankind since primitive recorded times. Yet it is only in the past 15 years that as a nation we have begun to develop programs to address the emotional needs of victims.

The Disaster Relief Act of 1974 (P.L. 93-288) provides for grants to States for crisis counseling programs in cases of Presidentially declared disasters, when available State and local resources and services are inadequate. In 1975, the first fiscal year of such funding, the total amount provided was $83,045 for programs in two States. In 1976, the amount provided was $98,923 for a program in one State. In 1985, the funding was $983,516 for programs in four States, and in 1986 it was $1,885,654 for programs in nine States. Funds come from the Federal Emergency Management Agency, after consultation with the National Institute of Mental Health (National Institute of Mental Health, 1975–1986).

The costs of ignoring the emotional needs of disaster victims are difficult to measure. Yet, one only needs to review personnel files and disability claims of fire and police agencies several months after they deal with the aftermath of an airline disaster to get some idea of the emotional toll a disaster can take on one identifiable population, the rescue workers.

The evidence of the need for service to victims of disaster and environmental emergencies is clear at this time. What is less clear is whose

239

responsibility it is to provide such assistance and what form that assistance should take.

The agencies that have traditionally provided disaster relief include the following:

- The Red Cross
- The Salvation Army
- The Federal Emergency Management Agency
- Local fire and police agencies
- The National Guard
- Local churches
- National and international church-related agencies

Most of these agencies will become involved in relief efforts following a community-wide disaster. Their focus is providing for the immediate physical needs of victims, including safe shelter, food, and clothing. They also become involved in the protection and reclamation of property. The ability to provide for these basic services is proven. Their efforts are, in fact, often heroic. Their ability to establish shelters and services quickly and efficiently is exceptional. Their staff and volunteers are well trained and know their roles.

However, given the tremendous physical needs that people have in the immediate aftermath of a disaster, it is unrealistic to expect that these agencies will be able to focus on the emotional needs as well. Yet, throughout their efforts in providing shelter, food, information, and first aid, they are also providing emotional support by their very presence and interventions. And because of the very nature of their intense involvement in early response to disaster, these workers themselves become disaster victims, often needing some assistance. Hartsough (1985) states:

> Certain types of event characteristics, either together or separately, have the potential for creating emotional distress in disaster workers: personal loss or injury, traumatic stimuli, and mission failure or human error. When all three of these characteristics are present . . . the potential exists for particularly intense stress reactions. Such effects, while debilitating, represent very normal reactions to quite abnormal situations. (p. 12)

Community mental health agencies are the most obvious organizations to be involved in the provision of services to victims. These agencies have staff whose skills can be adapted to the needs of disaster and emergency victims, with ability to assess, diagnose, and intervene in many different modalities. They have staff who are expert at reaching out to, listening to, and supporting people experiencing emotional distress.

The local community mental health agency is also frequently indigenous to the area impacted, has already established networks with other public service agencies, is part of the local government bureaucracy, and is most aware of all the potential public and private mental health resources in the community. It is in an excellent position to coordinate services from a community-wide perspective.

Providing services to victims of disaster is still a relatively new concept for public community mental health agencies. At best, some agencies may have developed a written disaster plan that gives some definition to the roles of staff following an emergency. Often these plans are specifically focused on providing care and support for existing caseloads and client populations (e.g., hospital inpatient or residential treatment facilities).

Often community mental health agencies in postdisaster situations will attempt to make the community aware that services are available at the local mental health clinic.

At worst, and in most cases, agencies have no written plan, have provided no training to staff, and have spent no time planning services for the victims of an emergency.

Given the current demand on mental health services, with large caseloads and shrinking resources, it is understandable why agencies have not set aside time to develop these plans. It has been only in recent years, since the Disaster Relief Act of 1974 and the availability of Federal resources and assistance, that the mental health community has begun to develop services and intervention strategies for disaster victims. Research findings, as well as experience of community mental health centers, the National Institute of Mental Health, the Federal Emergency Management Agency, the Red Cross, and many other agencies have clearly demonstrated the need for carefully planned community intervention after disasters.

Prior to the availability of Federal resources, or due to the length of time required to obtain the Federal resources, many community mental health agencies were reluctant to commit limited resources to a new population. Given the current levels of funding for most mental health agencies, the need to restrict services only to target populations has become a critical issue. In many cases, this need to prioritize has moved community mental health centers from being all things to all people to more clearly defining target populations to be served.

Generally, community mental health centers are moving towards serving abused children, the chronically mentally ill adult population and older adults who are at risk of institutionalization due to mental problems. The services to these populations generally include assessment, medication, medication monitoring, case management, day treatment, social and vocational rehabilitation, acute care, and crisis intervention. For the non-target populations, crisis intervention, assessment, and brief therapy are the most clinics can do.

VICTIM NEEDS

The victims of disasters are vulnerable and at risk. They need information, support, assessment and treatment, and public education. The major needs are the first two — that of information and support. With the availability of Federal funds to support these efforts after most major disasters and other available private community resources that can be mobilized to assist, there is no reason that a community mental health agency cannot serve the victims of emergencies within its priority services.

Many disasters can affect a community, but most, due to their limited scope and impact, will not be eligible for Federal funds. The local community mental health agency should have an implementation plan for these instances. These plans, when carefully considered, can have a real impact on the victims of these disasters while causing limited disruption of services for the ongoing caseload. Depending upon the size of the program and characteristics of the population affected, a specially trained core team of five or six staff or volunteers can provide immediate outreach to victims. With advanced training in disaster counseling and outreach and with printed educational information (described later in this chapter), these workers can provide invaluable services to the victims of these more limited disasters (e.g., airline accidents, hotel fires, etc.).

Given, then, that this population is in need of mental health services and that the local community mental health agency is the logical agency to coordinate and mobilize these efforts, the next section will focus on identifying the service needs.

Information

Anyone who has ever experienced an emergency, natural or man-made, in which there has been any isolation from the outside world can appreciate the tremendous hunger for information. Generally, the first information sought is about the extent of the damage, the safety of loved ones, the condition of one's property, and physical safety issues. However, within a day or two after impact, there is an ability to take in other information about other effects of the emergency. At this time, it can be most reassuring to receive information regarding possible emotional reactions. It is extremely important to remember that this information is being directed to the general population. In most cases, people have not previously thought about what emotional responses they might have under this kind of stress.

Support

As the victims of emergencies begin to assess the damages and "dig out" of the mess, the development of support becomes critical. In the immediate aftermath of a disaster, the community will experience tremendous cohesion and support. Neighbors who have previously never spoken to each other will often be working shoulder to shoulder in rescue and immediate clean-up efforts. As the days pass by and the media attention is focused elsewhere, the non-victim population of the community begins to resume an "everything is back to normal" routine. It is at this time that the victims need to look for ways to develop support for the months ahead. The mental health program can be very helpful in this process.

A victim of the 1982 winter rainstorms and mud slides in Santa Cruz, California, illustrated this need in describing her reaction.

The canyon in which she lived had been completely cut off from the outside community by a mud slide which had occurred near the entrance to the canyon. After hiking through mud and along a swollen creek, she and her husband reached the county road that led to town. They continued hiking to the bus stop. It was a beautiful sunny day and a bus driver, upon seeing them and their mud-coated dogs, refused to allow them on the bus. After a nearly violent confrontation, the bus driver relented, and they rode the bus into Santa Cruz. As they came into town they experienced tremendous anger as they noticed people eating in restaurants, and basically carrying on as though nothing had happened. As their anger subsided, it was replaced with a feeling of alienation. Within two years, this couple moved to another area of the state.

Later in this chapter, methods of providing support to victims of disasters will be discussed.

Assessment and Treatment

Beyond the need for education and support, some disaster victims will need treatment in order to facilitate their recovery from the experience.

Most often these victims have neither received counseling nor considered seeing a counselor previously. They are people who have, in the past, been able to solve their problems or deal with the normal stress in their lives. Suddenly they find that their usual coping methods aren't enough. They have no knowledge of how to access public services. They believe mental health services are for people who are "crazy" and think of state hospitals when mental health services are mentioned. Providing effective treatment services requires creative and effective outreach to help the victims feel comfortable in using the service.

With these basic service needs present and assuming that in most cases, the local community mental health agency has done little to prepare for this assignment, where to begin?

As early as physically possible (within the first 48 hours ideally) a mental health representative should tour the impact area to make an assessment of the need for mental health intervention. Usually this requires identification and clearance through either the Red Cross or the Office of Emergency Services. The person conducting the assessment should visit all emergency shelters, feeding stations, local fire departments, and police precincts or substations. If there has been reported injury or casualties, the hospital, emergency rooms and morgue should also be visited. Observations of both victims and rescuers should be made. If possible, there should be direct contact with victims in the shelter, not just with the shelter operators. Observation of the numbers of children in shelters and their level of anxiety should be noted.

The Red Cross nurse or first aid specialist also can provide valuable insights into the level of need for service. The observer is most likely to find, after most major disasters, an efficient system for distribution of blankets, cots, foods, and emergency supplies, and the availability of first aid. However, in most cases the shelter staff will have all they can handle in providing these basic services, and have little or no time to focus on other support to victims. Confusion will run high, with endless requests for information and frustration at the inability to act.

Given the above scenario, the next step is the deployment of staff to the shelters and other places victims are gathering. The earlier the visibility of these staff members, the more impact they will have in later interventions as people will remember that they were in the shelter and "know what it was like" in those first few days. Sending staff in pairs for mutual support is preferable. Mental health workers and public health nurses often work well in pairs and are able to provide emotional support, crisis counseling, and physical health information. Staff who live in the impacted areas are by far the most effective in these early assignments.

Remembering that the need for information is high, it is ideal if these early staff bring some of that information with them. Often, information about the purity of water, the spoilage of food, the need for care in salvage efforts, etc. is most appreciated. Information about how to reassure children and about common emotional reactions to the disaster is also useful.

As other services and agencies appear in the first week, it is important to assess the need for mental health staffing. For instance, in Presidentially declared disasters, when the Disaster Assistance Centers open, they are generally swamped with victims seeking assistance; this is an excellent opportunity to provide support and information. Cohen (1985) notes:

> As the mental health professional accepts a broader role in the shelter sites that house large populations in transition and crisis, he or she must develop the following solutions to problems inherent in that stressful situation: (1) create settings in nonclinical, physical locations within which to function; (2) provide emergency crisis services within a chaotic, unstructured environment; (3) make alliances with other professionals within the emergency system with whom there are few collaborative precedents; and (4) confront a rapidly changing adaptation/crisis phenomenology in the victim's behavior. (p. 11)

Some of these agencies are also actively engaged in damage assessment of the devastated areas. These assessments will help justify later expenditures for assistance to victims.

The use of on-call staff and the redirection of noncrisis staff to fill in behind the absent crisis workers can often be an interim solution.

There is usually a wealth of resources available in the private professional mental health community and a staff person should be designated to tap into this resource. Professionals are generally very willing to volunteer their time and expertise in endeavors such as this. These volunteers "can serve in numerous capacities, including crisis outreach, facilitators of debriefing groups, staff in day care centers, facilitators of community recovery groups, and trainers for new volunteers. Many private practitioners will make time available for providing brief therapy to disaster victims at no cost" (Peuler, 1985, p. 20).

Also during these early days, staff will need training and consultation for themselves as they begin to deliver these services. Those who have experienced a disaster or simply observed the effects of a disaster are deeply touched by the experience. It is very easy to underestimate the tremendous needs of disaster victims. Staff can be overwhelmed if not adequately prepared for what they will encounter. Kurault (1982) describes the effects of viewing the results of the storm of 1982 in Santa Cruz County, California:

> Once you have seen this, something changes inside. Once you have absorbed what nature and the forest can do; once you have seen the majestic, glorious redwoods turned into bludgeons and the good earth stirred to soup; once you have seen all this, you will never walk in the forest the same way again.

Identifying a consultant with whom staff can meet and confer becomes critical. The National Institute of Mental Health and many state departments of mental health have lists of available trainers and consultants for local programs.

Providing this level of mental health staffing can quickly deplete a local agency's resources and administrative records should be kept in order to document the costs of providing these services. In the case of Presidentially declared disasters, the Department of Mental Health of the affected State must immediately begin assessment of need for a Federal disaster grant. If the victim needs are greater than available resources, an application for such a grant should be made to the Federal Emergency Management Agency as soon as possible. The National Institute of Mental Health provides technical assistance in such assessments.

Public Education

The next step is an organized approach to educating the community about the mental health issues of disaster victims. In the early days following a disaster, the local news media are often eager to participate in this effort. Providing the media with simple, easy to read descriptions of common reactions that occur following a disaster can be very helpful. It is important to remember that this information is aimed at a population that, in general, has not utilized mental health type services. It's always helpful to remind victims that they are experiencing *normal reactions to an abnormal situation* and that with some attention to their emotional needs they will adjust in time. This information should specifically describe some of the experiences they or their children might have. An example is the following excerpt from a Project Cope handout, following the winter storms of 1982 in Santa Cruz County, California.

TAKING CARE OF YOURSELF EMOTIONALLY

During a disaster and for weeks or months after, people continue to experience emotional reactions. These are *normal responses* to living through an emergency.

Irritability	Anger
Fatigue	Disrupted sleep, appetite
Sleep disturbance	Unusual physical ailments
Anxiety and helpless feelings	Hyperactivity

Children are also susceptible to these feelings and may show them with anxieties, fear, worry, behavior problems, sleep disturbance, regressive behavior, bed-wetting.

Talk and listen to one another. Recount the experience of the disaster. Each time the experience is told you process what happened. The uncomfortable feelings will gradually diminish with each re-telling. Preparation will help to alleviate anxieties about the future. You have been through the worst; you know what it is like so you can prepare for it.

Allow children to voice their fears—reassuring them and telling them about the plans you are making. It is OK for them to express their fears. This is how they understand them. Allow them to tell how they felt during the disaster and what they experienced. (Project Cope, 1985, pp. 58–59)

Listing telephone numbers of agencies or services where people can get further information is also very important. Weeks and months later people will call for assistance with their personal or family issues. Such handouts can be distributed through the media, made available at shelters and food distribution centers, and posted in grocery stores, pharmacies, other markets, schools, and churches.

After time has passed, some cleanup has occurred and people have moved back into the devastated neighborhoods. Walking the neighborhoods and distributing information can be very effective.

The provision of information, simply written and appropriately timed, can have a very reassuring effect even months after.

APPROPRIATE ROLES FOR MENTAL HEALTH PROFESSIONALS

In this section the various roles for mental health staff will be discussed.

Project Coordinator

The Mental Health Disaster Project Coordinator obviously has a key role. The Coordinator clearly needs to have the full support of the agency administration and be able to access all the agency resources. This person should be, if possible, someone who is familiar with the agency staff, knowing their strengths and weaknesses, skills, and abilities. This is also the person who needs to make assessments of the mental health needs and to build networks with other agencies. If a functional mental health disaster plan is already in place, it can save valuable time setting up linkages after the disaster.

Outreach Workers/Crisis Workers

These are the early interveners who are deployed quickly (within 48 hours) and need to be able to adapt to changing situations. Staff who have the ability to make independent decisions, work without close consultation, and are comfortable doing outreach are most effective in this role. Generally, crisis workers, psychiatric emergency room staff, case managers, and community mental health nurses do well in this role. Also, staff who are indigenous to the area are extremely effective and nonprofessionals should be considered as well. Staff without these characteristics should not be used. A staff clerk who is sensitive to the situation and knowledgeable about resources can be a very effective neighborhood outreach worker in his or her community. These workers' duties frequently include information and referral, crisis assessment, counseling, and manual labor in shelters. They may be required to help people get medications, provide transportation to psychiatric inpatient units, protect vulnerable people from the media, do home visits to at-risk populations (e.g., elderly), and unload supply trucks.

Educators/Consultants

These are staff who are comfortable in making presentations, speaking in public, and talking to the news media, and who have an ability to write. Their duties would include developing the handouts that provide information on the emotional effects of the disaster, writing news releases, and providing consultation to other service agencies (such as schools, day care centers) regarding the potential effects of the disaster.

Trainers

The staff who are designated as the project trainers should have access to an outside consultant who has disaster expertise. The primary duties of these persons include training agency staff and volunteers in common disaster responses in intervention strategies, and in how to take care of themselves as disaster workers. All staff who become involved in the disaster outreach should be required to attend a training session first. The outreach staff should also have at least a basic understanding of the roles of other agencies in disaster relief such as the Red Cross, Federal Emergency Management Agency, and local agencies that are involved in relief efforts.

Debriefing Group Leaders

These leaders should have basic group facilitation skills and ability to facilitate groups of 6-8 workers, allowing for ventilation and debriefing of the day's experience in a safe and secure environment. Myers (1985) defines a debriefing as

> . . . an organized approach to the management of stress responses following a traumatic or critical incident. It is a specific, focused intervention to assist workers in dealing with the intense emotions that are common at such a time. It also assists workers by teaching them about normal stress responses, specific skills for coping with stress, and how to provide support for each other.
> A debriefing involves a one-to-one or group meeting between the workers and a trained facilitator. Group meetings are recommended, as they provide the added dimension of peer support.
> A debriefing is not a critique. A critique is a meeting in which the incident is discussed, evaluated, and analyzed with regard to procedures, performance, and what could have been improved upon. . . . A debriefing has a different focus: that of dealing with the emotional aspects of the experience. (p. 130)

Although mental health staff are accustomed to dealing with clients who are in a great deal of emotional pain and staff are also familiar with the symptoms of burnout from this, the impact of working with victims of disaster can be much more intensive. Although many mental health staff have experienced the loss of clients through suicide and have used the process of a psychological autopsy as a way of handling the feelings generated by such an unfortunate circumstance, this is not a routine occurrence. In providing services to disaster victims, experiences of this intensity can happen on a daily basis.

Community Recovery Group Leaders

These group leaders should have experience as group therapists and group facilitators. A recovery group will be described in detail in a later section of this chapter. Very simply, the recovery group's goals are to provide a forum for victims to vent their feelings and problem solve on issues related to their traumatic experiences. The role of the recovery group leaders is to provide support and encouragement, to give reassurance regarding some of the common symptoms, and to act as role models.

Therapists

Therapists also fill critical roles in working with victims needing more than peer support and information. All therapists should be given some training in postdisaster counseling. Whenever possible, the staff providing this assistance should have the opportunity to visit the impact area to get a firsthand sense of what took place. Therapy with this population is best accomplished in community-based offices and not in an office miles from the community affected. Home visits are frequently very effective. The private professional community is an excellent resource for volunteers to provide this service, especially those who are indigenous to the impact area.

These are just some of the roles that mental health staff and volunteers can provide. There are numerous others that may evolve during the delivery of postdisaster services. The more flexible and creative staff are, the more effective the service will be. All the staff who are serving the disaster project must have access to and, in many cases, be required to use some services themselves. The debriefing is a very important process that must be attended to or staff will burn out.

As the weeks go by, the community returns to normal, the major relief agencies close their centers, and families begin to return home, project staff are going to feel pressure from another source—their colleagues and peers. The pressure of the continuing caseloads at the mental health clinics is still there and the staff will typically begin to express some resentment towards the disaster project staff for their lack of availability to help with the regular caseload. In some situations, disaster project staff have reported receiving comments about "rescuing" victims and creating "dependent" relationships with victims. One way to keep this resentment from developing is to have agency staff informed and educated about the disaster project activities. Sharing caseload data and presenting cases for discussion at clinical grand rounds are methods that can be used.

POPULATIONS MOST VULNERABLE

All people who become victims of a disaster or of an environmental emergency potentially need services. However, there are certain populations who are especially at risk.

Older Adults

The older adult population is more vulnerable in several different ways. Often, older adults are on fixed incomes and live in structures that are especially at risk in environmental emergencies. Many live in older homes, mobile homes, or modular housing units that are especially vulnerable to the onslaught of nature. These housing units and mobile home parks are often in low-lying areas or along rivers and streambeds susceptible to flooding. In addition to these physical issues, older adults frequently have fewer resources, both financial and emotional, to set about rebuilding. They also are impacted more heavily by the loss of lifelong mementos, sentimental possessions, and family photographs. Their social support network can be small to nonexistent, depending on the circumstances.

The establishment of peer support groups and/or community recovery groups is a key service for the older population victimized by the disaster.

Typical responses and symptoms observed in this population in postdisaster situations include:

1. Depression, withdrawal, apathy;
2. Agitation, anger, irritability;
3. Sleep disturbances;
4. Disorientation, confusion, memory loss;
5. Decline in physical health.

This population also has a more difficult time seeking assistance from public or private agencies. This is often due to lack of knowledge about services. Inability to get to the disaster assistance center, feeling overwhelmed by the paperwork involved, pride in making it all their lives without public assistance, and valuing their independence from public assistance can all create barriers.

The most effective ways to overcome some of these barriers include: assertive outreach by making home visits; utilizing existing senior information and referral services to distribute information; posting information in the offices and recreation centers of mobile home parks; and accessing local community newspaper senior columns.

Children

Children are a second special population at risk in a disaster. The next chapter in this volume focuses on this population. There are, however, some specific interventions in the context of community outreach that are especially effective and worth discussing here.

It is particularly important to get information out early to parents, families, school teachers, day care centers, and any others who are in contact with children. Adults who are already under stress from the impact of the disaster or emergency find it especially reassuring to have information on what to expect of their children. Again, this information can be distributed at schools, shelters, churches, disaster assistance centers, through the mail and through the media. Remember to reassure readers that most of these responses are *normal reactions* to a very abnormal situation and experience. It is important to keep the language simple and to the point.

Immediately following a disaster, child care can be a very important outreach service. Parents need to know that their children are in a safe place while they focus on getting their lives back together. This need might be met by organizing a cooperative effort among parents in a neighborhood, or by asking a church or service group to take on the project. The following information can be helpful to anyone involved in establishing child care during a time of emergency or disaster.

1. *Finding a place.* It is important to have a safe environment and an accessible location for the child care center. Possible resources include churches, Red Cross Shelters, community or recreational centers, or preschools.

2. *Recruitment of volunteers.* Volunteers to staff Day Care Centers might be recruited by 1) contacting a Volunteer Bureau; 2) contacting local preschool or elementary school teachers; 3) asking parents who might use the center to participate; 4) contacting service organizations; 5) word of mouth.

3. *Food donations.* Possible resources for donations for food for the children include: 1) the Red Cross; 2) food and nutrition services; 3) local grocery stores.

4. *Staffing.* There should be a ratio of at least one adult for every six children. At least one person on each shift should have a solid background in care of small children. Shifts should be approximately four hours in length.

5. *Information from parents.* It can reduce confusion to have a sign-in sheet for parents and have them indicate the time they anticipate retrieving their children. Information on allergies, formula schedules, emergency phone numbers, and special needs of children should be detailed by parents.

HELPING CHILDREN COPE:
INFORMATION FOR CHILD CARE STAFF

Normal Reactions

Children are likely to react to the stress of the disaster with a variety of responses. You might find that they are hyperactive and excitable, or withdrawn and subdued. It is common for children to revert back to earlier behaviors such as thumbsucking or bedwetting. They might cling to their parents and whimper or cry more than usual. This is not unusual behavior under the circumstances.

Physical Contact

Children need lots of reassurance during these times and physical contact is especially important. Most children will welcome extra hugs, though others may be more comfortable with more subtle physical contact. Holding a child who is displaying aggressive or hyperactive behavior closely in a bear hug can give the message that you will help him/her regain control. A fatigued child may need to be held and rocked in order to drop off to sleep.

Physical Activity

Physical movement that involves large muscle activity is especially important during stressful times and can help relieve tensions. Skipping, jumping, hopping around the room are examples.

Play Reenactment

Availability of toys that encourage play reenactment of their experiences or observation during disaster can be helpful to children in their attempts to integrate these experiences. Toys might include building blocks, toy fire trucks or ambulances, clay or play dough, puppets, dolls, crayons and paper.

Food

During times of stress it is especially important to have plenty of finger foods (fruits, crackers, etc.) and fluids. The physical nourishment tends to be reassuring to children at a time when their security or survival seems threatened. They are better able to handle small amounts of food at frequent intervals rather than fewer larger meals.

Telling Their Stories

The children will need to talk about what happened — over and over again! This is a normal and healthy reaction to any frightening or extraordinary event. The more they can be listened to the better. Depending on the age of the children, they might distort or exaggerate what happened. Patient clarifications can be helpful, though the important thing is to tune in to the content of their feelings about what happened. Their feelings are real and shouldn't be contradicted or denied.

The aforementioned information and suggestions regarding children are adapted from *Project Cope: The Final Report* (California Department of Mental Health, 1983).

Ethnic Groups

A third population that can be vulnerable to disasters and environmental emergencies consists of specific ethnic groups. They can be physically vulnerable for many of the same reasons as the older adult. Often this population is housed in substandard physical structures in high-risk areas. Their support network can be small to nonexistent depending on the length of time they have resided in the community.

Very briefly, there are several important factors that should be kept in mind when providing outreach to particular ethnic groups:

1. language fluency and the need to provide information in the language of the victims;
2. their relationship to the community and ability to access services;
3. the cultural family roles, not only the male and female roles but also the roles of children and grandparents;

4. the role of religion and religious belief systems; beliefs about fate, causalty, responsibility, guilt, punishment, and the importance of religious mementos;
5. the importance of memories of previous experiences which can be triggered by disasters, especially for ethnic populations from war-ravaged countries.

Again, the use of indigenous and bilingual staff is extremely important in maximizing the impact of the outreach.

METHODS OF OUTREACH

Earlier in this chapter it was noted that the three major areas upon which community mental health agencies should focus outreach included providing information, support, and appropriate treatment-interventions. This section will focus on methods to handle information and support. Other chapters in this text will address treatment.

Information

Provision of information is an important service that mental health agencies can give to disaster victims. Although methods of disseminating information have been touched upon throughout this chapter, some of these will be highlighted here. Obviously, in all outreach efforts and support services, information is constantly being relayed to the victim population. In community recovery groups, in child care centers, and in treatment services, staff should be making information available to victims.

A project staff person or persons should be designated to develop a relationship with the media. Local television and radio talk show hosts and television newsrooms are often eager to assist in presenting practical information to their local viewers. Frequently, articulate disaster victims can be identified and with support are willing to share their experiences in order to help others receive service. Care should always be taken not to exploit these people.

Another excellent method of disseminating information is through children at school. Th.s can be particularly effective if the school staff is convinced of the valuable role children can play. This in itself requires education, since teachers, like most other people, tend to deny the emotional impact a disaster can have. Providing information and accounts of other community schools' efforts in this type of outreach can be helpful, especially coming from a fellow teacher. Teachers who spend even 30 to 60 minutes a week discussing the effects of the disaster will have an impact. Many of the children will carry this information into the home.

Methods of distributing information on common reactions to disasters are limited only by staff ingenuity. Pharmacies, beauty salons, medical clinics, churches, service organizations, community newsletters, club-houses are all places where information can be posted. Existing crisis lines and information and referral services can be utilized. In the 1986 floods in Michigan, the already established crisis line for farmers was utilized in outreach efforts. This crisis line had been established to assist farmers who were at risk of losing their farms because of the depressed farm economy. The staff of the crisis lines were targeted for special training on the effects of the flooding.

Support

Although the need for social support in postdisaster recovery has been clearly demonstrated, the methods by which an external agency might assist in providing that support still need further exploration and development. Solomon (1985) notes that research indicates victims first attempt to resolve problems on their own or within their immediate family, and only when that breaks down do they turn to their larger social network. She writes:

> Existing literature suggests that informal social support systems can help individuals cope with stresses associated with crises and that such systems are more likely than formal service networks to be called upon for emotional support. Kin network members appear to be the most crucial support sources for disaster victims' long term needs. In many instances, kin resources are supplemented by assistance from friends, co-workers, neighbors, informal care-givers, and professional community gate keepers.
>
> However, social networks are not always supportive. In disaster situations, victims may feel torn between the conflicting needs of different network members. Also the disaster may disrupt social networks. The loss of network support, in turn, may become a source of stress.
>
> Mental health professionals can take many steps to strengthen and build social support networks after a disaster. (p. 115)

One project which experienced some success with the development of local community support group was Project Cope (Counseling Ordinary

*P*eople in Emergencies) in Santa Cruz, California. The groups were called Community Recovery Groups and met in local churches and schools in the impacted areas. Efforts were made to provide group facilitators who were indigenous to the local communities. The groups met on a weekly basis. The importance of the locale of the group was demonstrated at one point when an attempt was made to merge two groups from two communities. The attendance fell off rapidly and people articulated a desire to meet only with their neighbors from the community. This also carried down to local neighborhoods where people who lived in one canyon preferred to meet only with other residents of that canyon and would not come into town for the meeting.

During the first two months, the facilitators followed a similar format each week. This consisted of introductions, with group members telling the group where they were living and what happened to them during the disaster. The repetitions seemed necessary and helpful. The facilitators encouraged participants to get more in touch with the emotional content of their stories. Active listening was an effective tool for supporting, validating, and drawing out the feelings of the participants. Sessions were characterized by the intensity of emotions and by the rapt attention that members gave each other. Many noted that friends and family had quickly tired of hearing them talk about the storm and that a clear need was met by the group. They experienced a unique receptiveness and depth of understanding from other storm victims which they could not get in most other relationships. Participants almost inevitably expressed feelings of relief and gratitude that they had the opportunity to retell their stories.

As the group needs changed, the format altered somewhat. However new members were encouraged to go through the process of retelling their experiences. As the need to repeat the story diminished, participants used their time to give updates on their situations, share information, or ask for help in problem-solving. They often shared their frustrations, anxieties, and accomplishments.

At each meeting with new participants, facilitators identified themselves and their function in the group. It seemed reassuring to members to have an experienced group leader who was able to provide direction to the group — to have someone in charge. Similarly, providing some structure to the groups seemed helpful and reassuring.

Dependence on group facilitators was avoided by strongly reinforcing peer support of members during groups. Outside of the groups, many participants exchanged phone numbers and contacted each other. when they felt the need for extra support.

The need for self-care on the part of the facilitators has to be emphasized.

Leaders noted that they could not have been adequately prepared prior to the first meeting for the tragic and gruesome stories they heard from group members. It was necessary for them to take full advantage of debriefing sessions and vent their feelings in order to be fully available to group participants each week. Leaders expressed feelings of personal frustration that the problems faced by victims were so complex. There were no simple solutions—they couldn't "fix things up" for group members. The fact that it was easy to identify with the victims—individuals who had arbitrarily suffered from an accident of nature—made it hard to not take on the victim's grief.

It is important to note that many of the same factors that made the groups demanding on the leaders' energies also contributed to making them a richly rewarding experience. Closeness and rapport with group participants were quickly established. There was a sense of playing a very special support role as victims moved toward recovery. The facilitators reported that the phases of emotional response among the group members tended to correspond with the phases of disaster identified in disaster literature: heroic, honeymoon, disillusionment, and reconstruction phases (Farberow, 1983).

The first four to eight weeks were marked by a sense of the group members being "in shock." They tended to be emotionally detached and thankful to be alive. Some were euphoric. Group members, without exception, reported poor sleep and nightmares. Some were angry. Most seemed preoccupied and restless. Denial was evident in various forms, including consistent denial by parents in the group that their children were affected. In some cases it was up to seven months later before they could acknowledge that the children had in fact been impacted.

The second six to 12 weeks were colored by the participants' irritation and frustration in dealing with bureaucratic hurdles as they attempted to get assistance. Group members reported feeling vulnerable and out of control. Bad dreams persisted. Many talked about being afraid to feel. There was a great need to have others who were affected less or not at all by the disaster understand how awful the victims' experiences had been. This was exemplified by their showing photographs of their damaged property to anyone who would look.

One of the more important functions of the facilitators during the second phase was to provide support and validation of group members' feelings. Members were encouraged to identify areas in their lives in which they could "take charge" or resume control.

In the four to six months following the disaster, the remedy phase began for most group members and they became more actively involved in their own recovery efforts. Group members exchanged practical information both within and outside the group. The group had become a solid support system for its members. Group members still reported bad dreams almost without exception.

Personality traits culturally reinforced by sex roles created observable differences in the impact of the disaster on men and women. These differences affected the type of interventions utilized by facilitators. Some typical traits observed in women group members were the tendencies to placate, to put others first, or to feel overly responsible for the welfare of others. These traits made it difficult for some women to give themselves permission to grieve their own sorrows and to tend to their own needs. Key interventions included encouragement to set limits on others' demands or requests, and in general to assert their own needs. It became important to help women members reestablish the boundaries of realistic self-expectation and responsibility. There was a need to validate themselves and to regain a sense of safety in their lives.

There was a tendency among male participants to have difficulty acknowledging and expressing feelings of helplessness and sadness. They tended to feel that they had failed in their protector and provider roles by "allowing" this devastation to strike their families. Men were more likely to identify strongly with their physical beings. To have been physically violated or threatened was to have their manhood jeopardized.

Facilitators found it necessary to provide special encouragement to men to express their feelings. Acceptance of feelings of vulnerability and helplessness as human beings was reinforced. Helping the men make realistic assessments of their own responsibilities and limitations was valuable. Attention was directed toward helping them accept their feelings of physical vulnerability and reconcile that acceptance with regaining the ability to trust their physical ability skills.

The group members in community recovery groups were predominantly female. This was consistent in all groups, with about 80% being female and 20% being male; a similar ratio also was noted in those victims seeking treatment from other resources.

Project COPE experienced little success in reaching males in the victim community. The outreach efforts that were successful in reaching men were those community meetings that were set up to disseminate practical information. One of the more successful efforts was a meeting where a geologist from the local university presented information about ground saturation and amount of rainfall that might trigger further mud slides — information that was useful in the men's role of protector.

The experiences of Project Cope underscore the need for the development of support networks. Development of new methods to reach the at-risk populations is an area where the need for further research is clearly indicated. As one victim of the Santa Cruz storm of 1982 stated: "Even my best friend is telling me she is sick and tired of my talking about my problems with the flood. Who do I turn to now?"

SUMMARY AND RECOMMENDATIONS

The establishment of peer support for victims is being utilized with many populations. Cancer victims, Vietnam veterans, families of the mentally ill, adult schizophrenics—all are discovering the value of the support of others who have shared their experience. Mental Health agencies, either directly or in consultation with other agencies or groups, can provide assistance in these efforts. Mental health, to be effective, must expand its traditional therapeutic role, and become more involved in community organization and education. People do have an amazing capacity to survive with emotional support and information. Research in methods of establishing social support will, hopefully, continue to identify successful models and approaches.

In the last 10 years, there has been a significant increase in disaster training resources at the State and Federal level. Ways in which to access this information must be made available to local agencies. Often, due to the lack of resources at the local level, agencies have not responded to local disasters with assertive outreach. The State Department of Mental Health must provide the leadership and support to local agencies to establish services after disasters. Furthermore, State Offices of Emergency Services and the Federal Emergency Management Agency must continue to require mental health involvement and input as they develop area disaster plans.

REFERENCES

California Department of Mental Health (1983). *Project Cope Final Report.* Sacramento, California.

Cohen, R. E. (1985). Crisis counseling principles and services. In M. Lystad (Ed.), *Innovations in Mental Health Services to Disaster Victims.* Washington, D.C.: DHHS Publication No. (ADM) 85-1390.

Farberow, N. (1983). *Training Manual for Human Services Workers in Major Disasters.* Washington, D.C.: DHHS Publication No. (ADM) 85-538.

Hartsough, D. M. (1985). Stress and mental health interventions in three major disasters. In D. M. Hartsough & D. G. Myers (Eds.), *Disaster Work and Mental Health: Prevention and Control of Stress Among Workers*. Washington, D.C.: DHHS Publication No. (ADM) 85–1422.

Kurault, C. (January, 1982). Good Morning America, CBS News.

Myers, D. G. (1985). Helping the helpers: A training manual. In D. M. Hartsough & D. G. Myers (Eds.), *Disaster Work and Mental Health: Prevention and Control of Stress Among Workers*. Washington, D.C.: DHHS Publication No. (ADM) 85–1422.

National Institute of Mental Health, Emergency Services Branch (1975–1986). *Annual Reports*. Rockville, Maryland.

Peuler, J. N. (1985). Family and community outreach in times of disaster: The Santa Cruz experience. In M. Lystad (Ed.), *Innovations in Mental Health Services to Disaster Victims*. Washington, D.C.: DHHS Publication No. (ADM) 85–1390.

Project COPE (1985). Preparing for disasters: The basics. In M. Lystad (Ed.), *Innovations in Mental Health Services to Disaster Victims*. Washington, D.C.: DHHS Publication No. (ADM) 85–1390.

Solomon, S. D. (1985). Enhancing social support for disaster victims. In B. J. Sowder (Ed.), *Disasters and Mental Health: Selected Contemporary Perspectives*. Washington, D.C.: DHHS Publication No. (ADM) 85–1421.

10

Intervention Programs for Children

RAQUEL E. COHEN

Worldwide catastrophic events are flashed daily by our press and communication media. We become aware of the effects of traumatic events when we see human faces contorted by pain and tragic expressions of grief. A small voice not generally heard is the child's voice, although we are told that children are part of the population affected. Child victims— refugees in lands torn by war or natural disasters who become displaced together with their families or wander as orphans—will be the subjects of this chapter. Therapeutic intervention approaches will be proposed based on theoretical constructs and clinical practices. The knowledge base to guide the operations will be obtained from contemporary research, clinical crisis intervention practices, and recorded multidisciplinary disaster activities (Orbaschel et al., 1980; Frederick, 1985).

Published descriptions of clinical and behavioral manifestations of children's reactions to traumatic events focus on biological, psychological, and social perspectives. Documented observations of post-traumatic child reactions suffer from the lack of research data and add to the difficulty of developing a comprehensive frame of reference (Garmezy, 1986).

In general, documented children's reactions after disasters are sketchy and fragmented because they are based on the experiences of different professionals who have reported them in their own style and perspective (Ahearn & Cohen, 1984; Eth & Pynoos, 1985). Missing from many publications are the descriptions of children's reactions and behavior patterns during the various time phases which are characteristic of the developmental crisis resolution process.

Scientific measures and methods to assess children's reactions are beginning to be employed (Cornely & Bromet, in press). A range of formats, including interviews, questionnaires and analyses of drawings, are being developed. Because the conceptualization of children's reactions is influenced by 1) the event itself; 2) the degree of disorganization of the family; 3) the impact on the social structures; and 4) the attention given to the children's subsequent needs, it is difficult to design a study which identifies and correlates all factors influencing child behavior. The importance of parental response to children's level of distress has been identified as a powerful influence, so this, too, has to be evaluated (Handford et al., 1986; Silber et al., 1957).

Increased attention by mental health professionals to this young, vulnerable population is due, in part, to several theoretical and research advances in the behavioral sciences. Among them are the following:

1. Increased knowledge of preventive programs following stressful life events in children.
2. Increased knowledge of the effects of stressors on health and illness (Rutter, 1981b).
3. Better understanding of interpersonal bond attachment processes and support systems (Bowlby, 1980).
4. New conceptualizations about the developmental perspectives of cognitive and affective systems (Kagan, 1984; Fisher, 1980).
5. New awareness of early appearance of children's capacities to process information and interact with their environment (Stern, 1985).
6. Further understanding of the effect of psychic trauma and emotional disorders in children, as differentiated from the outcome of grieving and mourning (Eth & Pynoos, 1985; Szapocznik, Cohen, & Hernandez, 1985).
7. Further accounts of children's postdisaster reactions (Burke, 1982; Cornely & Bromet, in press).

THEORETICAL BASES FOR APPROACH

Knowledge about what should be construed as a "healthy environment" for the development of a child stands in dramatic contrast to what has been learned about children in postdisaster situations (Cohen, 1976). The need to plan, develop, and offer assistance to the victims of these injurious events is promoting further study of programs designed to prevent pathological effects on the child's health and negative emotional consequences (Garmezy & Rutter, 1985).

The emerging knowledge about psychosocial processes that assist in adaptation at different levels of infantile development is very useful in disaster planning (Terr, 1984). Experiences are accumulating which are being shared, allowing professionals to develop tentative methods of intervention (Newman, 1976). Raising some questions about how to intervene with children after a disaster presents us with a classic dilemma in the clinical application of traditional theories. It is necessary to apply a consistent model to organize the obtained information, develop a diagnostic posture, and select the appropriate intervention approach. A useful conceptual approach in this specialized field of psychiatry can be obtained by focusing on the stressful situation in which the child finds himself and adopting a framework of understanding the child as an evolving interacting organism within a biopsychosociocultural model (Cohen, 1985).

There is a relation between the approaches by which problems are defined and the intervention which is chosen and then translated into action. Mental health problem definition reflects inferences and assumptions about the causes of the problem. In the case of post-traumatic stress reactions in children, the following can be conceptualized: The reactive-adaptive behavior that can be observed following the impact of the disaster is related to 1) the stage of development; 2) the gender of the child, ethnicity, economic status of the family; 3) usual coping defense style; 4) intensity of the stressor; 5) available and appropriate "fit" between the child's needs and support systems; 6) extent of dislocation; and 7) availability of relief and community disaster assistance resources. Collecting specific data about the victim and organizing the data to specify the problems produced by the situation in which the child finds himself offer guidance to develop the appropriate intervention. The way the data get organized, the unique characteristics that identify the victim, the hypothetical interaction among all the factors, and how they affect the child's capacity to cope are based on theoretical assumptions chosen by the therapist.

Several areas of theoretical knowledge will be highlighted because they are crucial to the understanding of behavior in postdisaster experiences and are key for intervention programs.

RELATION BETWEEN INFANTILE DEVELOPMENT STAGES AND POSTDISASTER REACTIONS

Periods of growth along developmental phases signal changes in several psychobiological systems. Depending on the age of the child traumatized by the event, the intervention should be designed by knowledge of the developmental stage of different systems—somatic, psychological, social, and behavioral. There is a relationship between the level achieved in these systems and the ability to deal with stressful events following the disaster. These adaptive processes can be understood as strategies, approaches, efforts that promote actions. The objective of these processes is to modify the impact of the stimuli unchained by the stressor and so tolerate, correct, modify, or diminish the effects on the organism and prevent reactive disorganization within the psychophysiological human system (Rutter, 1981a).

The manifestations of these adaptive skills and their effects on the vulnerable organism of the child will show a variety of behavior patterns. How we interpret these manifestations of the child's mechanism of adaptation, the social expectations toward him within the disorganized human environment, and the social and family conflicts that generally emerge in the crisis situation will all define diagnostic categories of healthy or pathological adaptation and, in turn, influence methods of assistance and intervention (Johnson, 1982).

The issues that need definition, for example, are as follows: How do children of different ages resolve a crisis? How do children of different ages adapt to bereavement and loss (Rutter, 1981)? How do children react to the experience of being lost and separated for specific periods of time from a mother and being cared for by strangers? What are the differences when the mother is dead, incapacitated, overwhelmed by the disaster, or wounded (Goodyear, Kolvin, & Gatzanis, 1985)?

It is well known, as a law of adaptation, that the child has to maintain his internal world and support the homeostatic systems functions. A working hypothesis considers the possibility that disruption of the systems produces effects on the social, psychological, and physiological levels of the organism (Longfellow & Belle, 1984). These changes will present behavior manifestations which are the expression of the organism's attempt to reduce tension by reestablishing a psychophysiologic balance. For instance, the reactions to an earthquake of a one-year-old child, who processes stimuli and information through an evolving cognitive system, will be different from that of an older child, who will use a symbolic-linguistic mode of information processing (Block et al., 1956).

PSYCHIC TRAUMA AND DEVELOPMENTAL EXPRESSION OF MOURNING POSTDISASTER

An important conceptual body of knowledge assists in the understanding of processes available to children during traumatic events that involve loss (Bowlby, 1963; Brown et al., 1985; Osterweis et al., 1984). For the child, the death or psychological unavailability of a nurturant person is not only a traumatic event, but also a developmental interference of a very serious nature (Bowlby, 1963). As the child advances through the multiple systems of growth, consolidating several psychological and emotional tasks needed to achieve maturity, a stimulating interaction with his love objects is essential (Bowlby, 1980).

Although the maturing developmental processes continue to surge ahead, the disruption to the interaction with the "synchronized" familiar stimuli will force the child to incorporate the abrupt, painful change while attempting to adapt to the shifting human environment. Depending on his stage of development and his cognitive/affective capacities, we will observe differing behavior patterns expressive of disrupted organization, regressive functions, infantile emotional manifestation and patterns of their cognitive functions that incorporate the developed level of their subunits— reality thinking, abstract reasoning, causality (Nagera, 1970).

In postdisaster experiences, in addition to consideration of the stage of development, there is a need to consider the dynamic implication of the loss and its interaction with reactive processes to the trauma set up by the disaster. All disasters are dramatic events accompanied by visual and auditory experiences that are incomprehensible at the moment of occurrence. The preliminary sounds of an earthquake, observing the earth opening up, and seeing buildings collapse produce anxiety reactions of different levels of intensity. There are concrete, frightening events that are mentally recorded and will be an internal traumatic repetitive stimuli to several infantile emotions (Terr, 1981). When these events are accompanied by a subsequent loss of a parent, it is difficult to sort out the child's reactions as belonging to psychic trauma or to early signs of mourning (Cohen, 1987; Eth & Pynoos, 1985).

Examples of affective displays are related to the nature of the relationship lost, the quality of the ambivalence, and the existence of hostile wishes with the accompanying guilt after the loss. If the survival need for nurturance is considered, it is evident that the child will demonstrate different needs during the maturing progression of his personality (Freud & Burlingham, 1943). Coupled with this differential need, the accompanying reactions to loss should be incorporated into the evaluation and intervention guidelines. The following points will bear on program planning:

1. Serious disruption of the developmental processes will produce disorganization in all psychological expressions.
2. Special significance of the event and postdisaster experiences will be related to the stage of development.

3. The quality of family relations will affect the expression of mourning manifestations.
4. Intensity of the physical and psychological trauma will influence the mourning process and lengthen the duration of the postdisaster reactions.
5. Special circumstances surrounding the life of the child predisaster (divorce, new school, surgery, immigration) will affect the child's reactions.
6. The reactions to these events by other important adults in the child's life will affect the child.
7. The multiple changes in the child's environment due to the loss of his family following the disaster are of special importance.
8. Plasticity and resiliency of the child as protective factors are also significant.

INTERVENTION PROGRAMS FOR CHILDREN—CRISIS INTERVENTION, CONSULTATION AND EDUCATION POSTDISASTER

Development and implementation of mental health services to help children suffering from the psychological consequences of a disaster have to be designed within the context of the disaster, the time frame postdisaster, and the identified population (Cohen, 1986). Although infantile responses may differ from event to event, it is possible to develop a broad-based guide for the design and execution of postdisaster psychological services. In this chapter, the elements that enter into the design of a plan will focus only on the child population. It is assumed that a major complex mental health program with different multilevel services is going on and the child program is imbedded and coordinated with other services so as to render psychological aid effectively to all victims (Cohen & Ahearn, 1980). The objective of the program described will be the implementation of mental health intervention services for the child affected by a disaster or catastrophic event. This is done with the understanding that there are many other types of services needed in this situation, such as feeding, housing, medical, and recreational services.

1. Direct Mental Health Intervention—Early Phase

The mental health intervention program can be organized along two major areas of professional activities. The first is the direct, face-to-face intervention with families housed in emergency sheltered sites. Professionals who start working directly with the families in the relocation centers will be available to offer psychological help to a gathered group of families in need. Guided by the knowledge of the time phase, sequential manifestations of crisis phenomenology, the professional can identify and organize a number of approaches developed to assist the children and their families through the early phases of crisis, coping, and adaptation. As these families move through their evolving emergency housing and changing human settings, their psychophysiological phases of crisis resolution will show different behaviors and will express different needs. The professional will develop therapeutic procedures to meet the objective of returning the family and the child to a functional level of adaptation.

As mentioned before, the objective of mental health intervention is a successful use of techniques that 1) restore the capacity of the child to a previous level of functioning by assisting him in handling the stressful situation in which he finds himself; and 2) assist the family in reorganizing its world through social and psychological interaction with the mental health professional. This can be done by the collaboration of the mental health professional with other support, care-giving emergency assistance groups, and all the family agencies helping the child and his caregivers.

Therapeutic crisis intervention. Therapeutic crisis intervention encompasses all the activities by which the professional seeks to relieve the distress of the child and assist the family through psychological means. It encompasses all helping activities that are primarily, although not necessarily, based on verbal communication. Many of the families display a sense of hopelessness and demoralization. All forms of therapy use certain approaches to combat and control this painful effect. Demoralized families show behavior that reflects the feeling of being unable to cope with the multiple tasks that families have when taking care of children, and that others expect them to handle well. These families' sense of self can vary widely after a disaster. Among the signs of demoralization, the following family reactions can be expected:

1. Families express feelings of diminished self-confidence and have difficulty remembering their ability to handle the children's and their spouses' needs.
2. They believe that failure will be the outcome of their decisions and actions, and they appear to be struggling with feelings of guilt and shame as part of the adaptive regression.
3. Families feel alienated, depressed, and isolated, as if they had been singled out for the worst outcome.

4. Families become enmeshed in a sense of increased dependency on agency workers, who may have difficulty in understanding both the intrafamilial confused reactive feelings and the family value systems based on traditional ethnic ways of behaving in a novel situation.

Techniques to assist across developmental phases of crisis resolution. Several techniques are available to the professional intervening during the crisis sequential phases manifested by the family and children traumatized by the disaster. These initial techniques can be grouped under the heading of "Auxiliary First Aid Techniques." These early approaches are directed toward restoring the family functions and adapting to the early transition experience, and can be instrumental in reintegrating and returning the total family system to balance. Intervention procedures are related to helping the family assess, problem solve, and make decisions day by day as they move through the emergency situation, the reconstruction, and, finally, return to a living situation that becomes more permanent. These psychotherapeutic approaches are defined as any active interaction between the professional and the family that tends to supplement, complement, reinforce, and promote the family systems mechanisms in the novel setting. When one restores the family functions of adaptive strategies, the child is assisted in functioning more effectively. The following is an example of this approach.

A family composed of a mother (36 years old) and father (41 years old) with two children (8 and 12 years old) were found in one of the shelters. A major avalanche had buried their neighborhood a few hours after they had climbed safely on a nearby hill. They had to spend six to eight hours in the cold night and had been rescued by emergency workers who brought them to the shelter, where they were fed and given cots and blankets. The professional who met them observed that the mother was crying and appeared somewhat dazed and depressed, while the father was trying to actively organize the family activities and cheer everyone up. The children seemed to adapt to the new surroundings and although their faces expressed tension, they did not appear to show gross behavior disturbances.

Following a preliminary evaluation of the situation, it was obvious that the most expressive disturbance of feelings was manifested by the mother. A short evaluation proved that she had been unable to relax, was depressed, and felt hopeless and helpless. On the other hand, the father appeared to deny the reality of the situation and tried to encourage the family with false and unrealistic hopes. After a few days, the children began to lose their ability to cope, became more demanding and restless, had difficulty in eating and sleeping, and did not want to separate from the mother to go out into the playgrounds that had been organized for the children of the shelter.

The objective of the therapeutic intervention was designed to complement the mother's ability to feel more competent and to reinforce the father's sense of "being in charge" in a realistic way so that he would not have to deny and distort reality to regain his composure. All family members were helped to express some of the sadness and feeling of disorientation by being provided with knowledge—daily news and explanations about what was going to happen in the present and in the next few days. The children were able to meet in small groups with other children, where they shared their memories about the event and were offered the possibility of expressing some of their fantasies through drawings so as to promote a sense of mastery of their feelings. The parents were asked to assist in the housekeeping of the shelter and to participate with organized adult activities.

The above process gives a prototypical example of the range of procedures (behavior, actions, speech, types of meetings, face-to-face interactions) through which process occurs and is adapted to the situation encountered. The child and his family in the early stages of relocation will express through behavior the manifestations of the crisis in psychophysiological disorganization. The resources available to the counselor will influence the procedures used, the time spent with the family, and the activities in the relocation center. The psychological assistance configuration varies in structure because the combination of factors differs according to the extent of the community disruption or the availability of resources. But the objective remains clear, as far as reconstituting the adaptive system of the family which, in turn, will help the child control the expected regressive behavior seen in all traumatized children.

Psychological assistance to children must be based on the ability to conceptualize and understand the crisis manifestations and the levels of infantile dysfunction during the various stages of postdisaster crisis resolution. The objectives of intervention are as follows:

1. To help the child develop an internal sense of perspective so that he will be able to organize his own environment.
2. To assist the recuperative process of sharing painful emotions provoked by the stressor events, helping the child (according to his age) put events in perspective.
3. To assist the child to reach out to both his family members and

the professionals on the emergency teams in order to use the resources that are available to develop a sense of comfort, security and affection.

The professional can mobilize available internal resources of the child to help him participate with his family in reordering its environment and alleviating emotional conflicts between family members so as to diminish emotional discomfort.

Risk factors in post-traumatic crisis resolution. The level of psychobiological functional status of the child is related to the vulnerability of the child's developmental stage, to his biological health, and to his personality strength. If the child is showing high anxiety, depression, withdrawal, regression, disturbance of sleep and eating functions, this needs to be ascertained as a measure of the manifestation of disorganized psychobiological factors. To be able to measure these signals, the professional must investigate the following:

1. The psychosocial maturity or immaturity of the child.
2. The social expectations of performance behavior as judged by the child, his family, and others living with them.
3. Continued environmental postdisaster stress, both in social and physical accommodations throughout the period of transition.
4. Accidental crisis events occurring in the child's life either before or after the stressor event.
5. Social settings as postdisaster stressors.

The setting where the child is located is an important variable that will affect the choice of psychological intervention. This is based on the realistic, practical experience of housing victims in crowded sheltered settings. The rapid turnover of large numbers of victims in and out of the shelter and the small number of trained staff to stay for continued periods of time with the same family influence the type of intervention. What can be the best type of useful intervention within the specific setting with the number of professional resources available?

Steps and guidelines for crisis intervention. The crisis counselor establishes a relationship with the family and the child by explaining to the family the psychological processes following a disaster. The objectives of intervention are set by (1) obtaining the information needed to plan an intervention; (2) establishing confidence and credibility in the family's awareness;

(3) describing the intervention plan; and (4) eliciting the family's cooperation with the plan. From all this data gathering, the crisis counselor arrives at a tentative formulation of the problem and/or the plan of action. The therapeutic objectives are first of all to alleviate the emotional distress in the family and the cognitive disorganization in the child.

The following key principles guide sequential steps of intervention:

Crisis counselors should assume that the families are potentially capable of handling their own problems, after being helped to recognize the areas of distress, and of redirecting their behavior towards exploring new solutions.

A counselor should allow the family to develop initial dependency so that the family can borrow confidence from the counselor and, at the same time, offer it to a child. This should be short-lived; long-term dependency should be discouraged.

Advice is generally given with caution, although this does not preclude informing the family about all relevant matters on which they are ignorant or misinformed. This will help the family direct their own energies to their own methods of problem solving.

Whenever possible, according to the age of the child, the interpretation that links feelings to behavior not previously connected by the child may be therapeutic. It may also assist the family in understanding the feelings and thoughts that signal the actual progression of crisis resolution. This will allow the family to make sense of feelings that are disturbing and, by putting those feelings in perspective, enhance their sense of mastery and control.

Emotions that are seen in the initial post-traumatic phases include sadness, fear, and anger. These are manifested in many forms and with a wide range of intensity. These emotions should be accepted as expressions of the pain the families have suffered and should be supported in the perspective of the event. Assistance to achieve resignation and acceptance of some of the reality situation in which they find themselves is an end point of grieving postdisaster.

Some families become cognitively and emotionally disorganized for a temporary period. The intervention needs to be acutely directed towards these functions, as they interfere with parenting tasks. Procedures must be implemented to increase competence and maintain their awareness that the situation generated by the disaster will demand increased individual mobilization of all parenting skills to help the child adapt to a traumatized environment. Support and encouragement is offered in strengthening parents' conscious awareness of the appropriateness of their social reactions in light of what is happening. This clarification is useful in reinforcing natural parental behavior. Continued cognitive disorganization will affect the parents' ability to deal with their problems and their children's problems.

One of the main considerations in this case is to help the parents diminish the effects of the disorganization and reinforce their cognitive mastery by offering psychological assistance that is useful according to their specific condition. By assisting the parents in diminishing their sense of helplessness, their indecisive or regressive behavior, and their disbelief that they lack coping skills, the therapist aids them in reconstituting themselves more rapidly and assuming responsibilities for child care. He assists them in the problem solving, dealing with the children directly when the children are showing expressions or the signs of emotional disturbance. As a result, the family members tend to pull together and continue to move forward in the crisis resolution pathway.

Strategies for intervention. The choice of priorities in intervention and selection of displaced families to assist in the first few days following the disaster is a difficult triage process. As soon as families are identified, they need help in regaining a sense of orientation, reinforcing reality, and developing support and trust. Ascertaining the needs of the family for the type of resources that can be obtained and provided by other agencies is the responsibility of the crisis worker.

A great array of resources in emergency programs that are available to the family must be organized to meet their specific needs. Many of these needs are material, but others are psychological. The crisis worker can mobilize appropriate help by observing the way staff from other agencies behave or approach the family. Required are special techniques that allow the worker to elicit directly and personally from the family, in their own communication style, what they perceive as immediate needs, to interpret these needs within the context of the shelter, and then to collaborate with other agencies in mobilizing the resources so that parents and children feel assisted, less helpless, less hopeless, and less destitute.

2. Direct Mental Health Intervention — Later Phase Postdisaster

As the families are relocated from emergency shelters to temporary lodgings or back to their own home, which may be damaged but safe, a new area of crisis work emerges which manifests itself through expressions of increased grieving and bereavement. The professional worker needs to develop a combination of activities which include outreach procedures to go out to the living site of relocated families and to follow the children's progression toward return of function. The family's level of adaptation is assessed and if the assessment does not reveal further decompensation, a message can be conveyed that the staff is available. If the family notices a psychological problem or is aware of further interest in using psychological resources, they can recontact the emergency assistance team.

It is during this sequential phase of postdisaster time frames that each level of development and previous experiences plays a role in the manifestation of coping mechanisms and level of adaptation in children. There appears to be a larger dependency on denial in the earlier years of development as a means of accommodating to the traumatic event. As the child develops a better command of expressing her ideas, she can talk more often about the frightening episodes, she is able to share experiences, she can reproduce in drawings some of the distressing visual experiences she lived through, and she can express through repetitive play her troubled conflicts. Older children appear to respond to explicit, directive, and encouraging discussion with the crisis counselors. The same objectives that were useful in the shelters—approaching daily activities through an accurate cognitive appraisal of the situation and enhancing the family's knowledge about its surroundings so that it can understand its own emotions and the external events—appear to aid during subsequent stages and increase adaptive mechanisms, diminishing the level of depression and anxiety.

If appropriate and feasible, group intervention with parents or teachers getting together with children to discuss how they are responding to stress and what is expected as natural, healthy crisis resolution behavior appears to enhance adaptation (Galante & Foa, 1986). The method of having parents and children in groups is helpful because the children's problems are often overlooked while family members are overwhelmed, not only by their own personal intrapsychic disorder and disorganized feelings but also because the enormous task of reconstructing their concrete world is a priority. The professional's function is to provide support, to offer himself as someone to whom the parents can come when in difficulties, to clarify the child's behavior, and to suggest methods of assisting it.

Often, too, other social agencies must be mobilized to help families which are having difficulty in adapting to their new setting and are disrupted or have difficulty in coping with the ordinary demands of family life. At times, working with the school may be essential to provide a child with additional assistance and contact with other adults who may be helpful to the family. To enable parents to use other community resources of social and practical support is part of educating them to the fact that they need assistance to carry out their task for a short time, but that does not mean that agencies should take over the parental role. Every decision must be the parents'; they must initiate every change in the sequence of life activities that will lead them to recuperate their family dynamic balance.

Indirect methods of assisting post-traumatized child populations. Two of the principal components of indirect intervention are: consultation and education. Through these activities directed at the problems of a child population, mental health professionals not only disseminate information and problem-solving skills, but also create a positive environment of support for the disaster relief program.

Mental health consultation is a cornerstone of all emergency intervention programs (Cohen, 1984). Consultation is the professional activity designed to promote the incorporation of psychological procedures in dealing with all the affected child population in an emergency situation. Specifically, its purpose is the early identification and use of psychological methodology to alleviate the disastrous effects of the traumatic experiences suffered by the child. As a method of problem solving, consultation generally addresses the issues of the case and program-centered problems in order to achieve this purpose.

Educational activities generally include education of the public and training and orientation of the disaster worker. Three groups have been selected to highlight the focus of these activities. The three groups are among the many involved in the care of children and are composed of 1) the family, 2) teachers, and 3) all professionals dealing with families in the disaster activities.

3. Consultation Objectives in a Postdisaster Program

Child victim-centered case consultation. This is a traditional type of consultation where the consultant is asked for his opinion, diagnosis, and assessment of adaptation problems in an individual victim.

In addition, the consultant might recommend a plan for effective approach to counseling the child. This is an appropriate method used with teachers when children return to their school settings. Teachers recognize age-appropriate cognitive and emotional behavior and can participate in the intervention program by adapting psychological knowledge of postdisaster reactions to problem solving in their classrooms.

Example: A teacher asked for help because he was unable to reach a six-year-old girl who appeared to have a change in her learning ability following a severe flooding in her town. Analysis of the situation showed that the family was closely meshed, with an additional infant and toddler who remained at home. Parents appeared to have trouble expressing their emotional postdisaster reactions and became distant to the six-year-old who was "sent to school and was a relief to the daily work of the mother." This perceived rejection was causing difficulties between the student and her family. Specifically, when she returned home after school, she demanded increased attention. Advice and suggestions were given by the consultant to the teacher on how the needs of the child could be balanced in school and at home. The consultant suggested a meeting with the family and the teacher to assist them in balancing the needs of both the family and the child.

Consultee-centered case consultation. The consultant focuses his attention on trying to understand the nature of the work difficulties for a consultee with regard to a victim and on helping him to remedy these difficulties. The consultee's difficulties may be viewed as: 1) lack of knowledge about the problems presented by the child victims; 2) lack of skill in making use of such knowledge; 3) lack of self-confidence in utilizing his knowledge and skills; or 4) lack of professional objectivity due to subjective emotional complication.

An example of how to increase the consultee's professional objectivity and to review the distortion of her perception of the victim's condition was highlighted by a community nurse working with a family that presented the following problem:

Mary, a seven-year-old girl who had lived through a major earthquake, was brought to the community medical-nursing center for diagnosis of her inability to sleep and night terrors. The nurse who was examining her had herself suffered from a loss of home and hospital job in the same disaster and was now volunteering at the nursing center. She had a child a few years older than the victim and was having conflicts about leaving her child with a neighbor while she came to work at the center. She had difficulty in being objective about the child's symptoms and her own guilt feelings in leaving her child in a care-giving situation. She appealed to the consultant because of her inability to obtain a clear story of the family situation.

As she presented the case history, it became apparent that the distortion was a result of difficulties with her own child and worries that her child might also develop symptoms. By helping her to separate the two children, supporting her feelings, and complimenting her on her professionalism by volunteering to help her community, the consultant was able to strengthen her sense of competence and her ability to develop an appropriate psychosocial history.

Program-centered administrative consultation. The work problem in this type of consultation is in planning the administration of the intervention program. The concern is how to best develop a program that will meet the needs of the population of children affected by the disaster. The consultant helps by using her psychological knowledge, administrative systems knowledge of disaster programs, and experience with problem solution in other areas of human behavior postdisaster. The primary goal for the consultant is to prescribe an effective course of action in planning the programs for children. The following example will highlight some issues:

A consultant who was working with the leader of a city that had been partially destroyed by a tornado was asked to participate in a series of meetings to plan the care of a large number of children housed in two welfare centers. The activities to be planned included housing, feeding, child health care, and placement in school and recreational facilities. The consultant participated with all the human service systems involved with the child population. After acquiring firsthand knowledge of the problems faced by the service organization and the needs of the children, the consultant was able to introduce psychological concepts into the program service plan.

Another major area of program consultation emerges after a disaster when there are a large number of orphans who are congregated in a site where there might not be appropriate child care facilities. The issues raised by child care workers are whether to relocate these children out of their geographical setting, where they were born and raised, and send them to distant cities where there is better schooling and health facilities. There is also a question of whether to send them in small groups or individually. The issue of foster care for these orphans and possible separation of siblings to suit the needs of the foster care system must be resolved. These are difficult and painful consultation issues that appear in almost all major catastrophic disaster events. The possibilities of assisting orphans are multiple, depending on the resources of the communities, but in general it is suggested that children should not be uprooted into unknown physical settings. If possible, they should be kept together in small groups that incorporate their own neighborhoods or family groupings for care in small homelike settings.

4. Education

An opportunity to implement educational activities promoting increased knowledge of the psychological reactions of children to disaster can be organized through a postdisaster mental health program. The primary educational need of a community which will include teachers, child care personnel, and disaster emergency personnel is the knowledge and understanding of how children react after an event. By reviewing the time phases of behavior reactions following a disaster, participants who work with children can examine the types of physical and emotional problems that can be expected at each phase of postdisaster time frames. Training is needed in the phenomena of psychic trauma, stress response, crisis resolution, loss and mourning in children, family disruption, and support systems, with recognition that the major objective is to enhance coping and adaptation in the children.

Teachers can be educated to assist children in their crisis resolution by: 1) allowing children free expression of feelings; 2) helping them correct misperception of the new situation; and 3) helping them to understand why they feel the way they do in order to increase mastery of emotions. Teachers should be aware that all children reenact in their play distressed memories that follow a postdisaster situation. This is a spontaneous process by which children master their experiences. For example, when a child is struggling to deal with problems of his parents' own confusing behavior and unpredictable expression of feelings, he may act this out in games and try to gain mastery of authority roles that have changed after the disaster.

At times, the teacher may feel that such games appear sadistic and callous and the impulse to intervene can be strong. It is not difficult, however, to educate the teacher to realize that this play has a therapeutic function and helps the child come to terms with the anxiety-arousing event she has recently lived through. The relief of anxiety through play has been observed after most traumatic events and it appears to help children gain control over their crisis feelings. The teacher may become aware of the child's reaction to the events and of the kind of reassurance and explanations appropriate for the specific expression of emotions.

Child care workers and teachers can be educated to allow the child to bring out in talk and in play his true thoughts and feelings about the event, even if these are aggressive, sadistic, and apparently callous. It is also helpful when the child reveals his misconceptions about what has happened that this be listened to. At the same time, the teacher with access to knowledge of the facts can offer this to the child for reality testing.

Teachers can be encouraged to set up special opportunities for children to express their feelings and thus encourage the crisis resolution process that emerges after a disaster. In this way, the child is helped in the crisis through some form of activity (playing, drawing, story telling) and the problem is not just avoided.

Children at risk in postdisaster situations are those who have lost their parents and who not only have to work through the psychic trauma of the event, the mourning and loss of the important figure in their lives, but also have to work through bonding to a new individual who takes on the role of a foster parent. Child care workers and teachers can be educated to understand not only the behavior of the child in their daily care, but their own responses. They should be aware of the complex phenomenology expressed by behavior, showing the processes that the child has to go through before he can have enough energy to bond again with the worker.

The complexity of the postdisaster situation for a child increases when the predisaster situation includes special problems of learning, physical illness, or social deprivation. Such children present very special problems. They have difficulty forming relationships with others, their capacities to express themselves in words are limited, their ideas about the world in general are immature for their age, and they usually display marked behavior disorders that are aggravated by the traumatizing event that they have gone through in the disaster. Aggressive outbursts, bed-wetting, soiling, stealing, and running away are common among these children who, in the past, found their way toward maturity full of barriers for normal development. Even though the basic need of such children is for a stable home situation, distressing changes provoked by the fragmented planning in postdisaster assistance programs often make them more reactive and unacceptable for permanent placement. It is important to teach the workers that the negativism that will prevent such children from coming close to their caretakers is an expression of traumatized trust.

It is helpful to educate the caretakers to recognize the regressive behavior, which is a stage of recapitulation of earlier stages of development that have been traumatized in the child and are going to emerge, postdisaster, as part of the new effort to mature. Programming for these children has the following aims: 1) to provide them in the present with experiences that they have missed in the past; 2) to allow them to process the traumatic event and the crisis that they have experienced during the disaster; and 3) to allow them to correct their distrust of human relationships. With a stable, understanding environment, children can use the human resources available to fill the gap in their growth process.

Again, the healing and reparatory process necessary to assist a child in a post-traumatic situation will depend on level of development and life experience before the disaster. Education given to the families who are having difficulty with the child assists them in conceptualizing and understanding the behavior. This allows the family members to understand the crisis behavior and separate themselves from pathological interaction with the child. It also allows them to feel comfortable in expressing their own crisis feelings and thoughts, which they were not free to tell the others before because of fears that the child might get worse. Parents who are confused about their own emotions and behavior towards their children or each other feel relieved in recognizing that the difficulties were based on the experiences that they have gone through. This knowledge allows them to face the daily, realistic tasks.

Educating the caretakers in child post-traumatic behavior puts them in a unique position to prevent further deterioration of coping abilities. Secondary crisis situations can be averted by preventing further separation experiences from developing into deprivation.

An effective way of providing regular inservice training for teachers, child care workers, and disaster workers is to develop postdisaster professional training groups. This can be part of the educational activities of an institution where such workers assist with children brought from disaster areas. The mutual exploration of problems and situations not only helps the participants with their ongoing work but provides a valuable extension to training in psychological child rearing methods. As the discussion focuses on the interaction between staff and children, it will highlight the fact that these children arouse feelings in the staff members such as anger, frustration, and anxiety, as well as affection and pleasure. Inevitably, too, irritations and frustration arise between staff members, often in relation to the organization of institutional life which is disrupted by the complicated postdisaster situation of a community in which they themselves are often victims of the disaster.

In summary, a child disaster team can be educated to view themselves as providing three different kinds of services to foster care units after a disaster:

1. An individual diagnostic and treatment service for children and their families who identify themselves as in need of help and who are referred for psychological assistance.
2. Special consultation services for social agencies that work in the postdisaster program. Direct links between the psychological teams and the agencies are cultivated. Special problem cases are referred for discussion and problem solving to assist the social agencies in obtaining resources for the family and the child.

3. A program of regular group discussions with professional groups helping children. The aim will be to help these professionals deal with their current problems and increase their therapeutic, supportive, and healing skills. Because assisting children who are orphaned or separated from their parents following a disaster is such a new component of social welfare systems, professionals need regular help and support in their dealings with the children and in their contact with relatives.

During a training workshop, a child worker spoke of her inability to understand a seven-year-old boy who appeared to be having difficulty in learning some of the rules and regulations of the home where he was placed after he became separated from his mother during an avalanche that covered his town. The boy had been rescued by a helicopter that plucked him from a mud cover where he was caught for several hours. It was explained to the worker that young children have a way of thinking that is not logical, cannot process cause and effect relationships, and tends to be concrete, rigid, nonreversible, and relatively inflexible. To help this child understand the relationship between the changed conditions of his life, the disaster, and why he had to live in this house with different rules would be unproductive. After a child is seven or eight years old, he develops a more logical, abstract, and complex understanding of events. The worker corrected the educator by pointing out that this child was beyond seven years. It was at this point that the educator could explain the fact that all children who have been severely traumatized will suffer regressive impact on their newly acquired functions. This means that adults need to know expected child development behavior, but must be aware of a shift toward infantile expressions younger than the stated age. As the traumatic memories and the daily quality of life interact, and if the environment is therapeutic, the child will regain his functions.

SUMMARY

This chapter has addressed the unique needs for intervention with a postdisaster traumatized child population.

Intervention activities are guided by a conceptualized body of knowledge based on the child as a biopsychosociocultural organism interacting with his environment (human and concrete). It is pointed out that a traumatized child will become dysfunctional for a specific length of time, but will recuperate his adaptive homeostatic balance if assisted by his family, environment, and community. The mental health professional who participates as a member of the disaster emergency team has the opportunity to help the child and his family through direct intervention, consultation, and education.

REFERENCES

Ahearn, F. L., & Cohen, R. E. (Eds.) (1984). *Disasters and Mental Health, An Annotated Bibliography.* Washington, D.C.: DHHS Publication No. ADM 84–131.

Block, D., Silber, E., & Perry, S. (1956). Some factors in the emotional reaction of children to disaster. *American Journal of Psychiatry,* 113: 416–422.

Bowlby, J. (1980). *Attachment and Loss, Vol. 3: Loss, Sadness and Depression.* New York: Basic Books.

Bowlby, J. (1963). Pathological mourning and childhood mourning. *Journal of the American Psychoanalytic Association,* 11: 500–541.

Brown, G., Harris, T., & Bifuleo, A. (1985). Long-term effects of early loss of parents. In M. Rutter, C. Izard, & P. Read (Eds.), *Depression in Young People: Developmental and Clinical Perspectives.* New York: Guilford Press.

Burke, J. D., Jr., Borus, J. F., Burnes, B. J., Millstein, K. H., & Beasley, M. C. (1982). Changes in children's behavior after a natural disaster. *American Journal of Psychiatry,* 139: 1010–1014.

Caplan, G. (1964). *Principles of Preventive Psychiatry.* New York: Basic Books.

Cohen, R. E. (1987). Armero tragedy: A lesson for mental health professionals. *Hospital & Community Psychiatry,* 38(12): 1316–1321.

Cohen, R. E. (1984). Consultation in disasters: Refugees. In N. R. Bernstein & J. N. Sussex (Eds.), *Psychiatric Consultation with Children and Youth.* Jamaica, NY: SP Medical and Scientific Books.

Cohen, R. E. (1985). Crisis counseling principles and services. In M. Lystad (Ed.), *Innovations in Mental Health Services to Disaster Victims.* Washington, D.C.: DHHS Publication No. ADM 85–1390.

Cohen, R. E. (1986). Developmental phases of children's reactions following natural disasters. *Journal of Emergency and Disaster Medicine,* 1(4): 89–95.

Cohen, R. E. (1982). Intervening with disaster victims. In H. C. Schulberg & M. Killilea (Eds.), *The Modern Practice of Community Mental Health.* San Francisco: Jossey-Bass.

Cohen, R. E. (1976). Post-disaster mobilization of a crisis intervention team: The Managua experience. In H. Parad, H. Resnik, & L. Parad (Eds.), *Emergency Mental Health Services and Disaster Management.* Bowie, MD: Charles Press.

Cohen, R. E., & Ahearn, F. L. (1980). *Handbook for Mental Health Care of Disaster Victims.* Baltimore: The Johns Hopkins University Press.

Cornely, P., & Bromet, E. (in press). Prevalence of behavior problems in three-year-old children living near Three Mile Island: A comparative analysis. *Journal of Child Psychology & Psychiatry.*

Eth, S., & Pynoos, R. (1985). Interaction of trauma and grief in childhood. In S. Eth & R. Pynoos (Eds.), *Post-Traumatic Stress Disorder in Children.* Washington, D.C.: American Psychiatric Press, pp. 171–186.

Figley, C. R., & McCubbin, H. I. (1983). *Stress and the Family, Vol. 2, Coping with Catastrophe.* New York: Brunner/Mazel.

Fisher, K. W. (1980). A theory of cognitive development: The control and construction of hierarchies of skills. *Psychology Review,* 87: 477–53.

Frederick, C. (1985). Children traumatized by catastrophic situations. In S. Eth & R. Pynoos (Eds.), *Post-Traumatic Stress Disorder in Children*. Washington, D.C.: American Psychiatric Press.

Freud, A., & Burlingham, D. T. (1943). *War and Children*. New York: Medical War Books.

Galante, M. A., & Foa, D. (1986). An epidemiological study of psychic trauma and treatment effectiveness for children after a natural disaster. *Journal of Community Psychiatry*, 25: 357–363.

Garmezy, N. (1986). Children under severe stress: Critique and commentary. *Journal of Child Psychiatry*, 25(3): 384–392.

Garmezy, N., & Rutter, M. (1985). Acute stress reactions. In M. Rutter & L. Herson (Eds.), *Child and Adolescent Psychiatry: Modern Approaches* (2nd ed.). Oxford, England: Blackwell Scientific.

Goodyear, I., Kolvin, I., & Gatzanis, S. (1985). Recent undesirable life events and psychiatric disorder in childhood and adolescence. *British Journal of Psychiatry*, 147: 517–523.

Handford, H. A., Mayes, S. D., Mattison, R. E., Humphrey, F. J. II, Bagnato, S., Bixler, E. O., & Kales, J. D. (1986). Child and parent reaction to the Three Mile Island Nuclear Accident. *Child Psychiatry*, 23(3): 346–355.

Howard, S. J., & Gordon, N. S. (1973). *Coping with Children's Reaction to Earthquakes and Other Disasters*. Van Nuys, CA: San Fernando Valley Child Guidance Clinic.

Johnson, J. H. (1982). Life events as stressors in childhood and adolescence. In B. B. Lahey & A. E. Kazdin (Eds.), *Advances in Clinical Child Psychology, Vol. 5*. New York: Plenum Press.

Kagan, J. (1984). *The Nature of the Child*. New York: Basic Books.

Lazarus, R. S. (1977). *Cognitive and Coping Processes in Emotion, in Stress and Coping*. New York: Columbia University Press.

Lehrman, S. R. (1956). Reactions to untimely death. *Psychiatry*, 30: 564–578.

Levinson, P. (1972). On sudden death. *Psychiatry*, 35: 160–173.

Longfellow, C., & Belle, D. (1984). Stressful environments and their impact on children. In J. Humphrey (Ed.), *Stress in Childhood*. New York: AMS.

Nagera, H. (1970). Children's reactions to the death of important objects: A developmental approach. *Psychoanalytic Study of the Child*, 25: 360–400.

Newman, C. J. (1976). Children of disaster: Clinical observations at Buffalo Creek. *American Journal of Psychiatry*, 133: 306–312.

Orbaschel, H., Sholomskas, D., & Weissman, M. M. (1980). *The Assessment of Psychopathology and Behavior Problems in Children: A Review of Scales Suitable for Epidemiological and Clinical Research (1967–1979)*. Washington, D.C.: Government Printing Office.

Osterweis, M., Solomon, F., & Green, M. (1984). Bereavement during childhood and adolescence. In M. Osterweis, F. Solomon, & M. Green (Eds.), *Bereavement: Reactions, Consequences and Care*. Washington, D.C.: National Academy Press, pp. 99–141.

Rutter, M. (1981a). *Maternal Deprivation Reassessed*. Harmondsworth, England: Penguin Books.

Rutter, M. (1981b). Stress, coping and development: Some issues and some questions. *Journal of Child Psychology & Psychiatry*, 22: 323–356.

Silber, E., Perry, S. E., & Block, D. A. (1957). Patterns of parent-child interactions in a disaster. *Psychiatry*, 21: 159–167.

Stern, N. D. (1985). *The Interpersonal World of the Infant*. New York: Basic Books.

Szapocznik, J., Cohen, R. E., & Hernandez, R. (Eds.) (1985). *Coping with Adolescent Refugees*. New York: Praeger.

Terr, L. C. (1981). Psychic trauma in children: Observations following the Chowchilla school-bus kidnapping. *American Journal of Psychiatry*, 138: 14–19.

Terr, L. C. (1984). Children at acute risk: Psychic trauma. In L. Grinspoon (Ed.), *Psychiatry Update, Vol. 3*. Washington, D.C.: American Psychiatric Press, pp. 104–120.

Wolff, S. (1969). *Children Under Stress* (pp. 194–213). London: Penguin Press.

11

Intervention Strategies for Emergency Workers

CHRISTINE DUNNING

There is growing recognition in emergency services management administration that those personnel deployed at scenes of disaster in the role of occupational duty are susceptible to physical and mental health sequelae. Anecdotal reports (Dunning & Silva, 1980; Forstenzer, 1980; Wilkinson, 1983; Mitchell, 1982; Jones, 1985) indicate immediate and delayed organizational dysfunction as a result of disaster duty assignment. Research based on retrospective accounts indicate that persons whose occupation requires them to participate in disaster response experience, at a minimum, physical and psychological discomfort (Keating, 1986; Mantell, 1986). However, no empirical data exist that provide comprehensive knowledge of the health sequelae of disaster deployment in duty-required participants such as police, fire, and protective service-connected emergency medical personnel.

While documentation of the potentially deleterious effects of a disaster on duty-assigned emergency workers would seem to be a necessary antecedent to the development of methods to prevent or resolve disaster-induced trauma, the negative consequences being experienced by present emergency workers point to the need to pursue immediately the development of relevant policy, procedure, and program recommendations. Creating effective organizational response under the complex and uncertain operating conditions of a disaster poses a sobering challenge to protective service and emergency medical agencies which bear the primary responsibility for its management. Emergency conditions place extraordinary demands on such personnel and their employing agencies to make optimum use of limited personal and professional resources under urgent constraints of time and skill.

The sudden, sharp increase in the number and kinds of demands for service during disaster can overwhelm routine agency functions. The general feeling is that a disaster is likely to occur only once in a lifetime so, since it is a unique event, there is little to be gained by allocating the already scarce resources of agencies involved to planning for its impact. Yet of concern is the development of mechanisms that will enhance ability to perform at the disaster site to facilitate optimum resolution of the event. Another important consideration for the agency would be to reduce the negative impact of disaster management participation on future organizational functioning. Lastly, by requiring workers to participate in an assignment which may prove injurious, the organization assumes responsibility for ameliorating negative consequences.

It is common for agencies whose governmental or geographic jurisdiction have experienced a disaster to receive numerous offers of consultative and intervention assistance, some coming from distant locations. Often these offers are refused, not because of a lack of interest or need, but rather because their number overwhelms the organization already burdened by the demands of the disaster response. The overextension of manpower and resources already occasioned by the need to respond quickly to stabilize and resolve the disaster strains most organizations; these organizations are still required to provide services as usual during and subsequent to the disaster. The operational aspects of the deployment, with its concomitant interorganizational coordinative requirements, occupy much of the administrative time of the agency.

Just making sure that shifts and assignments are staffed, supplies are replenished, the media are informed, and all the other time-consuming duties of a disaster response are performed causes most protective service agency administrators to place low priority on an intervention response for workers. The majority of agencies which might be called upon to respond to a disaster will not have considered the issue of the psychological trauma to workers prior to participating in a catastrophe; much less would they have promulgated an intervention strategy for the amelioration of traumatic stress symptoms.

Offers of the sort that pour in after media reports of the disastrous situation tend to bring this issue onto the organizational agenda. The response could be: do nothing, believing that such injury is not likely or that action requires more careful consideration, or accept one of the offers based on expediency or a generally cursory examination of the needs of the organization. Often, the accepted offer meets a minimal requirement of having done something, which does not cause much disruption or cost to the department. Little consideration is given to what course of action will provide the best resolution of disaster trauma among emergency and rescue workers. The eager offers, while sincere, allow the organization to put off or ignore much larger issues in relation to job-incurred psychological injuries.

The issue of traumatic stress related to the duties of protective service and other medical and rescue workers who respond to disaster incidents incites much disagreement in the professions. Most administrators are wary of any discussion that suggests job-related duties and conditions might produce psychological injury to workers. The protective services have generally believed that their selection and training process produces individuals who can adapt well under stressful conditions, and, in fact, that stress can bring out the best in a worker.

To recognize in any formal way the possible existence of trauma reactions that have as their precipitant duty deployment through officially recognized intervention and resolution programs might increase the likelihood of successful workers' compensation claims and duty disability retirements. The usual reaction of many protective service administrators is to assert that current training and support services provide sufficient protection against any injury, physical or psychological. Since 1955, when a landmark court case, *Bailey v. American General*, extended the workers' compensation law to psychological illness, there has been a burgeoning number of claims that assert that on-the-job stress or unsatisfactory work environment contributes to psychological disorders.

The task at hand for protective service administrators is to differentiate between stressors which clearly are job-related and those which are not, and to intervene in job-related stressors if the symptoms grow in intensity and frequency. Clearly, protective service administrators can no longer afford to ignore the issue of job stress, such as the traumatic stress of duty-related response to catastrophic events, as it has become a legal obligation. Much of the research currently emerging accepts a cause-and-effect relationship between workplace stress and many somatic illnesses. The task of administrators is to reduce liability for the legal risk associated with workplace stress, specifically the stress of response to an extraordinary event outside the realm of normal or even infrequent occurrence.

A particular issue to administrators is that in workers' compensation cases the law reflects a liberal definition of work-related injury. In *Wolfe v. Sibley, Lindsay and Curr Co.* (1975), the court accepted the link between the job stressor and the subsequent disability that caused incapability to function properly on the job without considering whether the job stressor caused the disability or aggravated an existing condition or vulnerability.

It should be noted that in the case of a psychological injury, the courts had been reluctant to compensate workers due to the difficulty in establishing either the cause or the extent of the injury (Ivancevich, Matteson, & Richards, 1985). The current advancement in research related to stress and specifically to the traumatic stressors of disaster experience will in all probability result in compensation for a wide range of conditions related to work-related stress. Claims that are currently successful generally result in compensation for psychological injury that arises from accidents involving physical injury or death. Discrete, specifically identifiable incidents that are unrelated to the usual performance of the duties of one's job and that result in psychological injury have frequently been upheld by the courts. These claims are further advanced when the issue of psychological injury has physical manifestations. The bottom line in decisions involving workers' compensation is whether the employee should be treated differently for inability to work because of a mental injury caused by employment as compared with a physical injury caused by employment (Lublin, 1980).

If administrators accept the premise that deployment at a scene of disaster or catastrophic event can result in a psychological reaction (and many don't), then efforts to initiate programs to reduce its negative effect and ensuing productivity and compensation costs must be addressed. Procedures that screen prospective employees rarely examine propensity toward stress manifestation. Such efforts would not appear to be cost-effective for most protective service agencies. Indeed, since no reliable procedures exist to measure stress other than reaction, one must look, like the court, to consideration of claims made by workers against protective service, medical, and rescue agencies subsequent to a catastrophic event.

Obviously, it is in the administrators' best interest to identify situations that are stressful before substantial legal liability is incurred. The present all-too-common supervisory response, ignoring lingering problems or disciplining workers, may prove detrimental not only to the operation of the department but to the financial well-being of the agency or governmental jurisdiction. Protective service, medical, and rescue administrators need to decide whether they accept the fact that sufficient evidence exists to link psychological injuries, temporary or permanent, with demands of the profession.

A review of the limited research examining disaster worker trauma (Keating, 1986; Mantell, 1986; Hartsough & Myers, 1985; Mitchell, 1985) and the anecdotal reports of emergency workers subsequent to disaster participation (Dunning & Silva, 1980; Dunning, 1985a; Hartsough & Myers, 1985; Mitchell, 1982) would suggest that deployment does cause psychological, physical, and/or behavioral impairment, both temporary and, in a few cases, permanent. Given that fact, administrators must address the manner in which the organization chooses to intervene in situations in which it has accepted that psychological injury might prove to be a factor. Points at which the administrator could choose to implement a program would be before the disaster, during the disaster, or subsequent to the disaster operation.

PREDISASTER STRESS MANAGEMENT

Ivancevich et al. (1985) suggest that an organization which is liability wary should develop a stress diagnostic system and a stress audit, especially in situations where stress can never be eliminated. Such diagnosis can occur prior to the disaster as the organization monitors those situations and incidents that result in obvious indicators of possible psychological injury—for example, chronic illness, changes in turnover, transfer, absenteeism, performance, and the state of union-management relations. Procedures developed for monitoring and diagnosis can form the basis for implementation subsequent to a catastrophic event and guide organizational action. The diagnosis and identification of potential job stressors and their manifestations increase the administrators awareness and sensitivity to worker concerns, in addition to providing valuable insight.

Ivancevich et al. (1985) opine that once stress diagnoses and legal determinations of potential liability have defined problem areas, top-level management must become involved in planning for amelioration. Administrators must play a leading role in instituting corrective and preventive programs, or the responsibility of management to provide assistance to help workers cope with traumatic stress may be downplayed and the programs developed underutilized.

Training curricula can incorporate the findings of the stress audit and include information concerning the physical and psychological impact of disaster and other catastrophic situations as part of regular recruit and in-service programs for protective service and rescue personnel. Unfortunately, given the wide range of tasks and information that it is necessary to cover in these programs, courses focusing on disaster are infrequent or nonexistent. It is generally thought that the skills brought to bear in a disaster response are substantially the same as those employed in day-to-day duty functioning, only on a larger scale. Body handling skills, extrication, emergency medical treatment, scene preservation, and a variety of other procedures utilized on disaster sites are familiar to most experienced emergency workers. The difference is obviously the scale of the event.

Since a catastrophic event is likely to be rare, it does not make sense for most training programs to spend much time focusing upon disaster psychological injury. However, if couched in a program which looks at rehabilitation for a variety of duty-related injuries, including back and knee, post-shooting, and accident, in addition to general physical conditioning and nutrition information, the training would be both timely and extremely helpful to the worker and to the organization which ultimately bears the cost, either financially or in lost manpower and productivity.

The training could include information concerning research focusing on psychological injury and duty deployment at scenes of mass casualty, disaster, catastrophe, or any potentially traumatic event. A one-car accident, murder, emergency medical run, shooting, or a variety of other work situations may be traumatic and produce stress in any given individual. By equating psychological injury with other more commonly known and accepted forms of duty-related injury, the likelihood of follow-through is enhanced. Psychological injury is thus not singled out as something unusual or more serious, but is seen as something that can normally happen in the course of performing one's job. Therefore, preventive and rehabilitative programming is beneficial both for the worker and the organization.

The goal of the training is to inform the worker of the natural conse-quences of disaster involvement and to indicate that the organization sees a range of reactions as normal, with the expectation that the worker participate in some form of intervention program when the symptoms prove unpleasant or interfere with work performance. The organization thus not only communicates organizational ownership of the symptoms, but also indicates that the individual worker shares responsibility for resolution. The training should include, as it would for physical injury, methods of rehabilitation and resolution for traumatic stress.

One way in which the protective service agency can protect itself from contrived claims of psychological injury is to document the steps taken to help the worker cope with the stress experienced by duty deployment. Ivancevich et al. (1985) point out that this can serve to be a two-edged sword, as duty to redress problems follows knowledge of their existence. An agency must be committed to developing and implementing some recommended course of action before it acts to recognize and analyze the effects of duty-related stress. Documentation without action leaves the agency liable, for problems will be well substantiated against the agency's failure to address resolution.

In addition to training, an evaluation of the effectiveness of current intervention programming serves to support the organization's claim that appropriate actions are being taken to resolve job or duty-related stress. Ivancevich et al. (1985) state that management should view the handling of stress-related liabilities as a process that includes problem identification, solution implementation, and follow-up to evaluate the effectiveness of the organizational response. An intervention programming plan should result that would lead to automatic implementation when a disaster occurs.

Agencies responsible for formal intervention in disaster and catastrophic situations have generally focused their planning efforts on securing sufficient material and manpower resources for response, on defining roles and responsibilities on-site, in negotiating responsibility for command and other functions, and in training personnel for specific tasks related to disaster resolution. If an organization conducts a traumatic stress audit and determines that certain tasks such as body handling (Hershisher & Quarantelli, 1976; Jones, 1985; Taylor & Frazer, 1982), victim identification, perimeter control, or victim extrication are susceptible to creating a stress reaction, then steps can be taken to determine what factors related to those duties contribute to stress and adapt procedures, policies, or assignment to reduce any harmful consequences.

In preparing a disaster manual, the administration could incorporate the findings of the stress audit which would look at the various tasks and responsibilities outlined in the response to determine if a less stressful method is available to accomplish whatever goal is under examination. For example, a frequently cited concern for many rescue workers is the failure to recover all body parts in situations where intact remains are rare. The use of a fan-out cordon to search the disaster site can result in overlooked bodily remains. The worker feels the need to complete the body, especially those workers trained in recovering evidentiary material. To miss any aspect of the material to be recovered is to fail at that task. The cordon procedure itself, which involves two line passes at right angles, and possibly a third at a diagonal, can leave the worker with a sense of lack of closure if additional human remains are found later.

A suggested alternative that may prove to be less stressful to the cordon search is the matrix approach, with teams assigned to scour specific sections which represent a small segment of the disaster site. By narrowing the physical responsibility of the search area, workers can gain a greater feeling of having conducted a thorough search, thus dispelling any fears that a body or its parts may have been overlooked. The segmented matrix also might reduce the enormity of the event for the worker, both in its devastating scope and the massive demand made on the work force. A disaster scene frequently looks as if resolution will be humanly impossible. The lack of prior experience with a similar situation could result in the perception that the response effort will be never-ending, with no relief or sense of time to completion. Predisaster stress audits might take a look at the various duties required in catastrophic situations and provide guidelines for time or task limits for personnel assigned to particularly stressful tasks.

TRANSDISASTER STRESS MANAGEMENT

Noy et al. (1984) found that providing brief respite therapy in a relatively secure, stress-free setting had great benefit toward returning a productive worker to the field. Complaints that seemed to be indicative of stress were mostly found to be somatic and resolvable through abreactive treatment. This would suggest that disaster-response agencies might find it advantageous to monitor workers in order to identify those who voice physical complaints and relieve them of duty for short periods of time, providing an environment that allows momentary removal from the disaster scene. In one case subsequent to an air crash, an air-conditioned public transit bus parked on site was used.

Some agencies have found it useful to allow specially trained mental health professionals on-site to conduct individual informal debrief sessions, keeping in mind that the lack of confidentiality afforded by the setting and the occupational need to keep face will probably interfere with a therapeutic process. The contact, however, does provide a sense of kinship between the mental health professional and the disaster-response worker.

First-line supervisors trained in identifying early warning signs of emotional upset may also serve to help identify and relieve workers in stressful task assignments before manifestations ensue. The positive aspects of intervention tied to proximity and immediacy (Solomon & Benbenishty, 1986) make such an approach appropriate to the disaster situation. Crisis intervention techniques employed on site (Bleich et al., 1986), particularly when administered by an integral, thus readily accepted, crisis intervention team, would serve the worker and the organization effectively for prevention and are much more desirable than instituting treatment subsequent to the event (Weil, 1985; Raphael, 1984). Treatment in the field, offered in as informal and unobtrusive manner as possible, may be more effective than treatment following the catastrophic event.

At issue is whether such services should be offered by mental health professionals on-site, particularly by those who do not regularly have contact or a relationship with the professions or agencies involved in the disaster response, or by some other body. Obviously, to have persons untrained in safety considerations on-site adds an additional stress to those already encountered by command personnel. Additionally, it would be distracting and even disruptive to incorporate two simultaneous functions—disaster response and treatment—to compete for workers' attention. Therefore, a more effective approach would be to have trained emergency service supervisors monitor time on task, task function, level of stressful exposure, indications of fatigue, and other factors as identified by the stress audit to determine respite rotation. Hartsough and Myers (1985) refer to this process as the need to remove and protect emergency workers who manifest the aftereffects of disaster exposure.

The respite or relief center should be staffed by support personnel who meet two criteria. First, the staff should have already been selected as part of the disaster-psychological recovery team for the participating departments, having made the commitment to provide treatment for as long as necessary to achieve resolution. Secondly, to facilitate acceptance of intervention, the team should have an established therapeutic rapport with members of the department so that their role in relation to job function is accepted at that level as well as by the organization. To attempt to establish legitimacy, credibility, and rapport concurrently with the disaster experience results in more intrusion than resolution. Curbstone consultation (Hartsough & Myers, 1985) has proved to be an effective method of monitoring personnel and establishing a therapeutic rapport with workers.

An additional approach to relieving the stress of responding to a traumatic event is to initiate a training perspective concurrent with task. Preselected field training officers may be assigned to monitor and instruct emergency workers detailed to those duties determined prior to the event to be the most stressful, thus potentially psychologically harmful. An example would be the requirement of field instructions while embarking on a task such as body handling. We assume that the skills necessary to pick up and bag body parts are known to the worker, and that performance will be mechanical and instruction unnecessary. Yet a disaster response requires that those skills be performed in an unfamiliar and unpleasant setting, beyond that probably experienced in the worker's professional career.

Often, the trauma of such a task causes some workers to respond inappropriately (Dunning & Silva, 1980). The worker needs to be told that what he is doing is correct, that progress/resolution is being made, that playful humor and macabre behavior must be placed in perspective, and that, above all, the bodies should be afforded the respect due to human remains. Acts of depersonalization, objectification, and sabotage could be monitored and pointed out, and inappropriate behavior rectified. The field training officer (FTO) may prove to be the appropriate contact for monitoring stress among workers. One potential disadvantage would be if workers perceived the FTO as performing an evaluative function for the department. Of course, if supervisory personnel were assigned the same monitoring duties, such a perception might also exist. Whether supervisory or field training personnel are used, their function to facilitate coping mechanisms and intervene when language alteration, humor, and desensitization are inappropriate (Dunning & Silva, 1980; Palmer, 1983) is advantageous. That instruction can occur on site or at a relief center established to allow the worker respite from the disaster site.

Consideration should be given as to whether personnel under considerable stress should be deployed in an assignment away from the disaster site or relieved of duty. Most experts would agree that it is beneficial to maintain group contact as part of recovery. It may be more appropriate to rotate workers to duties at the outer perimeter, such as in site security, evidentiary preservation, or support functions, rather than return to normal duties. The need for a weaning/transition experience was one lesson learned from the Vietnam war, where returning soldiers reported discomfort with leaving the war site and arriving to the normalcy of life in the U.S. within a matter of hours. Attention to the need for a transition or "decompression" period would be the ideal. However, since disasters rarely occur during a "downtime" and since normal services must also be maintained, this is not always possible. One procedure that might be used to provide a transitional/closure experience would be to hold an interagency meeting or a debrief session subsequent to the disaster response.

POSTDISASTER STRESS MANAGEMENT

Postdisaster programs aimed at intervention against the emergence of traumatic stress symptoms or toward resolution of their manifestations involve the greatest commitment on the part of the emergency response agency. If the pre- and transdisaster programs involving audit, training, and task refinement have been implemented, many agencies involved in emergency response tend to feel that all that has to be done to meet organizational responsibility has been accomplished. To recommend that the organization assume responsibility for any additional programming effort generally meets with the response that normal supervisory practices involving monitoring employees for symptoms of traumatic stress are sufficient for resolution. The fact that past efforts have not proven adequate to prevent or reduce disaster-related stress manifestations points to the need for postdisaster programming efforts to enhance the effectiveness of such procedures. Supervisory oversight might be augmented by linking first-line management personnel into the identification and treatment process that acts as a precursor to symptom resolution.

This approach would involve first-line supervisory personnel in training in the early warning signs of stress and emotional upset. The supervisor would be informed of the formal process for mandatory referral to an agency-determined or employee-selected treatment program. A much more advantageous approach would be to assist the first-line supervisor in techniques to facilitate and support voluntary informal referral. Such an approach maintains the demeanor that the symptoms are related to a duty-incurred injury and that the organization claims responsibility for its resolution in cooperation with the injured. The expectation of treatment for symptoms is conveyed as an official departmental policy. However, such an approach is not without impediments.

A problem that seems to exist with many agencies and with a significant number of personnel involved with disaster work is in the acceptance of the role and benefits afforded by disaster-response treatment. Indeed, an agency's mismanagement of its disaster aftercare response can precipitate its own form of psychological distress.

A general rule of psychotherapy is that treatment begins where the patient is, not where the therapist or the situation finds it convenient. To do otherwise would be to deny patient integrity. The starting point in any therapeutic alliance is the position or stage at which the patient finds himself or herself at the time of first contact. Depending on the individual who has been identified as the patient and the moment in life which that person is traversing, the approach selected for intervention will determine not only how amenable he or she is to treatment but also what is presented as the most critical problem(s).

Regardless of what professional opinion a therapist may have as to what the patient should or must be doing, the patient's perception and energies to bring about change are always determined by the view he brings to a therapeutic session. For the protective services involved in rescue and recovery in disaster situations, this consideration plays a major role in the selection and success of intervention strategies directed toward resolving the psychological, physical, and behavioral consequences of duty involvement.

Psychological support services for duty-incurred injury and trauma for police and fire personnel are still relatively rare. Such programs are generally limited to peer support programs, some connections with Employment Assistance Programs that serve the governmental jurisdiction generally, and, in some large departments, in-house counseling programs. Acceptance and utilization of these programs, where available, have been good, but have pointed to serious impediments that have served historically to prevent the use of the traditional human service delivery system based upon perceptions of occupational and organizational reaction.

The inclusion of on-staff psychological services and Employee Assistance programs is a relatively new phenomenon in the protective and emergency medical services. Only a very few large metropolitan departments had employed or retained the services of such specially trained personnel by the start of the decade. Historically, mental health specialists were associated with departments solely for the determination of fitness for duty of recruit and in-service personnel. These professionals were viewed as being the adversaries of workers since their function generally consisted of participating in the legal procedure necessary to prevent or terminate employment. Police officers, for example, as a group tend to denigrate the skills of human service delivery personnel because they regularly saw their failures, patients who were frequent customers for the street cop (Stratton, 1980). An occupational attitude that most police officers seemed to develop was that psychiatrists, psychologists, and social workers were generally ineffective and as a group were reputed to be more "screwed up" than the people they treated.

It is not surprising, then, that any professional with a social work/psychology background might be suspect in the eyes of the protective service worker. Human service delivery professionals experience a tough patient population in this group. The skepticism that prevailed before the 1980s was rooted in firsthand evaluation of the psychologist's skills as exemplified by patients met in the course of duty. To date, many organizations and emergency personnel have not changed that perception (Blackmore, 1978).

The prevailing occupational and organizational climate also discourages some emergency workers from seeking the assistance of mental health professionals. It seems to be difficult to convince protective service and emergency medical workers to utilize the same services as those persons identified as that portion of the population that were to be scorned. To sit in the same waiting room with someone you might have arrested last Saturday night, rousted from a vacant burning building, or picked up off the street for medical service was demeaning and embarrassing. To the self-esteem of the worker, just sitting on the "same side of the table" with society's losers is described as a blow.

In addition, seeking and utilizing the services of mental health professionals resulted in a loss of confidence with fellow workers who speculated that the display of a personal weakness such as some emotional problem made a peer's ability to provide back-up in case of an emergency extremely suspect. This attitude carries over into the administration of the department as well. Frequently, protective service supervisors and administrators have expressed concern that workers experiencing some sort of emotional problem that would lead them to seek counsel from a mental health professional might present a problem to the department if deployed in a stressful situation or even for the more mundane calls for service to which they frequently respond.

As a result, protective service workers, if they sought counseling at all, did so under the utmost secrecy. The loss of the respect and confidence of peers and concern for promotional opportunities and good duty assignments caused many workers to forego the benefit mental health counseling might have afforded. Old attitudes and values die hard. The perception that to undergo psychological counseling is indicative of a personal weakness, rather than an occupational injury, is still prevalent. In protective service and emergency medical departments which tend to be both small and conservative, mental health professionals are not likely to be on staff or even formally linked with the department.

The rocky legal grounds of duty-related disability and vicarious liability for the wrongdoings of employees, with consideration for negligent supervision, has further clouded the acceptance of professionals offering psychological asistance to duty-deployed disaster workers. The services of mental health professionals are looked upon skeptically by police administrators. Yet, more departments are recognizing the benefits to be gained by including such a component in their efforts to field a well-trained and prepared emergency medical or protective service worker.

When crisis occurs in the organization, the protective services do not have a history of established response, especially if the crisis involves an emotional/psychological component. Traditionally, the manner in which traumatic situations on the job are handled is to make the occurrence the basis for often very macabre humor or the center of self-aggrandizing war stories. Officers were expected to joke about the incident or become eager to return to action after discussing what happened.

The sentiment that a good police officer or fire fighter is not psychologically affected by duty assignments still pervades the service. In professions where one's own well-being depends upon the actions of coworkers, any indication of less than optimum functioning places doubts in the minds of those who might fear that their problem might affect their ability to provide back-up. Common fears associated with the effect that mental health treatment might have on career include loss of respect, failure to attain promotion, or having assignment to choice duty denied. These perceptions have all too frequently been found to be the case in fact as protective service administrators seek to determine appropriate qualification criteria for selecting personnel for position and duty assignment.

In-house or organizationally-sanctioned psychological counseling services have still not gained widespread acceptance in the protective services. Even in organizations which have such services, many personnel refuse to utilize their services. These prejudices have been hard to overcome. Despite the fact that many individuals have been satisfied, and indeed greatly helped by counseling, workers continue to reject the benefit such services may have for themselves personally. Only if mandatorily referred do they have contact with formal programs. Yet, the unwilling patient does not present the best therapeutic situation for successful intervention.

Intervention strategies must be couched with consideration for the prevailing attitudes of protective service workers toward mental health services. A major consideration for the protective service administrator is the assumption of responsibility for the resolution of the consequences of disaster deployment. Issues such as workers' compensation claims and disability retirement resulting from disaster deployment might prevent administrators from officially recognizing any ensuing psychological effect. Most would find it advantageous to ignore the possibility of any connection between duty assignment and subsequent psychological and behavioral manifestation. The low priority of intervention programs plus the general rejection of psychological services has resulted in the low incidence of intervention responses subsequent to disaster directed toward the rescue and emergency worker. While some programs have been conducted, their effect and impact have not been adequately documented.

The crisis nature of the disaster demand places both agency and workers outside of "business as usual." Routine function is disrupted, requiring new and innovative methods of performance. This state can result in suspension of normal value and expectation systems, allowing the introduction of unfamiliar procedures into an otherwise closed and nonaccepting culture. Such a situation makes the implementation of innovative programming much easier to accomplish. A relatively new procedure following a disaster is the inclusion of a formally structured debrief subsequent to the response (Davidson, 1979; Wagner, 1979a, 1979b). In the ensuing years since protective service and emergency medical agencies have elected to participate in postdisaster programs, three distinct types of debrief protocols have emerged. While not mutually exclusive in content, the distinction between the approaches is the emphasis on the context of the debrief session itself and on the anticipated goal following implementation. The three types include one teaching, or didactic, approach, and two approaches that address psychological, or therapeutic, functions.

The didactic debrief centers on an informational experience, generally providing participants with facts about what is known concerning psychological and behavioral reactions of others in like situations and professions. This method is employed in order to acquaint disaster workers with possible personal reactions and to begin preparation for any necessary therapeutic intervention. The objective of such an approach is to minimize the impact of any ensuing problems in emergency workers by normalizing the experience of symptoms in hopes that their emergence will not prove discomforting to the worker. If manifestations prove unpleasant or overwhelming, it is felt that such a straightforward and professional approach will induce the worker to seek appropriate mental health services through traditional resources.

The debrief session is seen as preparatory to receiving counseling, acquainting the worker with the symptoms associated with disaster duty response. The facilitators attempt to resolve the reticence of workers toward revealing personal information if appropriate, especially involving expressions of emotion, to persons outside of their family, whether nuclear or departmental. It is hoped that once stress manifestations are accepted as normal, the disaster-deployed worker will turn to normal support systems—those that are already perceived as acceptable and successful—for resolution. Contrary to a commonly held misperception, that support system is not generally work colleagues-peers (Fusilier, et. al., 1986; McCammon, et. al., 1986).

Persons who are employed in occupations with formal roles in disaster response are more likely to seek support and initiate coping strategies with family and selected friends. To use peer support and/or departmentally-supported programs represents a considerable departure from regular inclination. To impose an intervention by itself, especially in a manner not consonant with normal behavior, is stressful. Therefore, great care is taken to initiate a debrief approach that will be both beneficial for the worker and effective in terms of reaching the greatest number of personnel affected by the disaster.

Since the didactic-debrief is informational, not therapeutic, it can be easily adapted for presentation to the most likely caregivers: family members and significant friends. When apprised of the common reactions to traumatic deployment, these persons in closer contact and with greater knowledge about the emergency worker can better identify, understand, and react to the emergence of trauma-induced symptoms with support for their resolution. The organization may wish to consider whether it might be appropriate to hold separate or joint sessions with emergency workers and those closest to them. Either separate or apart, each group receives the same information, while allowing the opportunity to have their concerns addressed.

The didactic stress debrief session commences with the introduction of a two-person team composed of a mental health professional (who will subsequently serve to provide triage and/or treatment) and a member of the protective service profession (who represents occupational credibility and the departmental policy encouraging resolution). The parameters of the meeting—an informational and training exercise as opposed to a therapeutic session—should be made clear. This should allay the discomfort of those workers who are uncomfortable with participation in what will be construed to be a therapy session, especially one conducted by an "outsider" to their profession. Sometimes, workers will much more freely disclose their feelings, opinions, and reactions if they view the information as necessary to exercise evaluation than if the construed use is treatment or counseling.

By presenting the experiences of other protective service workers in like situations or performing similar tasks, the presenters educate participating officers in the possible effects, both physical and psychological, that may ensue from disaster rescue experience. These symptoms are couched in terms of their time-limited nature, underscoring the fact that their normal duration is usually six months or less. Emphasis is placed on the fact that in most cases these symptoms generally resolve themselves without professional intervention. However, it should be noted that it is not uncommon for some manifestations to last longer, to return after an additional traumatic experience, or to be exacerbated by the normal stresses of life and job.

The discomfort seen in most emergency workers seems to exist in professionals who pride themselves on their self-control and their ability to maintain their "edge," or invulnerability to attack (Deitz, 1986). Professionals who resolve other people's problems, whether social or medical, feel incompetent when confronted with these problems themselves. Solomon (1984) suggests that workers who by necessity face dangerous situations can condition themselves for fear through role rehearsal, information assessment, and peer support, a process that can be initiated in a didactic debrief session. This conditioning allows the worker to place fear or the sense of loss of control in perspective, within the realm of the manageable, while continuing to function on the job. The task of the mental health professional in a didactic debrief is to address this concern, focusing on imparting methods that will help regain or retain that advantage.

The mental health professional provides information on the type and course of symptoms associated with traumatic stress, explaining methods typically used in their resolution. Methods of treatment of these symptoms, including counseling, when discussed in the same context of any other duty-incurred injury, create the impression that symptoms and treatment are not unusual or indicative of personal weakness. Techniques for self-management of reactions to treatment through nonjudgmental official sanction of psychological counseling are presented, as with any other duty-incurred injury.

One goal of the didactic approach is to educate workers as participants in the triage process should their reactions or those of fellow workers require necessary intervention. Part of the purpose of the didactic debrief is to establish the structure of possible future treatment, to facilitate acceptance of psychological counseling for personal problems, and to begin to establish professional rapport with the mental health coleader, who would be part of the counseling delivery system. It is not the intention of the didactic debrief approach to perform therapy on debrief participants but to initiate the building of therapeutic rapport should subsequent contact be required.

It might be desirable, if decided by the participants, to remain together and achieve resolution through a group therapy approach. Such a choice would be left to group members, whose prejudices and inclinations might serve to inhibit any benefit from therapy conducted in a forced situation. Fears of disclosure, retribution, or some untoward consequence could serve to prevent the majority of emergency workers from accepting the information and assistance offered in a session where asked to participate in a treatment-oriented session.

The expression of the affective aspect of one's own experience in relation to the disaster deployment would not be discouraged in the didactic debrief, nor would it be expected. Nor should the session be monopolized by discussions of the aspects of the event at hand. The focus of the discussion should remain centered on the relationship between disaster duty, role, and experience and personal response. The department's expectation to be conveyed to the worker is that resolution is expected. The utilization of counseling services is to be seen as a natural, even desirable, method of intervening and resolving these symptoms before job performance is affected.

The advantage of the didactic debrief approach is the increased probability of acceptance among emergency workers and the promotion of subsequent action toward resolution. If workers know that flashbacks or nightmares are normal reactions to particular events, they will not view such events with as much alarm. Reactions such as these are likely to concern emergency workers more than vomiting, somatic complaints, numbing since they suggest a loss of control. If workers know that symptoms are common and predictable, their emergence is not as traumatic, hence not as likely to be exacerbated by anxiety or refusal to seek resolution.

To professionals concerned with self control, the ability to participate as an equal partner in the treatment process affords greater acceptance and success. To receive counseling in an atmosphere of peer and departmental acceptance and support also serves to facilitate success. The comfort of confidentiality afforded by the private session or voluntary group membership addresses the concern that information divulged might later be used to the detriment of the officer. Concern has been expressed that a one-shot cathartic experience in which the focus of the session centers upon ventilation of emotions and disclosure of reactions is insufficient for resolution. The problems created by the disclosure, including resistance to treatment, rejection of the reality of symptoms, and exacerbation of reaction due to the stressful experience of the individual focus, may outweigh its usefulness to the few who find such a session helpful.

It would appear useful to follow up a didactic debrief with a voluntary therapeutic group session. Unwilling participants would serve only to disrupt the group process as energies would be diverted to dealing with problems of group divisiveness. A more acceptable procedure would be to establish an acceptance of the role of supervisors and peers to monitor fellow workers for stress reactions which interfere with personal or professional performance. The administrator would need to inculcate the official departmental policy of the acceptance of professional counseling to resolve the duty-incurred psychological injury. The need to work through distressed feelings and their subsequent manifestations should be accepted as natural and desirable. However, the manner in which professional counseling is implemented must be carefully considered, as it is better to have a program that will be utilized than to have only a program.

The second type of intervention subsequent to a catastrophic situation is a psychological debrief. The protocol for a therapeutic intervention is based on the conception that ventilation or a cathartic experience precipitates the healing process necessary for resolution of the symptoms that are the result of disaster deployment. The psychological debrief has two common components—ventilation of feelings about the event and a discussion of the signs or symptoms of a stress response. The organized approach may operate in an atmosphere of informal discussion, in an agency or work group session, or in a more formalized program possibly involving other departments and jurisdictions. The focus of most psychological debriefs is on individual disclosure of emotion and personal revelation of symptoms related to the disaster experience. A training component which relates the experience of other disaster workers subsequent to the event is also present.

The manner in which the psychological debrief is presented differs between the two protocols currently used in emergency service agencies. While the intent of the debrief exercise is to seek integration of the disaster event into the life history of the duty-deployed worker, the manner in which the session is conducted and the goal sought from involvement differ.

The first protocol, labeled Critical Incident Stress Debrief or CISD (Mitchell, 1983) attempts to initiate emotional ventilation through disclosure and sharing of behavioral and physical responses subsequent to disaster deployment. The CISD involves a group or individual session with a caring facilitator who is able to help the worker talk about feelings and reactions to the disaster (Mitchell, 1983). The session has three parts: ventilation and assessment of stress response, support and reassurance, and resource mobilization through referral. The intervention takes place within 24 to 48 hours as effectiveness is said to decrease as time elapses after the incident. Mitchell (1983) claims that CISDs have an enormous potential to alleviate overwhelming emotional feelings and potentially dangerous physical symptoms.

The purpose of the debrief is to get workers to discuss their fears, anxieties, concerns, guilt, frustration, anger, and ambivalence about the event. The participants are urged to discuss what is going on with themselves physically, personally, and professionally. Additional components encompass a teaching phase about stress response syndromes and a reentry phase which offers reassurances that reactions are normal and help is available. A follow-up debrief session is recommended for several weeks after the critical incident to address any lingering concerns or problems voiced by the workers.

The main goals of CISD are to ventilate intense emotions, explore symbolic meanings in the event, generate group support, and initiate the grief process. The facilitator addresses the normalcy of reactions, hoping to correct the "fallacy of uniqueness" (Mitchell, 1985). In a survey of 360 emergency workers, Mitchell (1985) reported that 86.9% of the respondents felt that they had been emotionally and physically affected by their work and 93.3% felt that psychological debriefings were necessary after a major emergency event.

The second protocol (Bergmann & Queen, 1986a, 1986b) focuses upon coping skill-building and cognitive restructuring to master the disastrous event. This approach relies heavily on the continuum of care necessary to resolve the traumatic stress manifestations of disaster involvement. Disclosure is related to fact, thus avoiding problems of resistance and rejection, and is not seen as central to the success of the debrief session. Rather, the focus is on seeing the emergency worker as a success, having and using skills appropriate to survive the traumatic situation. The debrief facilitator explores pre-trauma coping skills, augmenting those that address reduction in intensity and frequency of symptoms. Since the family represents the most common source of coping support, families are asked to attend the debrief or a concurrent session so that the same information base exists. Action contracting is an integral part of the Continuum of Care (Bergmann & Queen, 1986a,b,c) as this increases the chances that workers experiencing stress will follow through with participation in appropriate treatment programs.

The Continuum of Care approach presents a comprehensive program that is not event limited. Components include recruit training emphasizing skills necessary to increase the probability of effective coping from the point of first exposure to a critical incident, the establishment of peer support programs focusing on attaining listening skills and counseling support, CIS debriefing training and services, and, finally, continuing individual and family counseling (Bergmann & Queen, 1986a). The Continuum of Care package emphasizes an ongoing relationship between the mental health care providers and the workers and department. The disaster intervention requires a relationship renewal (Bergmann & Queen, 1986b). The recommended continuing counseling is short-term, emphasizing existing coping and support systems.

If seen on a continuum, the two psychological debrief approaches presented share basic features, but are different in their perspective as to the place of the debrief in the larger organizational response to disaster aftermath. The Continuum of Care (Bergmann & Queen, 1986 a,b,c) presupposes a commitment on the part of the employing agency to providing or at least supporting the delivery of subsequent mental health care. The debrief is seen as an antecedent to that process. The CISD (Mitchell, 1983) highlights the debrief exercise as the major component in the recovery scheme. The didactic debrief resembles the Continuum of Care with its focus primarily on the informational aspect of the session, but incorporates the concepts of organizational ownership and need for subsequent formally designated intervention resources.

CONCLUSION

In instances of disaster, as with individual crisis, several basic principles of crisis intervention apply. The most obvious is to have resources, or at least knowledge of their existence and access, that might be put into use should the situation demand. The first step in intervention strategies for mass emergencies for emergency agencies is to determine the extent to which the organization is willing to program itself to mitigate possible deleterious effects on workers and department. The decision to commit the agency's resources, given organizational culture and level of policy/program development in employee assistance, directs the manner in which feasible programs can be implemented.

Programs that result from predisaster commitment on the part of emergency agencies would seem to have a greater chance of preventing and mitigating stress reactions in disaster-deployed workers. The organization must assume responsibility for analyzing tasks and training in relation to disaster effect, for planning and implementing policies and procedures related to deployment and supervision, and for creating links with mental health delivery systems that are likely to lead to usage of services. No one approach is appropriate for all agencies, as each reflects a different history, culture, sense of purpose, and style of operation.

Intervention requires that emergency organizations be proactive in developing a disaster response, treating the likelihood of the incidence of psychological injury with the same concern currently expressed for safety and physical injury. Reactive measures, accepting offers of one-shot debriefs or counseling services, should be examined in the light of what the organization wishes to accomplish—the prevention or rehabilitation of duty-incurred injury.

The most important aspect of disaster-intervention recovery is organizational understanding of the fact that occupational duty can result in psychological injury. If the department only wishes to have a window-dressing program, to say one is "on-the-books," then the program selected should not result in the creation of more stress for the worker. Care should be exercised in reviewing the ramifications, both negative and positive, of the course of action selected.

While the few research efforts that attempt to study the effects of disaster on emergency workers suggest the need for further data collection to document the extent and type of stress manifested, the information available points to the urgent need for administrators to act to prepare for incidences of psychological injury among workers. This not only represents good management practice, but has legal and ethical implications as well. At the very least, efforts that have been made thus far by various emergency agencies to ameliorate stress should be examined to determine their efficacy in preventing future problems for the emergency worker and agency at hand.

BIBLIOGRAPHY

American General Ins. Co. v. Bailey, 268 S.W. 2d (528) Tex., Civ. App. 1955.

American Psychiatric Association (1980). *Diagnostic and Statistical Manual of Mental Disorders (3rd Ed.)*. Washington, D.C.: American Psychiatric Association.

Berah, E., Jones H., & Valent, P. (1984). The experience of a mental health team involved in the early phase of a disaster. *Australia-New Zealand Journal of Psychiatry*, 18(4): 354–358.

Bergmann, L. H., & Queen, T. (1986a) Critical incident stress: Part 1. *Fire Command*, April 18–20.

Bergmann, L. H., & Queen, T. (1986b). Critical incident stress: Part 2. *Fire Command*, May, 52–56.

Bergmann, L. H., & Queen, T. (1986c). Responding to critical incident stress. *Fire Chief*, June, 43–49.

Blackmore, J. (1978). Are police allowed to have problems of their own? *Police*, July, 47–55.

Bleich, A., Chen, E., Katz, M., Levy, A., & Garb, E. (1986). A model for crisis intervention with Israeli soldiers during compulsory military service. *Israeli Journal of Psychiatry and Related Sciences*, 23(1): 17–28.

Burke, R. J., & Deszca, E. (1986). Correlates of psychological burnout phases among police officers. *Human Relations*, 39(6): 487–502.

Davidson, A. D. (1979). Air disaster: Coping with stress. *Police Stress*, 1(2): 20–22.

Deitz, I. J. (1986). Time-limited psychotherapy for post-traumatic stress disorder: The traumatized ego and its self-reparative function, *American Journal of Psychotherapy*, XL (2): 290–299.

Demi, A. S. (1983). Understanding psychological reactions to disaster. *Journal of Emergency Nursing*, 9(1): 11–16.

Diskin, S., Goldstein, M., & Grencik, J. (1977). Coping patterns of law enforcement officers in simulated and naturalistic stress. *American Journal of Community Psychology*, 5(1): 59–73.

Drabek, T. E. (1968). *Disaster in Aisle 13: A Case Study of the Coliseum Explosion at Indiana State Fairgrounds*. Columbus, OH: Ohio State University Press.

Dunning, C. (1985a). Prevention of stress. In *Role Stressors and Supports for Emergency Workers*. Washington, D.C.: DHHS Publication No. (ADM) 85–1408.

Dunning, C. (1985b). The burden of duty and psychosocial trauma resulting from life threatening and extinguishing events. In A. D. Mangelsdorff, J. M. King, & D. E. O'Brien (Eds), *Proceedings of the Fifth Users' Workshop on Combat Stress*. Fort Sam Houston, TX: U.S. Army Health Services Command.

Dunning, C., & Silva M. (1980). Disaster-induced trauma in rescue workers. *Victimology*, 5(2–4): 287–297.

Forstenzer, A. (1980). Stress, the psychological scarring of air crash rescue personnel. *Firehouse* 7: 50–62.

Frederick, C. J. (1977). Current thinking about crisis or psychological intervention in United States disasters. *Mass Emergencies*, 2: 43–50.

Frederick, C. J. (Ed.) (1981). *Aircraft Accidents: Emergency Mental Health Problems*. Washington, D.C.: DHHS Publication No. (ADM) 81–956.

Fusilier, M. R., Ganster, D. C., & Mayes, B. T. (1986). The social support and health relationship: Is there a gender difference? *Journal of Occupational Psychology*, 59 (2): 145–153.

Griffin, C. (1985). Community disasters and post-traumatic stress disorders: A debriefing model for response. Presented to Society for Traumatic Stress Studies.

Hartsough, D. M., & Myers, D. G. (1985). *Disaster Work and Mental Health: Prevention and Control of Stress Among Workers*. Washington, D.C.: DHHS Publication No. (ADM) 85–1422.

Hershisher, M. R., & Quarantelli, E. L. (1976). The handling of the dead in a disaster. *Omega*, 7(3): 195–208.

Hocking, F. (1970). Extreme environmental stress and its significance for psychopathology. *American Journal of Psychotherapy*, 24: 4–26.

Ivancevich, J. M., Matteson, M. T., & Richards III, E. P. (1985). Who's liable for stress on the job? *Harvard Business Review*, 63 (2): 60–72.

Jones, D. R. (1985). Secondary disaster victims: The emotional effects of recovering and identifying human remains. *American Journal of Psychiatry*, 142 (3): 303–307.

Keating, J. (1986). Psychological aftereffects of emergency workers at the Dallas/Fort Worth air crash. Presented at the annual meeting of the Society for Traumatic Stress Studies.

Lazarus, R. (1966). *Psychological Stress and the Coping Process*. New York: McGraw-Hill.

Lindemann, E. (1944). Crisis intervention—Symptomatology and management of acute grief. *American Journal of Psychiatry*, 101: 7–20.

Lublin, J. S. (1980). On-the-job stress leads many workers to file and win compensation awards. *Wall Street Journal*, September 17.

Mangelsdorff, A. D., King, J. M., & O'Brien, D. E. (Eds) (1985). *Proceedings of the Fifth Users' Workshop on Combat Stress*. Fort Sam Houston, TX: U.S. Army Health Services Command.

Mantell, M., Dubner, J., & Lipon, S. (1985). San Ysidro massacre: Impact on police officers. A report prepared for the National Institute of Mental Health, Rockville, MD (Mimeo).

Mantell, M. (1986). San Ysidro: When the badge turns blue. In J. Reese and H. Goldstein (Eds.), *Psychological Services for Law Enforcement*. Washington, D.C.: U.S. Government Printing Office. (027–000–012–66–3.)

McCammon, S., Durham, J. W., Williamson, J. E., & Allison, E. J. (1986). Coping theory related to emergency workers coping with traumatic effects. Presented to The Society for Traumatic Stress Studies.

Mitchell, J. (1982). The psychological impact of the Air Florida 90 disaster on fire-rescue, paramedic, and police officer personnel. In R. A. Crowley (Ed.), *Mass Casualties: A Learned Lesson Approach*. Washington, D.C: U.S. Dept. of Transportation.

Mitchell, J. (1983). When disaster strikes . . . . *Journal of Emergency Medical Services*, 8(1): 36–39.

Mitchell, J. (1985). Healing the helper. In *Role Stressors and Supports for Emergency Workers*. Washington, D.C.: DHHS Publication No. (ADM) 85–1408.

Modlin, H. (1986). Post-traumatic stress disorder. *Postgraduate Medicine*, 79(3): 26–44.

National Institute of Mental Health (1985). *Role Stressors and Supports for Emergency Workers*. Rockville, MD: NIMH.

Nielsen, E. (1985). Phases and Processes of Traumatic Stress Reactions. Seminar on Critical Incidents: Emotional Survival and Policing.

Nielsen, E. (1984). Understanding and Assessing Traumatic Stress Reactions. FBI Academy, National Symposium on Police Psychological Services.

Nielsen, E., & Eskridge, D. (1982). Police shooting incident: Implications for training. *Law and Order*, March: 16–18.

Noy, S., Levy, R., & Solomon, Z. (1984). Mental health care in the Lebanon War, 1982. *Israel Journal of Medical Sciences*, 20: 360–363.

Palmer, C. (1983). A note about paramedics' strategies for dealing with death and dying. *Journal of Occupational Psychology*, 56: 83–86.

Raphael, B. (1984). Psychiatric consultancy in major disaster. *Australia-New Zealand Journal of Psychiatry*, 18(4): 303–306.

Solomon, R. (1984). Mental Conditioning for Fear. FBI Academy, National Symposium on Police Psychological Services.

Solomon, Z., & Benbenishty, R. (1986). The role of proximity, immediacy, and expectancy in frontline treatment of combat stress reaction among Israelis in the Lebanon War. *American Journal of Psychiatry*, 143(5): 613–617.

Stratton, J. G. (1980). Psychological services for police. *Journal of Police Science and Administration*, 8(1): 31–39.

Taylor, A., & Frazer, A. (1982). The stress of post-disaster body handling and victim identification work. *Journal of Human Stress*, 4–12.

Wagner, M. (1979a). Airline disaster: A stress debrief program for police. *Police Stress*, 2(1): 16–20.

Wagner, M. (1979b). Stress debriefing—Flight 191: Department program that worked. *Police Star*, August: 4–8.

Weil, F. (1985). Treatment teams under war stress. *Psychiatric Journal of the University of Ottawa*, 10(1): 45–47.

Wilkinson, C. (1983). Aftermath of disaster: Collapse of the Hyatt Regency Hotel skywalks. *American Journal of Psychiatry*, 140 (9): 1134–1139.

Wilkinson, C., & Vera, E. (1985). The management and treatment of disaster victims. *Psychiatric Annals*, 15(3): 174–184.

Wolfe v. Sibley, Lindsay, and Curr Co., 33 O N.E. 2d 603 (N.Y.C.A. 1975).

PART III

Public Education/ Planning Programs

12

Big Bird Teaches Fire and Hurricane Safety

EVELYN PAYNE DAVIS

Children's Television Workshop (CTW), producers of *Sesame Street*, *The Electric Company*, *3-2-1 Contact*, *Square One TV*, is a multifaceted research oriented production company, dedicated to the education of young children.

From the very first broadcast season, *Sesame Street*'s Big Bird has demonstrated enormous power to influence young children. Parents everywhere attest to the skills and knowledge their children have gained from the series, while the educational effectiveness of *Sesame Street* has been well documented by independent groups such as Educational Testing Service.

The popularity, familiarity, and credibility of *Sesame Street* make it a powerful catalyst for mobilizing and organizing community resources to address issues of community and national concern. It has been demonstrated that the banner of *Sesame Street* can bring together groups as diverse as merchants' associations, day care and fire service personnel to discuss, plan, and carry out projects with specific objectives. *Sesame Street* is also a magnet for organizations hoping the series can assist them in reaching large audiences with important messages.

This combination of factors led the Federal Emergency Management Agency's U.S. Fire Administration (FEMA, USFA) to ask CTW if television, through *Sesame Street*, could be used to help teach fire safety to young children. Horrifying statistics indicate that children under the age of five account for 17% of the severe injuries and death from fire, although they constitute only 7% of the population.

311

Because television is a medium widely viewed by preschoolers (the average 2–to–5-year-old watches 25 hours or more per week), and because *Sesame Street* in particular has been successful in teaching educational messages to preschoolers (Ball & Bogatz, 1970; Bogatz & Ball, 1971), CTW agreed to explore ways of including important burn prevention/fire safety messages on television. Two major constraints in exploring the topic of fire safety for children were 1) to be sensitive to the range of effects that any programming might have and 2) to try to design that programming in such a way as to maximize desired educational effects and to preclude possible unwanted effects. The two considerations presented were the nature and capabilities of the 3–to–5-year-olds and the limitations of the television medium itself.

The basic finding of the study was that there are a number of highly limiting and fundamentally insurmountable limits on the capabilities of television for imparting to preschoolers precisely the messages they most need to know and understand about fire safety, and that preschoolers are largely dependent upon others for prevention and protection against fire and burns. The topics and messages that lent themselves most readily to television treatment for young children were added to the materials given to writers and producers to provide information and to stimulate creative thinking about a fire safety curriculum for the *Sesame Street* series.

The topics and messages include:

Understanding Fire

Fire has the following general characteristics:
- Fire is hot.
- Fire can be used to cook food, heat homes, and provide light.
- Fire can burn people and things.

Fire and Smoke Detectors

- Children can be taught about the form (appearance, shape, size, and sound) of smoke detectors.
- Children can be taught about the function of smoke detectors.

Firefighters

- The firefighter is an important person in the neighborhood who plays a role in educating neighbors about fire.
- The firefighter fights fires and rescues people from fire.
- The fire station is an important place in the town or city.
- A firefighter wears special protective clothing and uses many unusual tools (it's important to avoid the possibility that a firefighter may frighten a child during a rescue).

Scalds and Contact Burns

- Hot things burn and hurt.
- Children should not touch hot objects or appliances.

The conclusions of CTW's fire safety research led to a request from FEMA's U.S. Fire Administration for CTW to develop a comprehensive project to teach fire safety to preschool children.

To carry out this project, the Community Education Services Division of CTW went beyond those messages that could be demonstrated safely on television. Materials were developed to help firefighters, parents, and caregivers teach real-life safety skills for fire safety, with the necessary reinforcement and practice. Songs and skits teaching specific behaviors, as well as recommended teaching techniques for their effective use, were prepared. Dissemination of the information, tailored to regional needs, ranged from cable television teleconferences to face-to-face training workshops. The project linked firefighters, and fire safety educators to preschoolers, their parents, and their caregivers through fire safety festivals, training workshops to certify parents and teachers as *Sesame Street* Fire Safety Educators, and other activities planned to increase public awareness and action for fire safety.

There have been several important CTW spinoffs resulting from the fire safety project: inclusion of fire safety messages and practices as part of the ongoing safety curriculum of the *Sesame Street* broadcast; periodic articles about fire and fire safety in *Sesame Street* and *3-2-1 Contact* magazines; a Random House publication, *A Trip To The Fire House*, and a number of fire safety toys and games.

The effectiveness of the *Sesame Street* Fire Safety project resulted in a request to CTW from the Federal Emergency Management Administration to experiment with the development and dissemination of informational and safety messages for children about multinatural hazards. In late 1984, CTW began an investigation into the feasibility of using its productions to aid in teaching children, and in reaching their families with safety messages about a range of natural hazards.

General goals for the project were established. They are:

- to develop a level of awareness and information about the nature and characteristics of natural hazards among children and their families;
- to create an understanding and motivation for preparedness when faced with natural hazards among children and their families;
- to stimulate an interest in learning more about natural phenomena;

- to explore the use of various media for broad dissemination of natural hazards information.

The initial effort was to explore the relationship between natural hazards, children, and the media; develop an understanding of the information levels about natural hazards of 3–to–12-year-olds and adults; and to determine the opportunities and barriers to natural hazards education. This work was accomplished through a compilation and review of the literature on social science research of the population's response to natural hazards, with an emphasis on children and media, along with a compilation and review of existing public information and educational materials on natural hazards directed towards children.

In order to take a look at the opportunities and barriers to public education about natural hazards, a shared workshop was held with emergency managers, youth-serving organizations, voluntary organizations, and representatives of the private sector, media, and natural hazards research community. Viewpoints and information were shared about what information people need and what some of the obstacles are to the dissemination of information about natural hazards in general, and to children in particular.

The immensity of the work being undertaken by the community of practitioners, public educators, and community representatives and specialists was sobering indeed, but also very challenging. It was clear that the work being done by all of the groups and participants involved, as well as by others, complemented and supplemented each other. The opportunity to contribute and participate in all the activity around natural hazards information fit exactly into CTW's continuing mission to help provide information and programming of social value.

An informal investigation into the comprehension levels and sources of information about natural hazards was undertaken in order to provide guidelines for the development of age-specific messages. It then became evident that certain issues remain constant no matter which natural hazard is being considered. These issues, which guide the development of CTW's Natural Hazards project, are:

- Most children can cope with change if they are prepared for it.
- Children's responses to a natural hazards event or disaster depend on the adults around them.
- People can learn to be prepared for natural hazards.
- Most people receive their natural hazards information from the media.
- Just after a natural hazard occurs, people's interest is temporarily heightened.

Other considerations are:

- Information designed for children should progress from the familiar and simple to the more complex.
- There must be recognition of and sensitivity for different regional, family, and cultural contexts for natural hazards.
- The official cautionary terms "Watch" and "Warning" must be taught and reinforced.

The developmental levels and characteristics of our target age groups of preschoolers, and children 5 to 7, and 8 to 12 years old defined parameters for specific guidelines:

3–to–4–Year-Olds

- Look to adults if something goes wrong.
- Imitate what they see.
- Have difficulty understanding the relationship of one event to another.
- May fail to connect a problem with its portrayed solution.
- Do not have the experience or knowledge to understand words like "emergency" and "disaster."
- Are inexperienced at interpreting subtleties.

5–to–7–Year-Olds

- Begin to recognize cause and effect.
- Offer a wide range of explanations for why things happen.
- Begin to ask "what" and "how" questions.
- Demonstrate short-term recall of important safety and preparedness information.
- Can learn to follow instructions.

8–to–12–Year-Olds

- Look for patterns in the physical and social world.
- Create their own theories of how the world works based on their experiences.
- Want to define the range and limits of what's possible in the world.
- Enjoy problem solving, making "guesses," and refining their predictions.
- Are aware of cause and effect, reciprocal relationships and the influence of variables on one another.
- Enjoy colorful, modern graphics.

After checking into the information levels about natural hazards held by adults, we recognized that they:

- Have limited knowledge of natural hazards planning and preparedness for safety.
- Feel responsible for teaching children about natural hazards.
- Feel uncomfortable responding to children's questions about natural hazards.
- Have an incomplete picture of where hazards occur in the United States.

Added to the above issues are a variety of myths and misconceptions about natural hazards held by many, including:

- Outside organizations will come in and take care of everything.
- More help is available.
- People want to know about natural hazards.
- Information given one time is enough.
- The message intended is the one received.
- Information leads to appropriate behavior.
- "It won't happen to me."
- Local codes prevent danger.
- There is just one population.
- Tornadoes occur only in tornado alley, and earthquakes occur only in California.
- The danger of natural hazards is exaggerated.

A major step in the project development process was to hold a seminar bringing together natural hazards specialists with child development specialists and CTW staff representing the research, production, periodicals, music, products, and outreach divisions. Recommendations from this group guided the formulation of specific messages and guidelines for each age group. Although the following criteria are not exhaustive, they establish the contexts for the determination of the messages to be taught and the design of the materials.

3–to–4–Year–Olds

- Positive "can do" messages need to be reinforced.
- Frightening situations need to be resolved.
- Words and concepts should be age-appropriate.
- "If–then" descriptions should be avoided.

5-to-7-Year-Olds

- Guide and direct their understanding of the cause and effect of the weather and the earth.
- Strengthen and reinforce listening skills and the ability to follow instructions.

8-to-12-Year-Olds

- Combine new information with their preconceived notions.
- Take advantage of their interest in extremes.
- Build on their strong desire for competence.

Adults

- Adults need to reminded:
- That children need to feel connected to adults around a natural hazards event.
- That information should progress from the simple to the complex.
- That families should work together to plan and prepare for a natural hazard.
- That strategies and effort for getting accurate information may be required.

Planning and preparedness were the most important messages to be developed for the natural hazards family safety project. The theme chosen for the safety materials is *Big Bird's Get Ready*™ Family Kit. A major factor in setting the theme for the materials is the great need to reinforce the concepts of "watch" and "warning." The kit is designed to heighten the awareness that families need to "Get Ready," "Get Set," and "Go" (to safety), when the occasion calls for it.

The first natural hazards selected for kit development were hurricanes and earthquakes. These topics were selected because, first, hurricanes have warning time, and second, earthquakes have no warning time. Another determining factor was the difference presented between weather-related and geological phenomena. These contrasts, then, would help model the development of additional kits.

The first prototype *Big Bird's Get Ready*™ Family Kit deals with hurricanes. Although families generally have enough advance warning, hurricanes are erratic, often following unpredictable routes and leaving potential victims unsure about when, how, and whether or not to prepare to ensure safety for the family. The kit contains a brochure for parents with information on children and hurricanes, definitions of "watch" and "warning," basic hurricane facts, and suggestions for a family safety plan and safety kit. Music is very effective in conveying information to preschoolers; therefore, an original song was written to stress the primary message for that age. An original board game was designed for the older children to help them learn interesting facts and the science of hurricanes. It also contains information on how to help the family prepare safely for a hurricane.

For 3–to–5-year-olds, the song "Hurricane Blues" conveys two simple messages:

- Big winds, large waves, and a lot of rain make a hurricane.
- Listen to a grown-up carefully and do what they say when there is a hurricane.

Additional messages for the 3–to–5-year-olds are:

- Weather can be wet or dry, hot or cold, calm or stormy, clear or cloudy.
- A family safety kit has safety provision for a hurricane.
- A family safety plan tells you what to do in a hurricane.

8–to–12-year-olds will learn:

- A hurricane is a very powerful tropical storm that brings winds over 74 m.p.h., heavy rains, destructive waves, flooding, and sometimes tornadoes.
- Prepare for a hurricane by putting together a family safety kit and practicing a family safety plan. *Get ready.*
- A hurricane watch means that a hurricane is coming. *Get set.*
- A hurricane warning means that a hurricane is coming. *Go!* To Safety.
- Listen to a trusted grown-up and follow directions carefully during a hurricane.

Parents are reminded that hurricanes can be frightening to children. They are urged to encourage their children to express their feelings about them. Parents need to understand that some of these feelings may emerge when practicing family safety plans. Parents must help their children understand that hurricanes are part of life and that prepared families can cope with them.

The next step was to test the prototype with the target audiences. We wanted to know how parents living in hurricane areas would respond to the materials in the *Big Bird Get Ready*™ Family Kit. We wanted to find out whether the materials were appealing and comprehensible to adults, whether the information in the kit was considered useful and complete, whether and how adults would be likely to use the kit if they had an opportunity to have one at home, and whether parents perceived the song and board game as potentially appealing, comprehensible, and useful to their children.

By and large, the materials tested well. Parents had many helpful suggestions and comments that guided the final preparation of the *Big Bird Get Ready*™ Family Kit. The critical consensus of the parents was that the kit should be developed so that all of its components could be shared with their children.

It was clear that the materials are needed and wanted by parents living in areas vulnerable to the chaos caused by hurricanes. *Big Bird* and *Sesame Street* are perceived as appealing and potentially informative for children on the subject of natural hazards. Parents indicated they not only want to use the materials to teach their children, but also are enthusiastic about joining in the learning process themselves.

The test of any project is getting it to its intended target group and putting it into use. The *Big Bird Get Ready*™ Family Safety Kit offers a unique opportunity to motivate families to prepare for their safety before emergencies occur. On its own, it will be seen by parents as a trusted, educational, and informative resource for their children. Beyond that, however, it can be a powerful catalyst for agencies and organizations working to build and heighten public awareness about natural hazards. The kit can be used effectively as the basis for putting into motion activities and campaigns designed to promote safety and preparedness.

CTW has most often used the appeal of *Big Bird* and other *Sesame Street* characters to bring together parents, teachers, and others involved with children, so that face-to-face discussion and training can take place. This practice helps ensure that the materials will be used appropriately, and helps increase the understanding of the topic.

To facilitate this intent and process, CTW is producing a training videotape with accompanying guidelines to aid groups and organizations in the most effective use of the *Big Bird Get Ready*™ Family Kit(s). This "train the trainer" package will be made available to civil defense and emergency preparedness personnel, as well as to schools and child care, youth-serving, and community organizations, as a supplemental resource to their safety and preparedness programs. In addition, arrangements have been made to customize this training package for use by American Red Cross staff and volunteers.

The *Big Bird Get Ready*™ Family Kit emergency preparedness information will be spread through articles in CTW magazines, special segments in CTW productions, and inclusion in its various outreach programs. It is CTW's hope that the *Big Bird Get Ready*™ Family Kit can join with other ongoing efforts to help heighten awareness by the nation's population that planning and preparedness may lessen some of the destruction of a natural hazard. *Big Bird Get Ready*™ Family Kits will be distributed by FEMA.

The United States population is an increasingly mobile society, nationally as well as internationally. Because natural hazards can be encountered anywhere, awareness of safety measures for natural hazards prevalent in one's home area only will not suffice. A public attitude that calls for accepting major responsibility for one's own safety must be developed. This means having the necessary information at one's fingertips, and having some understanding that the information can help. To accomplish this, greater efforts must be made to get information to the public. Too often, the responsibility for obtaining the safety information is left to the individual. Thus, it is important to experiment with the most effective ways of reaching different groups of people, some of whom will be at greatest risk from natural hazards. CTW's contribution to this ongoing effort is the power and influence of *Big Bird* and *Sesame Street*.

REFERENCES

Ball, S., & Bogatz, G. A. (1970). A summary of the major findings. In *The First Year of SESAME STREET: An Evaluation*. Princeton, N.J.: Educational Testing Service.
Ball, S., & Bogatz, G. A. (1971). A summary of the major findings. In *The Second Year of SESAME STREET: An Evaluation*. Princeton, N.J.: Educational Testing Service.

13

Planning and Implementing Warning Systems

DENNIS S. MILETI and JOHN H. SORENSEN

Warning the public of impending disaster is an everyday occurrence in the United States. We estimate that warnings are issued at least once a day and perhaps more frequently for some American public at risk to some sort of geological, climatological, technological, or civil hazard. The number of people warned in these events varies; most episodes involve only a few persons. However, dozens of events occur annually in which warnings are issued to a population of substantial size. Considered nationally, public disaster warnings are hardly uncommon phenomena. At the local level, a warning event is often unique, although there are some communities for which warnings are commonplace—for example, flood warnings along the Mississippi.

History is riddled with warning events in which publics have been encouraged to engage in a variety of alternative protective actions. These actions, for example, include evacuation, sheltering, avoiding certain parts of a city, and so on. The record documents "successful" warning events in which loss of life and property were reduced because warnings were issued. History also catalogues warning systems "failures" where, despite warnings, many lives were lost when disaster struck. There is also emerging evidence which suggests that psychological impacts can emerge after even "successful" warning events. At the most general level, the purpose of this chapter is to seek an answer to the question of why variations occur in human response to warnings.

We are not the first to attempt an answer to this question. Researchers began to address the question of why publics respond as they do to

321

warnings of impending disasters some three decades ago. Early efforts (Mack & Baker, 1961; Moore et al., 1963; Withey, 1962) revealed that patterns did exist in public response to warnings. These efforts were followed by attempts to systematize and conceptualize findings (Mileti, 1975; McLuckie, 1970; Williams, 1957), as well as by systematic research on warning response events (e.g., Drabek, 1969). In recent years, research has continued, as have attempts to compile findings (Perry, 1985); in the last decade, the number of actual studies of public response to warnings has almost doubled. There are now about 200 empirical studies of public warning response.

It is the specific objective of this chapter to focus on the public response impacts of emergency warning systems in order to synthesize and appraise empirical findings, gaps in knowledge, and implications for research and policy.

THEORETICAL VIEWPOINT

A key purpose of a public warning system is to elicit protective actions by people in danger. Protective action, however, does not flow automatically from hearing a warning. An influential intervening factor between hearing and responding to a warning is the situational perception of risk that people hold. These perceptions impact what people do and do not do in response to warnings, as do perceptions about appropriate response actions. A key purpose for a warning system, therefore, is to provide the public with accurate situational perceptions of risk from the impending disaster commensurate with the actual or objective nature of the risk, and to provide sound situational perceptions of what to do to prevent personal harm and loss. As such, warning systems work through people's cognitive processes to influence behavior. Thus, the main challenge to any warning system is dissemination of information that leads a diverse public at risk to "correct" cognitions and perceptions.

These perceptions are shaped by dialectical forces. The first concerns the sender of warning information; the second concerns the information receiver. A dilemma for the sender is that there is typically, in any warning situation, more than one sender and more than one message. A dilemma for the receiver is that across a heterogeneous public, and even across time for one individual, there can be more than one perception of the impending event, risk, and appropriate response.

1. Dilemmas of Perception

In theory, there are four possible categorizations for warning events when one considers the juxtaposition of sender and receiver attributes.

These are poles of continuums: actual events are more likely to be variants of these ideal-types. First, only one warning message reaches the public, and a common public perception is formed. Second, only one message reaches the public, but multiple public perceptions are formed. Third, multiple messages reach the public who form multiple perceptions. Finally, multiple messages go out to the public, but only one common public perception is formed.

A circumstance in which a single warning would go to an endangered public, who would then form a single public perception about impending risk and appropriate response to it, is not likely in an open and free society. Events such as this have occurred in less pluralistic societies, and one of these is worth describing. A 7.3 Richter magnitude earthquake occurred on February 4, 1975, near Haicheng, China. Prior to the earthquake, elaborate monitoring led the provincial Revolutionary Committee to issue a public warning that a strong earthquake would hit within two days. The earthquake happened about five hours later, causing major destruction. Accounts suggest that the single warning was issued from the Revolutionary Committee; that almost everyone evacuated; and that evacuees remained in open fields in freezing winter temperatures (Mileti, Hutton, & Sorensen, 1981). Warning systems would not pose a complicated problem if all warning situations could parallel Haicheng. In a pluralistic society, information and warnings cannot be controlled as occurred in this case, and multiple and mixed public perceptions are more likely.

It is difficult to document other cases in which only a single public message was issued; however, the June 1972 Rapid City flood comes close. This flood occurred following two other historical floods. The most recent had occurred about a decade before; it was remembered by many as not a severe threat to life. Earlier in the century, however, a flood occurred that was much the same in magnitude and affect as the 1972 flood in which over 230 persons died. For all practical purposes, only a single warning message was issued for the 1972 flood—single, that is, in terms of content. It said a flood was coming and that people who lived abutting the creek should evacuate.

This single message resulted in multiple public perceptions. For example, some members of the public perceived that the impending flood would be like the minor flood remembered from the last decade, and this recollection constrained evacuation. Others perceived the impending flood to be like the earlier-in-the-century flood, and this was an incentive to evacuate. Additionally, some people perceived the word "abutting" to mean property backed onto the creek, while others correctly thought it to mean property within a block or two of the creek. The former perception constrained evacuation while the latter was an incentive to evacuate. This tale illustrates that a vague singular warning message can result in a heterogeneous set of public perceptions about the risk, and result in as varied a set of warning responses as there are perceptions.

We feel reasonable in the conclusion that the Three Mile Island accident in 1979 provides a textbook example of almost everything that could go wrong with a warning system from a public response viewpoint. The event catalogues a series of conflicting and inconsistent public messages. These include: a 25-mile area was at risk versus a five-mile area; there could be an explosion versus there would not be one; there was no danger versus the fact that the Catholic Church had granted general absolution of sins for local residents; and so on. An inspection of public perceptions elicited by these confused messages reveals multiple outcomes. For example, many people evacuated, but many did not, and many perceived that risk to life and health was high, but many did not.

Relatively complex multiple messages are needed to enable a heterogeneous public to reach single and accurate perceptions about who is and who is not at risk in an emergency, as well as who should and who should not do anything about it. The 1972 tropical storm Agnes provides an example. Agnes was one of the largest storms ever to hit the United States. Several states were impacted, thousands of people evacuated, thousands of others sheltered, and yet thousands more did nothing. For the most part, people responded "correctly" based on accurate perceptions of risk which were quite heterogeneous across the multistate area. The reason was that a multitude of different and detailed warning messages were disseminated and these helped almost everyone perceive risk, and then act, reasonably. In this hurricane, like others in recent years, many people came to a shared perception of the storm, and then took appropriate action. As a result, few people lost their lives in comparison to what could have occurred if the warnings were like those at Three Mile Island or in Rapid City. In the next section, we review the process by which multiple and single, inaccurate and accurate, perceptions are formed when the public receives a warning.

2. The Warning Response Process

Why do multiple public perceptions of risk arise among the members of an endangered public when all members receive the same single warning message? Why does human response to a warning differ among individuals when they receive the same information about how to respond? In this section, we elaborate upon the process by which these differences occur.

Human decision making when confronted by a warning resembles a lexicographic decision process: people go through a sequential process where various aspects of the decision confronting them are considered before acting. This process is illustrated in Figure 1. The sequence may not be the same for every person, and not each stage is necessary for response. The process is initiated by notification, or hearing an initial warning. This leads to various psychological and behavioral outcomes. The process is shaped by sender (those issuing the warning) and receiver (those hearing the warning) factors. Mediating the process are information-seeking and confirmation activities. Each component is now discussed in the order we believe characterizes a typical decision sequence.

The first stage of public warning response is hearing the alert or message. It cannot be assumed that broadcasting a warning or sounding a siren will be heard. Even when it is physically possible to receive the warning, it may fall on deaf ears, so to speak, because of habituation (e.g., they never really listen to television), selective perception (e.g., they hear only what they want to), or physical constraints (e.g., they are out of siren range). The failure to hear a warning generally precludes response.

Once heard, the warning must be understood. By understanding, we do not refer to interpretation, but rather to the attachment of meaning to the message. Those meanings can vary among people and may or may not conform to the understandings intended. For example, a flood warning may be understood as a wall of inundating water to one person, but ankle-high runoff to another. A 50% probability may be interpreted as certain by some or unlikely by others. In this sense, understanding includes the perception of risk.

It is also helpful for people to believe that the warning is real and that the contents of the message are accurate. Believability is influenced by a large number of factors associated with the method and contents of the warning. The classic case is the "cry-wolf" syndrome: people will not

ATTRIBUTES	NOTIFICATION	OUTCOMES	
		PSYCHOLOGICAL	BEHAVIOR
Sender Characteristics Receiver Characteristics	Hear	Understand Believe Personalize	Respond
← —————— Information Seeking and Confirmation —————— →			

Figure 1. The general warning-response sequential process model.

believe a true warning following frequent false alarms. This may be a legitimate concern but it has not been proven to be true for hazard warnings in general.

People think of warnings in personal terms — the implications for themselves or for a group such as their family. If people do not feel they are warning targets, they may well ignore the warning. This is illustrated by the "It can't happen to me" syndrome where people deny risk they do not want to face. Personalizing warnings is an important prerequisite of response.

At this stage of our model, a person has heard the warning, understood it, believed what was said, and established the belief that he or she will be personally affected by the hazard. Having gone through this process, one must decide what to do. People, in general, do what they think is best for them to do. Often this is interpreted by the expert as irrational, but it is in fact rational for the person making the response. Deciding does not automatically lead to protective action. After a decision, events may take place to prevent intended behavior from occurring. A family may decide to evacuate, but a missing pet may prevent the move.

Throughout the warning period, a person typically goes through the stages of the model (hear–understand–believe–personalize–decide and respond) just outlined each time new information is received. Thus, warning response is not a single decision, but instead follows from a series of decisions. Additionally, people do not passively await the arrival of more information; most people actively seek out additional knowledge and data. This behavior has typically been referred to as the confirmation process (Drabek, 1969; Mileti et al., 1975).

The confirmation process causes people to be "information hungry" following the first warning alert. Rarely are people overwhelmed by information in a disaster warning context. Instead, there is a void of information, particularly in rare or unfamiliar events. This often creates a demand for more information than is being disseminated in the warning message, and a need for repetitive messages to enable people to absorb all the knowledge they wish to possess.

Confirmation plays an important role in the model of warning response. It is an ongoing process that affects each stage of the process. It is more accurate to break the concept of confirmation into its basic components. A number of sender and receiver determinants are part of the confirmation process. These include the number and frequency of warnings received, the number of different sources utilized, the type and number of channels used to get information, and the role of social ties in the response process.

3. Conclusions

Our theoretical viewpoint is grounded in the premise that human response to warnings is based largely on the perceptions and definitions of the situation which people form about both risk and response options. These definitions are situationally determined and negotiated out of a dialectical process involving the information received by an actor in the warning setting, and characteristics of the actor receiving that information, for these characteristics can affect how warning information is processed. This symbolic interactionist perspective now forms the structure for our review of empirical research findings.

DETERMINANTS OF HUMAN RESPONSE

Empirical research to document the determinants of human response to warnings has a long-standing tradition. Research began in earnest in the 1950s as part of the research program in the National Academy of Sciences (NAS) to investigate natural and technological emergencies. Research was continued in the 1960s by individual researchers. In the 1970s and beyond, warning response studies placed less emphasis on describing human response to warnings and more on discovering how single factors (like sex, age, and others) covaried with response alternatives. Later studies emphasize attempts to model complex sets of determinants, their interaction and effects on warning response.

Available empirical studies, therefore, vary in terms of methodological soundness, theoretical quality, the hazard type case event being studied (floods, flash floods, hurricanes, a nuclear power plant accident, and so on), and the type of behavior and reasons for that behavior being examined. It is the purpose of this section to review and systematize available empirical findings. These findings focus on alternative explanations for the warning response process. Additionally, empirically documented covariants of warning response are catalogued according to two typologies suggested by the empirical evidence.

A review of research on human response to warnings suggests that determinants fall into two categories. These are sender determinants and receiver determinants. Sender determinants are attributes of the actual warnings received by members of the public. These fall into four general categories: attributes of the messages; attributes of the channels through which messages are conveyed; attributes of the frequency with which messages are given; and attributes of the person(s) and/or organization(s) from which the messages emanate which we label as source attributes.

Empirical findings suggest that message attributes important to consider vary in reference to both message content and style. Message content is relevant to consider along three lines: information about risk location; the character of that risk (e.g., effects of impact and time to impact); and guidance about what people should do before impact. Message style is also important. Important style attributes are: specificity (the degree to which the message is specific about risk, guidance, and location); consistency (the degree to which a message is internally consistent, as well as consistent across separate messages regarding risk, guidance, and location); accuracy (the extent to which message content about risk, location, and guidance is accurate); certainty (the degree to which those giving the warning message seem certain about what they are saying about risk, location, and guidance); and clarity (the degree to which risk, location, and guidance information in the message is stated in words that people can understand).

In addition to message attributes, other important factors are: the sender characteristics of channel attributes (the type of channel used—e.g., personal versus impersonal—and the number of different channels used); frequency attributes (the number of times a particular message is conveyed, the number of different messages, and the pattern between different conveyances—e.g., every 15 minutes, randomly, and so on); and source attributes (the level of familiarity of those giving the message to those receiving it, the degree to which the message giver is an official, and the credibility level of the message giver to those who receive the message).

Research also documents warning receiver characteristics that are important; these fall into four categories. The first is attributes of the receiver's environment when the warning is received. Environmental attributes worth noting are physical and social cues—for example, if it is raining when flood warnings are received or if neighbors are seen evacuating in concert with receiving evacuation advisements.

The second characteristic consists of the social attributes of the receiver. These have been grouped into five categories. Aspects of the social network of which the warning recipient is a member is one category, including factors such as whether or not the family is united, social ties and bonds, the existence of close-by friends and relatives, and so on. Resource characteristics is another category and refers to physical resources, such as having access to a car in which to evacuate; economic resources, such as having the money to pay for a hotel; and social resources, such as having a local social support system. Aspects of the role of the warning recipient is another important social attribute category. Role characteristics include, for example, sex and age. Cultural characteristics such as ethnicity, language, and social class are another illustrated dimension of social attributes. The last category, that of social attributes, consists of activity characteristics, that is, various dimensions of the social activities in which the warning recipient is participating when the warning is received. These include sleep, work, and recreation.

The third set of attributes of the warning recipient revealed by past research as important are psychological attributes. These include pre-warning knowledge about, for example, the risk associated with a particular hazard agent, protective actions, and the existence of emergency plans; pre-warning cognitions such as psychosocial stress level and locus of control of the warning recipient; and experience with the hazard agent, for example, type of experience and its recency.

The last set of warning recipient attributes in the typology consists of physiological attributes. Scant empirical research has been performed on physiological attributes; however, factors such as physical disabilities, deafness, blindness, and so on can affect warning process and response.

In the remainder of this section we document that portion of the research record on sender and receiver characteristics in reference to their effect on actual public warning response. In fact, the most frequently examined aspect of public warning studies has been the actual response of members of the public. Actual response can take a variety of forms, for example, evacuation, taking shelter, bringing in the lawn furniture, doing nothing. Some studies have examined the full range of potentially adaptive responses to warnings in an emergency; most studies have focused on evacuation. The findings catalogued from this research are now summarized in reference to sender, receiver, and process determinants.

1. Sender Determinants

The effect of message attributes on public response to emergency warnings is relatively well documented. A range of studies has concluded that the probability of a public engaging in protective response to warning is enhanced as the specificity of warning messages (location of risk, guidance about public response, the impending hazard, and time to impact) increases (Rogers, 1985a; Houts et al., 1984; Perry, 1979, 1981, 1983; Ikeda, 1982; Moore et al., 1982; Perry & Greene, 1982b; Paulsen, 1981; Perry, Lindell, & Greene, 1981; Simpson & Riehl, 1981; Carter, 1980; Flynn & Chalmers, 1980; Quarantelli, 1980; Dynes et al., 1979; Flynn, 1979; Mileti & Beck, 1975).

Also, the level of consistency within and between different warning messages concerning risk location, guidance about appropriate public response, the hazard, and time to impact increases the odds of an adaptive public response (Perry, 1981, 1983; Turner et al., 1981; Quarantelli, 1980; Flynn, 1979; Mileti et al., 1975). The clarity with which a warning message is spoken and the ease of understanding increases the likelihood of adaptive public response (Quarantelli, 1980, Mileti et al., 1975).

In addition to the three message attributes of specificity, consistency, and clarity impacting public warning response, the attribute of the type of channel through which the warning is communicated has also been empirically shown to affect public response, but in a confused way. Baker (1979) found communication channel to be unrelated to response. Gray (1981a) and Perry, Lindell, and Greene (1981) found that face-to-face communication channels had a higher probability fo eliciting adaptive public response than mass media channels, but Flynn (1979), Windham et al. (1977), and Mileti and Beck (1975) found the opposite to be the case. It seems logical to conclude that in historical cases, other factors such as warning specificity and consistency likely covaried with a particular form of communication channel, and that channel correlations with response were probably spurious.

The frequency attributes of number of warnings and warning pattern have both been demonstrated to enhance appropriate public response to warnings. The more warnings received, the greater the likelihood of adaptive public response (Perry, Lindell, & Greene, 1981; Quarantelli, 1980; Turner et al., 1979; Grunfest, 1977; Mileti & Beck, 1975; Drabek, 1969; Lachman et al., 1961; Fritz & Mathewson, 1957; Fritz & Marks, 1954). Additionally, the probability of response to warnings increases when the amount of forewarning is less (Perry, Greene, & Lindell, 1980; Quarantelli, 1980).

The source attributes of those giving the warning message, the last category of sender characteristics, has also been documented as affecting response to emergency warnings. Warnings from sources that are official (Baker, 1986; Rogers, 1985a; Saarinen & Sell, 1985; Baker, 1984; Perry, 1981, 1983; Goldstein & Schorr, 1982; Perry, Lindell, & Greene, 1981; Quarantelli, 1980; Windham et al., 1977; Treadwell, 1961) have a higher probability of eliciting adaptive public response than nonofficial warnings. Recently (Flynn, 1979; Sorensen, 1984) it was shown that scientists are an effective source of warning information. Also credibility of a warning source is positively related to adaptive public response (Stallings, 1984; Lindell & Perry, 1983; Perry, Lindell, & Greene, 1981; Simpson & Riehl,

1981; Quarantelli, 1980; Turner, 1976; McLuckie, 1970), as is familiarity with the source of the warning message (Perry & Lindell, 1986; Perry, 1981, 1983; Perry, Lindell, & Greene, 1981).

The set of findings on how sender characteristics affect public warning response reveals some relatively straightforward conclusions. These are that the likelihood of adaptive public response to emergency warnings is increased if those warnings are specific, consistent, clear, frequent in number, able to foretell a soon-to-impact event, and from sources which are official and scientific, credible and familiar.

2. Receiver Determinants

The effect of receiver determinants on public warning response is perhaps the best documented research area in warning system research.

Environmental cues function to affect warning response in a couple of ways. First, observing neighbors and others responding to warnings serves as a basis for modeling behavior and increases the odds that a warning recipient will engage in the same sort of adaptive response (Perry, 1981, 1983; Cutter & Barnes, 1982; Perry & Greene, 1982a; Christensen & Ruch, 1980; Baker, 1979; Dynes & Quarantelli, 1976; Treadwell, 1961). In addition, perceiving environmental cues consistent with the risk conveyed in a warning (e.g., heavy rain and flood warnings) also increases the likelihood that a warning recipient will engage in a protection response (Perry, 1981, 1983; Perry & Greene, 1982a; Liverman & Wilson, 1981; Perry, Lindell, & Greene, 1981; Flynn, 1979). Proximity to the potential impact site also enhances the probability of adaptive response (Houts et al., 1984; Liverman & Wilson, 1981; Perry, 1981; Baker, 1979; Dynes et al., 1979; Flynn, 1979).

Social attributes of warning recipients affect the odds of engaging in adaptive response to warnings. Aspects of the social networks in which a warning recipient is engaged have a set of well-documented response effects. First, persons immersed in elaborate social networks (as indicated by a variety of factors such as large local friend and kinship networks, long-term community residency, contacts or membership in community organizations, high level of community involvement, and so on) are more likely to engage in protective actions than persons with access to more limited networks (Anderson et al., 1984; Perry, 1983; Mileti, Hutton, & Sorensen, 1981; Perry, Lindell, & Greene, 1980, 1981; Turner et al., 1981; Baker, 1979; Dynes et al., 1979; Perry, 1979; Turner et al., 1979; Windham et al., 1977; Worth & McLuckie, 1967; Grunfest, 1977; Clifford, 1956). In addition, persons who are able to discuss the situation with other network members have a greater probability of engaging in protective action (Rogers, 1985b; Baker, 1979).

Network characteristics can also serve as constraints to engaging in protective actions. For example, Houts et al. (1984), Perry (1981), and Baker (1979) have documented that network aspects (e.g., not being able to leave from one's place of work) can constrain protective actions such as evacuation. Also, a variety of findings exist to suggest that protective actions such as evacuation have a higher probability of occurring if people are in a united as opposed to a separated nuclear family unit (Perry & Greene, 1982b, 1983; Perry, 1982; Perry, Lindell, & Greene, 1980, 1981; Flynn, 1979; Dynes & Quarantelli, 1976; Quarantelli, 1960), although there is some evidence to suggest that family unity is unrelated to response with very rapid onset emergencies (Mileti, 1975).

A small set of findings exists regarding the role of resources in affecting public warning response. It appears (Houts et al., 1984; Mileti, Hutton, & Sorensen, 1981; Baker, 1979) that possessing resources such as access to transportation, or cash in the case of protective actions requiring it, facilitate adaptive warning response.

The role membership of warning recipients has a clear effect on public response to emergency warnings. Persons in roles of responsibility for others (e.g., parents) are more likely to engage in protective action response to warnings than those not in such roles (Houts et al., 1984; Carter, Kendall, & Clark, 1983; Perry, 1981; Turner et al., 1981; Quarantelli, 1980; Flynn, 1979; Wilkinson & Ross, 1970). Socioeconomic status (level of education, income, and so on) is also positively related to adaptive warning response (Stallings, 1984; Mileti, Hutton, & Sorensen, 1981; Turner et al., 1981; Baker, 1979; Dynes et al., 1979; Flynn, 1979; Windham et al., 1977; Wilkinson & Ross, 1970; Lachman et al., 1961). Sex, in the sense that women are more likely than men to engage in adaptive warning response, is also related to response (Flynn & Chalmers, 1980; Flynn, 1979; Wilkinson & Ross, 1970).

Age has had mixed relationships with the performance of adaptive response to emergency warnings. It has been reported to have a negative effect (Perry, Lindell, & Greene, 1981; Dynes et al., 1979; Flynn, 1979; Perry, 1979; Grunfest, 1977; Mileti, 1975; Wilkinson & Ross, 1970; Moore et al., 1963); a positive effect (Cutter & Barnes, 1982; Perry, Lindell, & Greene, 1981); and no effect at all (Baker, 1979). A few studies (Stallings, 1984; Dynes et al., 1979; Flynn, 1979) report that having a job which precludes leaving can be a constraint to protective actions such as evacuation.

The cultural aspect of social attributes has also had an empirical effect on disaster warning response. Membership in a minority group decreases the odds of engaging in adaptive warning response (Perry, Lindell, & Greene, 1981, 1982a,b; Turner et al., 1981; Wilkinson & Ross, 1970; Drabek & Boggs, 1968). All other things equal, blacks are more likely than other ethnic groups to respond adaptively to warnings.

All three psychological attributes—knowledge, cognitions and experience— have been empirically demonstrated to impact upon emergency warning response. Knowledge about appropriate response (e.g., about evacuation routes in the case of evacuation) has a positive effect on response (Rogers, 1985b; Perry & Greene, 1982b; Leik et al., 1981; Liverman & Wilson, 1981; Perry, Lindell, & Greene, 1980, 1981; Perry, 1979; Windham et al., 1977). Warning response is also positively affected by knowledge about the hazard for which a warning is issued (Perry & Lindell, 1986; Dynes et al., 1979). Recent work (Sorensen, 1986) helps put this finding in context. Prior hazard knowledge is useful in upgrading warning response, but is likely not sufficient to elicit appropriate response in and of itself.

Cognitions have been documented to affect emergency warning response in the following ways. Persons with a fatalistic life outlook are less likely to respond adaptively to disaster warnings than those without this approach to life (Perry & Greene, 1982b; Turner et al., 1981; Flynn, 1979; Sims & Bauman, 1972). For the protective action of evacuation, fear over looting is negatively related to evacuation (Quarantelli, 1984; Perry, 1981, 1983; Flynn, 1979). A third cognition found to affect warning response is habitualized behaviors. Several studies have concluded that people have a tendency in responding to emergency warnings to do things as they do habitually—for example, evacuate over routes that they typically traverse (Glass, 1970; Anderson, 1968; Kilpatrick, 1957). Risk, or a person's perceived loss, also affects response (Houts et al., 1984; Mileti, Hutton, & Sorensen, 1981; Baker, 1979; Flynn, 1979; Windham et al., 1977). For example, mobile home dwellers are more likely to evacuate in response to hurricane warnings than regular homeowners because the perceived risk of staying is greater; and pregnant women were more likely to evacuate during Three Mile Island because they were labeled a high-risk group. The Three Mile Island accident also revealed another cognition as positively related to evacuation: it was fear over a possible forced evacuation which people sought to avoid (Perry, 1981; Flynn, 1979). Finally, it has been documented that in the case of evacuation, the perceived length of time that people think they will be away from their homes is positively related to the probability of evacuation (Liverman & Wilson, 1981) as well as the use of public shelters (Perry, Greene, & Lindell, 1980).

The third and last psychological attribute category, hazard experience, is also demonstrated to affect warning response. Experience with the hazard for which warning has been issued has a positive affect on adaptive warning response (Perry & Lindell, 1986; Perry & Greene, 1982b; Perry, Lindell, & Greene, 1981; Turner et al., 1981; Baker, 1979; Irish & Falconer, 1979; Perry, 1979; Smith & Tobin, 1979; Westgate, 1978; Hutton, 1976; Grunfest, 1977; Turner, 1976; Lachman, Tatsuoka, & Bonk, 1961; Treadwell, 1961). The effect of experience on warning response is not monolithic, however. It has also been found that it is the recency of experience which positively impacts warning response (Perry, Lindell, & Greene, 1980, 1981; Hutton, 1976; Anderson, 1969; Moore et al., 1963; Fogleman, 1958). There is also evidence to suggest that a lot of experience with a particular hazard can create routine and effective public response to warnings (Perry, Greene, & Lindell, 1980) as well as complacency and increased risk taking (Windham et al., 1977; Baker, 1979; Wilkinson & Ross, 1970).

It has also been concluded that physiological constraints can detract from adaptive public response to emergency warnings (Houts et al., 1984), as in the case of persons who are too sick or disabled to engage in evacuation.

There is, obviously, an elaborate research record to document the effect of receiver determinants on public response to emergency warnings, and the following conclusions have been reached. First, some members of the public are better equipped to respond to warnings because of pre-emergency knowledge about the hazard and response, education and socioeconomic status, resources to facilitate response, and being unencumbered by physiological constraints which preclude certain response options. Second, some people have incentives to respond adaptively to warnings, such as having responsibility for others, the presence of environmental and social modelling cues for adaptive response, experience, personal risk perceptions, being socialized into protector roles, proximity to impact area and therefore access to less distorted information and a clearer risk perception, and access to an elaborate social network to enhance response options like evacuation, the tendency to follow habit, and the general although not ironclad tendency to engage in some protective actions as a united nuclear family.

3. Process Determinants

All possible process determinants (hear, understand, believe, and personalize) have been empirically documented to affect response. Hearing a warning enhances the probability of an adaptive response (Saarinen &

Sell, 1985; Turner, 1983; Turner et al., 1981; Baker, 1979; Turner et al., 1979; Grunfest, 1977). Understanding warnings also enhances the odds of adaptive public response (Turner, 1983; Baker, 1979; Turner et al., 1979; Windham et al., 1977; Wilkinson & Ross, 1970). Believing a warning enhances adaptive public response (Perry, 1979, 1983; Perry & Greene, 1982b, Perry, Lindell, & Greene, 1980, 1981, 1982a; Lindell, Perry, & Greene, 1980; Baker, 1979; Hultaker, 1976; Mileti & Beck, 1975). Personalization of the risk conveyed in warnings has a positive effect on taking adaptive emergency warning response, and this is perhaps the most elaborately documented process relationship in warning system response research (Perry & Lindell, 1986; Quarantelli, 1984; Zeigler & Johnson, 1984; Perry, 1979, 1981, 1982, 1983; Goldstein & Schorr, 1982; Ikeda, 1982; Perry, Lindell, & Greene, 1981, 1982a; Mileti, Hutton, & Sorensen, 1981; Baker, 1979; Dynes, 1979; Turner et al., 1979; Flynn, 1979; Windham et al., 1977; Hultaker, 1976; Withey, 1976; Mileti & Beck, 1975; Glass, 1970; Bates et al., 1963).

Finally, one warning response is to seek to confirm the original warning message received. Confirmation has been documented to be a general descriptive response to receiving emergency warnings (Rogers, 1985a; Leik et al., 1981; Paulsen, 1981; Irish & Falconer, 1979; Drabek, 1969); a positive function of lead time (Perry, Lindell, & Greene, 1981), perceived personal risk (Leik et al., 1981; Danzig et al., 1958), messages received from the mass media (Dillman, Schwalbe, & Short, 1981; Drabek, 1969), and family unity (Drabek & Stephenson, 1971); and a negative function of the number of warning messages received (Mileti, 1975), which is itself confirmation, prior knowledge about the hazard (Rogers, 1985a) and the level of specificity contained in the original warning received (Cutter & Barnes, 1982).

CONCLUSIONS FOR POLICY AND APPLICATIONS

1. The Nonbehavioral Aspects of Response

Public response to warnings cannot legitimately be viewed solely as behavior. Although we have limited the review of the research record in this chapter solely to behavior, it is the case that people respond to warnings through a social process; to comprehend warning response means a comprehension of that process. Planning for future public warning response means that planning should address that process which ends in actual adaptive behavior. The process is a straightforward one: 1) the odds of an adaptive public response are enhanced if warnings are personalized by those who should personalize them, and not personalized by those not at risk; 2) the probability of effective personalization increases as a direct function of the level of belief elicted in emergency warnings; 3) belief can have its best effect on personalization, and eventually response, if it is prefaced by accurate public understanding of what is being said in a warning; and 4) understanding warning presumes that warnings must be heard.

The first general conclusion, therefore, is that public warning response is best understood, explained, and planned for if it is viewed as a series of sequential dependent variables, ordered as a social process, and comprised of hearing warnings, understanding what is said, believing what is heard, personalizing what is believed as appropriate, and then behavior. Of course, this process does not always function this way in the real world. For example, it is possible in any evacuation to find evacuees who did not believe that the disaster would impact the area. Consider a teenager who evacuated only because it was a chance to cut school and party with friends in another town. The point is that in general the process outlined will help explain most of the reasons why most people did or did not do whatever it is that they did in response to warnings. Exceptions to the general rule will exist, but these are not reason to dismiss the rule.

2. Response Process Determinants

Who in an endangered public does and does not hear, understand, believe, personalize, and respond adaptively to emergency warnings is not up to random chance. These process outcomes are the consequences of the effects of empirically demonstrated and known determinants which have been grouped into the categories of receiver and sender determinants. The following conclusions reached regarding these determinants are based on the reviewed empirical record.

First, different members of a public are members of different communication networks and have access to different communication linkages to the outside world. Consequently, the probability of maximizing the number who hear a warning is enhanced by warning systems which disseminate warning messages over the full range of communication networks through which that heterogeneous public receives information.

Second, the understand–believe–personalize–respond process appears to be facilitated by warning systems capable of providing emergency information that is both convincing and reasonable from the public's point of view, and the empirical record well documents what comprises reasonable and convincing warning information from the public's viewpoint. Warnings are perceived by the public to be convincing and reasonable if they are specific, consistent, and certain as to the location of the area of risk; if guidance is provided about what the public should do; if the character of the hazard is revealed as is the amount of time to its impact; if changes in the content of warnings which would make them appear inconsistent with others are explained; and if uncertainty in the content of warnings regarding, for example, the probability of impact is explained, as well as why the public should act upon inevitably uncertain information as if it were certain. Warnings should also be repeated frequently. It is insufficient to issue a warning once or so infrequently as to not provide for the public being able to hear the warning many times. Additionally, warnings should best come from a source that maximizes the credibility of the information. Who is credible for one person, however, may not be credible for another; therefore, it seems important that warnings stem from a panel of sources that could include, for example, scientists, officials, a familiar local personality, and a disaster response group familiar to most, such as the Red Cross. Credibility of warning information is also enhanced by the confirmation process and the frequency with which a particular warning message is heard.

Third, any public is a heterogeneous group. People have inherent differences of circumstance that would "predispose" them to different process outcomes were it not for sender determinants. These differences appear numerous when one views the empirical record. But these variables are a multitude of different indicators selected by different researchers which actually reflect different ways of operationalizing and measuring a handful of the same more general concepts. It is these concepts which provide an avenue of understanding as to how differences of fact and circumstance predispose variation in warning response. Four concepts stand out as capable of explaining and organizing the empirical record regarding the effect of receiver determinants on warning response process outcomes. These are variation in ability to process risk information; in access to social and physical networks; in incentives to be vigilant, take a warning seriously, or err on the side of caution; and in constraints on desirable warning response process outcomes.

People vary in their ability to process risk information, like that contained in warnings. Variability exists because of factual differences between people such as education, cognitive abilities, pre-emergency knowledge, experience with a hazard, and the degree of fatalism with which life is approached. Variability in the ability to process risk information also exists because of circumstances characterizing a warning event. For example, it is easier for people to impute meaning to risk information when their environment provides cues or models supporting the content of the received risk information—hearing sirens in the event of an invisible radiological emergency, or seeing neighbors evacuating. Human variation in the ability to process risk information, for either factual or circumstantial reasons, or both, will lead to variation in warning response process outcomes, all other factors being constant.

Warning recipients also differ in the access they have to social and geographical networks and events. These differences lead to differences in warning response process outcomes when all other factors are held constant. A range of social network attributes, for example, can make for differences in response process outcomes. Persons who are part of established pre-emergency social networks are more likely to receive informal warnings, or to give them, and therefore more likely to confirm warnings, as well as to understand, believe, personalize appropriately, and engage in adaptive response. Network membership also enhances the odds that people have someone to talk to as they seek to define the warning situation and arrive at a meaning for it. Network membership also increases options for response—for example, having the home of a friend to evacuate to, or receiving an invitation to do so.

Persons who by circumstance are not at home when they receive a warning are denied at least partial access to their networks and have a lower probability of achieving sound warning response process outcomes. Geographical proximity to the area at risk also affects process outcomes. The further away from the area, the more distorted is the emergency information one has access to and the less informed are warning response outcomes. Human variation in network access, either by factual differences between people regarding networks or differences due to circumstance, will lead to variation in warning response process outcomes, other factors being constant.

People who receive warnings also differ in terms of factors which act as either constraints or incentives to sound warning process outcomes. Some people have more of an incentive to be vigilant, take a warning seriously, investigate what is happening and confirm a warning, and/or to err on the side of caution; others simply lack some or all of these incentives. Incentives can exist for a variety of reasons including being in a role of responsibility for children, being socialized into and adhering to a protective/nurture role like that of female or mother, or being predisposed to perceive risk in one way or another to a particular hazard. Incentives can also be circumstantial—for example, having only a very short time to impact and, therefore, not being afforded the luxury of being able to socially negotiate the meaning of an impending disaster's warning. Incentives, either factual or circumstantial, will lead to variation in warning response process outcomes, holding all other factors constant, as will constraints.

Some people, again by virtue of factual or circumstantial differences, are constrained from sound warning understanding, belief, personalization, and response. Constraints are varied and include lacking the resources necessary to act (not having a car in which to evacuate), being unable to engage in some actions for physiological reasons, belonging to an ethnic group which simply discounts information that comes from the mainstream, being of a pre-emergency psychological state that precludes sound or unbiased judgement (being particularly stressed, or being frail and elderly so that movement is difficult), ascribing to unfounded fears and superstitions like the fear of looting, and simply not being willing to consider some actions until a person can check on or be assured of the safety of a loved one.

In sum, sender characteristics vary across warning events. In warning events that provide convincing and reasonable emergency warning information to the public, the understanding, belief, personalization, and response of the public can be sound. Receiver characteristics vary widely between members of a public in any one warning circumstance, as well as between different events; and receiver characteristics can be factual (things that simply exist and cannot be changed) as well as circumstantial (things that occur by chance during the emergency, like a heavy rain when flash flood warnings are issued).

The effects of receiver determinants on warning process outcomes are not unchangeable laws of nature. It is possible for a warning system to be designed to not only maximize the application of knowledge about how sender characteristics can elicit sound warning response process outcomes, but also eliminate, reasonably well, most of the negative impacts that receiver characteristics can have on process outcomes. The configuration of sender determinants which the empirical research record has revealed as important to achieving this follow. First, warning messages should be specific, consistent, accurate, certain, and clear about location and character of risk, guidance about what people should do, and how much time they have to do it. Changes in these items over time should be explained.

Second, the more communication channels used to reach a public, the better, because different people are part of different communication networks.

Third, warnings should be systematically repeated often in a predictable pattern.

Fourth, warnings should be labeled as from a set of sources, including a mix of scientists, officials, and a familiar local figure. These prescriptions could be achieved by a range of planning alternatives, and specific planning elements to achieve these goals would vary from hazard to hazard and across entities. The basic principles and planning goals, however, should be the same.

3. The Confirmation Process

The third conclusion is that underlying the warning-response process and the effect of sender and receiver determinants on the outcomes of that process is the concept of confirmation, which is itself a social process. People are not easily convinced that the unthinkable can happen. Concern that a public will panic when faced with news of an impending catastrophe and fear of public overreaction have been documented as constraints to issuing warnings in the first place. Many others presume that a warning will be immediately followed by prudent public action in response to the message. Still others speculate on the basis of misinterpreted evidence that some types of impending disaster, when warned for, will elicit dramatic and immediate public flight (e.g., fleeing American cities on the heels of initial notifications of an impending nuclear attack or a radiological emergency at a nuclear power plant). The accumulated empirical evidence strongly suggests that the first warning response (and perhaps even the second and third) of most people is to seek to confirm that message: to get more information, talk over the warning with others, and/or hear the same message again, instead of believing the news at first blush. Confirmation of warning messages is necessary for most people before they act in ways that go beyond seeking confirmatory information.

CONCLUSIONS FOR RESEARCH

The last conclusion in reference to public response to emergency warnings is, perhaps, best cast as extremely well informed speculation. It involves construction of a model, presumed to depict cause and effect, to summarize the process, determinants, and consequences of public response to warnings of impending disasters and catastrophes. Figure 2 presents our attempt to construct such a model informed by the empirical record recorded in earlier sections of this chapter. The boxes in the model represent the concepts that have been discussed in detail in this chapter, and the arrows represent cause and effect between the concepts.

The model presented in Figure 2 is best viewed as one in need of future

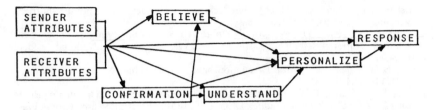

Figure 2. A model of the causes and effects of public response to warnings of impending disaster.

testing. It represents and then hypothesizes the character of cause and effect suggested by the empirical record. It was obviously induced from the existing data. To the best of our knowledge, no one research effort has sought to systematically measure each factor or concept in the model and analyze the entire system in a multivariate format. Although it is possible to hypothesize the model with empirical confidence, it is impossible to conclude that it is scientific fact.

There are few other areas of research in the social sciences that have compiled as extensive a record as public response to emergency disaster warnings. Additionally, even fewer areas exist in which the accumulated knowledge base promises to be as useful to society as does knowledge about public warning response.

REFERENCES

Anderson, J. W. (1968). Cultural adaptation to threatened disaster. *Human Organization,* 27 (Winter): 298–307.

Anderson, W. (1969). Disaster warning and communication processes in two communities. *The Journal of Communication,* 19 (June): 92–104.

Anderson, L., Keaton, J., Saarinen, T., & Wells, W., II. (1984). *The Utah Landslides, Debris Flows, and Floods of May and June 1983.* Washington, D.C.: National Academy Press.

Baker, E. J. (1979). Predicting Response to Hurricane Warnings: A Reanalysis of Data from Four Studies. *Mass Emergencies,* 4: 9–24.

Baker, E. J. (1984). *Public Response to Hurricane Probability Forecasts.* NOAA TM NWS FCST 29. Washington, D.C.: National Weather Service.

Baker, E. J. (1986). Hurricane Elena: Preparedness and response in Florida. *Florida Policy Review,* (Winter): 17–23.

Bates, F. L., et al. (1963). *The Social and Psychological Consequences of a Natural Disaster.* National Research Council Disaster Study 18. Washington, D.C.: National Academy of Sciences.

Carter, T. M. (1980). Community warning systems: The relationships among the broadcast media, emergency service agencies, and the national weather service. In *Disasters and the Mass Media* (pp. 214–228). Committee on Disasters and the Mass Media. Washington, D.C.: National Academy of Sciences.

Carter, T. M., Kendall, S., & Clark, J. P. (1983). Household response to warnings. *International Journal of Mass Emergencies and Disasters,* 9(1): 95–104.

Christensen, L., & Ruch, C. E. (1980). The effects of social influence on response to hurricane warnings. *Disasters*, 4(2): 205–210.

Clifford, R. A. (1956). *The Rio Grande Flood: A Comparative Study of Border Communities*. National Research Disaster Study 7. Washington, D.C.: National Academy of Sciences.

Cutter, S., & Barnes, K. (1982). Evacuation behavior and Three Mile Island. *Disasters*, 6(2): 116–124.

Danzig, E. R., Thayer, P. W., & Galater, L. R. (1958). *The Effects of a Threatening Rumor on a Disaster-Stricken Community*. Disease Study 10. Disaster Research Group. Washington: National Academy of Sciences.

Dillman, D. A., Schwalbe, M. L., & Short, J. F., Jr. (1981). Communication behavior and social impacts following the May 18, 1980, eruption of Mount St. Helens. In S. A. C. Keller (Ed.), Cheney, WA: Eastern Washington University Press.

Drabek, T. E. (1969). Social processes in disaster: Family evaluation. *Social Problems*, 16 (Winter): 336–349.

Drabek, T. E., & Boggs, K. (1968). Families in disaster: Reactions and relatives. *Journal of Marriage and the Family*, 30 (August): 443–451.

Drabek, T. E., & Stephenson, J. S., III. (1971). When disaster strikes. *Journal of Applied Social Psychology*, 1(2): 187–203.

Dynes, R. R., Purcell, A. H., Wenger, D. E., Stern, P. E., Stallings, R. A., & Johnson, Q. T. (1979). *Report of the Emergency Preparedness and Response Task Force from Staff Report to the President's Commission on the Accident at Three Mile Island*. Washington, D.C.: President's Commission on the Accident at Three Mile Island.

Dynes, R. R., & Quarantelli, E. L. (1976). The family and community context of individual reactions to disaster. In H. Parad, L. Resnik, & L. Parad (Eds.), *Emergency and Disaster Management: A Mental Health Sourcebook*. Bowie, MD: The Charles Press.

Flynn, C. B. (1979). *Three Mile Island Telephone Survey—Preliminary Report on Procedures and Findings*. Tempe, AZ: Mountain West Research.

Flynn, C. B., & Chalmers, J. A. (1980). *The Social and Economic Effects of the Accident at Three Mile Island*. Washington, D.C.: U.S. Office of Nuclear Regulatory Commission.

Fogleman, C. W. (1958). Family and community in disaster: A socio-psychological study of the effects of a major disaster upon individuals and groups. Dissertation. Baton Rouge: Louisiana State University.

Fritz, C. E., & Marks, E. S. (1954). The NORC studies of human behavior in disaster. *The Journal of Social Issues*, 10(3): 26–41.

Fritz, C. E., & Mathewson, J. H. (1957). *Convergency Behavior in Disasters*. National Research Council Disaster Study 9. Washington, D.C.: National Academy of Sciences.

Glass, A. J. (1970). The psychological aspects of emergency situations. In H. S. Abram (Ed.), *Psychological Aspects of Stress*. Springfield, IL: Charles C. Thomas.

Goldstein, R., & Schorr, J. K. (1982). The long-term impact of a man-made disaster: An examination of a small town in the aftermath of the Three Mile Island nuclear reactor accident. *Disasters*, 6(1): 50–59.

Gray, J. (1981a). Characteristic patterns of and variations in community response to acute chemical emergencies. *Journal of Hazardous Materials*, 4: 357–365.

Gray, J. (1981b). Three case studies of organized responses to chemical disasters. Misc. Report No. 29. Columbus: Disaster Research Center, The Ohio State University.

Grunfest, E. C. (1977). What people did during the big Thompason flood. Working Paper 32. Boulder, CO: Institute of Behavioral Science.

Houts, P. S., Lindell, M. K., Weittu, T., Cleary, P. D., Tokuhata, G., Flynn, C. B. (1984). The protective action decision model applied to evacuation during the Three Mile Island crisis. *International Journal of Mass Emergency and Disasters*, 2(1): 27–39.

Hultaker, O. E. (1976). Evakurea (Evacuate). *Disaster Studies*, 2. Uppsala, Sweden: University of Uppsala.

Hutton, J. R. (1976). The differential distribution of death in disaster: A test of theoretical propositions. *Mass Emergencies*, 1 (October): 261–266.

Ikeda, K. (1982). Warning of disaster and evacuation behavior in a Japanese chemical fire. *Journal of Hazardous Materials*, 7: 51–62.

Irish, J. L., & Falconer, B. (1979). Reaction to flood warning. In R. L. Heathcote & B. G. Thom (Eds.), *Natural Hazards in Australia*. Camberra: Australian Academy of Science.

Kilpatrick, F. P. (1957). Problems of perception in extreme situations. *Human Organization*, 16 (Summer): 20–22.

Lachman, R., Tatsuoka, M., & Bonk, W. (1961). Human behavior during the Tsunami of May, 1960. *Science*, 133 (May 5): 1405–1409.

Leik, R. K., Carter, T. M., & Clark, J. P., et al. (1981). *Community Response to Natural Hazard Warnings: Final Report*. Minneapolis, MN: University of Minnesota.

Lindell, M. K., & Perry, R. (1983). Nuclear power plant emergency warnings: How would the public respond? *Nuclear News*, (February): 49–57.

Lindell, M. K., Perry, R. W., & Greene, M. R. (1980). *Race and Disaster Warning Response*. Seattle, WN: Battelle Human Affairs Research Centers.

Liverman, D., & Wilson, J. P. (1981). The Mississagua Train Derailment and Evacuation, 10-16 November 1979. *Canadian Geographer*, XXV(4): 365–375.

Mack, R. W., & Baker, G. W. (1961). *The Occasion Instant*. National Academy of Sciences/National Research Council Disaster Study 15. Washington: National Academy of Sciences.

McLuckie, B. F. (1970). A study of functional response to stress in three societies. Dissertation. Departments of Sociology and Anthropology. Columbus, OH: The Ohio State University.

Mileti, D. S. (1975). *Natural Hazard Warning Systems in the United States: A Research Assessment*. Boulder, CO: Institute of Behavioral Science, University of Colorado.

Mileti, D. S., & Beck, E. M. (1975). Communication in crisis: Explaining evacuation symbolically. *Communication Research*, 2 (January): 24–49.

Mileti, D. S., Drabek, T. E., & Haas, J. E. (1975). *Human Systems in Extreme Environments*. Boulder, CO: Institute of Behavioral Science, University of Colorado.

Mileti, D. S., Hutton, J. R., & Sorensen, J. H. (1981). *Earthquake Prediction Response and Options for Public Policy*. Boulder, CO: Institute of Behavioral Science, University of Colorado.

Moore, H. E., et al. (1963). *Before the Wind: A Study of Response to Hurricane Carla*. National Academy of Sciences/National Research Council Disaster Study 19. Washington, D.C.: National Academy of Sciences.

Moore, W., Cook, E., Gooch, R., & Nordin, C. (1982). *The Austin, Texas Flood of May 24-25, 1981*. Washington, D.C.: National Academy Press.

Paulsen, R. L. (1981). *Human Behavior and Fire Emergencies: An Annotated Bibliography*. Washington: National Bureau of Standards, U.S. Department of Commerce.

Perry, R. W. (1979). Evacuation decision-making in natural disasters. *Mass Emergencies*, 4 (March): 25–38.

Perry, R. W. (1981). *Citizen Evacuation in Response to Nuclear and Non-nuclear Threats*. Washington, D.C.: FEMA.

Perry, R. W. (1982). *The Social Psychology of Civil Defense*. Lexington, MA: Lexington Books.

Perry, R. W. (1983). Population evacuation in volcanic eruptions, floods and nuclear power plant accidents: Some elementary comparisons. *Journal of Community Psychology*, 11: 36–47.

Perry, R. W. (1985). *Comprehensive Emergency Management*. Greenwich, CN: JAI Press.

Perry, R. W., & Greene, M. R. (1982a). *Citizen Response to Volcanic Eruptions: The Case of Mount St. Helens*. New York: Irvington.

Perry, R. W., & Greene, M. R. (1982b). The role of ethnicity in the emergency decision-making process. *Sociological Inquiry*, 52 (Fall): 309–334.

Perry, R. W., Greene, M. R., & Lindell, M. K. (1980). Enhancing evacuation warning compliance: Suggestions for emergency planning. *Disasters*, 4(4): 433–449.

Perry, R. W., & Lindell, M. K. (1986). *Twentieth Century Volcanicity at Mt. St. Helens: The Routinization of Life Near an Active Volcano*. Tempe, AZ: Arizona State University.

Perry, R. W., Lindell, M. K., & Greene, M. R. (1980). *The Implications of Natural Hazard Evacuation Warning Studies for Crisis Relocation Planning.* Seattle, WN: Battelle Human Affairs Research Center.

Perry, R. W., Lindell, M. K., & Greene, M. R. (1981). *Evacuation Planning in Emergency Management.* Lexington, MA and Toronto: Lexington Books.

Perry, R. W., Lindell, M. K., & Greene, M. R. (1982a). Crisis communications: Ethnic differentials in interpreting and acting on disaster warnings. *Social Behavior and Personality,* 10(1): 97–104.

Perry, R. W., Lindell, M. K., & Greene, M. R. (1982b). Threat perception and public response to volcano hazard. *Journal of Social Psychology,* 16: 119–204.

Quarantelli, E. L. (1960). A note on the protective function of the family in disasters. *Marriage and Family Living,* 22 (August): 263–264.

Quarantelli, E. L. (1980). *Evacuation Behavior and Problems: Findings and Implications From the Research Literature.* Columbus, OH: Disaster Research Center, The Ohio State University.

Quarantelli, E. L. (1984). Perceptions and reactions to emergency warnings of sudden hazards. *Ekistics,* 309 (Nov-Dec).

Rogers, G. O. (1985a). *Human Components of Emergency Warning.* Pittsburgh, PA: University Center for Social and Urban Research.

Rogers, G. O. (1985b). Decisions to evacuate in hurricanes: A social psychological model of evacuation decisions. Unpublished manuscript, University of Pittsburgh Center for Social and Urban Research.

Saarinen, T. F., & Sell, J. L. (1985). *Warning and Response to the Mount St. Helen's Eruption.* Albany: State University of New York Press.

Simpson, R. H., & Riehl, H. (1981). *The Hurricane and Its Impact.* Baton Rouge and London: Louisiana State University Press.

Sims, J. H., & Bauman, D. D. (1972). The tornado threat: Coping styles of the north and south. *Science,* 176: 1386–1392.

Smith, K., & Tobin, G. (1979). *Human Adjustment to the Flood Hazard.* London and New York: Longman.

Sorensen, J. H. (1984). Evaluating the effectiveness of warning systems for nuclear power plant emergencies: Criteria and application. In M. Pasqualietti & K. Pijawka (Eds.), *Nuclear Power: Assessing and Managing Hazardous Technologies.* Boulder, CO: Westview Press.

Sorensen, J. H. (1986). The Cheyenne flash flood: Warning and emergency response. Draft Report to the National Academy of Sciences. Washington, D.C.: National Academy of Sciences.

Stallings, R. (1984). Evacuation behavior at Three-Mile Island. *International Journal of Mass Emergencies and Disasters,* 2(1): 11–26.

Treadwell, M. E. (1961). *Hurricane Carla: September 3-14, 1961.* Denton, TX: Department of Defense, Office of Civil Defense, Region 5.

Turner, R. H. (1976). Earthquake prediction and public policy: Distillations from a National Academy of Sciences Report (1). *Mass Emergencies,* 1: 179–202.

Turner, R. H. (1983). Waiting for disaster: Changing reactions to earthquake forecasts in southern California. *International Journal of Mass Emergencies and Disasters,* 1(2): 307–334.

Turner, R. H., Nigg, J. M., Paz, D. H., & Young, B. S. (1979). *Earthquake Threat: The Human Response in Southern California.* Los Angeles: Institute for Social Science Research.

Turner, R. H., Nigg, J. M., Paz, D. H., & Young, B. S. (1981). *Community Response to Earthquake Threat in Southern California. Part Ten, Summary and Recommendations.* Los Angeles: Institute for Social Science Research, University of California, Los Angeles.

Westgate, K. (1978). Hurricane response and hurricane perception in the Commonwealth of the Bahamas. *Mass Emergencies,* 3: 251–265.

Wilkinson, K., & Ross, P. (1970). *Citizens Response to Warnings of Hurricane Camille.* Report No. 35. College Station, Mississippi: Mississippi State University, Social Science Research Center.

Williams, H. B. (1957). Some functions of communication in crisis behavior. *Human Organization,* 16 (Summer): 15–19.

Windham, G. O., Posey, E. I., Ross, P. J., & Spencer, B. (1977). *Reactions to Storm Threat During Hurricane Eloise.* Mississippi State University. Fort Worth, TX: National Weather Service.

Withey, S. B. (1962). Reaction to uncertain threat. In G. W. Baker & D. W. Chapman (Eds.), *Man and Society in Disaster.* New York: Basic Books.

Withey, S. B. (1976). Accommodation to threat. *Mass Emergencies,* 1: 125–130.

Worth, M. F., & McLuckie, B. F. (1967). *Get to High Ground! The Warning Process in the Colorado Floods June 1965.* Disaster Research Center Historical and Comparative Disasters Series. Columbus, OH: Disaster Research Center, The Ohio State University.

Zeigler, D. J., & Johnson, J. M., Jr. (1984). Evacuation behavior in response to nuclear power plant accidents. *Professional Geographer,* 36(2): 207–215.

14

Emergency Preparedness and Response Planning: An Intergovernmental Perspective

RONALD W. PERRY and JOANNE M. NIGG

Effective planning is vital to any successful emergency response operation, whether the disaster agent is natural or technological in origin. In its broadest sense, emergency planning refers to protection of the public from the effects of a hazard agent. With reference to organizations and governmental units, planning is the pathway to achieving a state of emergency preparedness, that is, the capacity to successfully cope with aberrations in the environment. Thus, preparedness should not be equated with the possession of a written plan, nor with just the ability to anticipate a specific negative event, nor with a simple extension of the routine operations of some emergency-relevant organization (cf. Quarantelli & Dynes, 1977). Instead, preparedness is a state of readiness to respond to threats that entails processes for threat identification, threat monitoring, and resource mobilization to ameliorate the danger. Consequently, there are both technical components to preparedness (such as possession of the "right" equipment) and social components (such as the establishment of necessary linkages or agreements between people and organizations).

Emergency planning is the semistructured process (including both formal and informal components and relationships) through which preparedness is achieved and maintained. We acknowledge that the planning process therefore includes and addresses the full range of emergency management issues—mitigation, preparedness, response, and recovery. In so doing, the ultimate objective is to enable the "emergency response system" to manage a given threat such that human suffering and loss of life and property are minimized.

The purpose of this chapter is to examine the nature and characteristics of the planning process designed to enhance community preparedness. Many of the technical issues and some of the social issues mentioned above have been carefully addressed in the literature (cf. Dynes, 1983; Dynes, Quarantelli, & Kreps, 1972, Perry & Lindell, 1987; Quarantelli, 1977; Wenger, Faupel, & James, 1980). What has not been addressed, however, is the reality that both the planning and response processes for any given community are *intergovernmental* in nature.

To develop a comprehensive emergency plan, a community certainly takes into account the matters of risk identification, risk assessment, and risk reduction. To a certain extent, there are geographical boundaries on such matters and they are inescapably "local" problems. Also, planning involves making inventories of local resources—personnel, skills, equipment, and material. It is well-known, however, that the need for resources to effectively manage disaster impacts frequently exceeds those available in any given community.

Obtaining supplemental resources and personnel from extracommunity sources is a strong tradition in American communities stricken by disasters. Some of these resources come "spontaneously" from private and governmental sources. This process has been documented in the popular press: for example, the outpouring of aid to San Francisco earthquake victims in 1906 *(San Francisco Examiner, 1906)* and described in the professional literature under the rubric of "convergence" (Fritz & Mathewson, 1957). In recent years, with the formalization of emergency planning, there has been an effort to encourage communities to formalize agreements for extracommunity assistance, primarily to enhance the effectiveness of the emergency response process (Foster, 1980, p. 232).

With the proliferation of such agreements, which are often stated as laws, statutes, ordinances or memoranda of agreement, arises the problem of official collaborative arrangements between different levels of government—municipal, county, State and Federal. To the extent that these different political units can agree on what needs to be done, who should take these actions, what actions are most important, and what resources are to be committed to the process, *intergovernmental coordination* is possible. Since intergovernmental coordination is the mechanism through which a community obtains the full complement of resources for its emergency response system, it is critical to the effective management of threats. Emergency planning, as the process through which resources (and agreements) are assembled, must consequently be seen in intergovernmental terms. When the process of intergovernmental coordination breaks down, whether during planning or response operations, the ability of the community to cope with environmental aberrations may be seriously impaired.

In this chapter the ways in which intergovernmental relations may be accounted for in the emergency planning process will be examined. Our discussion assumes that both emergency planning and response activities may be conceptualized as hierarchical and horizontal arrangements of expectations and responsibilities among and across different governmental units. Our approach to integrating intergovernmental issues with emergency planning focuses upon discussing the general principles of planning and the problems that arise in the formulation and adoption of such plans. Before reviewing planning principles, however, we recognize it is important to clarify the basic structure of intergovernmental relations in disasters.

WHERE RESPONSIBILITY RESIDES DURING EMERGENCIES

In connection with any community emergency, *local* government is responsible for managing the event. This responsibility, as we have mentioned above, includes determining where shortfalls in management resources exist and attempting to acquire supplements. An important means of acquiring supplemental resources is through agreements with other governmental units. These agreements may be horizontal (with units governing similar political jurisdictions) or hierarchical (with units governing larger, inclusive political jurisdictions). Interestingly, the conditions under which horizontal and hierarchical agreements are made differ.

In seeking supplementary resources for emergency management, local governments often look to geographically nearby governments of similar size. Such arrangements are normally concluded as "mutual aid agreements" in which two or more towns or cities agree to provide some constellation of services or resources to the other signatories under specified circumstances (usually disaster impact). These agreements are common among clusters of small communities (they often extend to "routine" emergencies such as fire protection and emergency medical services) and usually focus upon exchanges of the services of established emergency response organizations (Perry, Lindell, & Greene, 1981, p. 33). There are usually no (or few) statutory limits on a community's ability to enter into such agreements, except possibly limits on resources. Also, the agreements do not change the locus of responsibility for public safety; this continues to rest with the government of the afflicted community.

When a local community seeks aid in a hierarchical arrangement, different constraints are introduced. A county government is responsible for public safety in unincorporated areas and in such cases may be treated as a local government. Also, counties often negotiate with municipalities and towns to provide specific resources in emergencies; these arrangements are normally concluded in much the same way as "mutual assistance" pacts and in effect operate like a horizontal agreement. Hierarchical agreements (e.g., counties or towns seeking assistance from states or the Federal government) are usually bounded by legal restraints. Thus, it is only when a community's resources are exhausted or clearly insufficient to meet disaster-imposed demands that such requests for resources may be made.

Indeed, the Federal government is restricted, under section 301(a) of the Disaster Relief Act (Public Law 93-288), from involvement in response to any disaster situation unless "the situation is of such severity and magnitude that effective response is beyond the capabilities of the State and of the affected local governments." Consequently, to obtain State or Federal help, local and/or county governments must file disaster declarations. These formal declarations then result in assessments (conducted federally or by the State) to document the extent of loss (life and property), and the ability of the locality to manage the emergency, provide short-term relief, and to recover from the event. It should be emphasized that disaster declarations are both hierarchical and interdependent; a Presidential Disaster Declaration is dependant upon declarations being filed by State and local jurisdictions as well.

Although the process of *requesting* assistance is relatively mechanical, the problem of *coordinating* the resources that accrue from such declarations is considerably more involved and frequently a thorny problem. There are at least two aspects to the problem, which might arise 1) when programmatic assistance or response personnel are involved and 2) when the request involves a horizontal or hierarchical agreement. Actually, this separation is largely analytic since, in practice, there is a correlation between type of assistance and nature of agreement.

When intergovernmental assistance takes the form of an emergency response unit (e.g., a damage assistance team, police for evacuation management of security of the impact area, or shelter facilities for victims), the question of resource coordination is relatively straightforward. Normally a "loaned" unit operates as a whole (i.e., it is not broken up and integrated into other units), provides most of its own resources, and maintains its internal chain of command. Unit commanders or managers, however, are integrated into the host community chain of command or report to the Emergency Operations Center. In this way, the "loaned" unit continues to operate under familiar rules (presumably maximizing efficiency) but directs its operation toward objectives set by the emergency managers and political leadership of the stricken community. Such loaning of units and personnel characterizes most "mutual assistance" agreements which we have defined as horizontal assistance requests. When materials are part of such agreements, they are usually delivered to the host community and are distributed through that emergency response system. The exchange of funds is exceedingly rare in this type of agreement.

The important point is that under the conditions described above, resource coordination problems tend to be minimal. In essence, service units are loaned and their operational integrity is maintained; the host community remains in control of their deployment. Thus, because mutual assistance pacts are created as part of the planning process they have the advantage of offering the opportunity to establish preplanned authority relationships. That is, it is known in advance what resources or services are to be provided and how they will be integrated into the host emergency response system. While this is most common in horizontal arrangements, the situation may also occur in hierarchical arrangements when the assistance offered, even though it may not be preplanned, involves the loan of similar response units.

Problems of resource coordination appear to be most acute when the assistance involved takes the form of grants or loans of money or material. Furthermore, these types of assistance tend to be most common in hierarchical arrangements. What arises are conflicts between authorities representing different jurisdictions regarding the deployment and use of such resources. Such difficulties have been described under the rubric of "shared governance," and arise most frequently when major disasters require action from multiple levels of government.

> In such instances Federal and State officials each have separate but overlapping authorities for disaster relief, thus necessitating their negotiating the specifics of relief assistance. In principle the responsibility for life and property lie with State and local officials, but in practice the involvement of Federal officials and funding necessitates a sharing of authority. (May & Williams, 1986, pp. 6–7)

While the sharing of authority rests at the level of political authority and decision making, disagreements at this level tend to affect the emergency response system. Such impacts usually take the form of ambiguity over *who* is in charge of setting emergency management goals, objectives, and priorities relative to the disposition of resources. When decision making at this level is slow or when conflicting decisions are issued, the operation of the emergency response system may be severely impaired.

This is in part an organizational difficulty as well. Elected authorities by law are responsible for public safety decision making, and such decisions are made and disseminated to organizations designed to act in emergencies. The decision-making style mandated for elected officials, as well as intergovernmental relations at this level, falls within the democratic ethos and tends to be participative and inclusive. Emergency response systems, as well as the organizations that constitute them, tend to be organized along paramilitary lines. Although the two decision-making systems do not integrate well with one another, they can effectively coexist, as long as the deliberations at the political level yield prompt, consistent, and unambiguous directives for the emergency response system.

Shared governance creates a situation in which the number of interests represented by participants in the decisions made at political levels are increased. This tends to slow the process of decision making and introduces the opportunity for participants representing different governmental levels to engage in extended dialog. The dialog can become newsworthy, be picked up by mass media, and consequently create the appearance of considerable confusion and indecision. At its worst, public conflict can erupt between governments and agencies, confusing the public-at-large, the public-at-risk, and the emergency management system.

One of the most striking examples of such confusion arose during the Three Mile Island (TMI) nuclear reactor accident, where different authorities routinely discredited one another during news conferences presumably designed to disseminate information about the nature of the public threat (Martin, 1980). Interestingly, the accident at TMI was "slow-developing" enough to allow the event to be defined in political terms, at least initially, rather than emergency management terms. Thus, the "shared governance" disagreements resulted in not only confusing the public but also frustrating the emergency response system. Since the system can, at least legally, only be activated by elected authorities, emergency managers were in essence forced to watch the threat situation develop while they were often even excluded from deliberations at the political level (Perry, 1985, pp. 58–59).

Both problems arising in connection with shared governance and issues of control that might arise when emergency response units are exchanged are also related to characteristics of the disaster event. As has been pointed out, threats that develop gradually produce the opportunity for far greater authority conflicts than those that are characterized by rapid onset.

Similarly, when the impact period is prolonged, when the disaster event is characterized by multiple impacts, when the level of destruction is particularly high, when many secondary threats are involved, and when systemic or prolonged threats (e.g., to public health) are involved, the probability of authority conflicts is enhanced. Few emergency plans, if any, identify the way information and data from "resource controllers" will be integrated into the postimpact decision structure of the disaster-stricken community. It seems to be implicitly assumed that local elected authorities and their administrative structures will retain decision authority. However, locals commonly complain that representatives of State and Federal aid providers displace them or usurp their authority once disaster declarations are issued.

Although such difficulties are to a certain extent endemic to disaster situations, they can be reduced through careful planning processes. The remainder of this chapter is devoted to explicating general principles of emergency planning that are designed to enhance levels of community emergency preparedness to sufficiently ensure effective operation of the emergency response system, even within the potentially problematic context of shared governance.

GENERAL PRINCIPLES OF EMERGENCY PLANNING

There has been some confusion over the years regarding exactly what constitutes disaster planning and how it relates to community preparedness. Often, planning is equated with developing a written document, and preparedness is conceived as a product of written plans. Research on disaster planning and preparedness has suggested that this conceptualization is at best inappropriate and does not adequately represent activities that emergency managers themselves label as planning (cf. Quarantelli, 1977). Disaster planning is indeed one avenue to, and a necessary component of, community preparedness as was defined at the beginning of this chapter. But planning itself is best thought of as a *process*—a collection of documents, agreements, interpersonal and interorganizational relationships, and activities that are both perpetual and ever-changing.

Disaster planning is, in effect, an approach to dealing with the environment that is driven by three objectives: risk identification, risk assessment, and risk reduction. Thus, effective planning involves not only identifying threats that currently characterize the environment but also employing procedures that lead to prompt identification of new or potential threats. Once identified, the planning process should produce an assessment of risks. This activity includes a technical evaluation of the risk, as well as a social or societal evaluation aimed at determining what level of danger is "acceptable." Risk reduction involves an examination of the resources available and actions necessary to bring existing levels of danger into line with those judged to be acceptable. Risk identification and assessment are normally thought of as *procedures* through which the environment is measured, monitored, and evaluated. Risk reduction may be thought of in two lights: as the development and recording of activities aimed at mitigation, preparedness and recovery, *or* as the response operations (concrete actions) mounted at the time of disaster impact.

Even within the context of achieving the above objectives, the practice of emergency planning varies considerably among communities and organizations. This is not a problem; it is simply a reflection of the idea that planning as an activity depends upon resources, skills, and motivations of planners, and that there is variation in the extent to which these qualities are possessed. As a process, planning may be largely formal or informal. The products associated with planning may be mostly written or unwritten. To a certain extent, the elaborateness of the planning process will correlate with the size of the community in which it takes place. Larger communities—characterized by an extensive structure of governmental offices, many resources and personnel, and perhaps higher levels of staff turnover—tend to evolve formalized processes and rely more heavily upon written documentation and agreements. In smaller communities, the planning process may generate few written products and be largely reliant upon informal, personal relationships for risk identification, assessment, and reduction. In spite of such variation, it is possible to identify planning practices that appear to be effective and to empirically correlate with high levels of community preparedness. Such practices are probably best described as approaches to planning or principles of planning. In any event, the following 10 principles have been gleaned from the research literature and represent suggested orientations for the planning process.

One of the most important attributes of emergency planning is that it should be a *continuing process.* Clearly, if planning is conceived of as an approach to dealing with the environment, there is never a time when planning is "completed." The social, physical, and technological environments are constantly changing, and planning is in part the process of detecting, monitoring, and manipulating these changes. A piece of written documentation, or a particular plan, may be generated through the planning process, but as conditions change the written documentation must also change.

Wenger, Faupel, and James (1980) have found that ". . . there is a tendency on the part of officials to see disaster planning as a product, not a process" (p. 134). This research documents the problem of confusing tangible products with the activities that produced them. Planning is written documentation: elaboration of the nature and acceptability of threats, procedures, lists of resources, and records of agreements. But planning is also made up of intangibles: communication channels, social contacts between planners and potential responders, interorganizational linkages, and various practices oriented to obtaining and distributing information. To assume that the tangibles completely capture the process is simply inaccurate. Furthermore, by treating written plans as a final product, one risks creating the illusion of being prepared for an emergency when such is not the case (cf. Quarantelli, 1977). A finalized document does not change, while the threat environment (as well as the community's resources) is in a constant state of flux.

A second characteristic of effective *planning centers upon encouraging appropriate adaptive actions.* Particularly with regard to disaster operations, much emphasis has been given to the idea that careful planning promotes quicker response. Although this is true in many respects, there remains some question whether response speed should be the primary objective of planning or simply a byproduct. Quarantelli (1977) has argued that appropriateness of response is much more crucial than speed:

> It is far more important in a disaster to obtain valid information as to what is happening than it is to take immediate action . . . . Planning in fact should help to delay impulsive reactions in preference to appropriate actions necessary in the situation. (p. 106)

Two points are significant here. First, an important part of the planning process is threat assessment which must be performed continuously, even following periods of disaster impact. Second, quick reactions based upon incorrect, misleading, or incomplete information can lead to inadequate protective measures. For example, flooding along the Platte River in 1979 threatened a small Nebraska town (Perry, Lindell, & Greene, 1981, pp. 16–19). Traditionally, floods had approached the town from the north, causing highest levels of damage in the north and east sections of the community. As the height of the river steadily rose, there was pressure on the primary emergency manager to "get a jump on the situation" by setting up an emergency operating center (EOC) and evacuee shelter in the usually dry west end of town. The emergency manager resisted, opting to follow the flood emergency plan which provided for radio-equipped patrols along the river levees to determine the direction of approach of the water. Routes of egress for evacuees, shelter locations, and EOC location were to be determined after direction of approach was established. When the levees finally failed, the downstream levees went first, causing flood waters to approach the town from the west, consequently inundating the south and west parts of the community first. In this case, the emergency manager acted appropriately by following the plan that included provisions for intelligence gathering and making response decisions based upon the best available data. It is noteworthy that to have done otherwise would have involved undertaking a response that would have generated far more danger than doing nothing. In the high-pressure atmosphere that accompanies a community disaster event, it is undoubtedly difficult for an emergency manager to acknowledge that the "best" immediate action may be to gather more information and do nothing. It is in these circumstances that the discipline provided by the planning process may save both lives and property.

The preceding example also serves to highlight another guideline for effective planning. The changing direction of approach of the water from the Platte constitutes a reminder that it is impossible to cover every contingency that might arise in connection with a given disaster event. Hence, *the planning process should emphasize flexibility* so that those involved in response operations may adjust to changing disaster agency-generated as well as response-generated demands. Thus, the planning process should focus upon principles of management and response rather than trying to elaborate the process to include many specific details. The incorporation of great detail is problematic in at least four ways: 1) The anticipation of all contingencies is simply impossible (Lindell & Perry, 1980, p. 337); 2) very specific details tend to get out of date very quickly, demanding virtually constant updating of mechanistic aspects of written products (Dynes, Quarantelli, & Kreps, 1972); 3) very specific plans often contain so many details that the wide range of emergency functions appear to be of equal importance, causing response priorities to be unclear or confused (Tierney, 1980, p. 100); and 4) the more detail incorporated into written planning documents, the larger and more complex they become, making it more difficult to communicate the plan to personnel and, consequently, making it harder to implement.

From this perspective, planning should focus upon principles of response, minimize emphasis upon delineating operational details that tend to restrict flexibility, and clearly specify priorities. It should be assumed that "responder personnel" are reasoning professionals trained to evaluate situational contingencies before acting. Attempts by planners to specify all or even most of the actions of responders are unlikely to really cover all situational contingencies, and even in the unlikely event this was possible, responders would probably eschew preplanned assessments in favor of their own evaluations anyway. It is important to remember that one purpose of planning is to promote effective response and, in so doing, one must acknowledge the realities of the setting of disaster operations. Also, heavily elaborated plans have a tendency to become "sacred documents" to planners and community officials. As such they tend to be revered rather than questioned, changed, or adapted—a state of affairs that can ultimately hinder response capability.

A fourth principle of emergency planning rests on the idea that *it has an educational component.* The planning process has many audiences, in part because many different actors are involved in implementing emergency plans. Thus, planning involves educating administrators and personnel of those departments that will be involved in any phase of the emergency response with regard to the provisions of the plan. Also, public officials need to be educated with respect to community disaster plans, preparedness, and response operations, and this education should be a product of the planning process. The public-at-risk must also be educated; they should understand that planning for community threats is underway and that they will be expected to respond to these planning efforts. Education is consequently an integral part of the disaster planning process; and, when carefully attended to, it yields high dividends in terms of the effectiveness of emergency response. As an added benefit, the educational process can also become an important source of feedback regarding potential problems with the plan.

Another principle of *planning is that it should be based upon accurate knowledge,* both of the threat and of likely human responses. Disaster planning often devotes considerable time to assessing the efficacy of protective measures and appropriate procedures and timing for their implementation. Much less attention is traditionally devoted to examining research on how people are likely to perform in an emergency and building emergency planning around people's known reaction patterns. When emergency plans are simply administratively devised, they often reflect misconceptions of how citizens behave and create more operational response problems than they solve (Perry, 1979, p. 446). Quarantelli and Dynes (1972) have succinctly described a number of common myths regarding citizen disaster response which seem to persist in spite of much research that shows otherwise. For example, one often hears the claim that citizens routinely "panic" in the face of disaster threats. This claim is often given as justification for giving the public incomplete or no information at all about some environmental threats. More than 20 years of disaster field studies have documented, however, that panic is a very rare phenomenon which occurs under highly specific conditions. Furthermore, it is also known that when citizens are provided with vague or incomplete warning messages, they are more reluctant to comply with suggested emergency measures. In this instance, a misconception about human behavior can lead to actions that hinder emergency operations. Therefore, an important part of the planning process involves a review of not only technical literature on the hazard agent, but also the social science literature describing citizens response patterns.

Emergency *planning should address organizational issues,* as well as focus upon the public to be served. The success of disaster response operations is related to the achievement of effective interorganizational coordination among responding groups and organizations. Ideally, such organizations work in concert to accomplish a variety of disaster-relevant functions: threat detection, population warning, damage assessment, sheltering, and so on. To complete these tasks requires that organizations be aware of one another's missions, structures, and styles of operation, that a communication system exists, and that there are mutually agreed-upon response priorities and rules for determining which organization is responsible for which operations.

The process of planning is one of the most effective places (also the most desirable) for resolving these and related issues in advance of a disaster event. It is true that there are two other settings in which such issues are resolved. The first of these is by repeated drills and tests of the plan. Indeed, drills are the "planned" setting for "mistakes" to happen and for details to be ironed out. It could become a very tedious process, however, if drills were the only avenue for anticipating and correcting problems. Much time and frustration can be saved if the planning process is conducted in such a way that assumptions about response performance may be scrutinized even before the plan is tested. Another place, and by far the least desirable, where problems of coordination can be identified is during the response phase to a community disaster. Even in the absence of drills and effective planning, the repeated experience of dealing with disaster events will force organizations to devise workable coordination strategies. This option carries with it a very high cost, however, especially when it is acknowledged that alternatives are available.

As an example of the role of the planning process in detecting interorganizational problems, consider the southwestern city that wanted to upgrade its capacity to respond to hazardous materials incidents generated by airplane crashes. The city bordered a large regional airport. Although the city's police department had plans for responding to airliner crashes and its fire department maintained a hazardous materials response plan, there was minimal integration of these planning efforts. The newly created emergency management office was given the task of developing a comprehensive plan for crashes involving hazardous materials. Fortunately, the planning process established by the new emergency manager included full equipment lists of all resources to be used by an organization responding to such a disaster event. It was in reviewing these lists that the emergency manager discovered the police and fire department radio equipment was such that neither department could pick up a signal from the other's equipment. Yet, the police were charged with citizen management and the fire fighters with technical materials management in the same event. Had the emergency manager simply "folded" the two plans together instead of relying on review procedures as part of the planning process, this discrepancy may not have been discovered until the plan was tested, or worse, until an airliner crashed.

Still another principle of preparedness planning is that *it is almost always implemented and maintained in the face of resistance* (Quarantelli, 1982, p. 25). There are a multitude of truisms in emergency planning; one is that citizens don't like to think about the negative consequences of potential disasters. This attitude can be generalized as well to public officials: mayors, county executives, city and county managers, and city and county councils. A common objection to planning raised by such officials is that it consumes resources, and resources spent on planning cannot be spent on what, at the moment, may seem like more pressing community issues. In some cases (e.g., nuclear power plants), planning is mandated by Federal law and resistance is less formidable. In general, however, the initiation of planning activities requires strong advocacy from participants in the emergency response system.

Another important component of the planning process is the provision for *testing proposed response operations*. As was pointed out above, tests of plans or drills provide a setting in which operational details may be carefully examined. Testing of plans also serves other important functions. Testing forces responder organizations to meet, enabling personnel to begin to develop personal relationships with one another. Furthermore, drills constitute a comprehensive test of emergency planning; personnel, procedures, and equipment are all tested simultaneously. Not only do drills serve an educational function for the personnel involved, they constitute one form of "publicity" for the larger disaster planning and management process that informs both the public and community officials that plans are being tested and their efficacy evaluated.

Disaster preparedness planning should also be an *integrative process* with respect to the broader problem of disaster management. It is important to identify emergency functions that were important to perform across a variety of disaster events: warning, evacuation, emergency medical and mental health care, search and rescue, victim sheltering, and so forth. The planning process should be sensitive to multiple use opportunities for procedures and functions devised for use in one type of event which may also be useful in others. This property of generic functions is often cited as one of the strongest arguments for comprehensive emergency management, but it requires careful attention as part of the planning process before management benefits may be realized.

A final principle of preparedness planning may be found in the acknowledgment that *planning is not management;* rather, it is related to response (Quarantelli, 1985). Planning is preparing — isolating what are believed to be the important agent-generated and response-generated demands and developing strategies to meet them. Management, on the other hand, involves performance — actually responding to demands in part by carrying out those actions needed to meet the specifications of a plan. It can be argued that planning lays out the design for a shirt while management involves cutting the cloth and sewing. Confusing the two functions leads to poor performance of both.

PRODUCTS OF THE PLANNING PROCESS

The principles of emergency planning discussed above focus upon *process;* accounting for the organization of the emergency response in broadest context. The review of process emphasizes not only what needs to be done to assure community preparedness, but who is involved and how this involvement is organized. Ultimately, of course, intergovernmental coordination for emergencies may be greatly enhanced by the quality of the planning process, but when it comes to delivering promised resources the tendency is to depend heavily upon written documentation. Particularly when settling disputes that arise in a situation dominated by shared governance, formalized agreements are critical.

A principal byproduct of the planning process is the production of the written plan. It is in this format that both procedures and resource dependencies are formalized. To conclude this discussion of intergovernmental coordination issues in emergency planning, the structure of a community preparedness plan will be reviewed. In an effort to keep this review of plan content in perspective, it should be mentioned that the planning *process* is endorsed as the more significant activity. Written plans themselves may be seen as byproducts (not end products) of the planning process which change as planning adapts to new threats, new assessments of old threats, and new mechanisms for risk reduction. The written plan is a "slice of life" which simply reflects the state of planning at some given point in time. Thus, in our view, the "best" plans are concise, clear, well-structured, easily updated, and short. A document so constructed is more likely to be used by planners and responders, and less likely to become relegated to the status of simply another book to be stored indefinitely on a shelf.

It is not our intention to condemn the construction of written plans; they are an important part of the planning and response process when their function and role are understood. Just as there are many variants on the planning process, so are there many views on what elements make up a preparedness plan. Rather than try to describe all the varieties of plans, our tactic will be to simply describe our approach, which may then be distinguished as appropriate from competing approaches.

Our goal is to identify the elements of a comprehensive written plan that collects all of the documentation associated with a particular local government's (or organization's) strategy for coping with environmental threats. The basic premise here is that a plan is being developed which addresses general administrative and functional issues and deals with specific threats in a series of annexes. Hence, our presentation of plan elements will be divided into three parts: the general plan, generic functions, and special threat annexes.

Our discussion of these elements is purposely general; it is not our objective to provide the base for a "model plan." Like Quarantelli (1985), we belive that the concept of a model plan should be viewed very cautiously. It is simply *not possible* to devise an effective emergency response plan by copying or doing a "light adaptation" of someone else's plan to your jurisdiction. In some way, each jurisdiction is unique, with its own peculiar combination of communication problems and practices, resources, structure, and approach to managing people and the environment. An important part of the planning process and its products (the emergency plan) is working through the ways in which the unique character of the community can be (in effect, *must* be) dealt with to mount a response to environmental threats. The complete or partial adoption of a model plan subverts or shortcuts the planning process, thereby canceling many of the benefits of the process which are usually felt in the operations phase. Consequently, the primary function of model plans is to provide a guide for topics which should be considered and the structure for writing a jurisdiction-specific plan. In this spirit, the comments that follow are meant largely to identify important topics and issues that should be addressed in a formal emergency response plan.

The General Plan

This section contains provisions that establish the legal bases, technical bases, and administrative aspects of the plan. As a rule, these provisions are captured under six separate headings.

The Authority of the plan is routinely established at the beginning of the document. Government, whether local, state or federal, has both the authority and the responsibility to protect its citizens. During states of emergency, the power to act may be derived from a variety of sources, including laws, general police powers, and special statutes. The statement of authority is usually either an abbreviated listing or simple citation of the legal bases of the plan and the planning process.

The aim and scope of the plan represents an effort to concisely describe both the substance and breadth of the plan's general purpose. It is here that one establishes under what conditions the plan is activated. This specification should include the functional titles of the person(s) who can initiate plan activation. It is also appropriate to describe the conditions that call for plan deactivation and the individuals responsible for making such decisions. The statement of purpose is usually brief and serves to identify the major goals of the plan, the governmental unit that forms the focal organization (e.g., a municipality or county), and a listing of any protective obligations under the plan for jurisdictions other than the focal organization.

Comprehensive plans also typically contain a *hazard or vulnerability analysis.* Of course, a full analysis of the hazard environment of a community or region is completely outside the scope of what's called for in an emergency plan (cf. Truby & Boulas, 1983). It is appropriate, however, to identify all hazards addressed as special annexes and provide some minimal descriptive information. Ketchum and Whittaker (1982, p. 15) suggest that this information include disaster incidence, average severity of impact, probability of occurrence, and areas of the community that are most vulnerable.

The general plan should include a recounting of all *reciprocal agreements* for aid or support during the period of emergency operations. Such agreements might be established with other nearby local governments, private organizations, business concerns, or State and Federal government agencies. For each agreement with an organization, four items of information should be listed. First, there should be a declaration of the conditions under which the agreement takes effect, accompanied by the title of the individual who activates the assisting organization. Second, the precise nature of the assistance to be rendered should be specified. Third, a listing of resources available for loan (both equipment and personnel) and their locations should be included. Finally, there should be some specification of how personnel from the assisting organization will be deployed (whether they will work as a unit or integrate into host agency groups) and to whom they will report.

Another topic of concern in the general plan section is a description of the *provisions for testing the plan.* As was pointed out in the preceding section, all plans should be rehearsed on a regular basis. Such rehearsals provide an opportunity for personnel to develop working relationships with one another, for staff to learn the provisions of the plan, for testing interagency and intergovernmental agreements, and for positive (credibility building) publicity regarding emergency management efforts.

Finally, the sixth element of the general plan section addresses *administrative issues.* Typically, this involves specification of four procedural matters. First, there should be a description of the procedures to be followed in revising and updating the plan. It is a good practice to review plans twice each year for potential updates—personnel changes, telephone number changes, equipment list changes, new or expired mutual aid agreements. Second, there should be a record of plan distribution. This is necessary to ensure that all holders of plans are notified of revisions and to minimize the chance that a person or organization holds an "outdated" plan. Third, there should be a record of all previous plan amendments with the date they were undertaken. Fourth, there should be an authority and organization chart that shows the chain of command that will prevail during emergencies and the decision-making authority during nonemergency times.

Generic Functions

Generic functions are simply activities in which authorities must engage that are relevant to a variety of disaster events. Generic functions may arise in connection with either agent-generated or response-generated demands. The reason for explicitly including these issues in a comprehensive emergency plan centers on the idea that they are repeatedly used. In each case, the function described is carried out by a network of organizations, agencies, and individuals, sometimes acting relatively independently and sometimes in concert with one another. This condition raises two important points. First, each organization involved will have its own standard operating procedure (SOP) which serves as a detailed plan for executing its part of some given function. Consequently, while such SOPs need to be referenced in the comprehensive plan, the actual treatment of the function in the comprehensive plan can be brief and focused. Second, for every generic function discussed, there should be designation of the lead organization charged with seeing that the task is carried out, a list of all organizations involved in the function with a statement of their missions, and a contact or call list for activating the organizations.

Briefly discussed here are nine generic functions which might be addressed in a written plan. Our comments will focus upon the prime tasks associated with each function and identification of issues that arise in the operations setting.

Some form of *warning system* is used in almost every type of community emergency. In a comprehensive plan, a discussion of warning systems should include several components. The major monitoring systems through which alerts of environmental hazards reach community officials should be briefly described; this discussion usually includes mention of a "duty officer" system or some other mechanism used to ensure 24-hour coverage of the monitoring systems. The plan should designate which officials are to be notified of impending threats and under what circumstances notification will be initiated. The conditions for notifying the public-at-risk and the public-at-large would most likely be communicated to the agency or group charged with public information.

A discussion of warning systems must address relevant dissemination issues: 1) the identification of the individual who has the legal authority to issue public warnings; 2) the specification of who is responsible for warning message construction and choice of dissemination mode; 3) a listing of the organizations involved in warning dissemination; and 4) the identification of who will be responsible for constructing and ordering the dissemination of an all-clear signal.

Evacuation is probably one of the most commonly used generic functions that constitutes a protective measure in itself. For the most part, the actual movement of people is considered perfunctory and rarely elaborated in written form. Specific techniques depend upon the lead agency's standard operating procedure and upon the experience of the persons involved. There are a variety of issues, however, that merit comment in the comprehensive plan.

The decision to evacuate people and the warning to individuals themselves comes under the purview of what has been called warning systems. Most important, an evacuation annex will establish the lead agency for the relocation effort and lay out procedures for coordinating the timing and conduct of citizen movement with the agency or group responsible for establishing temporary shelters. The annex should contain a listing of resources that may be needed in evacuations (e.g., barricades, traffic cones) and the locations where such resources are stored. Decision-making rules should be established for choosing evacuation routes and for maintaining the flow of private vehicles.

Victim sheltering and welfare is a common operational demand placed upon emergency managers. We refer here only to what Quarantelli (1982, p. 75) has called "emergency sheltering" and "temporary sheltering," which involve the relatively short-term provision, from a few hours to a few days, of care for disaster victims. The emergency plan should designate a coordinator for shelter operations who would then be responsible for dealing with groups operating shelters (usually the Red Cross and Salvation Army, but other groups as well, including the local government). Procedures for coordinating the sheltering function with the emergency medical services function, the search and rescue function, and the mass feeding function should also be specified. A decision logic for locating the shelters to be opened is also necessary. The nature of the disaster impact — delineations of what areas are safe and for how long — and projections of the number of people involved will bear upon this logic.

Although provisions for either temporary or permanent housing of victims would not be part of a community's emergency response plan, some consideration must be given to the housing of victims after a disaster, especially one which results in a State or Federal disaster declaration. Within days after the event, special State and Federal programs can be activated to provide housing for disaster victims whose residences have become uninhabitable. In many instances, vacancy rates in disaster-stricken communities fall to zero, which may result in people leaving the community. One alternative that residents as well as local officials find initially attractive is the provision of mobile homes by the Federal Emergency Management Agency (FEMA). Victims can then use these facilities until more permanent housing becomes available or until their homes are rebuilt. However, the decisions of where to set up these "temporary" mobile home parks or whether to allow trailers to be established on private property that is not zoned for such use can become a source of major contention in a disaster-stricken community. This "temporary" solution often becomes a long-term headache for local officials during the recovery phase of a disaster, long after FEMA has withdrawn from the community (cf. Tierney, 1985), and is seldom used now by FEMA.

A prime concern in the operation of shelters is the development of a system for recording *who* is in the shelter. This allows for the process of reuniting separated families and enables accurate counts for feeding and sleeping facilities.

Emergency medical care and morgues constitute generic functions which are normally executed by specially trained individuals operating in specially equipped facilities. The comprehensive emergency plan usually specifies the lead organization or person for emergency medical services. There are often decision rules for the location of emergency medical facilities in the plan, as well as provisions for the transportation of people who require medical care. Lists of hospitals and other medical facilities (and the nature of their equipment and staff) are commonly included in disaster plans.

In most jurisdictions, the establishment of morgues and the handling of dead in disasters (and generally) are regulated by law (cf. Hershiser & Quarantelli, 1976, p. 195). Emergency plans normally specify the location of temporary and permanent morgues, the procedures for moving dead to the morgues, and the procedures for claiming bodies. Also, provisions are routinely made for maintaining records of both identified and unidentified bodies.

Research has documented that the *search and rescue* function often takes place in loosely structured situations with uncertain exercise of authority (cf. Quarantelli, 1980). This emphasizes the need for plan specification of 1) a coordinator for the search and rescue (SAR) effort, and 2) a listing of organizations (public and private) available for SAR work. Since volunteers (sometimes victims) are routinely involved in rescue, some plans include a procedure for documenting their presence and incorporating them into work groups.

Drabek et al. (1981, pp. 240–241) point out that unplanned contacts with the mass media form a key operational problem resulting in the inappropriate release of victims' names, harassment of victims, and inappropriate release of information about the progress of disaster operations. To minimize such difficulties, procedures can be developed in the plan to more explicitly manage media relations. This might be accomplished by excluding the media from rescue operations through controlling access to operations areas, by assigning a staff member to "media relations," or by briefing SAR workers themselves on what information can be appropriately released to whom.

Finally, the plan should carry some discussion of the "urban heavy rescue" component of SAR (Olson & Olson, 1985). Heavy rescue refers to recovering victims from urban building collapse and is currently an important issue in earthquake preparedness planning. The plan should contain several provisions regarding heavy rescue: 1) a list of available heavy rescue equipment; 2) a logic for what kinds of buildings to excavate first in the event of multiple collapses; and 3) a protocol for coordinating traditional heavy rescue efforts with "high technology" victim search efforts.

Damage assessment is another generic function which requires explicit treatment in the plan. One of the most important points about damage assessment is that it should be a continuing process rather than a one-time accounting of damage. Depending on the type of disaster impact, assessment teams may be required to report very frequently (perhaps hourly in some technological disasters). Without specifying a minimum timing, it is important to establish assessment as an ongoing activity. In this connection, there should be explicit communication links between the damage assessment coordinator and the Emergency Operations Center (EOC). Damage assessment must also deal with the full range of damages from primary as well as secondary threats and should involve provisions for anticipating short-term dangers (public health threats for example) associated with recorded damages.

For the most part, *security and property protection*—like evacuation—is a function considered to be perfunctory and not given extensive attention in a comprehensive emergency response plan. The details of such a function would be part of the standard operating procedures of the organizations delivering the service. Several issues do merit attention in the general plan, however. It is particularly important that a lead agency be established, and clear lines of authority and coordination be delineated among all organizations involved in security. Furthermore, a major initial priority (and one that persists throughout the emergency) involves securing the impact area. At a minimum, the plan should address: 1) What agency is in charge at the scene and the rules for relinquishing control to other agencies; 2) what type of controlled access plans should be instituted; and 3) what type of patrol system or surveillance is necessary to achieve property protection.

Public information is a particularly crucial generic function; it has been a high-planning priority since the communications fiasco was demonstrated to be an operational hindrance in the 1979 accident at the Three Mile Island nuclear power plant (Perry, 1985). In the comprehensive plan, care should be taken to clarify the structure through which information will be communicated to the public. Several issues must be dealt with in particular: 1) A chief of public information should be assigned; 2) all other officials, responders, and managers associated with the emergency response should be instructed to direct all media to the public information officer (PIO); and 3) the PIO should maintain open lines of communication and be in close contact at all times with the EOC and the overall coordinator of the emergency response. An effort should be made to centralize and formalize the public information effort through the assignment of specific space for press briefings and the scheduling of regular briefings. Also, it should be acknowledged that there are at least four primary audiences for public information: the public-at-risk, the public-at-large, governments in which a responding jurisdiction may be nested, and officials of relevant regulatory agencies. The responsibility of the PIO to communicate with the public-at-risk is shared with officials controlling the warning systems function. The PIO is the chief contact with the other three audiences. Each audience demands specialized information slightly different from the others. In particular, regulatory agencies and interested governments may require considerable technical information regarding the event (which may require careful coordination among those responsible for all of the generic functions listed here). Further, the public-at-large may be roughly divided into two segments, both requiring different types of event-relevant information: 1) the geographically nearby public, not yet in danger; and 2) the geographically distant public, not in danger.

Finally, the establishment of an *Emergency Operations Center* should be addressed in a comprehensive response plan. Most large municipalities and counties have a permanent EOC which is often a reinforced, perhaps specially designed, structure. In situations where there is no permanent EOC, the plan should contain provisions that specify the equipment necessary for the EOC, decision rules for the location of the EOC, and rules for when the EOC is to become operative and when it closes down.

The EOC is the hub of emergency response operations; it is from here that the overall assault on the environmental threat is managed. The prime function of the EOC is the gathering and relaying of information regarding all aspects of the emergency. Thus, the plan should establish the communications lines to be used and the authority between the EOC and all field command posts. The plan should establish what organizations should be represented in the EOC, with how many staff, and how the staff are to be rotated (cf. Stallings, 1971, p. 27). As the center of technical decision making during the emergency, EOC should have direct communications links to the relevant political authorities.

Specific Disaster Annexes

The number and types of specific disaster annexes included in a plan are a function of the hazard or vulnerability analysis for the particular community served. An annex is usually included for every threat for which planning is legally mandated (e.g., nuclear power plant accidents), all threats with a high probability of impact, and some low probability threats which carry high levels of negative consequences (e.g., volcanic eruptions).

Once again, the content of the special annexes is not meant to replace or duplicate the content of the standard operating procedures of the organizations involved in emergency response. A major concern in the annex is to focus upon specific issues of interorganizational or intergovernmental coordination. The lead organizations in each of the generic functions applicable to the threat should be established, along with rules for interacting with other responding organizations. Another major concern is the treatment of agent-generated demands and the specification of how they will be met. In particular, each annex should address the nature and types of protective measures to be implemented, as well as the strategies available for implementation. Specialized data on protective actions in a variety of disaster events are available in any number of event-specific planning guides (cf. Defense Civil Preparedness Agency, 1972; Hildebrand, 1980; U.S. Nuclear Regulatory Commission, 1980; Tierney, 1980; White & Haas, 1975). Such strategies should include consideration of any "unique" features of the threat, including psychological consequences for persons-at-risk, and secondary impacts that might require special management provisions.

MENTAL HEALTH PROGRAMS AND DISASTER RESPONSE PLANNING

As is obvious by its absence in the above discussions, the provision of mental health services following disaster events has not been well integrated into the emergency response planning process. However, through disaster declarations at different levels of government, special funding can be made available during both the immediate postimpact and short-term recovery periods to allow mental health professionals to provide assistance to residents of disaster-stricken areas as well as to those aiding in the response efforts (Lystad, 1985).

Although there has not been extensive research conducted on the prevalence, nature, dynamics, or duration of disaster-related emotional problems (Tierney, 1986), practitioner professionals in the field have identified some general principles to be used when postdisaster services are needed (Cohen & Ahearn, 1980; Farberow, 1979; Farberow & Gordon, 1981; Lystad, 1985; Solomon, 1985). Primarily, these writers have applied a community mental health ideology (Bloom, 1977) to disaster crisis intervention programs. This approach is based on preventing illness and encouraging positive psychological functioning of the entire community, not only of those who exhibit some type of extreme stress symptoms (Tierney, 1986).

From a review of this literature about how mental health efforts should be undertaken, it becomes clear that an attempt to merely "fold in" these programs under the generic response planning function which is concerned with disaster victims' welfare *after* the event is not feasible. For example, in her discussion of intervention strategies, Solomon (1985) suggests using indigenous personnel in naturally occurring support networks to transmit information, to develop case-finding strategies for the mental health professionals, and to identify unmet emotional and social needs among community residents. In order to use such strategies, mental health organizations must be incorporated in the *preparedness*, not just the response, planning process. This incorporation will provide them with timely information needed to assess the potential need for mental health services, legitimate access to disaster personnel and decision makers, and a role in the interorganizational process that is more commensurate with a community mental health perspective.

REFERENCES

Bloom, B. L. (1977). *Community Mental Health: A General Introduction.* Monterey, CA: Brooks/Cole.

Cohen, R., & Ahearn F. (1980). *Handbook for Mental Health Care of Disaster Victims.* Baltimore: Johns Hopkins University Press.

Defense Civil Preparedness Agency (1972). *Disaster Operations.* Washington, D.C.: Department of Defense.

Drabek, T. (1987). *Human System Responses to Disaster.* New York: Springer-Verlag.

Drabek, T., Tamminga, H., Kilijanek, T., & Adams, C. (1981). *Managing Multiorganizational Emergency Responses.* Boulder, CO: University of Colorado, Institute for Behavioral Science.

Dynes, R. (1983). Problems in emergency planning. *Energy,* 8(8): 635–660.

Dynes, R., Quarantelli, E., & Kreps, G. (1972). *A. Perspective on Disaster Planning.* Newark, DE: Disaster Research Center, University of Delaware.

Farberow, N. (1979). *Training Manual for Human Service Workers in Major Disasters.* DHEW Publication (ADM)79–538. Washington, D.C.: U.S. Government Printing Office.

Faberow, N., & Gordon, N. (1981). *Manual for Child Health Workers in Major Disasters.* DHHS Publication (ADM)81–1071. Washington, D.C.: U.S. Government Printing Office.

Foster, H. (1980). *Disaster Planning.* New York: Springer-Verlag.

Fritz, C., & Mathewson, J. H. (1957). *Convergence Behavior in Disasters.* Washington, D.C.: National Academy of Sciences–National Research Council.

Hershiser, M., & Quarantelli, E. (1976). The handling of dead in a disaster. *Omega,* 7(3): 195–208.

Hildebrand, M. (1980). *Disaster Planning Guidelines for Fire Chiefs.* Washington, D.C.: Federal Emergency Management Agency.

Ketchum, J., & Whittaker, H. (1982). Hazards analysis. *Comprehensive Emergency Management Bulletin,* 2(May): 1–17.

Lindell, M., & Perry, R. (1980). Evaluation criteria for emergency response plans in radiological transportation. *Journal of Hazardous Materials,* 3(3): 335–348.

Lystad, M. (1985). Facilitating mitigation through mental health services after a disaster. Paper presented for the American Bar Association, International Symposium on Housing and Urban Development after Natural Disasters, Miami, Florida.

Martin, D. (1980). *Three Mile Island.* Cambridge, MA: Ballinger Publishing Co.

May, P., & Williams, W. (1986). *Disaster Policy Implementation.* New York: Plenum.

Olson, R., & Olson, R. (1985). *Urban Heavy Rescue.* Tempe, AZ: Office of Hazards Studies, Arizona State University.

Perry, R. (1979). Incentives for evacuation in natural disasters. *Journal of the American Planning Association,* 45(October): 440–447.

Perry, R. (1985). *Comprehensive Emergency Management.* Greenwich, CT: JAI Press.

Perry, R., & Lindell, M. (1987). *Handbook of Emergency Response Planning.* New York: Harper & Row (Hemisphere Imprint).

Perry, R., Lindell, M., & Greene, M. (1981). *Evacuation Planning in Emergency Management.* Lexington, MA: Heath-Lexington Books.

Quarantelli, E. (1977). Social aspects of disasters and their relevance to pre-disaster planning. *Disasters,* 1(1): 98–107.

Quarantelli, E. (1980). *Evacuation Behavior and Problems.* Newark, DE: Disaster Research Center, University of Delaware.

Quarantelli, E. (1982). *Human Resources and Organizational Behaviors in Community Disasters and Their Relationship to Planning.* Newark, DE: Disaster Research Center, University of Delaware.

Quarantelli, E. (1983). *A Summary Research Observations Relevant to Sheltering and Housing in American Disasters.* Newark, DE: Disaster Research Center, University of Delaware.

Quarantelli, E. (1985). *The Functioning of Local Emergency Services Offices in Disasters.* Newark, DE: Disaster Research Center, University of Delaware.

Quarantelli, E., & Dynes, R. (1972). When disaster strikes. *Psychology Today,* 5(February): 67–70.

Quarantelli, E., & Dynes, R. (1977). Response to social crisis and disaster. *Annual Review of Sociology,* 2: 23–49.

San Francisco Examiner (1906). Examiner special first in relief. III (124): April 19, p. 1.

Solomon, S. D. (1985). Enhancing social support for disaster victims. In B. J. Sowder (Ed.), *Disasters and Mental Health: Selected Contemporary Perspectives* (pp. 107–121). Rockville, MD: National Institute of Mental Health.

Stallings, R. (1971). *Communications in Natural Disaster.* Newark, DE: Disaster Research Center, University of Delaware.

Tierney, K. (1980). *A Primer for Preparedness in Acute Chemical Disasters.* Newark, DE: Disaster Research Center, University of Delaware.

Tierney, K. (1985). *Report on the Coalinga Earthquake of May 2, 1983.* Sacramento, CA: Seismic Safety Commission. SSC Report No. 8501.

Tierney, K. J. (1986). Disasters and mental health: A critical look at knowledge and practice. Paper prepared for the University of Delaware Italy-United States Conference on Disasters, Newark, Delaware.

Truby, J., & Boulas, L. (1983). *Colorado's Vulnerability to Very High Risk Natural Hazards.* Golden, Colorado: Colorado Division of Disaster Emergency Services.

U.S. Nuclear Regulatory Commission (1980). *Report to Congress on the Status of Emergency Response Planning for Nuclear Power Plants* (NUREG–0–0755). Washington, D.C.: Nuclear Regulatory Commission.

Wenger, D., Faupel, C., & James, T. (1980). *Disaster Beliefs and Emergency Planning.* Newark, DE: Disaster Research Center, University of Delaware.

White, G., & Haas, E. (1975). *Assessment of Research on Natural Hazards.* Cambridge, MA: MIT Press.

15

Planning for Health/Mental Health Integration in Emergencies

BRUNO R. LIMA, HERNAN SANTACRUZ,
JULIO LOZANO, and JAIRO LUNA

Disasters, defined as "crisis occasions in which demands exceed capabilities" (Quarantelli, 1985), are common occurrences, but their impact on the psychiatric and psychosocial state of adults and children is still controversial. Various studies have either suggested little or no negative effects (Bromet, Schulbert, & Dunn, 1982; Dohrenwend et al., 1981; Mellick, 1978; Quarantelli & Dynes, 1977), whereas others have suggested significant consequences (Dunal et al., 1985; Glass, 1959; Hoiberg & McCaughey, 1984; Kinston & Rosser, 1974; Parker, 1975; Patrick & Patrick, 1981; Perry & Lindell, 1978; Popovic & Petrovic, 1964; Shore, Tatum, & Vollmer, 1986; Titchener & Kapp, 1976; Wilkinson, 1983). These consequences include long-term effects (Gleser, Green, & Winget, 1981; Leopold & Dillon, 1963) and effects on children (Burke et al., 1982; Newman, 1976). The controversy relates both to the assessment of certain characteristics of the disaster, such as the scope of the impact, the speed of onset, the duration of the impact and the social preparedness of the

Supported by the Johns Hopkins University School of Medicine; the University Javeriana School of Medicine, Bogota, Colombia; the Divisions of Mental Health of the Tolima Health Department and the Colombian Ministry of Health; the Pan American Health Organization; and the Natural Hazards Research and Applications Information Center, University of Colorado.

community (Barton, 1969), and to the research methodology utilized, which includes sampling processes, criteria for case identification, and timing of the study (Green, 1982). For disasters in developing countries, clinical observations (Lima, 1986a), empirical evidence (Ahearn, 1984; Cohen, 1985), and preliminary research data (Lima et al., 1987) indicate that psychosocial consequences are usually significant and need to be handled promptly and effectively.

The primary case worker has been effective in providing mental health care in routine clinical situations both in developed (Strain et al., 1983) and in developing countries (Busnello, Lima, & Bertolote, 1985), but his/her mental health interventions in disasters, particularly in the medium- and long-term care of victims, have remained largely unexplored. This chapter is partially based on our experience in planning, implementing, and evaluating the delivery of primary mental health care in routine clinical settings, and partially based on our experience in managing and evaluating the psychiatric and psychosocial problems of victims of the volcanic eruption in Colombia in 1985, which destroyed the town of Armero. To be initially reviewed are selected issues on primary mental health care in general as a background for understanding their relation-ship to a disaster situation. A description of the Armero project will follow, outlining its origins and development. The implications of this project are discussed as they relate to research design and implementation, to the education and training of primary care workers in mental health, and to health planning. It is expected that the Colombian experience of delivering mental health care to disaster victims through the primary care sector, immediately relevant to disasters in other developing nations, will also be applicable to disasters occurring in developed countries, where for logistic, clinical, or cultural reasons, the delivery of mental health care through the specialized mental health sector may be inadequate, ineffective, or unacceptable.

PRIMARY MENTAL HEALTH CARE

The importance of primary care as the main strategy for attaining the goal of "health for all by the year 2000" (Pan American Health Organization, 1980) has been widely accepted. Primary health care has been defined by the World Health Organization (WHO) as:

essential health care made universally accessible to individuals and families in the community by means acceptable to them, through their full participation and at a cost that the community and country can afford. It forms an integral part both of the country's health system of which it is the nucleus and of the overall social and economic development of the community. (World Health Organization, 1978)

The main steps used to ensure primary care include:

- extension of health care coverage and improvement of environmental conditions;
- community organization for active participation of the community in its own well-being;
- development of intersectorial collaboration;
- development of appropriate research and technology;
- availability of human, financial, and physical resources; and
- international cooperation.

Primary health care services must be organized to ensure that they will be delivered longitudinally, locally, comprehensively, in a personalized manner, and with the full participation of the community. Primary health care involves a variety of priority areas, such as maternal and child health, immunizations, acute respiratory diseases, malaria, food and nutrition, cardiovascular and degenerative diseases, cancer, occupational diseases, and mental health (Pan American Health Organization, 1980).

Mental health is one of the essential elements of primary care both in developed countries (Shepherd, 1980), where it has been called the "keystone of community psychiatry" (World Health Organization, 1973), and in developing nations (World Health Organization, 1975), where the success of mental health programs largely depends on how successfully mental health care is integrated with primary health care (Lin, 1983). Mental health is part of the various activities developed for health promotion and disease prevention and it aims at achieving the following goals (Gulbinat, 1983):

- prevention and treatment of psychiatric disorders, which is the classic model;
- increased application of mental health knowledge to general health programs; and
- prevention of the harmful consequences of accelerated social changes.

The need to provide primary mental health services is widely supported by clinical epidemiological studies. Fifteen to twenty-five percent of patients attending primary care clinics in both the developed (Shepherd, 1967) and developing countries (Climent et al., 1980; Harding et al., 1980) have diagnosable mental health problems. Furthermore, even in the United States, where extensive specialized mental health resources are available, 60% of the patients with emotional and psychiatric problems are managed through the general/primary care sector (Regier, Goldberg, & Taube, 1978), and almost one half of all office visits to a physician resulting in a mental disorder diagnosis are to nonpsychiatrists, mostly in primary care (Schurman, Kramer, & Mitchell, 1985). It can be assumed that a similar pattern of service utilization exists in developing countries where specialized mental health resources are blatantly inadequate (Harding, 1976).

Hence, various efforts have been made to develop the capability of the primary care sector for the identification and management of patients with emotional problems. The WHO study on "Strategies for Extending Mental Health Care" has identified crucial programmatic aspects for the successful design and implementation of a primary mental health care program (World Health Organization, 1984):

- formulation of a national policy on mental health and the establishment of a mental health department or unit within each country's national or regional administration;
- adequate financial provision for
  —the recruitment, training, and employment of personnel,
  —the adequate provision of drugs,
  —a network of facilities, including transportation,
  —data collection and research;
- the decentralization of mental health services, integration of mental health services with the general health services, and the development of collaboration with nonmedical community agencies;
- the utilization of nonspecialized health workers at all levels, from primary health worker to nurse or doctor, for certain tasks of basic mental health care;
- the utilization of specialized mental health workers for most of their working hours in training and supervising the nonspecialized health workers who will provide basic mental health care in the community;
- the training of mental health professionals in this new task of training and supporting nonspecialized health workers.

In developing countries, the primary care worker may be the general doctor or the nurse, but more frequently he or she is a person with limited education and training, selected by the local community, or with the community's agreement, to perform basic health actions (World Health Organization, 1980). His mental health training has included the conditions seen in routine clinical practice, such as (Harding et al., 1980):

- first aid in neuropsychiatric emergencies;
- maintenance treatment of the chronically mentally ill;
- advice and support to high-risk families;
- referral of mentally ill people in a nonacute or unclear state to the nearest health facilities;
- family education about psychosocial development and the needs of the elderly and the handicapped;
- support and education of the mentally ill about self-care; and
- collaboration with community leaders in activities aimed at protecting and promoting mental health.

In developed countries, the primary care worker has been variously defined (Spiegel et al., 1983), but may include the family doctor, the internist, the gynecologist or the pediatrician (Draper & Smits, 1975), as well as the specialist (Aiken et al., 1979), or the intermediate-level health professional, such as the physician assistant or the nurse practitioner (Lamb & Napodano, 1984; Rosenaur et al., 1984). Mental health training of these workers may vary considerably (Burns & Scott, 1982; Cohen-Cole & Bird, 1984).

To increase the effectiveness of mental health interventions by the primary care worker, priority mental health problems for the primary level of care have been identified by the WHO (1984) and include:

- psychiatric emergencies;
- chronic psychiatric disorders;
- mental health problems of patients attending health units, general clinics, and other curative services; and
- psychiatric and emotional problems of high-risk groups.

These broad categories have to be adjusted to local needs following the criteria developed for pediatric priorities in developing countries (Morley, 1973) and adapted for psychiatric problems in primary care (Giel & Harding, 1976). These criteria include the point-prevalence and seriousness of the problem, the existence of simple techniques for its management, and the concern of the community. When these criteria are applied to disasters, victims can be considered a priority population for primary mental health care for various reasons:

- disaster victims are known to be a group at high risk for developing emotional problems;
- it has been shown that significant psychological problems are indeed present among disaster victims;
- the community is usually concerned about the disaster and its health and mental health consequences for the victims; and
- it has been shown that the primary care worker can be trained to carry out relatively simple and well-defined mental health interventions for the identification and management of problems seen in primary care settings (Harding et al., 1983), and it can be expected that he/she can be equally trained to intervene with similar effectiveness with disaster victims.

Primary mental health care for disaster victims, however, has been an area of surprising neglect in disaster relief planning (Lechat, 1979). Attention has been paid to mental health interventions in the more immediate postimpact phase (Cohen, 1982), but the primary care worker has not been involved in the management of the medium- and long-term psychological consequences of a disaster (Pan American Health Organization, 1981). Disasters are more likely to affect socioeconomically disadvantaged populations, in both developed and developing countries, as the fast rise in the population of some cities, the pressure on the land, and the steadily deteriorating economic conditions have forced the underprivileged population into more hazardous areas, hence rendering them more prone to disasters (Seaman, 1984). Socioeconomically disadvantaged populations have little access to specialized mental health care, and are the prime group for whom primary care has been recognized as the most appropriate strategy for mental health service delivery. Excluding disasters in the United States (Table 1), in this century there have been 2,392 disasters in the world, but 86.4% occurred in developing nations, producing a total of 42 million deaths and 1.4 billion affected individuals. Seventy eight percent of all deaths occurred in developing countries, where 97.5% of all affected individuals are located. The observed ratio between affected and killed, of only 2.9 for the developed nations, is ten times greater for developing countries (United States Agency for International Development, 1986). Hence, not only are disasters disproportionately more frequent events in the Third World, but they are also responsible for a much higher

TABLE 1
Worldwide Disasters (Excluding United States)
Killed and Affected Individuals and Number of Disasters
1900–1986

Individuals	Total	Developed Countries		Developing Countries	
	N	N	%	N	%
Killed	53,245,836	12,056,683	22	42,040,168	78.0
Affected	1,419,351,000	35,822,000	2.5	1,383,529,000	97.5
Total	1,472,596,836	47,878,683		1,425,569,168	
Ratio	26.7	2.97		32.9	
Number of Disasters	2,392	327	13.6	2,036	86.4

Source: United States Agency for International Development, 1986.

proportion of victims who, having survived the impact, need long-term management of their biopsychosocial needs.

Even if disaster victims have access to specialized mental health services, however, they may still be reluctant to utilize them (Heffron, 1977). Disaster victims see themselves as normal individuals who have been subjected to an extreme situation (Cohen, 1985). It is reasonable to expect then that they will utilize the primary care worker, rather than the specialized mental health professional, for the management of their emotional and social difficulties alongside their physical problems. The disaster literature is very sparse on this particular subject, but some information is available from the studies done by McFarlane (1984, 1986) with bush-fire victims in Australia. The data show that victims presented various complaints to their general practitioners, including nonspecific emotional distress, sleep disorders, psychological symptoms and, for the significant majority, decline in their physical rather then psychological health. The latter included mostly patients suffering from post-traumatic stress disorders and major depression. It was further noted that victims preferred to utilize existing general health services in their districts, rather than consulting outside specialists. It is proposed that one of the first priorities in the postimpact situation should be to increase the level of detection and management of victims with emotional problems by general practitioners.

In summary, the review of the literature on primary care, mental health, and disaster reveals the need for exploring alternative strategies for mental health service delivery to disaster victims through the effective utilization of the primary care worker. The Armero disaster represented an opportunity for probing into this issue in a developing country.

ORIGINS OF THE ARMERO PROJECT

The Division of Mental Hygiene of the Colombian Ministry of Health had the task of designing, implementing, and evaluating a primary mental health care plan, for which it requested consultation to the Pan American Health Organization. The Division invited one of this chapter's authors, Bruno R. Lima, to consult in August 1985 (Lima, 1985). A subsequent national meeting was scheduled for November 27–29 in the town of Ibague, capital of the State of Tolima, when the state mental health directors would discuss the proposed plan. The State of Tolima was selected as the site for the meeting due to the excellence of its community-based mental health services, where the Plan would be pilot-tested. However, neither the meeting nor the visit to the important regional psychiatric hospital in the neighboring town of Armero was to take place. A volcanic eruption on November 13 produced a mudslide that completely destroyed Armero, leaving in its wake a total of 22,000 dead, 5,000 injured, and scores of homeless survivors in dire economic conditions (Sigurdsson & Carey, 1986).

Immediately following the tragedy, it was agreed that Dr. Lima would pursue his work on primary mental health care, adjusting it to the disaster situation, with the objective of developing mental health services for the disaster victims within the broader scope of the primary mental health care plan (Lima, 1986b).

The initial evaluation of the disaster characteristics underscored its likely psychological consequences for the survivors and neighboring communities. Eighty percent of the 30,000 inhabitants of Armero had died in the tragedy, and the small towns of Lerida and Guayabal, with an original population of about 3,000 people each, had to assimilate approximately 6,000 homeless victims. Survivors were mostly drawn from peripheral segments of society, being mostly unskilled workers with limited possibility for alternative gainful employment. The population had been unprepared for this unanticipated disaster, in which it was rapidly and deeply involved; the events were totally unfamiliar to the community. These features have been identified by Quarantelli (1985) as being highly predictable of subsequent emotional difficulties among victims.

Subsequent discussion with health care providers in the disaster area confirmed the high frequency of emotional difficulties among the victims of Armero. Two weeks after the eruption, various psychosocial problems were noted, particularly depressive states and acute anxiety, with recurrent nightmares and intrusive fantasies that recapitulated the disaster experience of the victims. In the following months, psychophysiological disorders and complaints increased in frequency and/or severity, and included backache and headaches, hypertension, cardiovascular problems, and gastrointestinal complaints. Chronic disorders that required careful management (such as diabetes and epilepsy) were being poorly controlled. Six to twelve months later, additional problems had become more conspicuous. As temporary shelters were still being used for housing and jobs had not become available to most, growing dissatisfaction with living conditions was seen. A higher frequency of alcohol and drug abuse was observed, as well as episodes of conduct problems, such as violence and thefts. Thus, in the course of one year a wide variety of problems, which encompassed biological, psychological, and social areas, was noted. An integrated biopsychosocial approach was therefore thought to be the most appropriate for detection and management of victims' health problems.

In addition to these special characteristics, this particular disaster also produced a decrease in the specialized mental health resources. The psychiatric hospital of Armero had 5,000 yearly outpatient visits and a 90-bed inpatient service that represented 87% of the state's psychiatric beds, in addition to various community-oriented programs and consultation services to neighboring schools and health centers. The hospital was totally destroyed by the mudslide, and many of its professional staff were killed.

This combination of events—an increase in the level of emotional problems among victims and a decrease in the already limited psychiatric resources—created an opportunity for studying the role of the primary care worker in delivering mental health care to disaster victims in a developing country.

THE ARMERO PROJECT

On the basis of the previous observations and assumptions, a research project was designed to evaluate the psychiatric morbidity of victims of the volcanic eruption and mudslide. This project is a collaborative effort of the Departments of Psychiatry of the Johns Hopkins University and the University of Javeriana, in Bogota, and the Division of Mental Hygiene of the Tolima Health Secretariat and the Colombian Ministry of Health. The project has the following goals:

1. to ascertain the frequency and kinds of psychiatric morbidity seem among victims in camps and among patients in primary care clinics;

2. to assess the primary care worker's capability for adequately identifying patients with mental health problems.

The project design involved a two-phase examination of adult victims living in shelters and camps of the disaster area: an initial screening of all adult residents of two shelters and one camp, as well as a convenience sample of a second camp. The screening was done by mental health professionals of the disaster area: two psychologists, a psychiatric nurse, and a social worker. A subsample of these subjects were subsequently interviewed by a psychiatrist. The data collection was carried out seven to 10 months after the disaster, and it is now complete. The analysis, however, is still in progress.

The screening instrument used was the Self-Reporting Questionnaire (see Appendix, pp. 392–393), an instrument that has been validated (Mari & Williams, 1985) and used extensively in primary care settings in developing countries (Harding et al., 1983). It detects cases with neurotic and psychotic symptoms, with a sensitivity of 83% and a specificity of 80%. For this particular project, specific questions on alcoholism and epilepsy were added. Victims were identified by the Self-Reporting Questionnaire as suffering from emotional distress if they had a positive score of eight or more on the 20-item neurotic subscale, or a score of one or more on the 4-item psychotic subscale, or a score of one on either the question on epilepsy or alcoholism.

In order to assess the relationship between cognitive capacity of victims and their postdisaster coping and adaptation, an evaluation of their cognitive status was also done. The Mini-Mental State Examination was used to screen for cognitive problems. The Mini-Mental is a simple and reliable method for the detection of cognitive disorders (Folstein, Folstein, & McHugh, 1975), which has been used in inpatient settings (Knights & Folstein, 1977) and outpatient settings (Cavanaugh, 1983) as well as in community surveys (Regier et al., 1984).

Additional information was also obtained on the demographic characteristics of the study subjects, the disaster experience, perceived physical and emotional health, utilization of health and mental health services, level of current social support, current living conditions, and plans for the future.

All subjects scoring positively on the Self-Reporting Questionnaire and a subsample of the subjects with negative scores were given a semistructured psychiatric interview, in which the clinicians followed their routine outline for a clinical exam. Even though the utilization of a fully structured psychiatric interview could have yielded more reliable and valid data, the clinicians were confronted with the realities of a postdisaster situation: the pressing demands on the clinicians' time for meeting other responsibilities, and the need to collect the data without much delay. Hence, it was felt that clinicians should follow their usual clinical practice, but in addition they were asked to complete selected sections of a simple symptom checklist to generate DSM-III diagnoses.

Data were also collected on a systematic sample of 100 patients attending two primary care clinics of the neighboring towns of Lerida and Guayabal, where the same research design was used. In addition, the primary care workers were also asked to complete the "Health Staff Review" to assess their ability to detect emotional problems among their patients. This simple questionnaire had been used in primary care settings elsewhere (Sartorius & Harding, 1983) and asks whether the patient suffers from: (a) a physical disorder only; (b) an emotional disorder only; (c) both a physical and emotional disorder; or (d) neither. Its brevity makes it appropriate to a primary care setting and it was readily accepted by the primary care workers.

IMPLICATIONS OF THIS EXPERIENCE

The experience thus far gathered in the Armero project has significant practical and theoretical implications for disaster mental health in the areas of research design and implementation, education/training of primary care workers, and health planning.

Research Design and Implementation

Even though the origins of this project are partially the result of serendipity, two of its essential strategies should be highlighted as guidelines for replication elsewhere.

1. Predisaster relationship between health authorities and researchers. It seems to be both difficult and easy to develop a disaster project. If no previous relationship existed with the health authorities of the disaster area, it may be extremely difficult to develop a successful collaborative research. If a relationship preexisted the disaster, however, it can evolve very rapidly into an effective research effort. Communications with the health sector and other sectors of the disaster relief system are facilitated by the special disaster-related context, promoting intra- and intersectorial collaboration. To increase the likelihood of having a successful entry into the disaster system, an ongoing relationship between a disaster research center and health officials of a disaster-prone areas could be proactively established as an avenue for subsequent collaborative work. Furthermore, it seems more appropriate and more effective for the research team to participate directly or indirectly in the service delivery activities as well. This collaboration will not only assist the disaster relief operations, but will permit a better understanding of the health and mental health issues of the affected individuals and communities. Once the collaborative relationship is established and some of the basic service delivery issues are settled, research questions can be jointly formulated on the basis of the shared experience, and a project can be jointly designed. Particularly for developing countries, the research should be service-oriented, or at least have well-defined practical and immediate consequences, which will make it more clearly applicable to the pressing realities of service provision.

   2. *Relevance of research to service delivery.* The data collection in this project was carried out by a team of mental health professionals who had worked very closely with the affected community in delivering routine mental health care. Thus, they were accepted members of the community, rather than outsiders with no perceived commitment to the welfare of the community. This special strategy circumvented a variety of problems related to victims' uncooperativeness with research projects.

   The service-research intertwining was present as an essential theme throughout the project: in its antecedents, as the project had its origin in the development of a primary mental health plan for Colombia; in its design, as the information obtained aims at the identification of individual and environmental characteristics that render victims at a high risk for the development of emotional distress, with clear implications for health care delivery and social interventions; and in its implementation, as the data collection was carried out by professionals who shared research and service-delivery roles. For a disaster situation, the establishment of a clear relationship between the proposed research and the services that need to be provided to victims seems to be a very important ingredient for the successful completion of the project, particularly for developing countries and, most likely, for underserved areas of developed nations.

Education and Training of Primary Care Workers in Disaster Mental Health

   In the Armero disaster, participation in a project on primary mental health care has increased the interest of the primary care workers in the psychosocial problems of their patients. At the completion of the data collection, they requested of the state mental health officers a formal training program in mental health (Lima et al., in press).

The high levels of psychiatric morbidity identified among the victims in the temporary camps and shelters indicate that primary care workers should be trained to meet the victims' mental health needs adequately. The contents and methodologies developed for routine primary mental health care can be adapted to a disaster situation. Important content areas include (Cohen & Ahearn, Jr, 1980):

- interviewing skills and mental status exam;
- knowledge of disaster behavior (e.g., coping and adaptation);
- identification of psychiatric problems commonly seen in a postimpact situation (e.g., post-traumatic stress disorder, alcohol and drug abuse, marital and family conflicts, anxiety, depression and sleep disorders);
- skills in managing various therapeutic modalities (e.g., crisis counseling, supportive psychotherapy, group therapy, basic pharmacology);
- identification of thresholds for referral to the specialized mental health sector (e.g., psychotic symptoms, suicidal risk, violent behavior);
- knowledge of the disaster-relief system (e.g., housing, financial aid, employment, social services, medical care); and
- utilization of family and community resources.

Various methodologies have been designed for the training of the primary care worker in mental health care. Manuals have been developed in various settings, and successfully implemented (Lima, 1981; Murthy, 1985). Flow charts have been developed for the identification and management of problems seen in routine clinical settings which bypass more complex diagnostic formulations and focus on abnormal behaviors, such as violence against other people and self, delusions, abnormal and withdrawn behavior, abnormal speech, anxiety and depression (Essex & Gosling, 1983). These instruments must now be adjusted to a disaster situation. Other methods should be considered as well, such as videocassettes that have already been used successfully (Brownstone et al., 1977). According to the technological resources of the affected communities, videocassettes could represent a significant educational strategy. Experience gathered in the WHO collaborative study on "Strategies for Extending Mental Care" has shown that two or three hours for each of the identified priority conditions sufficed for the primary care worker to master the necessary contents (Murthy & Wig, 1983). Drawing from our experience, we estimate that training the primary care worker on basic disaster, mental health interventions could be implemented in 15–20 hours, a time frame that seems compatible with the time constraints and pressure for service.

It may be virtually impossible to include, in the limited mental health training for the primary care worker, content related to a future disaster that may never occur. After a disaster strikes, however, the primary care workers local to the disaster area will of necessity become involved with its health consequences, and are likely to be motivated to develop additional skills to meet the varied health needs of their patients. As we have observed in Armero, the heightened tension and anxiety seen in the postimpact period facilitated the learning process and created a climate that was conducive to the optimal development of new skills, knowledge, and attitudes. Furthermore, there seems to be ample time for the mental health training of the primary care worker, as it has been observed that very few cases come to the clinics in the first days after a disaster (Chamberlin, 1980), the majority of victims dating the beginning of their symptoms two months after the disaster, with new cases still occurring 24 months after it (McFarlane, 1986).

Health Planning

A program for developing the primary care worker's capability for actively participating in the delivery of mental health care to disaster victims needs to be designed, implemented, and evaluated. This involves a series of strategies that include the formulation of a clear national policy on disaster mental health, the establishment of a specialized unit within the department of mental health, and minimal financial provisions for operating the program (World Health Organization, 1984).

The role of the specialized mental health sector in the comprehensive care of disaster victims needs to be reexamined as well. Certainly the role should not be of routine and direct service delivery, not only because the demands are likely to be far greater than the resources available, but also because mental health care delivered though the primary level of care may be more appropriate to the victims' health needs (Bromet & Schulberg, 1987). The role of the specialized mental health sector, therefore, should relate to program design, implementation, and evaluation; to the training and education of the primary care worker; and to providing him or her continuing support through consultation and supervision. Particularly in disaster-prone countries, a small national disaster mental health team should develop and master a simple and well-structured educational and training package adjusted to the particular country (Figure 1). Once a disaster strikes, this team becomes responsible for training the mental health team local to the affected community. The local mental health team will then provide training and continuing support to the general health

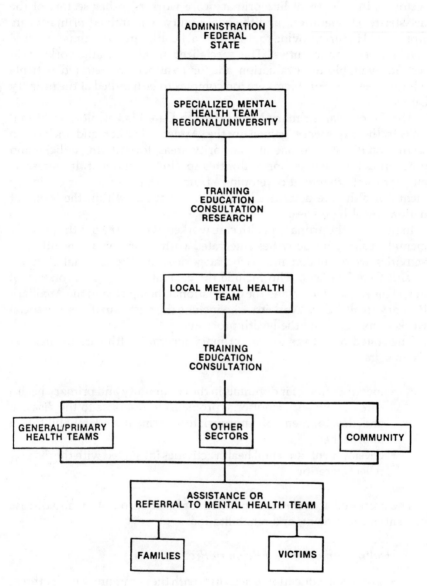

Figure 1. Mental health care integrated into the disaster relief aid.

sector and to the front-line primary care workers, other sectors of the disaster-relief operation, and the community. The trained primary care worker will in turn provide routine mental health care to victims, families, and affected communities. The specialized mental health worker will remain available for evaluation and/or treatment of referred patients whose psychiatric problems are too complex to be handled at the primary care level.

The Colombian Primary Mental Health Care Plan (Colombia, 1986) reflects the experience gained in the Armero disaster and includes a section on disasters as one of its priority areas, formulating policies and procedures for the development of this specific component. It represents an important attempt at developing a framework for structuring primary mental health care activities in disaster situations within the scope of national health policies.

In the Plan, the primary health care workers who carry out the primary mental health care activities integrated with their general health care activities were divided into two categories: the Professional Primary Health Care Workers, who include the general doctor, the professional nurse, the social worker, and the occupational therapist; and the Auxiliary Primary Health Care Workers, who include the nurse auxiliary, the social worker auxiliary, and the health promoter.

The stated objectives for the primary mental health care for disaster victims are:

- identification of individuals in the community and primary health care centers with emotional problems in response to the disaster, and development of appropriate treatment and rehabilitation approaches;
- development of mental health activities integrated with the disaster relief operation.

The proposed activities are specified for health promotion and disease prevention, treatment, and rehabilitation:

Health Promotion and Primary Prevention

- to develop educational activities with the community under threat of an impending disaster to address frequent emotional problems, such as denial or anxiety;
- to collaborate with programs being developed by the health sector or other sectors, integrating mental health in all the proposed activities;

- to coordinate the mental health activities with other sectors in the community which will become active in the forthcoming disaster;
- to be familiar with the disaster relief system being developed, the health and community resources available, and the mechanism for accessing these services;
- to develop community activities to foster solidarity and support to obtain a collective response to the disaster situation.

Secondary Prevention

- to train the Auxiliary and Professional Primary Care Worker to identify and manage victims who present emotional problems;
- to train the Auxiliary Primary Health Care Worker to utilize various approaches to manage the emotional problems of victims which include:
  - providing ventilation and emotional support;
  - facilitating access to other health services or community resources as needed;
  - providing accurate information to victims; and
  - involving the family and other support persons to manage the emotional problems.
- to support the Auxiliary Primary Health Care Worker through scheduled supervision, consultation, or referral by the Professional Primary Health Care Worker.
- to train the Professional Primary Health Care Worker to utilize various approaches for managing the emotional problems of victims who are referred to him or her by the Auxiliary Primary Health Care Worker, which include:
  - prescription and administration of required medications;
  - evaluation and treatment of physical problems, and
  - evaluation of psychosocial problems;
- to support the Professional Health Worker through scheduled supervision, consultation, or referral with the Specialized Mental Health Worker (e.g., psychiatrist, psychiatric nurse).

Tertiary Prevention

- to ensure that the Primary Health Care Worker maintains close collaboration with victims and affected families to promote their community adjustment, facilitating the utilization of available resources;
- to ensure that the Primary Health Care Worker works with the community to facilitate the assimilation of displaced victims who have been relocated to this community.

CONCLUSION

The integration of mental health and general health services, particularly at the primary level of care, has been a significant policy objective in developed (Burns et al., 1979; Coleman & Patrick, 1976; Pincus, 1980) and developing countries (Baasher et al., 1975, World Health Organization, 1975), although its realization has been fraught with difficulties (Broskowski, 1982; Brown & Zinberg, 1982; Goldman, 1982). Disasters may represent an opportunity for developing a decentralized primary health care system (Soberon et al., 1986) and for integrating mental health care into general health services (Pucheu, 1985) as victims are at risk for suffering significant emotional distress, and the primary care worker is likely to be more motivated to develop his or her mental health capability.

Given the scarcity of health resources and the increasing frequency and magnitude of disasters, both developed and developing countries are forced to engage in creative strategies to meet the victims' mental health needs, which include the active participation of the primary care worker. The conceptual service delivery model proposed in this chapter is partially derived from our experience in Colombia, but it may be applicable to those areas of the United States or other developed countries where, for various reasons—such as scarcity of specialized mental health resources (Burns et al., 1983) or cultural stigmatization of psychiatric treatment (Lindy, Grace, & Green, 1981)—the primary level of care may be the most appropriate one for the delivery of mental health care to disaster victims. This integrated approach, however, may be desirable irrespective of the availability or acceptability of specialized mental health treatment, as it has been shown to be more responsive to patients' biopsychosocial needs (Engel, 1977; Kessler, Tessler, & Nycz, 1983). It is hoped that our efforts, in addition to meeting the pressing health needs of developing countries, may in the long run prove to be an adequate model for integrating mental health and general health services in the care of disaster victims in developed nations as well.

REFERENCES

Aiken, L. H., Lewis, C. E., Craig, J., et al. (1979). The contribution of specialists to the delivery of primary care. *New England Journal of Medicine*, 300: 1363–1370.

Ahearn, F. (1984). Ingresos en servicios de psiquiatria despues de un desastre natural. *Boletin de la Oficina Sanitaria Panamericana*, 97: 325–333.

Baasher, T. A., Carstairs, G. M., Giel, R., et al. (1975). *Mental Health Services in Developing Countries*. Geneva: World Health Organization.

Barton, A. L. (1969). *Communities in Disaster: A Sociological Analysis of Collective Stress Situation*. New York: Doubleday, Archor Books.
Bromet, E. J., & Schulberg, H. E. (1987). Epidemiologic findings from disaster research. In R. E. Hales & A. J. Frances (Eds.), *Update: American Psychiatric Association Annual Review* (Vol. 6; pp. 676–689). Washington, D.C.: American Psychiatric Press.
Bromet, C., Schulberg, H. C., & Dunn, L. (1982). Reactions of psychiatric patients to the Three Mile Island Nuclear accident. *Archives of General Psychiatry*, 39: 725–730.
Broskowski, A. (1982). Linking mental health and health care systems. In H. C. Schulberg & M. Killilea (Eds.), *The Modern Practice of Community Mental Health* (pp. 486–513). San Francisco: Jossey-Bass.
Brown, H. M., & Zinberg, N. E. (1982). Difficulties in the integration of psychological and medical practices. *American Journal of Psychiatry*, 139: 1576–1580.
Brownstone, J., Penick, E. C., Larcen, S. W., et al. (1977). Disaster-relief training and mental health. *Hospital & Community Psychiatry*, 28: 30–32.
Burke, J. D., Borus, J. F., Burns, B. J., et al. (1982). Changes in children's behavior after a natural disaster. *American Journal of Psychiatry*, 139: 1010–1014.
Burns, B. J., Burke, J. D., & Ozarin, L. D. (1983). Linking health and mental health services in rural areas. *International Journal of Mental Health*, 12: 130–143.
Burns, B. J., Regier, D. A., Goldberg, I. G., et al. (1979). Future directions in primary care/mental health research. *International Journal of Mental Health*, 8: 130–140.
Burns, B. J., & Scott, J. E. (1982). Mental health training for family practice residents: An annotated bibliography of recent literature (1975–1981). *Family Medicine*, 14: 1–9.
Busnello, E., Lima, B., & Bertolote, J. (1985). Psychiatric and psychosocial issues in Vila Sao Jose do Murialdo setting in Brazil. In A. Jablensky (Ed.), *International Perspectives on their Diagnosis and Classification* (pp. 383–390). International Congress. Series 66g. Amsterdam: Excerpta Medica.
Cavanaugh, S. (1983). The prevalence of emotional and cognitive dysfuntion in a general medical population: Using the MMSE, GHQ, and BDI. *General Hospital Psychiatry*, 5: 15–24.
Chamberlin, B. C. (1980). Mayo seminars in psychiatry: The psychological aftermath of disasters. *Journal of Clinical Psychiatry*, 41: 238–244.
Climent, C. E., Diop, B. S. M., Harding, T. W., et al. (1980). Mental health in primary health care. *World Health Organization Chronicle*, 34: 231–236.
Cohen, R. E. (1982). Intervening with disaster victims. In H. C. Schulberg & M. Killilea (Eds.), *The Modern Practice of Community Mental Health* (pp. 397–418). San Francisco: Jossey-Bass.
Cohen, R. E. (1985). Reacciones individuales ante desastres naturales. *Boletin de la Oficina Sanitaria Panamericana*, 98: 171–180.
Cohen, R. E., & Ahearn, F. L. Jr., (1980). *Handbook for Mental Health Care of Disaster Victims*. Baltimore: The Johns Hopkins University Press.
Cohen-Cole, S. A., & Bird, J. (1984). Teaching psychiatry to nonpsychiatrists: II. A model curriculum. *General Hospital Psychiatry*, 6: 1–11.
Coleman, J. V., & Patrick, D. L. (1976). Integrating mental health services into primary medical care. *Medical Care*, 14: 654–661.
Colombia, Ministerio de Salud (1986). *Plan de Atencion Primaria en Salud Mental* (Primary Mental Health Care Plan). Bogota, Colombia: Author.
Dohrenwend, B. P., Dohrenwend, B. S., Warheit, G., et al. (1981). Stress in the community: A report to the President's Commission on the accident at Three Mile Island. *Annals of the New York Academy of Sciences*, 365: 159–174.
Draper, P., & Smits, H. L. (1975). The primary-care practitioner—Specialist or jack-of-all-trades? *New England Journal of Medicine*, 293: 903–907.
Dunal, C., Gaviria, M., Flaherty, J., et al. (1985). Perceived disruption and psychological distress among flood victims. *Journal of Operational Psychiatry*, 16: 9–16.
Engel, G. L. (1977). The need for a new medical model: A challenge for biomedicine. *Science*, 196 (4286): 129–136.

Essex, B., & Gosling, H. (1983). An algorithmic method for management of mental health problems in developing countries. *British Journal of Psychiatry*, 143: 451–459.

Folstein, M. F., Folstein, S., & McHugh, P. R. (1975). Mini-mental state. A practical method for grading the cognitive state of patients for the clinician. *Journal of Psychiatric Research*, 12: 189–198.

Giel, R., & Harding, T. W. (1976). Psychiatric priorities in developing countries. *British Journal of Psychiatry*, 128: 513–522.

Glass, A. J. (1959). Psychological aspects of disaster. *Journal of the American Medical Association*, 171: 222–225.

Gleser, G. C., Green, B. L., & Winget, C. (1981). *Prolonged Psychosocial Effects of Disaster.* New York: Academic Press.

Goldman, H. H. (1982). Integrating health and mental health services: Historical obstacles and opportunities. *American Journal of Psychiatry*, 139: 616–20.

Green, B. (1982). Assessing levels of psychological impairment following disaster: Consideration of actual and methodological dimensions. *Journal of Nervous and Mental Disease*, 170: 544–552.

Gulbinat, W. (1983). Mental health problem assessment and information support: Directions of WHO's work. *World Health Statistical Quarterly*, 36: 224–231.

Harding, T. W. (1976). Psychiatry in rural-agrarian societies. *Psychiatric Annals*, 8: 302–310.

Harding, T. W., Climent, C. E., Diop, M. D., et al. (1983). The WHO collaborative study on strategies for extending mental health care, II: The development of new research methods. *American Journal of Psychiatry*, 140: 1474–1480.

Harding, T. W., deArango, M. V., Baltazar, J., et al. (1980). Mental disorders in primary health care: A study of their frequency in four developing countries. *Psychological Medicine*, 10: 231–241.

Harding, T. W., D'Arrigo Busnello, E., Climent, C. E., et al. (1983). The WHO collaborative study on strategies for extending mental health care, III: Evaluative design and illustrative results. *American Journal of Psychiatry*, 140: 1481–1485.

Heffron, E. F. (1977). Project outreach: Crisis intervention following natural disaster. *Journal of Community Psychology*, 5: 103–111.

Hoiberg, A., & McCaughey, B. G. (1984). The traumatic aftereffects of collision at sea. *American Journal of Psychiatry*, 141: 70–73.

Kessler, L. G., Tessler, R. C., & Nycz, G. R. (1983). Co-occurrence of psychiatric and medical morbidity in primary care. *Journal of Family Practice*, 16: 319–324.

Kinston, W., & Rosser, R. (1974). Disaster: Effects of mental and physical state. *Journal of Psychosomatic Research*, 18: 437–456.

Knights, E. B., & Folstein, M. F. (1977). Unsuspected emotional and cognitive disturbance in medical patients. *Annals of Internal Medicine*, 87: 723–734.

Lamb, G. S., & Napodano, R. J. (1984). Physician-nurse practitioner interaction patterns in primary care practices. *American Journal of Public Health*, 74: 26–29.

Lechat, M. F. (1979). Disasters and public health. *Bulletin of the World Health Organization*, 57: 11–17.

Leopold, R. L., & Dillon, H. (1963). Psychoanatomy of a disaster: A long-term study of post-traumatic neuroses in survivors of a marine explosion. *American Journal of Psychiatry*, 119: 913–921.

Lima, B. R. (Ed.) (1981). *Manual de Treinamento em Cuidados Primarios de Saude Mental.* Porto Alegre, Brasil, Secretaria de Saude e do Meio Ambiente do Rio Grande do Sul.

Lima, B. R. (1985). *Final Report.* Consultation to the Division of Mental Hygiene of the Colombian Ministry of Health to design, implement, and evaluate a primary mental health care plan, August 4–16, Washington, D.C., Pan American Health Organization.

Lima, B. R. (1986a). Primary mental health care for disaster victims in developing countries. *Disasters*, 10: 203–204.

Lima, B. R. (1986b). Asesoria en salud mental a raiz del desastre de Armero en Colombia. *Boletin de la Oficina Sanitaria Panamericana*, 101: 678–683.

Lima, B. R., Lozano, J., & Santacruz, H. (in press.) Atencion primaria en salud mental para victimas de desastres. Actividades desarrolladas en Armero, Colombia. *Boletin de la Oficina Sanitaria Panamericana.*

Lima, B. R., Santacruz, H., Lozano, J., et al. (1986). Armero: Uma Cidade Desaparece (Armero: A Town Disappears). Paper presented at the meeting of the World Association for Social Psychiatry, Rio de Janeiro, Brazil.

Lima, B. R., Pai, S., Santacruz, H., et al. (1987). Screening for the psychological consequences of a major disaster in a developing country: Armero, Colombia. *Psychiatrica Scandinavica,* 76: 561–567.

Lin, T. (1983). Mental health in the Third World. *Journal of Nervous and Mental Disease,* 171: 71–78.

Lindy, J. D., Grace, M. C., & Green, B. L. (1981). Survivors: outreach to a reluctant population. *American Journal of Orthopsychiatry,* 51: 468–478.

Mari, J. J., & Williams, P. (1985). A comparison of the validity of two psychiatric screening questionnaires (GHQ-12 and SRQ-20) in Brazil, using relative operating characteristics (ROC) analysis. *Psychological Medicine,* 15: 651–659.

McFarlane, A. C. (1984). The Ash Wednesday bushfires in South Australia. *Medical Journal of Australia,* 141: 286–291.

McFarlane, A. C. (1986). Post-traumatic morbidity of a disaster. A study of cases presenting for psychiatric treatment. *Journal of Nervous and Mental Disease,* 174: 4–14.

Mellick, M. E. (1978). Life change and illness: Illness behavior of males in the recovery period of a natural disaster. *Journal of Health and Social Behavior,* 19: 335–342.

Morley, D. (1973). *Paediatric priorities in the developing world.* London: Butterworths.

Murthy, R. S. (1985). *Manual of Mental Health for Multipurpose Workers.* Bangalore, India.

Murthy, R. S. & Wig, N. N. (1983). The WHO collaborative study on strategies for extending mental health care. IV: A training approach to enhancing the availability of mental health manpower in a developing country. *American Journal of Psychiatry,* 140: 1486–1490.

Newman, C. J. (1976). Children of disaster: Clinical observations in Buffalo Creek. *American Journal of Psychiatry,* 133: 306–312.

Pan American Health Organization (1980). *Health for All by the Year 2000. Strategies.* Washington, D.C.: Pan American Health Organization.

Pan American Health Organization (1981). *Emergency Health Management After Natural Disasters.* Scientific Publication No. 407. Washington, D.C.: Pan American Health Organization.

Parker, G. (1975). Psychological disturbance in Darwin evacuees following cyclone Tracy. *Medical Journal of Australia,* 1: 650–652.

Patrick, V., & Patrick, W. K. (1981). Cyclone '78 in Sri Lanka—The mental health trail. *British Journal of Psychiatry,* 138: 210–216.

Perry, R., & Lindell, M. K. (1978). The psychological consequences of natural disasters: A review of research on American communities. *Mass Emergencies,* 3: 105–115.

Pincus, H. A. (1980). Linking general health and mental health systems of care: Conceptual models of implementation. *American Journal of Psychiatry,* 137: 315–20.

Popovic, M., & Petrovic, D. (1964). After the earthquake. *Lancet,* 2: 1169–1171.

Pucheu, R. C. (1985). Atencion primaria y fomento a la salud mental. *Cuestion Social,* 2: 74–82.

Quarantelli, E. L. (1985). What is a disaster? The need for clarification in definition and conceptualization in research. In B. J. Sowder (Ed.), *Disasters and Mental Health. Selected Contemporary Perspectives* (pp. 41–73). DHHS Publication No. (ADM) 85-1421, Washington, D.C.

Quarantelli, E. L., & Dynes, R. R. (1977). Response to social crisis and disaster. *Annual Review of Sociology,* 3: 23–49.

Regier, D. A., Goldberg, I. D., & Taube, C. A. (1978). The "De Facto" US mental health service systems. *Archives of General Psychiatry,* 35: 685–693.

Regier, D. A., Myers, J. K., Kramer, M., et al. (1984). The NIMH epidemiologic catchment area program. *Archives of General Psychiatry,* 41: 934–941.

Rosenauer, J., Stanford, D., Morgan, W., et al. (1984). Prescribing behaviors of primary care nurse practitioners. *American Journal of Public Health,* 74: 10–13.

Sartorius, N., & Harding T. W. (1983). The WHO collaborative study on strategies for extending mental health care. I: The genesis of the study. *American Journal of Psychiatry,* 140: 1470–1473.

Schurman, R. A., Kramer, P. D., & Mitchell, J. B. (1985). The hidden mental health network. Treatment of mental illness by nonpsychiatrist physician. *Archives of General Psychiatry,* 42: 89–94.

Seaman, J. (Ed.) (1984). *Epidemiology of Natural Disasters.* Basel, Switzerland: Karger.

Shepherd, M. (1967). *Psychiatric Illness in General Practice.* London: Oxford University Press.

Shepherd, M. (1980). Mental health as an integrant of primary medical care. *Journal of the Royal College of General Practitioners,* 30: 657–664.

Shore, J. H., Tatum, E. L., & Vollmer, W. M. (1986). Psychiatric reactions to disaster: The Mt. St. Helen's Experience. *American Journal of Psychiatry,* 143: 590–595.

Sigurdsson, H., & Carey, S. (1986). Volcanic disasters in Latin America and the 13th November 1985 eruption of Nevado del Ruiz Volcano in Colombia. *Disasters,* 10: 205–217.

Soberon, G., Frenk, J., & Sepulveda, J. (1986). The health care reform in Mexico: Before and after the 1985 earthquakes. *American Journal of Public Health,* 76: 673–680.

Spiegel, J. S., Rubenstein, L. V., Scott, B., et al. (1983). Who is the primary physician? *New England Journal of Medicine,* 308: 1208–1212.

Strain, J. J., Bender-Laitman, L., Gise, L. H., et al. (1983). Mental health training programs in primary care: A bibliography. *Journal of Psychiatric Education,* 7(3): 208–231.

Titchener, J. L., & Kapp, F. T. (1976). Family and character change at Buffalo Creek. *American Journal of Psychiatry,* 133: 295–299.

United States Agency for International Development, Office of U.S. Foreign Disaster Assistance. (1986). *Disaster History. Significant Data on Major Disasters Worldwide, 1900–Present.* Washington, D.C.

Wilkinson, C. B. (1983). Aftermath of a disaster: The collapse of the Hyatt Regency Hotel skywalks. *American Journal of Psychiatry,* 140: 1134–1139.

World Health Organization. (1973). *Psychiatry and Primary Medical Care.* Report on a working group. Copenhagen: World Health Organization.

World Health Organization. (1975). Organization of mental health services in developing countries. Sixteenth report of the Expert Committee on Mental Health. *World Health Organization Technical Report Series,* 564.

World Health Organization. (1978). *Primary Health Care.* A Joint Report by the Director-General of the World Health Organization and the Executive-Director of the United Nations Children's Fund. Geneva: World Health Organization.

World Health Organization. (1980). *The Primary Health Worker.* Geneva: World Health Organization.

World Health Organization. (1984). Mental health care in developing countries: A critical appraisal of research findings. Report of a WHO Study Group. *World Health Organization Technical Report Series,* 698.

APPENDIX:
ITEMS OF THE SELF-REPORTING QUESTIONNAIRE

Nonpsychotic

1. Do you often have headaches?
2. Is your appetite poor?

3. Do you sleep badly?
4. Are you easily frightened?
5. Do your hands shake?
6. Do you feel nervous, tense, or worried?
7. Is your digestion poor?
8. Do you have trouble thinking clearly?
9. Do you feel unhappy?
10. Do you cry more than usual?
11. Do you find it difficult to enjoy your daily activities?
12. Do you find it difficult to make decisions?
13. Is your daily work suffering?
14. Are you unable to play a useful part in life?
15. Have you lost interest in things?
16. Do you feel that you are a worthless person?
17. Has the thought of ending your life been in your mind?
18. Do you feel tired all the time?
19. Do you have uncomfortable feelings in your stomach?
20. Are you easily tired?

Psychotic

1. Do you feel that somebody has been trying to harm you in some way?
2. Are you a much more important person than most people think?
3. Have you noticed any interference or anything else unusual with your thinking?
4. Do you ever hear voices without knowing where they come from or which other people cannot hear?

Epilepsy

1. Do you ever have attacks where you fall down, your arms and legs shake, you bite your tongue and lose consciousness?

Alcohol

1. Do you often get drunk?

Author Index

395

Subject Index